yury lotman

analysis of the poetic text

Edited & Translated by D. BARTON JOHNSON

with a bibliography of Lotman's works
compiled by Lazar Fleishman

ardis / ann arbor

ISBN: 0-88233-106X

Table of Contents

THE STRUCTURAL POETICS OF YURY LOTMAN

I

INTRODUCTION

Professor Lotman is the preeminent figure in Soviet literary structuralism. The first full-scale exposition of his general theoretical views was his book *Lectures on Structural Poetics: Introduction, The Theory of Poetry (Lektsii po struktural'noi poetike: vvedenie, teoriia stikha)* which appeared in 1964 in an edition of 500 copies. (Based on his 1958-1962 lectures at Tartu State University, the Russian text of this small volume was reprinted by Brown University in 1968.) In it, the author briefly expounds a general theory of art as a semiotic system subject to interpretive modeling and structural analysis. The central part of the work is an attempt at a structural analysis of poetry on its various levels ranging from those of rhythm and rhyme, the phonological, the grammatical and the lexical up through more abstract levels such as the line and the stanza to such general problems as composition and plot *(siuzhet).* The final section considers the problem of the poetic text and its relationship to extra-textual structures.

In 1970 a second book, *The Structure of the Artistic Text (Struktura khudozhestvennogo teksta),* appeared. Although still primarily focusing on the belletristic literary text, this new volume offered a wider perspective on structuralism as an approach to all of the representational arts which are seen as secondary modeling systems derived from and overlaying the primary modeling system constituted by natural language. Of a more theoretical nature than the earlier work, *Structure* treats in considerable detail such problems as art as a language, meaning in the artistic text, and the concept of the text and its relationship to the system it manifests. The constructional principles of the text are examined in terms of its paradigmatic and syntagmatic axes while the various levels and their organizing entities on each axis are considered in separate chapters. Extremely general questions of composition such as framing, artistic space, character, plot, plane and point of view are also treated.

Both of the foregoing are essentially theoretical works containing only enough actual analysis of specific texts to illustrate the theoretical points under discussion. Since much of the theorizing is quite abstract and since Lotman assumes a detailed familiarity with much of Russian literature, especially poetry, the non-Russian reader may feel a certain discontinuity between theory and practice.

Professor Lotman's most recent work *The Analysis of the Poetic Text: The Structure of Poetry (Analiz poeticheskogo teksta: struktura stikh)* (1972) is at least in part an attempt to provide abundant illustration of the relationship between his theory and the actual critical analysis of poetic language. The first half of the book presents a recapitulation of Lotman's basic theoretical constructs, his principles of analysis, the levels of analysis, and their operative elements. In large part this portion of the volume duplicates the material of his first book which is, however, relatively poor in illustrative materials. The second half of *Analysis* demonstrates the application of Lotman's structuralist theory of criticism to the detailed analysis of some dozen-odd Russian poems ranging from Batyushkov to Zabolotsky. Each analysis focuses on a particular structural organizational principle or level. In sum, the individual treatments are intended to illustrate various aspects of the methodology of structural analysis. This approach offers the reader a bridge from a highly abstract set of theoretical concepts to critical practice.

The three Lotman volumes mentioned here contain a high degree of duplication. Consequently readers of the present book may obtain a fair idea of all three of these works which thus far collectively constitute the only major exposition of Soviet literary structuralism.

II

GENERAL THEORETICAL CONCEPTS

The present essay is directed toward two general goals. The first is to present an integrated overview of Lotman's theory while the second is an attempted assessment of the value of these ideas in practice.

There are perhaps two reasons why an overview of Lotman's theoretical positions may be of value. The reader probably already has some degree of familiarity with current European literary structuralist thought.[1] Although Professor Lotman shares much of the same theoretical foundation, i.e., de Saussure's view of language, his approach differs substantially from that of current Western European and especially French structuralist theoreticians. Hence a preliminary overview of Lotman's basic positions and methodology may assist the reader in more clearly seeing the author's work as an independent entity. The second reason is that Professor Lotman's exposition is sometimes rather diffuse with a single topic or its different aspects being discussed in various places. A preliminary survey hopefully may provide the reader with a somewhat more integrated approach to the material.

In the following section, we shall survey the fundamental concepts of Professor Lotman's theories by setting them out in three more or less separate but interdependent categories; 1) general theoretical foundations, 2) organizing processes and analytic principles, and 3) levels of analysis and their units. The content of each of these categories basically reflects various topical sections of the *Analysis* although somewhat reordered. A concluding section raises a number of questions about the nature of literary structuralism.

Professor Lotman's theory of literature rests upon two closely related sets of fundamental concepts—those of semiotics and structuralism.[2]

Semiotics is described as that science of signs and sign systems which studies the basic characteristics of all signs and their combinations, e.g., the words and word combinations of natural and artificial languages, the metaphors of poetic language, and chemical and mathematical symbols. It also treats systems of signs such as those of artificial logical and machine languages, the languages of various poetic schools, codes, animal communication systems and so on. The presence of two aspects are obligatory for each sign, the *signifying* (material) aspect apprehended by the sense organs and the *signified* aspect, i.e., meaning. For words of natural (ordinary) language, pronunciation or writing is the signifying aspect while content is the signified aspect. The signs of one system, e.g., the words of a language, can be the signifying aspect for complex signs of another system (such as that of poetic language) superimposed on them.

From the semiotic point of view, poetics, viewing the literary text as a complex sign, singles out the intermediate levels (plot, tropes, rhythm, etc) existing between the signified aspect, the subject matter, and the designating aspect, its verbal embodiment.

The basic theory goes on to outline a series of fundamental oppositions which provide organizing frameworks for the consideration of signs and sign systems. For present purposes the most important of these is the division of signs into conventional wherein the relationship between the two aspects of each sign is arbitrary as is the case in all natural languages (excepting onomatopoeic words) and into iconic wherein the relationship between elements is based on some sort of resemblance. Poetic language (including that of belletristic prose) tends toward the iconic.

The idea of system is inherent in semiotics. System implies structure and no body of related data can be understood without these concepts. In its most general sense structuralism may be defined as "the idea of a system: a complete self-regulating entity that adapts to new conditions by transforming its features while retaining its systematic structure." Although formulated in these terms only since the advent of cybernetics and information theory, this idea has long been a basic postulate of science. Most simply put, it means that any properly chosen object of investigation must be viewed as an interrelated and interdependent system made up of a number of elementary units and the rules of their permissible combinations. Although self-regulating via some type of internal feedback mechanism, the system may be a part of and interact with one or more other systems. This view initially took hold in the physical sciences and, subsequently, in the natural and social sciences, especially linguistics. In recent years attempts have increasingly been made to extend this approach to the humanities.

The relevance of structuralism to literary studies and questions of how it might apply are matters of dispute in both Eastern and Western Europe. Soviet scholars who favor such an approach make the following points. In reference to literary studies "structure" implies the study of the constructive elements of the poetic work in their dependence on the artistic whole, i.e., a functional point of view. The study of literature is set in the framework of semiotics and involves the idea of binary oppositions permitting the isolation of the distinctive features of the constitutive elements of a literary work. During the sixties the object of the structural analysis of literature came to be seen as the determination of structural levels in a work. These levels constitute a hierarchy and the elementary units of each successive higher level are built from those of the lower level. No less vital is the determination of the permissible combinatory rules within and among levels.

Structure may be extremely complex. In order to determine the structure of an entity (including works of art), it is often necessary to engage in a modeling process wherein the invariant properties of the entity may be isolated and examined in their interdependent relations.

Another equally fundamental dichotomy which Lotman takes over into his poetic semantics is that of the paradigmatic and syntagmatic axes. Paradigmatics is the associative plane of language wherein each structural element is viewed in relation to some set whose members are associated by a relationship of opposition. Sets may be of various kinds ranging from the set of noun case endings to a set of lexical synonyms. In the areas of both linguistics and poetics one member of such a set may be represented by a zero unit which is interpreted against the background of the system represented by the set as a whole. Syntagmatics refers to the linear unity of language and the serial unification of different items in a text. The basic relationship of the syntagmatic axis is that of contrast. For narrative literature the syntagmatic axis dominates, whereas for poetry, especially lyric poetry, the paradigmatic aspect predominates.

If the functions of such entities as a natural language are to be understood, it is helpful (if not indispensable) to restrict our view, at least initially, to the invariant units and their interconnections. This is possible because only invariant entities are characterized by meaning. The establishment of the invariant elements of a system enables us to set aside a vast amount of data known to be functionally extraneous and to focus upon a simplified (although still immensely complex) body of data and the rules of its organization. This abstracted version of the system is called a model and is a powerful tool in understanding the workings of complex entities such as language or literature.

Virtually all systematic entities are parts of still other structures. In this sense natural language is a model of the world while specific languages are models of their various cultural systems. It is in Lotman's terms "a primary modeling system." Poetic or belletristic language and other art forms constitute "secondary modeling systems."

Language and literature are perhaps the most complex human systems. The very number of apparent factors and the intricacy of their interrelations, their functional interactions, makes comprehension of these systems difficult if not, in some cases, impossible. The sound aspect of a natural language is a good illustration of this point. A sophisticated analysis of the sound system of any natural language will show many dozens and even hundreds of distinguishable sounds. In fact, the numbers of sounds that can be discriminated within a language is limited only by the sensitivity and sophistication of the transcriber and/or his equipment. The rules of collocation of this myriad of sounds will be even more complex. All of this is actually occurring data. By virtue of its complexity it is very difficult to order and perceive it as an integrated functional whole, i.e., a system.

"Functional" is the operational word here. The function of the sound system of a language is communication and it can easily be demonstrated that most of the vast number of sound variants that occur in a language are not essential to its communicative function. A very considerable portion of the even casually identifiable similar sounds in a language are variants of a single invariant unit, i.e., they play the same functional role. To illustrate briefly: the "t" sound in "tin" may in fact be recognizably pronounced in a considerable number of variants. Although most of the variants will sound somewhat strange or foreign to a native speaker, from the functional-communicative point of view the word "tin" will continue to be understood so long as the pronounced versions of the "t" do not slip over into the range of pronunciation of variants characterizing a different functional sound unit in that language, such as for example, "d" or "s" or "p" which would result in different words with different meanings. The entire range of pronunciational variants of a single functional sound is termed a phoneme and any given representative of that class is an allophone. The phoneme, the minimal sense-discriminating unit within a given language, is an invariant element within the functional sound system of that language and all of its allophones are its variants. The number of phonemes in the languages of the world varies from about 15 to 50.

There is still another dimension to the description of a sound system or more precisely to the basis for the discrimination of invariant sound units. Phonemes in their turn are describable and definable in terms of a still smaller set of organizational oppositions which are applicable to all natural languages. These are a series of binary oppositions which form a multidimensional matrix specifying the relationship among the systemic invariants. For example, "t" and "d" are members of a correlated pair opposed by the distinctive feature of voicing. In all other respects, i.e., their other distinctive features, they are identical. Correlation and opposition are basic operations in the establishment of structural units and levels. In this way all of the invariant sounds of a language can be seen and understood as an interlocking system constituted by a set of basic invariant entities and their permissible combinations.

The phonological level is of course only one of the levels of language and literature which may be examined in this way. Language is made up of a number of different levels (e.g., morphology, syntax, semantics, etc.), all of which may be modeled and all of which are subsets of ever larger models ending ultimately in the culture of a people. Lotman's view that each natural language constitutes a primary modeling system is related to the hierarchic view just described but also to another extremely general proposition. Although language structure through its grammatical categories such as number and tense seems to reflect certain universal properties of both the natural world and the human mind, it is clear that this process is not entirely unilateral. The structure of language, the model of the world it represents, in turn influences the way in which the individual and the culture perceive and understand reality. The extent of this interaction is disputed but the process itself is not. Thus natural language is in fact a primary modeling system in the most literal sense. Virtually all aspects of man's perception and understanding are in some measure shaped by this primary interpretive system.

Language as the central mode of human communication underlies a large number of other social systems—tradition, social convention, ritual, religion and, most importantly for our purposes, the representational arts. These constitute secondary modeling systems. In the field of literature, the most concrete unit of organization is that of the text which, however, is decipherable only in terms of its organizing system. The text manifests the secondary modeling system of literature. Its relationship to this system is parallel to that prevailing between other types of variants and invariants such as *parole* and *langue,* allophone and phoneme, performance and competence, and so on. Items of the non-literary text are normally unambiguously assigned by the reader to their invariant representations in the system. In a non-belletristic work the text and the system interpreting it are in close accord. The system structures the text to such an extent that actual textual slips such as misprints are usually automatically brought into accord with the system.

In ordinary non-artistic language the content of a text is generally interpreted in terms of a single code. For belletristic works the relationship between text and system is crucially different. All elements including normally variant ones may assume meaning on all levels of such a work. The allo-elements may become part of the system and bear their own informational load. This is of course not to say that all variant elements in an artistic text are significant. In a successful work of art we do not automatically "correct" apparently a-systemic elements as we do in ordinary language usage. (If we do, we may inadvertently destroy some part of the text's artistic meaning.) Lotman asserts that apparent deviations in a work of art are elements of one or more *other* systems (or interpretive codes) commingling with that of the original or background code. Indeed all such "deviations" reflect other systems, and this multi-systemicity is considered to be an obligatory characteristic of art. Art's effect is due to the tension resulting from the clash of the collocation of elements of two (or more) systems. This conflict has the function of breaking down automatism of perception and occurs simultaneously on the many levels of a work of art—phonic, grammatical, lexical, compositional, etc. Such conflicts are often to be observed between different organizational levels of a work. A well-known example is that of poetic enjambment where the semantic sense unit fails to coincide with the formal unit of the poetic line. It is the task of structural analysis to examine the work of art in terms of these levels, their systems, and their interplay.

In the broadest sense both ordinary language and verbal art are semiotic systems designed for the transmission and storage of information. In non-artistic language, the relationship between language structure and message content is fairly loose. The same information can be relayed in various ways. The particular mode of linguistic formulation does not carry a substantial amount of content. Barring some inadvertent ambiguity, the addressee attends only to the content of the message while his perception of the carrier is fully automatic. The message and the code are largely independent.

In artistic language the situation is quite different. As we have noted, the language of verbal art is multi-systemic and, consequently, perception of it is non-automatic. All levels may carry meaning—not just lexical meaning but a full range of esthetic, ideological, and cultural meanings. This means that in the artistic text, unlike that of ordinary prose, the language is more than the neutral bearer of meaning. It is a part of the meaning. Hence the information of a particular belletristic work can be conveyed *only* via that particular ordering of language. It is also this multi-systemicity within a single text with its resulting shattering of automatized perception that results in the exceptionally high information content of artistic prose. In terms of information theory, information is a function of the available number of choices. A single system has a limited number of choices available. Two or more systems functioning within a single text will obviously be capable of affording a greater number of choices and hence have a higher potential for transmitting information. Hence a work of verbal art has a higher information load than a non-belletristic text of equal length. It should be noted here that "information" is used in a much broader sense than that of lexical meaning. It includes everything contributing to the impact of the work on the reader.

The foregoing provides Professor Lotman with the basis for his answer to perhaps the key question of art. A number of West European structuralist theoreticians such as Tzvetan Todorov tend to dismiss the matter of the evaluation of the work of art as being beyond the limits of their approach. Professor Lotman suggests a criterion in the light of the ideas sketched above. Bad poems do not carry sufficient information with the result that they are overly predictable and lacking in tension. Good poems bear more information and their elements are less predictable.

The greater part of Professor Lotman's theoretical and applied work has focused on poetry, on the grounds that theory should proceed from simple to more complex cases. This choice of subject matter seems odd since poetry is structurally more complex than belletristic prose. This leads us to Professor Lotman's interesting views on the relationship of poetry and prose and the nature of poetry. In a striking way, Lotman's stress on poetry rather than belletristic prose as the basis for his theory of literature parallels his view of the historical development of the two forms. Prose in the sense of ordinary language is obviously antecedent to poetry. Poetry arose as a marked form maximally distinct from ordinary language. For a long period poetry was the *only* form of verbal art. Only with the establishment of poetry as the dominant form of verbal art did belletristic prose evolve through a process of dissimilation. Thus belletristic prose is originally projected against the background of poetry, not of prose. In time in certain cultures once belletristic prose has become firmly established as the dominant form of verbal art, poetry comes to be seen against the background of prose.

A somewhat similar process may be noted within the history of Russian poetry. In the period just prior to Pushkin, the Romantic style á la Zhukovsky had become dominant. For most poetry readers the Romantic way *was* poetry. Against the backdrop of this lush system Pushkin's spare lines produced a startling impression. Pushkin's work was read in the context of the earlier system and struck the reader by its deliberate avoidance of the typical features of the older Romantic model or, as Lotman puts it, by its saturation of minus devices. This is a version of the multi-systemic conflict discussed above. It is, however, one with exceedingly important implications for structuralist criticism. Criticism must consider both what is physically present in a text and, no less importantly, what is missing in terms of the reader's system of expectations.

This is a part of a more general principle. Artistic simplicity is more complex than artistic complexity for it arises via the simplification of the latter and against its backdrop or system. In this view poetry although in a sense more complex is a more informative area of investigation because its esthetic mechanisms are more in evidence than are those of belletristic prose which arose from poetry via simplification. Poetry in general has fewer "minus devices" than belletristic prose and is hence more accessible to investigation.

Virtually all of Professor Lotman's analyses of poems are internal or immanent in their orientation. This is not however an inherent feature of literary structuralism. Although the literary text and the system(s) it manifests are thus far the chief focus of literary structural analysis, this restricted view is a function of the present limitations of the state of the art. Whereas the technique of the structural study of single poems is fairly well, albeit far from fully, elaborated our understanding of the many larger structures which subsume and provide the context of a poem is quite limited. A truly structural understanding of a poem involves both the immanent analysis of the work and equally of a wide range of overlapping and congruent systems. These include such entities as the genre of the poem, the system of the Russian lyric of a certain period, Russian poetry, belle lettres, the cultural milieu of the period and so on. A full appreciation of the individual work implies all of these and much more. This is obviously more of an ideal than even a potential reality. Nevertheless some presently existing poetic analyses do show striking and insightful correlations between immanent features of the work and aspects of our rudimentary models of higher levels.

III

ORGANIZING PROCESSES AND ANALYTIC PROCEDURES

The data of the various levels of a text are organized according to certain very general principles. Textual analysis requires an awareness of these constitutive principles. The organizational process that unifies the topics considered here is that of repetition or recurrence. These include rhythm, meter, and rhyme. Additionally the categories of the concepts of "the alien word" and plot are considered in this section.

Recurrence:
Perhaps the most fundamental phenomenon which characterizes the organization of literary art is that of heightened repetition or recurrence. The recurrence of textual segments cuts across all of the levels of textual construction—from the metrical and phonetic to the compositional. The analytic process for the determination of recurrence is, according to Lotman, that of contrast-comparison *(so-protivopostavlenie)* which apparently means no more than the search for whole and/or partial duplications on different levels of the text. Recurrences may be realized as either those of identity or those of antithesis. Lotman's definition of these last items seems to be founded on paradox. Identity describes the combination of elements of comparison that seem different; antithesis—that which marks

the opposing in the similar, i.e., the correlative pair. Analogy, the isolation of the similar in the different, is a variety of antithesis.

These entities describe basic logical concepts and are parenthetically alluded to by Lotman in a number of places. The reader gets the impression that they are systematically applied as part of structural analysis. This is somewhat misleading. While it is true that no analytic effort can be undertaken without the use of these concepts, it is not true that Lotman systematically applies these standards on the successive levels of a text. Much of the result would be utterly trivial and in any case the application of these concepts depends upon the recognition of the units of comparison. These are far from clear especially on the higher analytic levels—those wherein semantic meanings are heavily involved.

The concepts of recurrence and of parallelism are discussed both jointly and in separate sections although no clear line of demarcation is maintained. Perhaps the nearest approach to a delimitation is to be found in Robert Austerlitz's observation that "parallelism can be viewed as an incomplete recurrence." This distinction is blurred, however, in that Lotman quite properly notes that no recurrence is ever complete due to differences of context. Since, however, recurrence or repetition is the more encompassing of the terms it shall be used here.

Various poetic systems are at least partly definable by the extent to which they utilize recurrence of various levels. Indeed the recognition of a text as poetic or not may depend on this.

The existence of partial recurrences permits the establishment of paradigms, i.e., unified sets of variant forms of some functional entity. The actually occurring forms are also compared by the reader (and writer) against the tacitly known full membership of the paradigm. This comparison of the actually occurring elements in a recurrent structure against the physically absent but tacitly present members of its paradigm is a phenomenon extant on various levels—from the phonetic, e.g., alliteration, to the genre. As Lotman points out by way of example, each XVIII century Russian tragedy is read as a realization of the abstract paradigm "tragedies of the XVIII century." This paradigm constitutes a model for the entire class. Each realization is a variant unit, one of those which collectively constitute the invariant unit. The invariant, although absolute on its own level, is a variant with respect to higher level invariants such as "tragedy," "literature," "language," and "culture."

Rhythm and Meter:

Rhythm is the cyclical recurrence of position. In addition to its metronomic function it also plays a semantic role. The similarity of very different elements or, conversely, the differences in very similar elements can be emphasized through their occurrence in identical metrical positions. Rhythm is a textual entity as opposed to meter which is systemic. Rhythm is the variant; meter—the invariant. Meter, whose abstract pattern is recognized through scansion, creates its own system of expectation, its own inertia. Its perception quickly becomes automatized. The variety introduced into meter by rhythmic variants disrupts the automatism of perception and is an essential ingredient in the overall esthetic impact of the text. Lotman sees the conflict of these two levels as a manifestation of the dialectic process. Here too we find the same pattern as elsewhere in the poetic process: the establishment of a rule system with its own inertia and then the partial disruption of that system.

The metrical system interacts not only with its own rhythmic interpretation but also with the elements of other levels such as the lexical. Metrical position and recurrence unquestionably alter lexical meaning in poetry. In fact, the history of Russian poetry shows a long and complex interaction of the two systems. Early syllabo-tonic verse is rigidly metrical often to the point of obscuring lexical meaning. As the metrical norm became more firmly set, the lexical aspect of verse came to play a more central role, eventually displacing metrics in some twentieth century poetry. Lotman asserts that the history of poetry has proceeded by such a series of dialectical oscillations. The dominance of various structural stages is assertedly reflected by such labels as Classicism, Romanticism, etc.

Metrical systems not only have some impact on the lexical level but even tend to assume semantic value themselves. In demonstration of this Lotman shows the gradual development of fixed associations between types of meters and types of poetic content and the potential for either mutual reinforcement or dissonance between them. Both possibilities are sources of esthetic reaction.

Rhyme:

Rhyme no less than meter and rhythm is based on recurrence (and non-recurrence). It is, however, based on the recurrence of sound as well as of position. In addition to its obvious integrative role on the phonetic level, rhyme plays an important semantic role. Words which by chance share similar phonetic elements are juxtaposed throwing their lexical meaning into vivid contrast. Words which outside of a given text have little in common throw each other into high relief. Evidence of the semantic nature of rhyme is afforded on the one hand by the prohibition of rhymes depending on recurrence of the same word (i.e., exact duplication of sound and sense) and, on the other, by the rise of inexact rhyme which vastly expands the possibilities for startling semantic juxtapositions.

The level of rhyme also interacts with that of rhythm. Lotman argues that relaxations in rhythmic systems have been paralleled by increased stringency in rhyme requirements. Interaction with still other levels is reflected in Lotman's assertion that a weakening of metaphorism is generally accompanied by a weakening of the structural role of rhyme.

"The Alien Word":

This is a concept that functions on a variety of levels. On each level a certain system or "language" prevails. This "language" is the dominant system on that level. There are, however, on each structural level elements which are not part of the dominant language. It is a basic tenet in Lotman's theory that these intruding elements are not asystemic but are representatives of another system. The tension arising from the concurrent presence of more than one system is an obligatory feature of art. These elements of a second (or third) "language" constitute "the alien word." Their effect is that of deautomatizing the reader's perception of the dominant system of that level. Only by contrast is it possible to foreground a central system. Following the Soviet scholar Bakhtin, Lotman sees this process as one of the "dialogization" or a "polylogization" of a text wherein each system represents one of the speakers.

Plot:

Plot *(siuzhet)* or thematic treatment is one of the higher levels of belletristic organization. It too is subject to the same sorts of factors as are lower level structural entities. Poetic plot essentially differs from prose plot due to its greater abstractness. The enormous variety of human experience is not represented directly in the poetic plot but via reduction to one of a small number of culturally and chronologically determined models. All actual plots are surface variants, i.e., transformations of a small number of plots. Each basic plot model is built upon a set of oppositions, e.g., freedom/slavery, town/country, etc. Both the nature of the oppositions and the accepted mode of resolution of the opposition varies with time and place.

IV

THE LEVELS OF ANALYSIS

Structural analysis of the poetic text derives from the outlook and procedures elaborated in structural linguistics. One of the central tenets of structural linguistics is that language is composed of a number of different levels such as the phonetic, the morphological, the syntactic, the lexical and so on. Although there is interaction among these levels, each, insofar as possible, is generally treated on its own terms using its own basic units of analysis. The description of these levels is obviously germane to the study of poetic language.

Poetry language in addition to these general linguistic levels has a number of structural entities which are uniquely the province of belletristic language. These include the poetic line, the stanza, and the text itself.

All of these levels, both the linguistic and the purely poetic, are hierarchically related to each other. We shall summarize Lotman's views and uses of these various levels in his structural analysis of the poetic text.

The Graphic Level:

Lotman's inclusion of a graphic level is likely to strike the linguist as strange since graphic systems are often a distorting overlay concealing the phonological and morphological levels of language. It is also unusual from the viewpoint of most non-structurally oriented literary critics. That Lotman should incorporate such a level into his model is indicative of his broadly based theoretical stance. Art as a whole is a communicational system and representational graphics may be just as much a part of the overall semiotic system of literature as is the overtly semantic component. More specifically the logic underlying this is as follows. One of the most general features of natural language is that the relationship between form and content is conventional and that our normal perception of the language is automatized. Attention to structure is suppressed and content is the focus. Poetic language features an iconic rather than a predominantly conventional relationship of form and content in which all language (and cultural) elements, variant as well as invariant, may be involved in the expression of the content. The graphic level is a particularly striking example of the special nature of poetic language, for in non-belletristic writing typographical data are apprehended automatically whereas in poetic language such data are non-automatic and may carry meaning. In extreme cases, typographical considerations alone, such as the coincidence of verse line and graphic line, mark a text as poetic.

The graphic level provides illustration of another regularity that recurs on all levels of the structural hierarchy. On each level, a historical oscillation may be noted between an initial period of the rigid observation of a newly established set of rules (i.e., a new system) which has become firmly fixed as a norm in the reader's consciousness, and a subsequent period of increasing deviation from that norm ultimately tending toward a new system which in turn undergoes the same sort of process.

In earlier times graphic devices were often an integral part of poetry. Not only in the use of the poetic line but in the use of frames, vignettes, and so on. In extreme cases the very shape of the poem mimicked some aspect of content, e.g., a love poem printed in the shape of a heart. This is an extreme case of iconicity in which visual appearance carries esthetic information. Such features in their less extravagant forms came to be viewed as markers of poetry as opposed to prose. However, with the eventual establishment of poetry as a category distinct from belletristic prose, these elements gradually dropped away leading ultimately to poetry graphically marked only by line arrangement and certain other orthographic peculiarities. The history of the metrical and rhythmic levels of poetry display a like process.

Deviations from established systems disrupt the automatism of perception and by calling the reader's attention to particular points result in a higher level of information flow. This, according to Lotman, is one of the main characteristics of art.

The Phonological Level:

Specially ordered sound patterning is the dimension of poetry which most obviously separates poetry from non-poetry. Of all of the structural levels of language, that of sound is the best understood and it is not surprising that linguistics has made its greatest contribution to the study of poetry in this area. Alliteration and rhyme both rely on the recurrence of similar sounds. Although considering these topics, Lotman focuses upon a different aspect of sound in poetry. In ordinary language, sound structure is for the most part informationally neutral. Phonemes *per se* do not bear meaning and the association of sound and meaning is a matter of convention. In poetic language this is not true. The levels of sound and meaning interact and this interaction may either take the form of the sound system reinforcing the lexical level or of entering into conflict with it by linking antithetic lexical items through the recurrence of identical or similar sounds which previously have been identified with one of the two terms. This semanticization of phonemes is specific to the particular work of art and is quite apart from onomatopoeic and synesthetic phenomena which also play an important role in poetry.

Cases of this sort of interplay manifest a general principle. The role of recurrent sound units in linking the lexical units of a poem increases as grammatical cohesiveness within the poem diminishes. Where syntactic linkage, for example, is obscure, sound recurrence may compensate.

The Morphological Level:

Perhaps the most insightful aspect of Lotman's structuralist approach to literature is his analysis of the grammatical level. Consonant with his general principle that in artistic language all (not just invariant) elements may bear esthetic information Lotman argues that purely formal grammatical meanings do in fact become artistic devices in poetry. Taken on a low level, this assertion is neither novel nor profound. The writer's conscious selection of one morphological or syntactic possibility over another has long been recognized as a standard artistic device. Lotman, however, deriving his interpretation from Roman Jakobson, sets this process in another dimension. Rather than focusing on low level choices (the traditional domain of stylistics), Lotman considers the role of high level grammatical categories in the meaning of the work of art.

The grammatical category of personal pronouns, for example, represents a closed system whose elements are devoid of lexical meaning. Supremely abstract, pronouns segment the world of experience in a certain stereotyped way and express the full range of possibilities open to the speakers of a given language. All of the data of experience must be coded or recoded to fit the pronominal categories. Lotman shows how this formal skeleton of grammatical meaning may constitute a counterpoint to the meaning of a poem. This intermeshing profoundly contributes to the esthetic impact of a poem.

On an even more general level Lotman shows that the pronominal structures of literary works typically vary by genre. Lyric poetry, for example, is expressed largely in terms of the first and second person with the latter generally dominant over the former. Narrative poems on the other hand tend to involve the grammatical third person. Pronouns are only one of the many grammatical categories which may play semi-covert roles in verbal art in their interaction with other levels of artistic structure.

Grammatical categories are features inherent in human language and generally function below the level of consciousness. Lotman's surfacing of these categories is a thoroughly convincing presentation of their importance in producing esthetic impact.

The Lexical Level:

The lexical component of a poem is both the entire vocabulary of that particular poetic universe and also a subset of a particular national language. Words which are externally identical in the two lexicons may or may not coincide in meaning. The lexicon of a poem is a model of that particular restricted universe and its lexical items of necessity play a much weightier relative role than their equivalents in the general language. The shorter a text, the more important each word is. The restricted context of a poem may and often does result in words assuming meanings different from and even contrary to their non-belletristic ones. Poetic synonyms and antonyms may thus be quite different from their non-poetic counterparts.

These facts of the poetic lexicon have led Russian structuralist critics to compile micro-glossaries of individual poems and of individual poets in an attempt to demonstrate the distinctive nature of poetic language.

A closely related matter is that of the concept of the "unknown word." The lexical meaning of such items may often be unfamiliar to the reader and even to the poet. Such lexical items may play an important role in poetry for while their meaning is unclear they are all the more significant and implication-laden for the reader.

The Line:

The poetic line in contrast to the prose line is an enormously complex entity. The prose line is an external unit defined by typographic considerations of spacing. The poetic line is an internal integral entity defined by a complex of factors drawn from various levels of poetic structure. These include the levels of metrics, intonation, syntax and rhyme. All of these levels have their own meanings which may either complement or conflict with the "surface" lexical meaning of the line. One such traditionally recognized conflict often used for artistic effect is a clash between various types of meter and the emotional tonality of a poem.

Like other elements of poetic language, the line, a non-significant feature of prose, strives for independent meaning while it simultaneously is part of a larger structure. It shares this tendency with other lower and higher level entities of poetic language. This continuum includes such smaller entities as the phoneme, sound patterning, the morpheme, and such larger ones as that of the rhyme pattern, the stanza, and the text. Lotman asserts that in poetry each of these entities functions as an *ad hoc* word, an integral meaning.

The Stanza:

The stanza like all of the other structural entities discussed has an internal and an external aspect. Unlike the preceding structural levels, it is facultative. If present however, it functions as a unit and has its own well-defined internal structure. The minimal stanza consists of two lines, a couplet. In its more complex forms, the lines forming a stanza may constitute a hierarchy. This hierarchy is structured in terms of interlocking unities of various levels such as meter, rhyme, and sense. In extreme cases these units may blend into highly structured entities, such as a poem with an initial quatrain advancing a thesis, a second quatrain with an antithesis and a concluding synthesizing couplet.

On the stanzaic level, as on all others, the relationship of the constitutive elements may be either mutually supportive or, once a pattern is established, such elements may be set in juxtaposition to each other. The latter may equally be a source of esthetic judgment.

The Compositional Level:

A poetic text is an indivisible sign whose integrality is assured by the interaction of its constituent levels of organization. The interrelations of these levels is the sphere of the compositional level although, practically speaking, only the larger structural units such as the supra-phrasal tend to be considered. Such sequences constitute the syntagmatics of the text while individually, in comparison with each other and their unrealized variants, they form structural paradigms.

The Text:

The term "text" which is one of the central concepts in structuralist criticism is used at various levels of abstraction. In one sense the "text" is the highest level of the immanent analysis of a poem. It is the sum of the poem's constituent levels, i.e., the graphic, the phonemic, that of grammatical categories, the lexical level, the line, and the stanza. It is the poem itself.

The term also has a more general supra-meaning akin to a general principle of structural linguistics. In this sense, a text is a particular manifestation of an invariant. It is a surface representation of an underlying deep structure or structures. Thus any given poem is a manifestation of some larger model or system of texts which gives it some part of its meaning. At the highest level this system of texts represents the entire culture. Any given poem (or text in the lower sense) is a particular realization of this much larger invariant.

V

CONCLUDING COMMENTS

In the foregoing we have attempted to set forth Professor Lotman's view of the structural analysis of the poetic text with a minimum of evaluative commentary. Our attention will now be directed toward a number of problems raised by Lotman's arguments.

The claims made for the results, both attained and potential, to be derived from the application of the structuralist view and techniques to literature are impressive. At the one extreme we have the extravagant macro-structuralist dictum of Tzvetan Todorov that given a structuralist view of literature a single feature of a genre specimen should be sufficient to reconstruct the entire genre just as a paleontologist reconstructs an extinct creature from a fossil bone.[3] At the other end of the spectrum, we have phono-stylistic studies which often are too restricted in scope and implication to serve as the basis of significant generalization. The benefits of the structural approach in the sciences and more recently in linguistics are undeniable. The desirability and potential benefit of a structuralist view of literature is equally beyond dispute. The real question is the extent to which literature lends itself to structuralist techniques of description and analysis. It is certainly true that literature as a subtopic of the category "language" must constitute an integral system or structure. Literature as an object of structural analysis is, however, much more complex than language.

During the twentieth century, scholars have arrived at a conception of language which in its broad outline has achieved general concurrence. Language has been placed within the wider context of information theory and semiotics. There is, again in general terms, agreement that language contains a number of interrelated hierarchical levels such as phonetics, phonology, morphology, syntax, semantics, etc., and that each of these

xxv

levels operates with a small number of prime units such as distinctive features, phonemes, morphemes, etc. It is understood that these basic units and the levels they represent interact according to certain principles and rules.

The "structuralist situation" for literature is much less impressive. Even among structurally oriented critics, agreement is truly general only on the point that literature does constitute a structure and is to some degree susceptible to rigorous analysis.

The idea of literary structuralism is most appealing. The concept of the variant/invariant relationship which has proved so fertile for linguistic analysis when applied at various levels in the analysis of a literary work seems to provide a framework for hitherto loosely defined relationships. Let us take a closer look at one such parallel. Perhaps the classic case in linguistics illustrating the variant/invariant relationship is that involving the concept of the phoneme. Most of the applications of the variant/invariant relationship to morphology, syntax, etc. are extensions of and derived from its use in the elaboration of the concept of the phoneme. The standard definition of a phoneme is that it is an abstract entity representing a number of physically similar sounds which have a single function and which are in complementary distribution or free variation with other members of that class. All actually occurring sounds are allophones, i.e., variants, while the phoneme, the invariant unit, is an abstract construct. The requirement that complementary distribution prevail among the allophones of a given phoneme (if they are to be classed as members of that phoneme) means that each allophone must occur in its own distinctive environment and nowhere else. If two different allophones of a given phoneme were to occur in the same environment, they would be in contrast and hence, by definition, not members of that phoneme. It should be noted that the necessary parameters of physical similarity and functional identity are susceptible of precise definition. It should be emphasized that the entire concept of the phoneme is meaningless without the idea of complementary distribution.

If we now examine some literary entity in the light of a structural model such as that of a phoneme, we shall see a number of parallels and a number of divergencies. Let us take the literary category of "genre." Like the phoneme, the prototype invariant unit, the genre is an abstract unit consisting of a large number of literary texts of a particular sort. These are the real, actually occurring entities which collectively constitute the genre. They are the variant units. Each text, like each allophone, bears a certain physical resemblance to the other texts which make up the genre and all have a similar function. Roughly the same sort of parallels can be drawn for many of the literary entities discussed by Lotman. It would appear that the variant/invariant principle provides a powerful tool for studying individual texts in terms of their relationship to a central invariant unit, the genre. This sort of parallel gives the impression that one of the fundamental principles of modern science can be systematically and fruitfully applied to literature.

A closer look, however, suggests that the parallel is less satisfactory than it initially seemed. If we carry our analogy a bit further, difficulties arise. We noted that complementary distribution was a key constitutive element in the definition of the phoneme. What might be the literary equivalent of complementary distribution? On the surface of the matter it seems plausible to take two love lyric texts and on the grounds of similarity of function and form to describe them as particular manifestations of a single genre, i.e., variants of a single invariant. That is, they appear to stand in the same sort of relationship to each other and to their genre as do two allophones of a single phoneme. The allophones of a phoneme are in complementary distribution however. Is it meaningful to say that the two poetry texts are in this relationship? Are their differences describable in terms of environmental differences? Would a given environment invariably assure the production of one particular text and not the other? What does environment mean in this context? It is clear that if the variant/invariant relationship which has been so productive in linguistic analysis is pushed very far in literary analysis the analogy which first seemed so promising is a relatively weak one. One of the chief problems is that most purely literary entities, unlike phonological ones, do not lend themselves to sharp definition. Literary constructs although undoubtedly real and useful are often hybridized. Any "pure" example of a literary genre is a rare bird indeed. Individual texts clearly cannot be related to each other or to a hypercategory such as genre in the same sense that allophones or allomorphs are to phonemes and morphemes. These difficulties apply not only to the literary category of genre but equally to other literary constructs.

The analogy between the structural analysis of language and of literature is less than satisfactory in other ways as well. Structural linguistics views language as the sum of a number of different levels, e.g., phonological, morphological, syntactic, lexical, etc. Each of these levels has its own rigorously defined units of analysis and rules of combination and permutation. The different levels interact with each other in fairly well understood ways. The situation for literature is quite different. Inasmuch as literature is a form of language the basic levels of analysis that apply to language must also apply to literature. On the other hand, any theory of poetic language must contend with a large number of levels and entities which are either not at all or only very marginally part of general linguistic theory. This includes such compositional elements as the line, the stanza, dialogization (the alien word), and plot, on the one hand, and such matters as parallelism, rhythm, meter, and rhyme on the other. These constitute at least two additional dimensions to poetic language over and above those characteristic of "ordinary language." These "poetic" levels and/or entities are of a quite different order from those constituting ordinary language. The basis of their definitions is quite different and the nature of their interaction with each other and with the data of the "linguistic" levels is far from clear. If we agree in principle that a poem is a coherent structure, we must concede at once that our grasp of its constitutive entities and particularly their interrelationships is greatly inferior to our understanding of the structure of ordinary language or that of a chemical compound. The relationship between the levels and entities of poetic language is too poorly understood to allow the use of structural analysis in the sense that it is utilized in structural linguistics.

There is yet another problem of literary structuralist analysis which derives from its linguistic prototype. Beyond any question, structural analysis can reveal patterning on many if not all levels of an artistic work. Much of this patterning is inherent in language itself. Without this structuring, language could not serve a communicative function. It is the language patterning which is over and above that of its communicative informational function that constitutes those aspects of a work that make it an object of esthetic attention. The difficulty is that the demonstration of the existence of these additional patterns is in no way equivalent to showing that they are the source of the esthetic effect of the work.

Some of the unresolved problems of literary structuralism which have been discussed here are manifested in the second half of Professor Lotman's book. The analyses of some dozen Russian poems are often informative and occasionally brilliant. It is only in retrospect that one realizes that the relationship between the theoretical portion of the book and the analysis of the poems is often problematical. In the general introduction to the poem analyses, the author notes that each analysis focuses upon only the dominant level of each individual poem. (In passing, one might ask how this dominant is determined.) Some of the analyses do focus on levels and entities discussed in the earlier theoretical portion of the book. The analysis of the phonologic-metrical level in Batyushkov's "Thou Awakest, O Baiae, from the Tomb..." ("Ty probuzhdaesh'sia, o Baiia, iz grobnitsy") or of the grammatical level in Lermontov's "We Parted; But Thy Portrait..." ("Rasstalis' my; no tvoi portret...") may serve as examples of the integration of theory and practice. It is probably significant that such cases are the ones closest to "traditional" structural *linguistic* analyses of poetry. Other of the analyses focus on aspects of poems which are not treated at all in the theoretical portions of the book. In the analysis of Zabolotsky's "The Passerby" ("Prokhozhii") the focus is on the spatial relations evinced in the text and an attempt is made to infer the author's philosophical symbolism from these. Most of the analyses fall somewhere between these examples in the extent of their relationship to Lotman's structuralist theory of poetics.

Some of the discrepancy between theory and critical practice stems from the fact that the theory is not a coherent integrated body of knowledge. Consequently the results of its critical application are sporadic although at times insightful. One suspects that most of the critical analyses could well have been made without reference to the theoretical part of the work. Although oriented toward an analysis modeled on the techniques of structural linguistics, Lotman's approach is at times distinctly eclectic.

Professor Lotman's work has presented us with what is thus far one of the broadest expositions of literary structuralism. As an effort to bring the most humane of the humanities into the same philosophical framework as the social and natural sciences, literary structuralism is attractive. On the larger scale it appears that the structural approach and particularly the ideas of function and of the variant/invariant relationship succeed in throwing some light on how a poem "works," how it relates to other poems, and to such larger entities as literature and culture. It may even help explicate some of the mystery of esthetic impact. At the lower levels the picture is less satisfactory. The correspondence between literary and linguistic structuralism is not nearly so strong as Professor Lotman suggests. In fact in many ways the idea of literary structuralism is metaphorical. While this is not the viewpoint of most structuralist literary critics, it is by no means a bad thing. The metaphor is an extremely interesting one and has been remarkably productive during its relatively brief existence. If the idea of literary structuralism is adopted and used in a heuristic way, it will certainly continue to inspire the production of both interesting analyses and new theories which perhaps may be truly structural.

Translator's Note

The original language of Professor Lotman's book is quite complex and at times verges on opacity. This is reflected in the translation although Professor Lotman has been kind enough to clarify a number of matters for me. In general, I have tried to provide a close rendering of the original.

The translation of a volume involving the analysis of Russian poetry offers particular problems for the obvious reason that the author's commentary on sound patterning or any other language-specific aspect of a poem will often be virtually meaningless if the reader has only an English translation of the poem before him. I have tried to meet this problem by giving all of the poetic materials in both English and transliterated Russian. The English versions are as literal as I could make them. Insofar as possible, the original word order has been retained especially where the passage is discussed in the text. This procedure has resulted in a great many awkward lines but has the advantage that the reader can more nearly follow Lotman's argument by a close comparison of the transliterated Russian text and its literal English rendering.

part 1

Introduction

This book is devoted to the analysis of the poetic text.

Before proceeding to the exposition of the material itself, we shall make several preliminary observations and, first of all, define what goals *have not been set* for the present volume. Knowing in advance what is not to be found here, the reader may be spared disenchantment and spend his time on studies more directly pertaining to the area of his interests.

Poetry belongs to those spheres of art whose essence is not ultimately clear to science. Approaching its study, one must recognize that many extremely important problems are still beyond the scope of contemporary science. Moreover, their solution now seems to be even more remote than formerly: that which recently seemed obvious now seems incomprehensible and enigmatic to the modern scholar. This, however, must not discourage us. False clarity in replacing the scientific approach with that "common sense" which assures us that the earth is flat and that the sun goes around the earth is characteristic of the pre-scientific state of knowledge. This stage was a necessary step in the history of humanity. It must precede science. For during this period a mass of empirical data is accumulated and a feeling of the inadequacy of simple ordinary experience arises. Without this period there can be no science. Science arises as the transcendence of everyday ordinary experience, the transcendence of "common sense." In this process, the original "clarity," which arose from a failure to comprehend the complexity of the questions under investigation, is replaced by that fruitful lack of comprehension which is the basis of science. The naive bearer of pre-scientific knowledge, having accumulated a large body of data and having discovered that it cannot be synthesized, calls science to his aid supposing that it will give him brief and exhaustive answers that will show where the inconsistency lies and will impart integrality and stability to ordinary experience, while preserving his customary view of the world. Science presents itself to him in the guise of a physician who is summoned to a patient so that he may establish the reasons for the indisposition, prescribe the simplest, cheapest, and most effective medications and depart after having entrusted subsequent events to the care of the relatives.

The naive realism of "common sense" supposes that it will pose questions and science will answer them.

Appealed to with this wholly specific goal, science conscientiously tries to answer the questions put to it. The results are most discouraging: after prolonged effort it often becomes clear that it is impossible to answer such questions, that the questions are *incorrectly posed,* and that the correct posing of the question presents enormous difficulties and demands an effort considerably exceeding that which was initially thought sufficient for the complete resolution of the problem.

It subsequently becomes clear that science does not even constitute an instrument for obtaining answers, for no sooner than a problem obtains a definitive solution, it descends from the sphere of science into the province of post-scientific knowledge.

Thus, the task of science is *the correct posing of a question.* But to determine the correct posing of a question is impossible without a study of the methodology of the progression from ignorance to knowledge and without a determination of whether a given question can, in principle, be answered. Consequently, a whole circle of methodological questions, everything that is connected with the *route* from question to answer (but not with the answer itself), belongs to science.

Science's realization of its own specific nature and its rejection of any pretence toward activities for whose realization it lacks means constitutes a huge step on the path to knowledge. However, it is precisely this step which most frequently evokes disenchantment among the adherents of "common sense" in science, which begins to appear an overly abstract occupation. Naive realism regards science as a pagan does his idol: in the beginning, supposing that it is capable of helping him overcome all difficulties, he prays to it; then, having become disenchanted, he chops it to pieces and throws it into the fire or into the river. Having turned away from science, by-passing it, he attempts to conclude a direct alliance with the world of post-scientific resultative knowledge, with the world of answers. Thus it is, for example, when participants in the debate "physicists and lyric poets" assume that cybernetics is called upon to answer the question of whether "machine poetry" is possible and how quickly a computer will replace the members of the Union of Writers. They think that science must answer a question thusly formulated.

When we observe the mass infatuation with popularized books which are supposed to acquaint the reader not with the *course* of science and with its *methods,* but with its results and solutions—we have before us typical cases of an alliance of the pre-and post-scientific states of knowledge *against* science. However, this alliance is lacking in perspective: the answers given by science cannot be separated from science itself. They are not absolute and lose their value when the methodology which advanced them is replaced by a new one.

One must not think, however, that the contradiction noted among the pre-scientific, the scientific, and the post-scientific stages of knowledge is an irreconcilable antagonism. Each of these components requires the others. In particular, science not only draws raw material from the sphere of everyday experience but also requires a regulatory correlation of its own movement with the world of "common sense" for it is in this unique but naive and coarse world that man lives.

It follows that science must not undertake the resolution of questions that are incorrectly posed or that are non-scientific in their nature, and that the user of scientific knowledge must not make such demands on science if he is to escape disenchantment. Thus, for example, the question "Why do I like the poetry of Pushkin (Blok or Mayakovsky)?" does not lend itself to scientific scrutiny in such a form. Science is not called upon to answer *all* questions and is bound by a certain methodology.

In order that the adduced questions can become the object of science we must decide in advance whether a question interests us from the viewpoint of the psychology of personality, of social psychology, of the history of literary norms, of readers' tastes, of critical evaluation, etc. The question must then be reformulated in the language of the appropriate science and resolved by the appropriate means. Of course, results so obtained may seem to be too narrow and specialized, but science cannot propose anything other than *scientific* truth.

In the present book the poetic text will be examined not in all the wealth of the personal and social experiences evoked by it, i.e., not in all its cultural significance, but only from the relatively restricted point of view that is accessible to contemporary science.

The present work has in view the *critical literary analysis of the poetic text* and, notwithstanding all of their obvious importance, excludes from scrutiny *all questions* that go beyond the limits of literary analysis, i.e., problems of the social functioning of the text, the psychology of the readers' perception, etc. We do not examine questions of the creation and historical functioning of the text. The object of our attention will be the poetic text taken as a separate, already completed, and internally independent whole. How is this whole to be studied from the point of view of its ideational, artistic unity? Are there scientific methods that would permit us to make art an object of investigation without "killing" it? How is the text constructed and why is it constructed in precisely such a fashion? These are the questions the present book must answer.

Still another major reservation is necessary. The resolution of every scientific problem is determined by the method of investigation and by the scholar, his experience, his talent, his intuition. We shall touch only upon the first of these constituent parts of scholarly creativity.

In the humanities one frequently meets with the assertion that an exact working methodology, specific rules of analysis, limit the creative potentialities of the investigator. It is permissible to ask: "Can it really be that the knowledge of formulae, the presence of algorithms according to which a given problem is solved restrict a mathematician and make him less creatively active than a person with no idea of formulae?" Formulae do not countermand individual creativity but rather lead to its economization by freeing one from the necessity of "inventing the bicycle" and directing our thoughts into the area of the as yet unresolved.

Contemporary literary criticism is on the threshold of a new phase. This is expressed in its ever-growing striving not so much toward unimpeachable answers as toward the verification of the correct way of posing questions. Literary criticism is learning to ask; previously, it hastened to answer. Now it is not the individual experience of this or that investigator, nor that which is inseparable from his personal experience, tastes, and temperament but a considerably more prosaic, more strict standardized methodology of analysis that is brought to the fore. Accessible to every literary scholar, it does not replace personal scientific creativity but serves as its foundation.

Goncharov once wrote of civilization, ''. . . that what was an inaccessible luxury for the few, thanks to civilization, becomes accessible for all: in the North a pineapple costs five or ten rubles, here—half a kopeck; the task of civilization is to transport it quickly to the North and to drive its price down to five kopecks so that you and I may enjoy it.''[1] To a certain extent the task of science is analogous: obtaining certain results, the scholar elaborates certain fixed methods of analysis, investigational algorithms, that makes his result replicable. What a surgeon of genius was doing yesterday in unique conditions, will become accessible to *every* physician tomorrow. It is precisely the sum of this replicable research experience that constitutes scientific methodology.

In principle the analysis of belletristic text allows several approaches: a work of art can be studied as secondary material for the examination of historical, socio-economic, or philosophical problems or it can be a source of information about the daily existence, the juridical, or moral norms of another era, etc. In each case a distinctive methodology of investigation will correspond to the specific features of the scientific problem.

In the present book the object of investigation will be *the artistic text as such.* The specifically artistic meaning of a text that enables it to perform a particular function, i.e., an esthetic one, will be the object of our attention. This will also determine the peculiarities of our approach.

In the real life of a culture, texts, as a rule, are multifunctional: the same text fulfills not one, but several (sometimes many) functions. Thus, a medieval icon, a temple of the Classical era, of the European Middle Ages, of the Renaissance, or of the Baroque period, simultaneously have both a religious and esthetic function. The military regulations and governmental legislative documents of the epoch of Peter the First were simultaneously juridical and publicistic. The proclamations of the Generals' Convention, Suvorov's "Science of Victory" or the divisional orders of Mikhail Orlov can be examined either as military historical texts or as monuments of publicistics, of the orator's art, or as belletristic prose. Under certain conditions similar combinations of functions are not only an individual phenomenon but an indispensable one: so that a text can have its *own*

6

function, it must also have a supplementary one. Thus, under certain conditions, so that an icon may be perceived as a religious text and perform this social function, it must also be a work of art. The reverse dependence is also possible. In order to be perceived as a work of art, the icon must have the religious function that is proper to it. Therefore, its transfer to a museum (and, in a certain sense, the absence of religious feeling in the viewer) violates the effect, historically inherent to the text, of the unity of the two social functions.

All this directly relates to literature. The unification of the artistic function with the magical, juridical, moral, philosophical, and political constitutes an inalienable feature of the social functioning of an artistic text. A bilateral connection is frequently present: so that it may perform a particular belletristic function, a text must simultaneously have moral, political, philosophical, and publicistic functions.

Conversely, in order to play a particular role (for example, a political one), a text must also realize an esthetic function. Of course, in a number of cases, only one function is realized. The investigation of which clusters of functions can be combined within a single text would give interesting indices for the construction of a typology of culture. Thus, for example, in the eighteenth century, the unification of the artistic and moralistic functions was a condition for the esthetic perception of a text. For Pushkin and Gogol, the unification of these two functions in a single text was no longer possible.

Fluctuations in the limits of the concept "belletristic text" continue even in the literature of the modern period. Memoir literature is of great interest in this regard in that it is initially opposed to bellestristic prose, to "flights of imagination," and then begins to occupy an important place in its constituency. This applies equally to the "sketch" with its specific role in the 1840s, 1860s, and 1950s. Mayakovsky composing the texts for the display windows of the Russian Telegraph Agency or verse ads for the State Department Store (GUM) scarcely pursued purely poetic aims. (See "Order No. 2 for the Army of the Arts.") For us, however, the place of these texts in the history of Russian poetry is beyond dispute.

The relativity of the boundaries of "belletristic" and "non-belletristic" texts is evident in the history of the documentary film.

The complexity, sometimes the diffuseness, of the social functioning of texts naturally pushes the investigator toward a diffuseness of approach to his subject: it is regarded as completely natural to avoid the fractionalization of objects of investigation that in life function together. However, one must resolutely protest this. In order to understand the complex interaction of the diverse functions of a single text, one must preliminarily inspect each of them separately, and investigate those objective features that define a given text as a work of art, a monument of philosophical, juridical or other form of social thought. Such an inspection of the text's various aspects does not replace the study of the entire wealth of its associations but must precede it. The analysis of the interaction of the text's social functions must be preceded by their articulation and description. Violation of this sequence would be at odds with the elementary demand of science to proceed from the simple to the complex.

The present work is devoted precisely to this initial stage of the analysis of the belletristic text. From the entire wealth of problems arising in the analysis of a work of art, we isolate a comparatively narrow one: the strictly esthetic nature of a literary work.

We are forced to proceed to an even greater circumscription of our topic. One can approach the examination of a work of art variously. Let us suppose that we are studying the Pushkin poem "I remember a marvellous moment..." ("Ia pomniu chudnoe mgnoven'e..."). The character of our study will be different depending upon what we select as the topic of investigation, and what we shall consider to be the limits of this text. We can examine Pushkin's poem from the point of view of its internal structure or we can take as our text more general aggregates, as for example, "Pushkin's lyrics from the period of the Mikhailovsky exile," "the Pushkin lyric," "the Russian love lyric of the 1820s," "Russian poetry of the first quarter of the nineteenth century," or, broadening the theme not chronologically but typologically, "European poetry of the 1820s." In each case, different aspects of the poem are revealed.

Therefore, several types of investigation will be appropriate: a monographic study of the text, an investigation of the history of the national literature, a comparative typological investigation, etc. Thus, the topic of investigation and its limits, but not its method, will be determined. Both the text of an individual poem and the art of an individual epoch can be presented in the form of a single structure organized according to certain internal laws that pertain only to it.

The incompletely enumerated aspects of our study constitute in their totality a complete description of the artistic structure of the work. However, such a description would be so cumbersome that to realize it within the limits of the single investigative text would be an unrealistic task. The investigator, willingly or unwillingly, is forced to limit himself to selecting one or another aspect of the object of study. The initial approach will be that which will limit itself to the examination of the text of a work "from the first word to the last." This approach will permit us to bring out the internal structure of the work, the nature of its artistic organization, and a certain, sometimes considerable, part of the artistic information included in the text. Such an approach constitutes an indispensable but nonetheless initial stage of the study of the work. It will not inform us about the text's social function nor will it reveal the history of its interpretations, its place in the poet's subsequent evolution, nor will it answer a multitude of other questions. Nevertheless, the author wishes to stress that, according to his deep conviction, such a "monographic" analysis of the text constitutes an indispensable first step in its study. Apart from this, such an analysis occupies a special place in the hierarchy of scientific problems, for it answers the question "Why is the present work a work of art?" If on other levels of investigation the literary scholar attacks problems that also attract the cultural historian, the student of political studies, of philosophy, of everyday life, etc., then here he is completely original in studying the organic problems of literary art.

It is hoped that the foregoing fully justifies the excerption of the monographic investigation of the individual text to be examined as an artistic whole as the special subject matter of this book. The posing of such a theme also has another basis.

Soviet literary studies have achieved certain successes, especially in the area of the history of Russian literature. Extensive experience in research methodology has been accumulated and its mastery, as experience shows, does not meet with great difficulties. The methodology of the analysis of the internal structure of the artistic text is considerably less well developed, notwithstanding the fact that Soviet scholarship can point to works that have become classic and have received wide acknowledgment.

The present book expounds the principles of the structural analysis of poetry.[2]

For many literary scholars, terminology is a major obstacle to the mastery of the essentially simple ideas of structural-semiotic analysis. The history of our science has taken shape in such a way that many fertile ideas touching upon all systems of communcation between transmitter and receiver were first advanced in linguistics. Because of this, because language is the major communicative system in human society and many general principles are manifested in it more clearly, and because all secondary modeling systems in some measure experience its influence, linguistic terminology occupies a special place in all of the sciences of the semiotic cycle—including structural poetics.

If the reader wishes to obtain more detailed information regarding the terminology that has been accepted in modern structural linguistics and that, under its influence, has penetrated into works on semiotics, it will be useful to refer to the following handbooks: O. S. Akhmanova, *A Dictionary of Linguistic Terms (Slovar' lingvisticheskikh terminov),* (M. 1966); note that a reference guide by V. F. Beliaev called *Basic Terminology of Metrics and Poetics (Osnovnaia terminologiia metriki i poetika),* has been appended to the *Dictionary* making it especially valuable for our purposes; J. Vakhek, *A Linguistic Dictionary of the Prague School (Lingvisticheskii slovar' prazhskoi shkoly),* (M. 1964); Eric P. Hamp, *A Glossary of American Technical Linguistic Usage* (Utrecht/Antwerp, 1957).

Purposes and Methods of the Structural
Analysis of the Poetic Text

Structural analysis is based on viewing a literary work as an organic whole. The text in this analysis is not perceived as a mechanical sum of its constituent elements and the "separateness" of these elements loses its absolute character: each of them is realized only in relation to the other elements and to the structural whole of the entire text. In this sense, structural analysis is opposed to the atomistic metaphysical scientific tradition of the positivist investigations of the nineteenth century and corresponds to the general spirit of the scientific quests of our century. It is not by chance that structural methods of investigation have won a place for themselves in the most diverse areas of scientific knowledge: linguistics and geology, paleontology and jurisprudence, chemistry and sociology. The attention given to the mathematical aspects of the attendant problems and the creation of a theory of structures as an independent scientific discipline attest that the question has moved from the sphere of the methodology of a separate discipline into the area of the theory of scientific knowledge as a whole.

Structural analysis, thus understood, does not constitute anything new. Its specific property lies in the very conception of integrality. A work of art constitutes a certain reality and as such can be broken down into parts. We presuppose that we are dealing with a certain part of a text. Let us assume that it is a line of a poetic text or a painted representation of a human head. Now let us imagine that this fragment is incorporated into some more extended text. Accordingly, this same drawing of a head may now be one of the numerous details of the picture, say its upper half, or it may fill (as, for example, in preliminary rough sketches) the whole canvas. Comparing these examples we shall be convinced that the textually coinciding detail, entering into different unities of a more general character, is not equal to itself.

The viewing of a film frame provides some curious observations in this regard. A single film representation taken at different distances (for example—a long shot, a medium shot, or a close-up) will enter into the artistic construction of the film print as *different* depictions, depending on the relationship of the filled part of the screen to the unfilled part and to the picture frame. (The very difference of *planes* becomes a means for the transmission of artistic meanings.) However, the change of the size of the representation depending upon the dimensions of the screen, the size of the hall, and other conditions of projection does not create new artistic meanings. Thus size, not as some absolute magnitude equal to itself outside of any connection with the artistic environment but as the *relationship* between the detail and the limits of the frame, will be in a given case the source of esthetic effect, the artistic reality.

This observation can be expanded into a general law. *One of the basic properties of artistic reality will be revealed if we set ourselves the task of separating that which enters into the very essence of the work, without which it ceases to be itself, from features, sometimes very important, but separable to the extent that given their alteration, the specific character of the work is preserved and it remains itself.* Thus, for example, without any hesitation we equate all editions of the novel *Eugene Onegin* independently of their format, type, and quality of paper.[3] In another regard we identify as one all the performed treatments of a musical or theatrical work. Finally we look upon a black and white reproduction of a picture or engraving from it (until the end of the nineteenth century this was the only way of reproducing paintings) and we identify it, in certain respects, with the original. (Thus, for example, the copying of etchings was long the basic mode of teaching the classical art of drawing and composition. An investigator analyzing the placement of figures on a canvas could completely illustrate his text with a black and white reproduction having identified it in this regard with the picture itself.) On an old fresco the scratches or spots may be far more noticeable than the drawing itself, but we "erase" them or strive to remove them in our perception. (Our enjoyment of them bears an esthetic character and is clearly secondary. It is possible only as a layer on perception extracting the text from the damage.) Thus, the reality of the text does not include all that is materially inherent to the text if one understands the concept of materiality in a naive empirical or positivistic sense. The reality of the text is created by its systemic relationships, by its meaningful antitheses, that is, by what enters into *the structure of the work.*

The concept of structure above all else implies the presence of systemic unity. Noting this property, Claude Lévi-Strauss wrote: "Structure has a systemic character. The correlation of the elements constituting it is such that the change of any one of them involves the change of all the others."[4]

The second important consequence of the observations made above is the *delimitation in the phenomenon under study of the structural (systemic) and extra-structural elements.* Structure always constitutes a model. Therefore, it differs from the text by its greater systematicity, by its "correctness," by its greater degree of abstraction. (More accurately, it is not a single abstract structure-model that is opposed to the text, but a hierarchy of structures organized according to their degree of increasing abstractness.) The text itself in relation to the structure is its realization or its interpretation on a certain level. (Thus, Shakespeare's *Hamlet* in book form and on the stage, are, from one point of view, a single work in antithesis to Sumarokov's *Hamlet* or to Shakespeare's *Macbeth;* from another point of view, they are two different levels of interpretation of a single structure.) Consequently, the text is also hierarchical. *This hierarchism of internal organization is also*

11

an essential feature of structurality.

The delimitation of system and text (in reference to language one speaks of the opposition of "language" and "speech" which is treated in more detail in the following chapter) has fundamental significance for the study of all disciplines of the structural cycle. Meanwhile, without touching upon many of the consequences of such an approach, we shall pause upon only a few in a preliminary way. Above all, it must be stressed that the opposition of text and system bears not an absolute but a relative and frequently purely heuristic character. In the first place, by virtue of the previously noted hierarchism of these concepts, a single phenomenon may appear in certain connections as a text, and in others, as a system that deciphers texts of a lower level. Thus, an Evangelical parable or a Classical fable represent texts that interpret various common religious or moral propositions. However, for people who must utilize these precepts, they constitute models interpretable on the level of worldly practice and of the readers' behavior.

The connection of the concepts "text" and "system" is also manifested elsewhere. It would be a mistake to oppose them, ascribing to text the feature of reality, and viewing structure as speculation, as something whose existence is considerably more problematical. Structure exists being realized in the empirical reality of the text. But one must not think that the connection here is unidirectional and that the fact of empirical existence is a higher criterion in the definition of reality. In the empirical world we constantly reject, exclude from our experience, particular facts. A driver observing street traffic through his windshield notices a group of pedestrians crossing the street. He instantly estimates their speed and his direction and notes those features necessary to predict their behavior in the roadway ("children," "drunk," "blind," "country-bumpkin"). He will not note (must not note!) those features that only distract his attention and have no influence on the selection of a strategy for his own behavior. For example, he must train himself *not to notice* the color of their apparel or hair, or their facial features. Meanwhile, a police detective and a young admirer of the fair sex, being on the same street at the same time, will see a completely different reality—each his own. The ability to observe implies in equal degree the ability both to notice something and not to notice it. Empiric reality appears before each of these attentive observers in a particular guise. The proofreader and the poet look differently at one and the same page. It is impossible to see only one fact if a selection system does not exist just as it is impossible to decipher a text without knowing the code. Text and structure mutually condition each other and assume reality only in this mutual correlation.

The example of the street that we have given can serve us in still another respect: it may be interpreted as the presence of three texts within the framework of one and the same situation (the street filled with people and cars functions as the text), decipherable with the aid of three different codes. However, we can also interpret it as a single text that permits three different modes of decoding. We shall meet such cases fairly frequently. The case where a single structure permits its embodiment in several different texts will afford us no less interest.

Full comprehension of the specific character of structural methods in the humanities requires the isolation of still another aspect of the question. Not every structure serves as a device for the storage and transmission of information, but any information-bearing device is a structure. Thus arises the question of the structural study of semiotic systems—systems that utilize signs and that serve for the transmission and storage of information. Structural methods are characteristic of the majority of contemporary sciences. For the humanities, it would be more accurate to speak of *structural-semiotic methods.*

* * *

Viewing the poetic text as a special sort of organized semiotic structure, we naturally will rely on the achievements of earlier scientific thought.

Given all the differences and diversity of initial scientific principles conditioned both by the correlation of each investigative method with a particular type of ideology (and, more broadly, culture) and also by the laws of the progressive development of human knowledge, two approaches to the study of the artistic work are typologically possible. The first proceeds from the idea that the essence of art is hidden in the text itself and that each work is of value by virtue of the fact that it is what it is. In this case attention is concentrated on the internal laws of the construction of the work of art. The second approach implies a view of the work *as a part,* the expression of something more significant than the text itself, e.g., the personality of the poet, the psychological moment, or the social situation. In this case the text will interest the investigator not for itself, but as material for the construction of the above-enumerated models of a more abstract level.

In the history of literary studies each of these tendencies has known periods when it was forced to attempt the solution of the most pressing scholarly problems, and times when, having exhausted the possibilities afforded it by a given level of the development of science, it yielded to the opposing tendency. Thus, in the eighteenth century, the science of literature was, in the first instance, the science of rules for the internal construction of the text. Whatever the estheticians of the nineteenth century may have said about anti-historicism, about norms, or the metaphysics of the science of literature in the eighteenth century, it must not be forgotten that it was precisely at that time when Boileau's *L'Art poétique,* Lomonosov's *Rhetoric (Ritorika),* and Lessing's *Hamburgische Dramaturgie* were written. To theoreticians of the nineteenth century the judgments of their predecessors about art seemed "trivial" and too much absorbed in the technology of the writer's craft. However, one must not forget that it was precisely in the eighteenth century that the theory of literature, as never since, was connected with criticism and with real literary life and that, in concentrating on the question of how a text must be constructed, the theoreticians of the eighteenth century created a huge capital of belletristic culture on whose basis nineteenth century European literature actually existed.

Theoretical thought of the following epoch absolutely refused to see a work as something self-contained. The text was searched for *the expression of the spirit,* of history, of the epoch, or of some other essence that lay outside of the work. And insofar as the essence lying beyond the text was thought of as living and infinite and the work itself was its ultimately inadequate clothing, "the soul's imprisonment in material manifestation," a finite image of the infinite, the task of the reader and the investigator (formerly it was supposed that this was a single task and that the investigator was simply a qualified reader) was to *break through the text* to the essences lying beyond it. From this point of view, the relationship of the text to other texts, their merger into a single stream, or the relationship of the text to external reality (however this reality might be understood—as the development of a world spirit or as a battle of social forces) assumed decisive significance. Taken in and of itself, the text did not constitute anything significant. It was reduced to the level of a "monument."

In the twentieth century battle of literary opinions, upon which the general character of the epoch has laid an imprint of profound dramatism, voices have frequently been raised decrying the fundamental depravity of first one, then the other, of the tendencies named above. It has been lost from view that each of these tendencies reflects a certain aspect of the reality of the material under study and that each, at certain stages in the development of scholarly thought, has advanced powerful and fertile conceptions, and in other stages—epigonic and doctrinaire constructs.

For a number of historical reasons, the conflict between these two tendencies has assumed a particularly acute character in the twentieth century. The degradation of academic literary studies evoked a reaction in the works of the young literary scholars of the so-called Formal school—the Moscow Linguistic Circle in Moscow, the Society for the Study of Poetic Language in Petrograd (OPOJaZ), the critics and theoreticians of Futurism, and later of the Left Front (LEF). The fundamental position and basic merit of this trend was the assertion that art is not merely secondary material for psychological or historical studies, but that the study of art has its own proper subject matter. Declaring the independence of subject matter and investigative methodology, the Formal school advanced the problem of the text into the foreground. Assuming that they stood on a materialist foundation, Formalism's adherents affirmed that meaning is impossible without a material substratum, without the sign, and depends on its organization. Many brilliant surmises about the semiotic nature of the artistic text were advanced. A number of the postulates of the Formal school antici-pated the ideas of structural literary studies and have found confirmation and interpretation in the latest ideas of structural linguistics, of semiotics, and of information theory. Through the Prague Linguistic Circle and the works of R. Jakobson, the theory of the Russian Formal school exerted a profound influence on the worldwide development of the humanities.

At the very beginning of the polemic which was not long in bursting into flame around the works of the young literary scholars, a number of vulnerable points in the conception of the Formal school were pointed out. Criticism of the Formalists was first heard from the pillars of Symbolism who occupied eminent places in literary criticism at the beginning of the 1920s (V. Ia. Briusov and others). Having become accustomed to see in the text only an external sign of profound and hidden ideas, they could not agree with the reduction of the idea to a construct. Other aspects of For-malism evoked protest among scholars connected with classical German philosophy (G. Shpet) who saw culture as movement of the spirit and not as the sum of its texts. Finally, sociological criticism of the 1920s pointed to the immanence of the Formalists' literary analysis as their basic failing. If for the Formalists, the explication of a text was reduced to answering the question "How is it constructed?," then, for the sociologists, all was defined by another question—"By what is it conditioned?"

An exposition of the dramatic history of the Formal school would lead us beyond the limits of our immediate task. One must, however, note that major Soviet scholars such as B. M. Eikhenbaum, V. B. Shklovsky, Iu. N. Tynyanov, and B. V. Tomashevsky have come from the ranks of the Formal school. Its principles also influenced G. O. Vinokur, G. A. Gukovsky, V. V. Gippius, P. A. Skaftymov, V. M. Zhirmunsky, M. M. Bakhtin, V. V. Vinogradov, V. Ia. Propp, and many other scholars. The evolution of the Formal school was connected with the effort to overcome the immanence of intra-textual analysis and to replace the metaphysical concept of the "device" as the basis of art with the dialectical concept of artistic function. Here one must especially single out the works of Iu. N. Tynyanov. The transition of Formalism to Functionalism is clearly visible in the example of the noteworthy Czech and Slovak school of literary studies and is to be seen in the works of Jan Mukarovsky, J. Hrabak, M. Bakos, and other members of the Prague Linguistic Circle, and also of N. S. Trubeckoi and R. Jakobson, who were closely connected with it.

However, after rendering their full due to the ideas advanced by the theoreticians of the OPOJaZ, one must strongly protest the frequently expressed idea of Formalism as the chief source of Structuralism or even of the identity of these two scholarly tendencies. Structural ideas crystal-lized both in the works of the Formalists, and also in the works of their opponents. If some spoke about the structure of the text, then others studied the structure of wider, extra-textual, entities: a culture, an epoch, or political history. It is impossible to include within the framework of the Formal school such investigators as M. M. Bakhtin, V. Ia. Propp, G. A. Gukovsky, V. M. Zhirmunsky, D. S. Likhachev, V. V. Gippius, and S. M. Eizenshtein, as well as Andrei Bely, B. I. Jarkho, P. A. Florensky, and many others. Nonetheless, the significance of their works for the development of Structuralism is indisputable.

Structural-semiotic literary criticism takes into consideration the experience of all preceding literary scholarship. It has, however, its own specific character. It arose in the environment of that scientific revolution that has marked the middle of the twentieth century and is organically connected with the ideas and methodology of structural linguistics, semiotics, information theory, and cybernetics.

Structural literary studies do not represent a fully constituted and definitively formed scholarly tendency. For many, even very important, problems no essential unity or even scientific clarity exists. The author of the present book fully understands that such a situation will unavoidably add new shortcomings to those that are conditioned by his own defects as a scholar. However, he does not set himself the goal of giving a complete and systematic exposition of all questions pertaining to the structural-semiotic analysis of the text. He only wishes to introduce the reader to the range of the problems and the methods of their resolution and to show not so much final results as possible roads to their attainment.

Language as the Matériel of Literature

The particular place of literature among the other arts is determined in considerable degree by the specific features of that matériel which it uses for the re-creation of circumambient reality. Without examining the entire complex nature of language as a social phenomenon, let us pause to consider those of its aspects that are essential to our question.

Language is the matériel of literature. From this definition it follows that language in relation to literature functions as a material substance similar to paint in painting, stone in sculpture, and sound in music.

However, the character of the materiality of language and of the matériels of the other arts is different. Paint, stone, etc., until they come into the hands of the artist are socially indifferent. They stand outside of any cognition of reality. Each of these matériels has its own structure but it is given by nature and is not correlated with social (ideological) processes. Language, in this sense, constitutes a special matériel characterized by its high degree of social activeness even before the hand of the artist touches it.

In the semiotic sciences, language is defined as a mechanism of sign communication serving the goals of storage and transmission of information. The concept of the *sign—the meaningful element of a given language* lies at the basis of all language. The sign possesses a binary essence: being invested with a certain material expression that constitutes its formal aspect, it also has within the limits of a given language a certain meaning that constitutes its content. Thus, for the word "decoration, medal" ("orden"), a particular sequence of Russian phonemes and a certain morpho-grammatical structure constitute its expression, and the lexical, historical, cultural, and other meanings, its content. If we address ourselves to the decoration itself, for example, the Order of St. George, First Class, then the decoration's regalia— the insignia, star, and the ribbon—constitute the expression, whereas the honor connected with this award, the relationship of its social value to other decorations of the Russian Empire, the idea of the services which this decoration attests, constitute its content.

One may conclude from this that the sign is always a *substitute.* In the process of social intercourse it figures as a substitute for some essence that is represented by it. The relationship of that which substitutes to that which is substituted, of expression to content, constitutes the *meaning* of the sign. From the fact that meaning is always a relationship, it follows that content and expression cannot be identical, for in order that an act of communication be possible, expression must have some other nature than that of content.

However, this distinction can have different degrees. If expression and content have nothing in common and their identity is realized only within the confines of a given language (for example, the identity of a word and the object indicated by it), then such a sign is called conventional. Words are the most widespread type of conventional sign. If a certain similarity exists between content and expression, e.g., the relationship of a locality and a geographic map, a person and a portrait, a person and a photograph, the sign is called representational or iconic.

The practical discrimination of conventional and iconic signs is not difficult and the theoretical opposition is indispensable for the functioning of a culture as an integral communicational organism. However, one must keep in view that the concept of the "similarity" of a sign and the designated object is distinguished by a high degree of conventionality and always belongs to the postulates of a given culture: a sketch equates a three-dimensional object to a two-dimensional representation; from the point of view of topology, any square is homomorphic to any circle; a stage depicts a room but takes as given the absence of a wall on the side where the spectators sit. An actor's monologue performs the function of an iconic sign of the hero's thought flow, although the similarity of that which is designated and that which designates can be accepted only after taking into consideration an entire system of conventions, that is, the language of the theater.[5]

Signs do not exist in language as a mechanical accumulation of independent essences that are not interconnected: they constitute a system. Language is systemic in its essence. The systemic character of language is shaped by the presence of certain rules that determine the correlation of the elements among themselves.

Language is a hierarchical structure. It breaks down into elements of different levels. Linguistics, in particular, differentiates the levels of phonemes, morphemes, lexicon, word combinations, sentences, and supraphrasal units. (We adduce only a gross segmentation: in some cases one must additionally isolate syllabic, intonational, and a number of other levels.) Each of the levels is organized according to a certain system of rules that is inherent to it.

Language is organized along two structural axes. On the one hand, its elements are distributed according to equivalency classes of various sorts: e.g., all the grammatical cases of a given noun, all the synonyms of a given word, all the prepositions of a given language, etc. Building an actual phrase in a given language, we select from each class of equivalencies the needed word or form. This ordering of language elements is called *paradigmatic.*

On the other hand, so that the selected linguistic units form a correct chain (from the point of view of a given language), a sentence must be constructed so that the words agree among themselves with the aid of special morphemes, so that the syntagmas agree, and so on. This ordering of language will be termed *syntagmatic.* Every linguistic term is ordered along these paradigmatic and syntagmatic axes.

On whatever level we examine a text we shall discover that some of its elements are repeated and others vary. Thus, examining all texts in the Russian language, we shall discover the constant repetition of the thirty-two letters of the Russian alphabet, although the contours of these letters in various type faces and in manuscript drafts by different persons may vary greatly. Moreover, in actual texts we shall meet only *variants* of the letters of the Russian alphabet, while the letters as such will represent *structural invariants* (ideal constructs) to which the meanings of the letters are ascribed. The invariant is the meaningful unit of structure and however many variants it may have in actual texts, they will all have but one meaning—that of the invariant.

Recognizing this, we can isolate in each communication system that aspect of its invariant structure, which, following F. de Saussure, we call *language,* and that aspect of its variant realizations in different texts, which, in the same scientific tradition, is termed *speech.* The division of the plane of language and the plane of speech is one of the most fundamental propositions of modern linguistics. In information theory, the opposition of code (language) and communication (speech) approximately correspond to it.

Discrimination of the linguistic positions of speaker and hearer, on whose basis the principally different synthetic (generative) and analytic language models are constructed, is critical for understanding the relationship of language (code) and speech (communication) which is parallel to the relationship "system—text."[6]

All classes of phenomena that satisfy the definitions given above qualify in semiotics as languages. It is evident that the term "language" is used here in a broader sense than is generally accepted. The following are considered as "languages":

1. Natural languages: a concept equivalent to the term "language" in its usual usage. Examples of natural languages are Russian, Estonian, French, Czech, etc.

2. Artificial languages: sign systems created by man and serving narrowly specialized spheres of human endeavor. To these belong all scientific languages and systems of the traffic signal type. (Systems of conventional signs and the rules of their usage, such as those of algebra or chemistry, are, from the semiotic point of view, objects equivalent to language.) Artificial languages are created on the basis of natural ones as a result of the conscious simplification of their mechanism.

3. Secondary modeling systems: semiotic systems constructed on the basis of a natural language but having a more complex structure. Secondary modeling systems include ritual, all aggregates of social and ideological sign communications, and art, all of which merge into a single complex semiotic whole—a culture.

The relationship between natural language and poetry is determined by the complexity of the correlation between primary and secondary languages in the unified complex whole of a given culture.

The specific character of natural language as the matériel of art largely determines the distinctness of poetry (and, more broadly, of verbal art in general) from other types of artistic creativity.

The languages of the world's peoples are not passive factors in the formation of culture. On the one hand, languages themselves are products of a complex multi-century cultural process. Insofar as the vast, continuous, surrounding world appears in language as discrete and constructed, i.e., as having a distinct structure, natural language, which is correlated with the world, becomes its model, a projection of reality upon the plane of language. And insofar as natural language is one of the major factors in national culture, the linguistic model of the world becomes one of the factors regulating the national perception of the world. The formative influence of national language on secondary modeling systems is a real and indisputable fact.[7] It is especially important in poetry.[8]

On the other hand, the process of the formation of poetry on the basis of a national linguistic tradition is complex and contradictory. In its day, the Formal school advanced the theory that language is a material whose resistance is overcome by poetry. In disputing this position there arose the view of poetry as an automatic realization of linguistic laws, as one of the functional styles of language. B. V. Tomashevsky, polemicizing against one of the most extreme points of view which argues that everything that exists in poetry is already present in the language, observed that language actually does contain everything that is present in poetry except poetry itself. True, in his works of later years B. V. Tomashevsky began increasingly to emphasize the communality of linguistic and poetic laws.

At the present time both theories, the "conflict with language" and the denial of the qualitative uniqueness of poetry in relation to natural language, may be seen as unavoidable extremes of the early stages of a science.

Language forms secondary systems. This is what makes the verbal arts indisputably the richest in their artistic potential. It must not be forgotten however, that significant specific difficulties are connected with just this aspect of language which is so advantageous for the artist.

Language, by its entire system being so intimately associated with life, copies it, enters into it, so that man ceases to distinguish object from appellation, the plane of reality from that of its reflection in language. An analogous situation exists in cinematography: the fact that photography was intimately and automatically bound to the object being photographed was long an obstacle to the transformation of cinematography into an art. Only after the appearance of montage, and the mobile camera made it possible to film an object in at least two different ways and the sequence of objects in real life ceased to specify automatically the sequence of film images, was cinematography transformed from a copy of reality into its artistic model. *The cinema had acquired its own language.*

Much effort was necessary for poetry to acquire its own language, one created on the basis of a natural language but not equivalent to it, i.e., for poetry to become an art. A categorical imperative arose at the dawn of verbal art: the language of literature had to be differentiated from ordinary language; the linguistic reproduction of reality with an artistic intent had to differ from that with informational intent. This determined the necessity for poetry.

Poetry and Prose

Assertions that ordinary speech and the language of artistic prose are identical and, consequently, that prose is a primary prior phenomenon in relation to poetry are generally accepted axioms in the theory of literature. The eminent specialist in poetic theory, B. V. Tomashevsky, summing up his many years of study, wrote: "The axiom that the natural form of organized human language is prose is a prerequisite to opinions about language."[9]

Poetic language is thought of as something secondary, more complex in structure. Zygmunt Czerny proposes the following transitional ladder from simplicity of structure to complexity: "utilitarian prose (scientific and scholarly, administrative, military, juridical, commercial, industrial, journalistic, etc.), ordinary prose, literary prose, poetry in prose, rhythmic prose, *vers libre,* free stanzas, free line, classical verse of strict obligatoriness."[10]

We, on the other hand, shall try to show that the disposition of genres on the typological ladder from simplicity to complexity is: conversational speech, song (text plus motif), "classical poetry," belletristic prose. Of course, this scheme is highly approximate, but one cannot concur that belletristic prose constitutes a historically primary form of the same type as conversational, non-belletristic speech. (The question of *vers libre* will be stipulated separately.)

Indeed, the correlation is different: poetic speech (as well as singing) was originally the only possible language of verbal art. The "dissimilation" of the language of belletristic literature, i.e., its separation from ordinary speech, was attained by this means. Only later did "assimilation" begin. From this already relatively sharply "dissimilar" material, a [new] picture of reality was created. A model-sign was constructed by the devices of human language. If language functioned in relation to reality as a reproducing structure, then literature constituted a structure of structures.

Structural analysis assumes that the artistic device is not a material element of the text but a relationship. There exists a difference in principle between the absence of rhyme, on the one hand, in verse that does not yet imply the possibility of its existence (for example, ancient poetry, Russian bylina verse, etc.) or in verse having already rejected it so that the absence of rhyme enters into the readers' expectation, into the esthetic norm of that kind of art (for example, contemporary *vers libre),* and, on the other hand, its absence in verse that incorporates rhyme into the characteristic features of the poetic text. In the first case, the absence of rhyme is not an artistically significant element; in the second, the absence of rhyme is the presence of non-rhyme, of minus-rhyme. In the epoch when the reader's consciousness, raised in the poetic school of Zhukovsky, Batyushkov, and the young Pushkin, identified Romantic poetics with the very concept of poetry, the artistic system of "Anew, I visited..." ("Vnov', ia posetil...") produced an impression not of the absence of "devices" but of their maximal saturation. But these were "minus-devices," a system of consistent and conscious rejections felt by the reader. In this sense, in 1830, a poetic text written according to the accepted norms of Romantic poetics produced a more "naked" impression and was more devoid of elements of belletristic structure than a Pushkin text.

Descriptive poetics resembles the observer who only fixes on certain of life's phenomena (e.g., a "naked man"). Structural poetics always proceeds from the fact that the observed phenomenon is only one of the constituents of the complex whole. It is like an observer who is constantly asking: "In what situation?" It is clear that a naked man in a bath is not the same as a naked man at a social gathering. In the first case, the absence of clothes is a general feature. It says nothing about the individual. An undone necktie at a ball is a greater degree of nudity than the absence of clothes in a bathhouse. A statue of Apollo in a museum does not seem naked, but attach a tie to its neck and it will strike us as indecent.

From the structural point of view, the actual material text set in type loses its absolute self-sufficient meaning as the unique object of artistic analysis. The idea that the text and the artistic work are identical must be decisively rejected. The text is one of the components of an artistic work, albeit an extremely important component, without which the existence of the work of art is impossible. But the artistic effect as a whole arises from comparisons of the text with a complex set of ontological and ideological esthetic ideas.

In the light of the foregoing, we can now offer a definition of the historical correlation of poetry and prose.[11] One must first note that the numerous non-poetic genres in folklore and in Russian medieval literature differ in principle from the prose of the nineteenth century. The use of shared terms is only a result of the diffuseness of concepts in our discipline.

These genres are not in opposition to poetry inasmuch as they developed before its appearance. They did not form a contrasting binary pair with poetry and were perceived outside of any connection with it. The poetic genres of folklore are not opposed to prose genres but simply are not correlated with them inasmuch as they are perceived not as two varieties of a single art, but as different arts—the sung and spoken. The relationship of folklore and medieval "prose" genres to conversational speech is completely different from that of nineteenth century prose due to the absence of any correlation with poetry. Nineteenth century prose is opposed to poetic language which is perceived as "conventional," "unnatural," and gravitates toward the conversational element. This process is but one of the aspects of esthetics that implies similarity with life, movement toward reality, is the goal of art.

"Prose" in folklore and medieval literature observed other laws: it had just been born of the conversational element and strove to separate itself from it. At this stage in the development of literature, a story about reality was not yet perceived as art. Thus, a chronicle was not experienced by the readers and chroniclers as a belletristic text in our understanding of this concept.

Structural elements such as the archaization of language in hagiographic literature, the fantastic unreality of the fairy tale plot, the emphasized conventionality of narrational devices, and strict adherence to genre ritual, all create a kind of style consciously oriented toward distinctness from the element of "ordinary language."

Without touching upon the complex question of the place of prose in the literature of the eighteenth and the beginning of the nineteenth centuries, we shall note only that, whatever the real situation might have been, literary theory of that epoch slighted the novel and other prose genres as low varieties of art. Prose still was either blended with philosophy and political journalism, being perceived as a genre exceeding the bounds of elegant literature,[12] or was considered as trash reckoned for the undemanding and esthetically uncultivated reader.

Prose in the modern meaning of the word arises in Russian literature with Pushkin. It simultaneously unites the idea of high art and of non-poetry. Behind this stands the esthetic of "real life" with its conviction that the source of poetry is reality. Thus, *the esthetic perception of prose is possible only against the background of poetic culture.* Prose is a later phenomenon than poetry, arising in a period of chronologically more mature esthetic consciousness. Precisely because prose is esthetically secondary in relation to poetry and is perceived against its background, the writer can boldly bring the style of a prose belletristic narrative close to that of conversational speech without fearing that the reader will lose his feeling of dealing not with reality but with its recreation. Thus, notwithstanding its seeming simplicity and its closeness to ordinary speech, prose is esthetically more complex than poetry while its simplicity is secondary. Conversational speech is actually equivalent to the text; belletristic prose = text + the "minus devices" of poetically conventionalized speech. One must note anew that in a given case a prose literary work is not equal to the text: the text is only one of the components of a complex belletristic structure.

Subsequently, artistic norms emerge that permit us to perceive prose as an independent artistic formation outside of its correlation with poetic culture. At certain moments in the history of literature, a reverse relationship comes about: poetry begins to be perceived against the background of prose, which performs the role of the norm of the artistic text.

In this connection, it is appropriate to mention that in the light of structural analysis, artistic simplicity is shown to be something contrary to primitiveness. It is by no means a love of paradox that forces us to affirm that artistic simplicity is more complex than artistic complexity for it arises as the simplification of the latter and against its background. Thus, it is natural to begin the analysis of belletristic structures with poetry as the more elementary system, as a system whose elements obtain much of their expression in the text but which are not realized as "minus devices." In the analysis of the poetic work, extra-textual associations and relationships play a smaller role than in prose.

The investigatory path from poetry to prose, as to a more complex structure, repeats the historical course of the literary process that initially gives us that poetic structure which constituted the entire domain of the concept of "verbal art" and which is contrastively correlated (by the principle of isolation) with its background. This background consists of conversational and all forms of written, non-artistic (from the contemporary viewpoint) speech.

The next stage is the displacement of poetry by prose. Prose strives to become a synonym for the concept of literature and is projected against two backgrounds: the poetry of the preceding period, according to the principle of contrast, and "ordinary" non-artistic language as a limit toward which the structure of a literary work strives (without merging with it).

Subsequently, poetry and prose emerge as two independent but correlated artistic systems. The concept of simplicity in art is considerably more comprehensive than the concept of prose. It is even broader than such a literary generalization as "realism." Definition of the simplicity of a work of art presents great difficulties. Nonetheless, as a working approximation, it is indispensable for the demonstration of the specifics of prose. In this, the evaluational aspect of the question is most essential.

One must note that the concept of simplicity as a synonym for artistic merit appeared in art quite late. The works of Old Russian literature which seem so simple to us did not seem at all so to contemporaries. Kirill Turovsky believed that "chroniclers and bards" "pay heed to the tales" of ordinary people in order to retell them later "in refined language" and to "exalt with encomia."[13] Daniil Zatochnik depicted the process of artistic creation thusly: "For let us trumpet, o brethren, as through a gold-forged trumpet, through the reason of our minds and let us begin to beat silver instruments [argany] in proclamation of wisdom and let us sound the tympans of our mind."[14] The idea of "ornamentality" as an indispensable sign that art be perceived precisely as art (as something "made," a model) is characteristic of many early artistic methods. This also applies to human maturation: for a child, "pretty" and "ornamental" almost always coincide. The same phenomenon is evident in modern esthetically underdeveloped "adult" taste, which always views beauty and magnificence as synonyms. (One must not, of course, infer from this the inverse syllogism that all magnificence is in and of itself evidence of esthetic ill-breeding.)

The concept of simplicity as an esthetic value comes with the following stage and is invariably connected with the rejection of ornamentality. Perception of artistic simplicity is possible only against a background of "ornamental" art whose memory is present in the consciousness of the viewer-listener. In order that the simple be perceived as simple, not as primitive, it must be simplified, that is, the artist consciously does not use certain constructional elements and the viewer-hearer projects the text against a background in which these "devices" might be realized. Thus, if an "ornamented" ("complex") structure is realized chiefly in the text, then a "simple" structure is, in considerable measure, beyond its limits being perceived as a system of "minus devices," of non-materialized relationships. (This "non-materialized" aspect, which is completely real in the philosophical but not in the everyday sense of the word, is entirely material and enters into the stuff of the work's structure.) Consequently, simplicity is structurally a much more complex phenomenon than "ornamentality." That this is not paradox but truth is something of which anyone may persuade himself, if he will undertake an analysis of the prose of Marlinsky or Hugo, on the one hand, and of Chekhov or de Maupassant, on the other. (In the case at hand, the issue is not relative artistic merit, but rather that it is, of course, significantly easier to study the belletristic nature of the more ornate work, i.e., that of the first-named writers.)

It follows that the concept of "simplicity," typologically secondary and historically quite variable, depends upon the system against which it is projected. It is understandable, for example, that we, involuntarily projecting Pushkin's work against the familiar realistic tradition from Gogol to Chekhov, perceive Pushkin's "simplicity" quite differently than did his contemporaries.

To bring the concept of "simplicity" within fixed measurable limits, we must define one further, extra-textual component. If, in the light of what has been said, simplicity is "non-complexity," a *rejection* of the implementation of certain principles ("simplicity/complexity" is a binary oppositional pair), then at the same time, the creation of a "simple work" (like any other) is simultaneously a striving toward the *implementation of certain principles.* (It is the realization of a design that may be regarded as an interpretation of a particular abstract model by a model of a more concrete level). If we do not take into account the relationship of the belletristic text to this ideal model of simplicity (which also includes such concepts as, for example, "the limit of the potential of art"), its essence will remain incomprehensible. Not only the "simplicity" of the neo-realistic Italian film, but also the "simplicity" of Nekrasov's method would probably be beyond the limits of art for Pushkin.

From the above, it is clear that it will be considerably simpler to artificially model "complex" forms than to model simple ones.

In the history of literature, the parallel between prose and artistic simplicity has been frequently adduced.

"Precision and brevity, these are the primary merits of prose," wrote
Pushkin, criticizing the school of Karamzin. "It [prose—Iu. L.] demands ideas
and ideas—lacking them, brilliant phrases serve no purpose."[15]

Belinsky, who in his "Literary Reveries" had characterized the dominance of Karamzin's school as the "century of phraseology," equates the
terms "prose," "wealth of content," and the concept of artistic realism in his
review "Russian Literature in 1842."

"And what do you think has killed our dear and innocent Romanticism...? Prose! Yes, prose, prose, and more prose..." By "verse" we mean not
merely measured lines sharpened by rhyme... Thus, for example, Pushkin's
Ruslan and Lyudmila, The Prisoner of the Caucasus, and *The Fountain
of Bakhchisarai* are real poetry; *Onegin, The Gypsies, Poltava,* and *Boris
Godunov* are already a transition to prose, while such poems as *Mozart
and Salieri, The Covetous Knight, The Water Nymph, Galub,* and *The Stone
Guest* are already pure unadulterated prose where there is no longer poetry
at all, although these poems are also written in verse... By "prose" we understand a wealth of inner poetic content, steadfast maturity and firmness of
thought, which has distilled into itself strength of feeling, the true measure
of reality.[16]

Pushkin's and Belinsky's statements must not be categorized as random
couplings of concepts. They reflect the basis of the esthetic experiencing of
prose. The concept of simplicity is infinitely broader than the concept of
prose but the promotion of prose to the rank of belletristic phenomena
proved possible only after the concept of simplicity had already been elaborated as the basis of artistic merit. The historically and socially conditioned
concept of simplicity made possible the creation of models of reality in
art, certain elements of which are realized as "minus devices."

Belletristic prose arose against the background of a particular poetic
system as its negation.

A similar interpretation of the relationship between poetry and prose
permits us to view dialectically the problem of the boundary between these
phenomena and the esthetic nature of borderline forms of the *vers libre* type.
Here a curious paradox develops. The view of poetry and prose as independent constructs which can be described without mutual correlation
("poetry is rhythmically organized speech while prose is ordinary speech")
unexpectedly leads to the impossibility of delimiting these phenomena.
Encountering an abundance of intermediate forms, the investigator is com-
pelled to conclude that it is generally impossible to establish a fixed boundary
between poetry and prose. B. V. Tomashevsky wrote:

It is more natural and more fruitful to regard poetry and prose not as two areas with a firm boundary between them but as two poles, two centers of attraction, around which the actual facts have historically arrayed themselves. . . It is legitimate to speak of more or less prosaic and more or less poetic phenomena.

And further:

Inasmuch as different people possess varying degrees of perceptivity about individual problems in poetry and prose, their assertions "This is poetry," "No, this is rhymed prose," in no way contradict each other as it seems to the disputants themselves.

For the resolution of the fundamental question of the difference between poetry and prose one must address oneself, first of all, to the most typical, the most marked forms of poetry and prose. Study of borderline phenomena and their definition via the establishment of some quite possibly false boundary between them is not a productive approach.[17]

B. Unbegaun holds approximately this same point of view.[18] Proceeding from the idea that poetry is ordered, organized, that is, "non-free speech," he declares the very concept of *vers libre* a logical antinomy. M. Ianakiev also adheres to this view:

"Free verse" *(vers libre)* cannot be an object of poetic investigation insofar as it in no way differs from ordinary speech. On the other hand, poetics must concern itself with even the most talentless "non-free verse."

M. Ianakiev considers that "palpable, albeit unskillful, material poetic organization may be revealed in this way."[19] Citing Elizaveta Bagriana's poem "The Clown Speaks," the author concludes:

The general impression is that of belletristic prose. . . The rhymed assonance *the places—the earth (mestáta—zemiáta)* is insufficient to convert the text into "poetry." Similar assonances are met from time to time even in ordinary prose.[20]

But such treatment of "palpable material poetic organization" is overly narrow. It scrutinizes only the text, which is understood as "everything that is written." The absence of an element, when it is impossible and not expected in a given structure, is equivalent to the removal of an expected element. The rejection of distinct rhythmicness in the epoch before the rise of the verse system is equivalent to its rejection afterwards. The element is taken outside of its structure and function, the sign—outside of its background. If one adopts such an approach, then *vers libre* really can be equated with prose.

J. Hrabák's view in his article "Observations on the Relationship of Poetry and Prose, Especially in the So-Called Transitional Forms" is considerably more dialectical. J. Hrabák proceeds from the idea of prose and poetry as an opposed structural binomial. (Incidentally, the reservation should be made that such a correlation far from always exists, just as it is not always possible to make a distinction between the structure of ordinary speech and belletristic prose—a distinction which Hrabak does not make.) J. Hrabák, as if paying tribute to the traditional formulation, describes prose as language "that is constrained only by grammatical norms."[21] Further on, however, he proceeds from the assumption that contemporary esthetic responses to prose and poetry are mutually projected and, consequently, it is impossible not to reckon with the extra-textual elements of the esthetic constructs. J. Hrabák poses the question of the delimitation of prose and poetry in a completely different fashion. Believing that the structure of poetry and the structure of prose are sharply delineated in the consciousness of the reader, he writes of "cases where the border is not only not eliminated, but, on the contrary, assumes greater reality."[22] And further:

> The fewer the elements in a poetic form that distinguish verse from prose, the more clearly one must determine that it is not a matter of prose but of verse. On the other hand, in works written in free verse, certain individual poems, isolated and taken out of context, may be perceived as prose.[23]

In consequence, the boundary that exists between free verse and prose must be clearly distinguishable and, for this reason, free verse requires special graphic construction in order to be understood as a form of poetic speech.

Thus, the metaphysical concept "device" is replaced by the dialectical concept "the structural element and its function" and the idea of the boundary between poetry and prose comes to be connected not only with positive but also with negative elements of structure.

Contemporary molecular physics has the concept of "holes" that are not at all equal to the simple absence of matter. These "holes" display an absence of matter in a structural position that implies its presence. In these conditions, a "hole" behaves so that it is possible to measure its weight, in negative quantities, of course. Physicists regularly speak of "heavy" and "light" holes. The poetry specialist must also reckon with analogous phenomena and it follows from this that the concept "text" is considerably more complex for the literary scholar than for the linguist. If one equates it to the concept "the real data of an artistic work," then it is also necessary to consider "minus-devices," the "heavy" and "light holes" of artistic structure.

Subsequently, in order not to diverge too much from traditional terminology, we regard the word "text" as something more usual: the entire sum of structural relations that have found linguistic expression. (The formula "that have found graphic expression" is not suitable, since it does not cover the concept of the text in folklore.) However, given this approach, we must, along with intra-textual constructs and relationships, single out extra-textual ones as a special topic of investigation. The extra-textual part of an artistic structure is a completely real (sometimes very significant) component of the artistic whole. Of course, it differs from the textual part by its greater instability, its greater variability. It is clear, for example, that for people who have studied Mayakovsky from their early school years and who accept his poetry as an esthetic norm, the extra-textual part of his works presents itself in a completely different form than it did to the author himself and to his first listeners. For the contemporary reader of Mayakovsky the text moves into the complex general structures; the extra-textual part of his work also exists for the contemporary reader, but, in many respects, it is already quite different. Extra-textual connections contain much that is subjective, idiosyncratic, and which does not lend itself to analysis by modern means of literary study. But these associations also have their own regular historically and socially conditioned aspect and, in their structural aggregate, can even now be an object of study.

We shall subsequently examine extra-textual ties only partially, i.e., in their relationship to the text. The strict delimitation of levels and the search for clear boundary criteria accessible to contemporary scientific analysis will be the token of scientific success.

The question of the difficulty of constructing generative models[24] is evidence of the greater complexity of prose in comparison with poetry. It is quite clear that a poetic model will be distinguished by greater complexity than a general language one (the second will enter into the first), but it is no less clear that the modeling of a belletristic prose text is a task incomparably more difficult than modeling a poetic one.

Hrabák is indisputably right when along with other poetry specialists such as B. V. Tomashevsky, he stresses the significance of graphics for the discrimination of poetry and prose. Graphics figure here not as a technical device for the establishment of the text, but as a structural signal following which our mind "fits" the text into a certain extra-textual structure. One can only agree with Hrabák when he writes:

> Some may object, for example, that P. Fort or M. Gorky wrote some of their poetry without line divisions *(in continuo),* but in these cases, it is a matter of poetry of traditional and stable form, of verses which include pronounced rhythmic elements that exclude the possibility of confusion with prose.[25]

The Nature of Poetry

When people ask, "Why is poetry necessary since one can speak in plain prose?" they are posing an incorrect question. Prose is not simpler but more complex than poetry. On the other hand, the question arises: "Why must we transmit certain information by means of belletristic speech?" This question can also be put in another way. If we leave aside other aspects of the nature of art and consider only the transfer of information, does belletristic speech then have a distinctive character compared with ordinary language?

Modern poetics is an extremely well-worked area of literary scholarship. One can not but note that numerous critical works of international reputation are based on studies of poetry specialists of the Russian school, which tooks its beginnings from A. Bely and V. Ia. Bryusov and which has produced such scholars as B. V. Tomashevsky, B. M. Eikhenbaum, R. O. Jakobson, V. M. Zhirmunsky, Iu. N. Tynyanov, M. P. Shtokmar, L. I. Timofeev, S. M. Bondi, and G. A. Shengeli.

This tradition has been further developed in the works of foreign scholars, especially in the Slavic countries: K. Taranovsky, J. Levý, M. R. Mayenowa, L. Pszczołowska, A. Wierzbicka, J. Woronczak, Z. Kopczińska, and others.[26]

The last decade has brought a new surge of poetic studies in the Soviet Union. Articles have appeared by A. Kvyatkovsky, V. E. Kholshevnikov, P. A. Rudnev, Ia. Pyldmiaè and others. The investigations of Academician A. N. Kolmogorov's group (A. N. Kondratov, A. A. Prokhorov, and others) have enriched the discipline with a series of precise descriptions of the metrico-rhythmic structures of individual poets. One must especially single out the works of M. L. Gasparov, which are distinguished by their wide semiotic perspective.

That the investigation of poetry has advanced significantly first of all on its lowest levels cannot be considered accidental. Precisely these levels, by virtue of the marked discreteness of the units, their formal character, and the possibility of operating with large numbers (that is, large for literary studies) have proved a suitable field for the application of statistical methods with their well-elaborated mathematical apparatus. The use of extensive statistical material has permitted the creation of such works as K. Taranovsky's classic investigation of the Russian binary meters[27] and the application of exact mathematical apparatus has permitted the construction of convincing models of the extremely complex rhythmic structures that are typical of twentieth century poetry.[28] However, the transition to higher levels, for example, attempts at the creation of frequency dictionaries of poetry, has convincingly shown that given the sharp increase in the semanticity of the elements and the decrease in their number, statistical methods must be supplemented by structural ones.

Future advances in poetics will require the resolution of general problems of poetic structure. Thus, the hiatus between the study of the lowest poetic levels and the thoroughly studied area of literary history will be filled in.

Science begins when we, looking at the commonplace and the seemingly well understood, unexpectedly discover in it the strange and inexplicable. A question arises to which some conception is advanced as an answer. As the starting point for the study of poetry, we have our awareness of the paradoxical nature of poetry. If poetry's existence were not an indisputably established fact, one could, with a degree of cogency, show that it could not possibly exist.

The initial paradox of poetry lies in the following: it is known that no natural language is free of rules, that is, the combination of its constitutive elements is not disorderly. Certain limitations, which comprise the rules of a given language, are imposed on their combinability. Without such limitations, language could not serve a communicative function. However, the increase of the limitations imposed on language, as is well known, is simultaneously accompanied by a decline in its informativeness.

The poetic text is subject to all of the rules of a given language. However, new limitations, which are supplementary in relation to language, are imposed on it: the requirement that it observe certain metrico- rhythmical norms and be organized on the phonological, rhyming, lexical and ideo-compositional levels. All this makes the poetic text significantly more "non-free" than ordinary conversational speech. As the adage has it, "you can't throw a word out of a song." It would appear that this must result in a monstrous growth of redundancy in the poetic text[29] and that its information content must be sharply reduced in this process. If one regards poetry as an ordinary text with supplementary limitations imposed upon it (and from a certain standpoint such a definition is completely convincing) or, paraphrasing the same thought in simplified form, if one believes that the poet expresses the same ideas as do ordinary speakers of the language but imposes on it certain external ornamentations, then poetry obviously becomes not only unnecessary, but even impossible. It is transformed into a text with infinitely increasing redundancy and sharply diminishing information content.

Experiments show the opposite, however. The Hungarian scholar Ivan Fónagy, having conducted special experiments, writes:

Notwithstanding meter and rhyme, in Endre Adi's poetry sixty per cent of the phonemes require prompting, whereas in an experiment with a newspaper article, only thirty-three percent necessitated prompting. In the poem only forty sounds out of a hundred proved to be redundant, while in a newspaper editorial, sixty-seven percent were devoid of information. The redundancy in the conversation of two young girls was still higher. Only twenty-nine sounds were necessary in order to guess the remaining seventy-one.[30]

The data adduced here agree also with the reader's intuition. We all know that a brief poem may contain information beyond the capacity of thick tomes of a non-belletristic text.[31]

Thus, the information content of a poetry text increases, a fact which, at first glance, diverges from the basic postulates of information theory.

To resolve this problem, to understand wherein lies the source of the cultural significance of poetry, means to answer basic questions in the theory of the poetic text. In what way does the imposition on the text of additional poetic restrictions lead not to a reduction but to a sharp increase in the potential for new meaningful combinations of elements within the text?

The present book is an attempt to answer this question. Anticipating ourselves, we isolate the following elements in non-poetry.

1. Structurally meaningful elements which belong to language, and their variants which are arrayed on the speech level. The latter do not have their own meaning and acquire it only as a result of their correlation with certain invariant units on the level of the *langue.*

2. Within the limits of each linguistic level elements having semantic meaning are discriminated, i.e., correlated with some extra-linguistic reality. There are also formal elements, i.e., those having only intra-linguistic (e.g., grammatical) meaning.

Turning to poetry, we discover that:

1. Any element on the *parole* level can be elevated to the rank of meaningful elements.

2. Any formal element appearing in the language may in poetry acquire a semantic character thereby obtaining supplementary meanings.

Thus, certain supplementary restrictions imposed on the text compel us to perceive it as poetry. As soon as one assigns a given text to the category of poetry, the number of meaningful elements in it acquires the capacity to grow.

However, not only does the number of elements increase but the system of their combinations also becomes more complex. F. de Saussure said that the entire structure of language is reducible to the mechanism of similarities and differences. In poetry this principle assumes a significantly more universal character: elements which in a general language text appear to be unconnected, belonging to different structures or even to different levels of structures, turn out to be compared or contrasted in the poetic context. The principle of the contrastive comparison of elements is a universal structure-forming principle in poetry and verbal art in general. It comprises that "coupling" of episodes (for prose, the plot level is the most meaningful), about which L. Tolstoi wrote, seeing in it the source of the text's specifically artistic significance.

The author's conception is realized in a certain artistic structure and is inseparable from it. L.N. Tolstoi wrote of the central idea of *Anna Karenina:*

> If I wanted to say in words all that I intended to express by my novel, then I would rewrite it just as I wrote it from the beginning. If myopic critics think I wish to describe only what I like, how Ob[lonsky] dines and what beautiful shoulders Karenina has, then they are mistaken. In everything, in almost everything, that I have written, I have been guided by the need to assemble ideas linked together for the expression of myself, for each idea expressed by words alone loses its meaning, is terribly diminished, when it is removed from that conjunction in which it is found. . . If the critics now understand and can say in a newspaper sketch what I intended to say, then I congratulate them.[32]

Tolstoy vividly expressed the thought that the artistic idea realizes itself through "couplings," through structure, and does not exist outside of it and that the artist's conception is realized in his model of reality. Tolstoy writes:

> . . . art criticism requires people who would demonstrate the senselessness of picking out isolated ideas in a belletristic work and who would constantly guide the reader through that infinite labyrinth of couplings that comprises the very essence of art. This should be done according to those laws which serve as the foundation of these couplings.[33]

The definition "form corresponds to content," true in the philosophical sense, is far from adequately precise in expressing the relationship of structure and idea. Iu. N. Tynyanov has demonstrated its awkward (in reference to art) metaphorical nature:

> Form + content = glass + wine. But all spatial analogies that are applied to the concept of form are important in that they only simulate analogies: in fact, a static feature closely connected with spatiality invariably slips into the concept of form.[34]

For a clear idea of the relationship of idea to structure, it is more convenient to show the connection between life and the complex biological mechanism of living tissue. Life, which constitutes the property of the living organism, inconceivable outside of its physical structure, is a function of this working system. The student of literature who hopes to grasp an idea detached from the author's system of modeling the world, from the work's structure, reminds one of the scholar-idealist, who tries to separate life from that concrete biological structure whose function it is. The idea is not contained in any however successfully chosen excerpts, but is expressed in its entire artistic structure. The scholar who does not understand this and who seeks the idea in isolated citations resembles a person who, having learned that a house has a plan, starts to break down the walls in search of the place where this plan is immured. The plan is not immured in a wall, but is realized in the proportions of the building. The plan is the architect's idea; the structure of the building is its realization. The ideational content of a work is its structure. The idea in art is always a model for it reconstructs the image of reality. Consequently, an artistic idea is inconceivable apart from its structure. Dualism of form and content must be replaced by the concept of an idea that realizes itself in an adequate structure and that does not exist outside of this structure. Altered structure reports a different idea to the reader or viewer.

Poetry is a complexly constructed meaning [smysl]. All of its elements are semantic elements and are designations of certain content. We shall try to show the validity of this position in reference to such "formal" concepts as rhyme, rhythm, euphony, the musical sound of verse, etc. It follows from the above that any complexity of construction not engendered by the requirements of the information to be transmitted, any self-contained formal construct in art that does not bear information, contradicts the very nature of art as a complex system, particularly one having a semiotic character. Would anyone be satisfied with the construction of a traffic signal that transmits its informational content of three commands ("proceed," "caution," and "stop") by twelve signals?

Thus, *a poem is a complexly constructed meaning.* This signifies that entering into the integral structure of a poem, the meaningful elements of a language are connected by a complex system of correlations, comparisons, and contrasts impossible in an ordinary language construct. This gives each element separately and the construction as a whole an absolutely unique semantic load. Words, sentences, and utterances, which in the grammatical structure are found in different positions which are devoid of similar characteristics and, consequently, are non-comparable, prove in the artistic structure to be in positions of identity and antithesis and, consequently, comparable and contrastable. This reveals in them unexpected new semantic content impossible outside of poetry. Moreover, as we shall try to show, elements obtain a semantic load that they lack in the usual language structure. As we know, the speech construct is protracted in time and perceptible in segments in the process of speaking. Speech, a chain of signals unidirectional in the time sequence, is correlated with the language system that exists outside of time. This correlation also defines the nature of language as a bearer of meaning: the chain of meanings is revealed in temporal succession. The decoding of each linguistic sign is a one-time act whose character is predetermined by the correlation of a given *signifié* and a given *signifiant*.

The belletristic construct is also protracted in space; it requires a constant return, it would seem, to the text which has already fulfilled its informational role. It requires its comparison with subsequent text. In the process of such comparison, the old text is revealed anew, manifesting formerly hidden semantic content. The principle of return is a universal structural principle of the poetic work.

This, in particular, explains the fact that the belletristic text—not only poetic but also prose—loses the relative freedom of the transposition of elements on the syntactic level of utterance construction which is so characteristic of ordinary Russian speech. Repetition in the belletristic text is the traditional name for the relationship of its belletristic structural elements of comparison which can be realized as antithesis and identity. Antithesis designates the singling out of the opposite in the similar (the correlative pair); identity—the combination of that which seems different; analogy, the isolation of the similar in the different, is a variety of antithesis.

These systems of relationships constitute the general principle of the artistic structure's organization. On the different levels of this structure, we deal with its different elements, but the structural principle itself is preserved.

Being a principle of the organization of structure, comparison (opposition, identity) is also an operational principle of its analysis.

Belletristic Repetition

The belletristic text is a text with heightened features of ordering [uporiadochnost'].

The ordered quality of any text can be realized along two lines. In linguistic terms it can be characterized as ordering in terms of *paradigmatics* and *syntagmatics;* in mathematical terms—of equivalency and order. The character and function of these two types of ordering are different. If in narrative genre the second type predominates, then texts with a strongly expressed modeling function (and it is precisely here that poetry, especially lyric poetry, belongs) are constructed with marked predominance of the first. Repetition figures in the text as the realization of ordering on the paradigmatic plane, of ordering in terms of equivalency.

In the linguistic sense, paradigmatics is defined as the associative plane. The text is articulated into elements that are formed into a single structure. In contradistinction to the syntagmatic nexus that unites different elements of the text[35] by contrast, paradigmatics provides the comparison-contrast of elements which on a certain level form mutually differentiated variants. In each concrete case, the text selects one of these. Thus, a paradigmatic relationship is the relationship between an element that actually exists in the text and a potential multiplicity of other forms.

In natural language the paradigmatic relationship is the relationship between the element actually given in the text and the potential set of other forms that are present in the system. Therefore, the case in which the paradigm would be fully adduced in a natural language text is either impossible or extremely rare. A scholarly grammatical text (a meta-text) can give a sequence (list) of all of the possible forms, but it is difficult to construct a normal utterance in this way.

Poetry is a different matter. A secondary poetic structure, being imposed on language, creates a more complex relationship: a poem as a fact of the Russian language is a speech text; not a system, but its partial realization. However, as a poetic picture of the world, it gives the system fully and already functions as language. The secondary semantic paradigm is realized in the text as a whole. The basic mechanism of its construction is parallelism.

I am not amused when an inept dauber	Mne ne smeshno, kogda maliar negodnyi
Besmears Raphael's Madonna for me,	Mne pachkaet Madonnu Rafaelia,
I am not amused when a despised buffoon	Mne ne smeshno, kogda figliar prezrennyi
Dishonors Alighieri with a parody.	Parodiei beschestit Alig'eri.
—*Mozart and Salieri*	—A. Pushkin, *Motsart i Sal'eri*

The excerpt is laced with parallelisms. The twice repeated "I am not amused when..." ("Mne ne smeshno, kodga...") creates a unity of tonal inertia. "Dauber-buffoon" ("maliar-figliar") and "inept-despised" ("negodnyi-prezrennyi") are both synonymic pairs, but "dauber" and "buffoon" are synonyms in a different sense than are "inept" and "despised." In the second case, we can speak of synonymy in the general linguistic sense. In the first, parallelism is manifested in the communality of the archiseme "practitioner of art" and of pejorative meaning. "Raphael" and "Alighieri" in this context are also synonyms thanks to the disclosure of their common archiseme—"exalted artist." Thus, a semantic construct of the type "I am not amused when incompetence demeans genius" is invariant for both parts of the excerpt. Simultaneously, *parallelismus membrorum* is observed, a communality of rhythmico-syntactic and intonational constructions and a coincidence of stylistic characteristics. The communality between the parts of the text is so great that the second of them may seem redundant.

Comparing various types of poetry in world cultural history we see that coincidences among the segments of any poetic work can be very essentially varied, embracing the most diverse levels of language in extremely different combinations. Even the parameters of the concept "coincidence" change. In some systems it will strive toward a maximum; if a certain number of levels in a given system must obligatorily be drawn into the mechanism of parallelism for the text to be conceived of as poetic, then the author will strive to increase their number, including facultative (that is, facultative from the standpoint of the given system) types of coincidences, but pursuant to the structure-forming principle, to its striving toward their maximum increase.

At the opposite pole, we have the structural type that tends toward the minimalization of features of parallel organization. If a certain minimum number of features is recognized by the author and the reader without which the text ceases to be perceived as poetic, then the poet will strive to reduce the meaningful structure of the text to just this minimum and periodically even exceed this limit, creating passages that are perceived as verse only because they are included in more extensive contexts that possess the minimal set of features of poetry, but, which taken in isolation, cannot be differentiated from non-poetry.

Both of these tendencies underlie the typology of texts as possibilities. Their realization and functioning is determined by specific relationships that arise within human society, by the history of its culture and, especially, by the history of its literature.

But whether we shall take semantic parallelisms (such as the psychological parallelisms of folklore studied by A. N. Veselovsky, the psalmic parallels which D. S. Likhachev wrote about, or the songs about Foma and Erema that have been so interestingly analyzed by P. G. Bogatyrev), syntactic parallelisms, prosodic or phonological parallelisms, we shall encounter a certain system of segmentation of the text and an ensuing establishment of repetitions that permit us *to equate* these segments.

Of no less importance is the fact that in any poetic structure, along with the levels of coincidences, levels of *non-coincidences* are obligatorily present. Even if we assume the presence of absolute repetition (a possibility more theoretical than real inasmuch as even given the complete coincidence of two pieces of a text, their place in the work as a whole changes as does their relation to it, their pragmatic function, etc.), some difference will be present as an "empty sub-set," a structurally active, although unrealized, possibility.

In calling such a construction paradigmatic one must, however, state a reservation. In a general language text, as we have already noted, the paradigm exists in the consciousness of the speaker and the hearer, but in the text only one form is realized, the one that is abstracted from the paradigm. Such is also encountered in literature. Thus, for example, we can view all of the tragedies of the eighteenth century as realizations of some abstract paradigm called "tragedies of the eighteenth century." This is not, however, what we are discussing here. In poetic text the paradigmatic principle is manifested in a different fashion. A poetic work is not to be compared with a general language text, but with that grammatical meta-text which includes all possible members of a given paradigm.

So that the parallel will be still more complete, let us imagine a paradigm from the structure of an unfamiliar language. Here it is not the selection of the appropriate form from a known set of variants, but rather the clarification of the boundaries and the nature of the set of equivalent forms that will constitute the basis of the poetic construct. It is precisely because of this that the speech text, which any poetic work remains in the eyes of the linguist, becomes a *model*. The quality of *being a model* is inherent in any poetry. As examples of various kinds of models, we may cite: man in a given epoch, man in general, the universe. All this depends upon the character of the culture into which the poetry in question enters as a particular group of texts that constitute the culture.

Thus we can define the essence of poetic structure as the presence of certain orderings not implied by the structure of the natural language which permit us to identify in certain relationships the intra-textual segments and to examine the set of these segments as one or several paradigms. Within these segments not only similarity but also difference must be present. This permits us to see in them not simply the frequent repetition of one and the same thing, but a system of *variants* which are different from each other and which are grouped around a certain invariant type. One can learn what comprises this central invariant meaning only by considering all its variants inasmuch as the capability to be, in certain circumstances, either this or that variant is its basic property.

Why must we resort to such a strange expedient for the construction of the text, strange, that is, from the point of view of everyday speech practice?

Before answering this question, we shall show that two types of disruption of recurrence are possible. This, as we shall see, has great significance.

In the first place, we encounter ordering on one structural level (or on certain structural levels) and absence of ordering on others.

In the second place, within the limits of a single artificially isolated level we encounter *partial* ordering. Elements can be ordered to the point that a feeling of the organized nature of the text is evoked in the reader but cannot be ordered to the extent that the feeling of the incompleteness of this ordering is extinguished.

The combination of both of these principles is so organic for art that it may be considered a universal law of the structural building of the belletristic text. The striving for maximal informational saturation underlies the structure of the artistic text. To be suitable for the storage and transmission of information, every system must possess the following features.

1. It must be a system, that is, it must consist not of chance elements. Each of the system's elements is connected with the remaining ones, that is, one in some measure predicts the others.

2. The connection of elements must not be completely automatized. If each element unambiguously predicts the following one, it will be impossible to transmit information by such a system.

For the system to bear information, each element must predict a certain number of subsequent possibilities of which one is realized, that is, two mechanisms must work simultaneously: the automatizing and the de-automatizing.

In the natural sciences the plane of expression has a tendency toward automatization whereas content is not automatic. Therefore, the mechanism of expression is not meaningful in and of itself and is ignored by the information receiver who notes it only in cases of malfunction. (Thus we do not notice a typesetter's good work but only the bad; we do not notice good pronunciation in our native language but we note speech defects, etc). In poetry, all levels of language are meaningful and the conflict of automatization and de-automatization is distributed over all elements of the structure. The reality of the artistic text always exists in two dimensions[36] and the work of art can be described on every structural level via two modalities: the system of the realization of certain rules and the system of their violations. In this process, the "meat" of the text can be identified neither with the one nor with the other aspect taken separately. Only the relationship between them, only the structural tension, the mixture of incompatible tendencies, creates the reality of the work of art. If such an approach still sometimes surprises literary scholars (who sometimes polemicize about the nature of reality and what constitutes "the investigator's fiction," i.e., foot or "hypostasis," rhythm or meter, phoneme or sound, literary tendency or the text of the work and the "correct" way of writing literary history, i.e., as a conceptual construct "without people" or as a series of "creative portraits" without the abstractions that "kill" art), then for the linguist or the logician the very discussion of this topic seems an archaism.

Since the time of F. de Saussure the idea that the system of language involves two realities—language and speech—is more of a commonplace than a novelty requiring discussion. The logician is not surprised by the fact that the subject matter of any science may be studied on two levels: on the level of models and of their interpretations. Both of these conditions answer to the concept of reality, although they relate in different ways to that reality from which the subject matter of various sciences has not yet been isolated.

The model and the object of modeling belong to different levels of knowledge and in principle cannot be studied in a single series. Instead of their diffuse, undifferentiated examination, which at times leads literary historians and sometimes even poetry specialists[37] to study objects belonging to different levels of knowledge, e.g., text and meta-text as a single aggregate, scholars must learn to isolate levels of knowledge and to establish subordination in the material under study, i.e., to discriminate between objects and meta-objects of different degrees. Equally important is the subsequent definition of the rules of the relationship between them and material generally beyond the limits of a given science.

The subordination of the study of the literary work to the general rules of scientific logic and to that apparatus which has been elaborated in linguistics only more clearly isolates the specifics of the material to be studied. In the artistic text the very subordination of levels can be displaced and the usual situation wherein the elements which disturb the system are arrayed on a hierarchy of levels lower than the system itself is often not possible in the analysis of artistic creations. The very concept of "systemic" and "extra-systemic," as we shall see, is considerably more relative than had been imagined initially.

41

Rhythm as the Structural Basis of Poetry

The concept of rhythm belongs to the most general and commonly accepted features of poetic speech. Pierre Quiraud, defining the nature of rhythm, writes that "metrics and versification constitute a primary area of statistical linguistics inasmuch as the correct recurrence of sound is their subject matter." And further: "Thus, the line is defined as a segment that can be easily measured."[38]

"Rhythm" is generally understood as meaning correct alternation, the repetition of identical elements. (It is precisely this property of rhythmic processes, their cyclic nature, that defines the meaning of rhythm in natural processes and in man's work. In scholarly literature a tradition has been established [often perceived as "materialistic"] underlining the identity of the cyclic nature of natural and labor processes with rhythm in art in general and in poetry in particular.) G. Shengeli wrote:

> Let us take any sort of process flowing in time, for example, rowing (assuming good, uniform, skilled rowing). This process is broken down into segments, stroke to stroke, and in each segment there are exactly the same elements: raising the oar requiring almost no expenditure of effort; pulling the oar through the water requiring a considerable expenditure of effort. . . Such an ordered process, divisible into links of equal length in each of which the weak is supplanted by the strong, is called rhythmic and the ordered quality of the elements rhythm.[39]

It is not difficult to note that cyclicity in nature and rhythmicity in verse are phenomena of a completely different order. Rhythm in the cyclical processes of nature requires that certain conditions be repeated throughout certain intervals of time. (The transformation has a closed character.) If we take the cyclicity of the earth's position relative to the sun and isolate a chain of transformations: W—Sp—Sm—F—W—Sp—Sm—F—W (where W is winter, Sp—spring, Sm—summer, and F—fall) then the sequence W, Sp, Sm, F constitutes an exact repetition of the corresponding point of the preceding cycle.

Rhythm in poetry is a phenomenon of a different kind. The rhythmicity of poetry is the cyclical repetition of different elements in identical positions with the aim of equating the unequal or revealing similarity in difference, or the repetition of the identical with the aim of revealing the false character of this identity, of establishing differences in similarity.

Rhythm in poetry is a sense-discriminating element while those linguistic elements that do not possess it in ordinary usage assume a sense-discriminating character upon entering into a rhythmic structure. It is also important to note that poetic structure does not merely manifest new nuances of word meanings but reveals the dialectics of concepts, that internal contradictoriness of the phenomena of life and language for whose designation ordinary language lacks special means. Of all the investigators who have studied prosody, it was, in all probability, Andrei Bely who first clearly saw the dialectical nature of rhythm.[40]

Rhythm and Meter

Rhythmic recurrences have long been regarded as one of the basic features of Russian verse. After Lomonosov's reform and his introduction of the concept of the foot, recurrences of alternate stressed and unstressed syllables came to be viewed as an absolute condition for the perception of a text as poetic.

At the beginning of the twentieth century, however, in the light of changes then being experienced by Russian poetry, the classical verse system appeared in a new form.

The foundation for this new trend of scholarly thought was laid by Andrei Bely. In a 1909 study in the anthology *Symbolism,* he demonstrated that in Russian classical verse the stress was often not located where it might be expected according to Lomonosov's theoretical scheme. As Kiril Taranovsky's computations have since shown, the number of tri-stressed lines of Russian iambic tetrameter (that is, those with a single omitted stress) had already attained the startling figure of 63.7 percent during the nineteenth century.[41]

Bely himself, and later Bryusov, attempted to reconcile the theory of the poetic foot as it appeared in the Lomonosov system with their own observations of the realities of poetic stress with the aid of a system of "figures" or "hypostases" which were admissible within the limits of a given rhythm and which created its variants. They advanced the fruitful idea of regarding empirically diverse data as variants of an invariant system of constants. In the works of Bely, with his organic feeling for dialectics, the tendency toward the singling out of contradictions between text and system, on the one hand, and the elimination of this contradiction through the establishment of their equivalence, on the other, was especially palpable. Bryusov's approach was more dogmatic and attempted to resolve the question by rejecting the Lomonosov model and describing only a single aspect of poetry—the empiric. This latter approach, carried on by V. Pyast, S. Bobrov, and A. Kvyatkovsky has proved to be considerably less fruitful than those studies based on Bely's work, albeit as anti-Bely polemics concerning the description of Russian classical verse seen as a *contradiction* between a certain structural scheme and its realization. On this basis, at the beginning of the 1920's, V. M. Zhirmunsky and B. V. Tomashevsky developed a theory of the opposition of rhythm and meter—of the empiric reality of poetic stresses and of the abstract scheme of an idealized poetic meter. Zhirmunsky's and Tomashevsky's early theoretical postulates have preserved their fundamental scholarly significance, notwithstanding certain refinements subsequently introduced both by the authors themselves and by other investigators.[42] At present their theories have been adopted by K. Taranovsky, V. E. Kholshevnikov, M. L. Gasparov, P. A. Rudnev, by Academician A. N. Kolmogorov's group, and by a number of other investigators. The empirically given poetic text is perceived against the background of an ideal structure that is realized as rhythmic inertia, as "structural expectation." Inasmuch as the pyrrhic feet are distributed irregularly and their place in the line is relatively accidental (more accurately, their ordering is on another level), an ideal scheme of a higher level arises (in the consciousness of the transmitter and the receiver of the poetic text) in which rhythmic violations are cancelled out and the recurrent structure is given in a pure form. Tomashevsky also pointed out the true mode of the materialization of the metrical construct—scansion. He wrote:

> The concrete metrical system regulating the composition of classical verse amounts to the calculation of the expected canonized (metrical) stresses. Like any method of reckoning it is clearly manifested neither in the normal reading of poems nor in declamation, but in a special reading that clarifies the laws of stress distribution, i.e., in scansion. . . This artificial scansion is not an arbitrary act for it only demonstrates that constructional law which is invested in the lines.[43]

Tomashevsky has essentially never rejected this position. Thus, in his final summing up he wrote: "Scansion for correct verse is a natural operation since it is nothing but an emphatic clarification of the meter." And further: "Scansion is analogous to counting aloud in learning a song or in the movement of the director's baton."[44]

Tomashevsky's position elicited the objections of A. Bely who wrote:

> Scansion does not exist in reality; the poet does not scan his lines when reading to himself; nor does any performer, whoever he be, poet or artist, ever read the lines "Spirit of denial, spirit of doubt" ("Dukh otrican'ia, dukh somnen'ia") as "Of stuffiness sayings, spirit from opinions" ("Dukhot rican'ia, dukhso mnen'ia"). We flee aghast from such misreadings as "dukhot," "ricanii," and "mnenii."[45]

L. I. Timofeev agrees: "The celebrated concept of scansion is an unconcealed violence on language."[46]

Both objections stem from the fact that scansion is not encountered in linguistic and declamatory practice. But this objection is based on a logical error. No one has ever asserted that scansion realizes a norm for the reading of an empiric poem. What is being discussed is the reality of a construct, a second order reality. Demonstrating the absence of a feature in the object-language is insufficient grounds for affirming its absence in the meta-language. In nature there is no object having the form of a geometrically perfect sphere.

It is not difficult to show the extremely low probability of such an object occurring. But this is not to be viewed as a denial of the existence of the sphere as a geometric figure. As a geometrical object the sphere exists. Real physical spheres, from the geometric point of view, exist only to the extent that we disregard chance deviations. In natural language texts, the grammatical rules are not expressed. Moreover, in the utilization of our native language we have no more need of grammar than the poet does of scansion. But neither consideration denies the existence of grammar as an object of the second degree, as a meta-system in whose light much that exists in the text is unreal. (The text may contain typographical errors, handwriting differences, and other features that will be "eliminated" by the meta-system and which lose their reality to the point that they cease to be noticed.)

At the same time we must stress that scansion (or the related feeling that an accent should fall where it is foreseen by the metrical scheme but which is absent in the actual text) in no way implies the equation of the fully stressed segment and the pyrrhic one. Quite the contrary. Not only does it permit us to feel that there *might be* a stress at this point but brings out the fact that *it is not there.* Scansion never functions (for the contemporary adult reader)[47] as a text; it creates the *background* for the perception of the text. Against this background, the text is perceived as a simultaneous realization and disruption of certain rules, as recurrence and non-recurrence in their mutual tension.

The opposition of meter and rhythm continues to provoke objections. B. Ia. Bukhshtab in a work containing many observations, writes:

> This theory raises a number of questions. Why should classical Russian verse not exist in and of itself, as it were, rather than arise from the imposition of a metrical scheme, from a transparency, whose features we cannot consider attributes of the empirical verse? Why is the metrical scheme so inadequately embodied in the poem it underlies? Why does this counterforce that supports a building incapable of independently supporting itself appear and how is it formed in the consciousness of the hearer or reader of poetry?[48]

We now have a basis for the directly contrary assertion: not only must the opposition "meter-rhythm" not be rejected as an organizing structural principle, but rather the opposite. It is precisely here that poetics encounters one of the most general laws of verbal artistic structure.

Language contains a number of different levels. The description of separate levels as immanently organized synchronic slices is one of the fundamental postulates of modern linguistics. The fact that in a belletristic structure each level is comprised of structural mechanisms of opposing tendencies, one of which establishes constructional inertia, automatizes it, while the other de-automatizes it, leads to a characteristic phenomenon: in the artistic text *each* level has a two-tiered organization. The relationship of text and system here is not the simple realization it is in [ordinary] language, but is always a conflict, a tension. This creates the complex dialecticalism of belletristic phenomena. The task lies not in "overcoming" this duality in our understanding of the nature of poetic meter, but rather in learning how to detect its two-tiered and functionally opposed mechanism on other structural levels. The relationships of the phonetic series to the phonemic (sound—phoneme), the clausula (rhyming position) to assonance, plot to fabula [framework to narration, DBJ], and so on, form not a dead automatism but the vital interplay of the correlated elements on each level.

The two-tiered character of each level can be formulated either as a contradiction between the different sorts of constructional elements (thus in rhyme tension arises between the rhythmic, the phonological, and, as we shall see, the semantic elements) or between the realization or nonrealization of a single constructional series (the metric system). Tension between a variant of an element and its invariant form is also possible, e.g., the correlations "sound—phoneme" and "phoneme—grapheme." The possibility of such tension in a series is conditioned by the fact that, as we have said, in poetry the variant form can be promoted in function and become equal in rank to its invariant.

Finally, conflict is possible between different organizations on a single level. It is most typical for the plot. Thus, Dostoevsky frequently lends his plot development the inertia of the detective novel, which subsequently enters into conflict with the construction of his ideological-philosophical and psychological prose. However, such construction is possible also on lower levels.

Tyutchev's poem "Last Love" ("Posledniaia liubov' ") is constructed in this fashion.

> O, how in the decline of our years
> More tenderly we love and more superstitiously...
> Shine, shine, farewell light
> Of my last love, of evening twilight!
>
> The shadow embraced the half-sky
> Only there in the west wanders the radiance,—
> Linger, linger, evening day,
> Stay on, stay on, enchantment.
>
> Let the blood run thin in my veins,
> But in my heart scant not the tenderness...
> O thou, last love!
> Thou and bliss and hopelessness.

		No. of syllables
O, kak na sklone nashikh let	U´U´U´U´	8
Nezhnei my liubim i suevernei...	U´U´UU—U´U	10
Siiai, siiai, proshchal'nyi svet	U´U´U´U´	8
Liubvi poslednei, zari vechernei!	U´U—UU´U´U	10

47

		No. of syllables
Polneba obkhvatila ten',	ÚU−ÚÚ	8
Lish' tam na zapade brodit siian'e,	ÚÚUÚUU−U	11
Pomedli, pomedli, vechernii den',	ÚUU−UU−U−	10
Prodlis', prodlis', ocharovan'e.	ÚU−U−U−U	9
Puskai skudeet v zhilakh krov',	ÚÚÚÚ	8
No v serdce ne skudeet nezhnost'...	ÚU−ÚÚU	9
O ty, posledniaia liubov'!	ÚÚU−Ú	8
Ty i blazhenstvo i beznadezhnost'.	U−ÚUU−ÚU	10

The rhythmic construction of the poem is a complex correlation of orderings and their disruptions. Moreover, the disruptions themselves are ordering, but of another type.

Let us look first at the problem of isometrism insofar as in Lomonosov's syllabo-tonic system, metrical ordering also specifies the recurrence of the number of syllables in a line.

The first stanza affords a certain inertia of expectation by creating the correct alternation of the number of syllables: 8–10–8–10. True, there is already an anomaly here: habit in reading Russian iambic tetrameter, the most widespread meter in post-Pushkin poetry, disposes one to expect the correlation 8–9–8–9. The extra syllable in the even lines is distinctly heard by the ear. Thus, against the background of preceding poetic tradition, the first stanza is a violation. But from the point of view of immanent structure, it is ideally ordered, and this forces us subsequently to expect precisely this type of alternation.

The second stanza, however, violates these expectations in a different way. First, the arrangement of the short and long lines is converted from interlacing to embracing. This is all the more sharply felt because the rhyme remains interlacing. And insofar as the lengthening of interlacing lines in Russian poetry is connected with the combination of masculine and feminine rhymes and is its automatic consequence, the divergence of these two phenomena is unusual and, therefore, highly significant. But the matter is not limited to this: each of the two combined types of lines, counter to our expectation, is lengthened by a syllable that is also extremely noticeable to the ear. The 10 syllable line is replaced by the 11 syllable, and the 8 syllable line by the 9 syllable. Here an additional variation is introduced: in the long lines the syllable is lengthened in the first of them (the second is perceived as *shortened),* and in the short lines—in the first (the second is perceived as *lengthened).*

The diverse violations of the established order in the second stanza require in the third stanza a resurrection of the inertia of expectations: the inertia 8–10–8–10 is reintroduced. But here too there is a disruption: in the second line instead of the expected 10 syllable unit, there are 9 syllables. The significance of this interruption is that the 9 syllable unit in the second stanza was a lengthening of the short stanza and structurally constituted its variant. Here it is positionally equal to a long one, structurally not being equal to itself. At each step we see that poetic structure is an excellent school for dialectics.

In the syllabo-tonic line the disposition of stresses is just as important a factor as the number of syllables. Here we can observe the "play" of the orderings and their disruptions. The poem begins with a form I iambic tetrameter (according to K. Taranovsky's nomenclature). This is the most widespread variant. According to Taranovsky's calculations, between twenty-one and thirty-four percent of all of Pushkin's iambic tetrameter verse belong to this type, and this variant is actually this meter's signature, affording a certain metrical inertia and readers' expectation.

This disposes the reader to expect the usual iambic tetrameter intonation. However, the second line introduces into the iambic ordering an element similar to an anapestic foot, something not permitted by the poetic norms of that epoch. This interspersion might seem a mistake did it not obtain heightened development in the second stanza. In spite of the rhyme, a distinct compositional ring effect is found here: in the first and fourth lines, the correct iambic forms (III and IV) are utilized, but the stanza's compositional center is formed by the two lines with two interspersed bisyllabic intra-ictic intervals which create an anapestic inertia. However, the development of this intonation which is alien to the poem's basic construction takes place against the background of a strengthening, not a weakening of the iambic inertia. It is instructive that if the first line of the second stanza represents the comparatively rare form III (about ten percent in the Pushkinian tradition), the fourth is the most frequent form IV, while the following line begins with a fully stressed form which is especially important for the creation of the iambic inertia.

The last stanza begins with the resurrection of the shattered iambic inertia; three lines of correct iambs are given seriatim. However, they are followed by the line that closes the entire poem which is therefore especially weighty and which returns us to the mixed iambic-anapestic intonation of the first stanza.

This situation is an extremely rare one not only in classical Russian poetry but also in the twentieth century. While the combination of incongruent stylistic elements or the convergence of opposed semantic units has become one of the most widespread phenomena in poetry since Nekrasov, the increasing complexity of metrical constructions has gone a different route.[49] The development of the relationship "meter-rhythm" can be seen in the appearance of a stress system, which, for its artistic functioning, requires the syllabo-tonic system just as the rhythmical model requires the metrical one.

If the law of the dual stratification of an artistic structural level determines the text's synchronic construction, then the mechanism of de-automization functions on the syntagmatic axis. The "law of three-quarters" is one of its manifestations. It is as follows: if one takes a text, which on the syntagmatic axis is articulated into four elements, then we shall find, almost universally, that the first two quarters establish a structural inertia while the third violates it, and the fourth reestablishes the original pattern preserving, however, some token of its deformation.

Notwithstanding the fact that in actual texts this law, of course, becomes considerably more complex, its connection with the structure of memory and attention and with the norms of the de-automatization of the text assures it considerable scope.

Thus, for example, in iambic tetrameter the overwhelming majority of stress omissions are in the third foot. Taranovsky's data convincingly demonstrate this. If one takes not the line but the quatrain as the basic unit, one easily sees that in the great majority of cases the third line is the most disorganized on all levels. Thus, in the tradition arising in the numerous Russian translations of Heine, a tradition which obtained wide currency in the second half of the nineteenth and early twentieth centuries, the third line "has the right" not to observe the rhyme pattern, i.e., ABCB. Usually this deliberate lack of order also appears on the phonological level. Let us examine the distribution of stressed vowels in the first stanza of Blok's poem "Fiesole" ("F'esole," 1909).

Rings the ax, and from the campanile
Toward us the valley's Florentine peal
Swims, arrived, and awoke
Sleep golden and ancient...

Stuchit topor, i s kampanil	i o i
K nam florentiiskii zvon dolinnyi	i o i
Plyvyot, doplyl i razbudil	o y i
Son zolotistyi i starinnyi...	o i i

The first two lines set the inertia, the third violates it, and the last synthetically resurrects it, while incorporating a reminiscence of the third line.

Analogous regularities can also be found on the plot *[siuzhet]* level.

Thus, we see that more general principles of the construction of the belletristic text underlie the rhythmico-metrical structure of the poetic line. One must, however, emphasize that of the two tendencies (the ordering and the dissolution of order) the first is basic.

The articulation of the text into equivalent segments is one of the basic belletristic functions of the metrico-rhythmic structure. In natural language, lexico-semantic meaning is inherent only in the word. In poetry, the word is broken down into segments, from morpheme to phoneme, and each of these segments obtains independent meaning. The word is simultaneously divided and not divided. In this process, metric recurrences play a critical role.

Thus, the line is simultaneously a sequence of phonological units perceived as divided, existing separately, and a sequence of words seen as fused entities of phoneme combinations. Both sequences exist in a unity as two hypostases of a single reality, a line constituting a correlating structural pair.

The relationship of word and sound in verse is different from that in conversational speech. Grossly schematizing and breaking down the unity into provisional sequential phases, one can present this relationship in the following form: words are initially divided into sounds, but insofar as this division does not destroy the words, which exist simultaneously as chains of sounds, lexical meaning is transferred to the individual phoneme.

Such a division of the text into two types of segments, lexical and non-lexical (phonological, metrical), increases the number of consciously organized and, consequently meaningful elements in the text. But it also fulfills another function.

Meaningfulness of all textual elements (or, more accurately, the idea that the extra-systemic and, consequently, non-meaningful elements of a non-belletristic text can become systemic and meaningful given its realization of an esthetic function) constitutes the presumption of the perception of poetry. As soon as a set of texts is defined as poetry, among the aggregate of texts that constitute a given culture, the receiver of information is disposed toward a special perception of the text—one in which the system of meaningful elements shifts. (The shift may involve expansion, restriction, or zero change; in the latter case, we are dealing with the *abrogation* of a shift.)

So that a text can function as poetic, the recognition of this possibility, the expectation of poetry, must be present in the consciousness of the reader; certain signals, which would permit us to recognize that text as poetic, must be present in the text. The minimal set of such signals is perceived as "the basic properties" of the poetic text.

The function of metrical structure is that in dividing up the text into segments, it signals that the text belongs to the category "poetry." That metrical structure is called upon to separate poetry from non-poetry and to serve as a signal of a special esthetic experiencing of textual information is evident in those societies in which verse is just beginning to be recognized and in which the very concept of poetry is still being elaborated. In this process the metrical scheme is often put forward at the cost of eclipsing the lexical meaning. The way in which children read verse is instructive. Anyone who has thoughtfully observed a child's recitation of a poem cannot but concede that scansion is real. Inasmuch as for a child establishing the fact that "this is poetry" is much more important than determining "what it is about," scansion becomes the natural mode of declamation. Children apperceive "adult" reading with great reluctance, firmly insisting that their childish reading is better, prettier. One might compare with this the obligatory nature of stressed, emphatic declamation in a milieu that is still insufficiently experienced in poetic culture. Thus, in the poetry of the 1740s, during the elaboration of the syllabo-tonic system as the new type of belletristic structure which had assumed the function of poetry in the cultural system of the times, deviations from the metrical norms were an uncharacteristic phenomenon and were perceived as "poetic license," permitted but nonetheless a mistake.

The development of a belletristic structure is subject to a curious regularity: initially a general type of artistic structure is established and the types of meaning accessible to it become manifest. The content is determined by the *difference* of a given structure (genre, type of rhythmic construction, style, etc.) from all others possible within the limits of this culture. Then we begin to observe the internal differentiation of meanings within this structural formation, which from something singular turns into a set and a hierarchy of possibilities, from an individual object, into a class, and then, into a class of classes.

The rules are formulated most rigidly in the first stage of development. The sum total of prohibitions which define a given structural type is immediately introduced. Subsequent development lies in the shattering of the prohibitions and their reduction to a minimum. If initially the observation of an entire system of rules is required in order to recognize that we are dealing with tragedy, an ode, an elegy, with poetry in general, then, subsequently, an ever greater number of the rules become facultative. Each new removal of a formerly obligatory prohibition is perceived as a step toward simplicity, toward naturalness, a movement from "literariness" toward "life-likeness." This process has great significance and it is not by chance that it is invariably repeated in each cultural cycle.

Art strives toward the augmentation of information possibilities. But the possibility of bearing information is directly proportional to the number of structural alternatives. The greater the number of alternative possibilities, the greater the extent to which we find: (1) supra-linguistic prohibitions and (2) the subsequent replacement of an unambiguous prescription for each structural bundle by a set of alternative possibilities.

Without the preceding prohibition its subsequent abrogation cannot become a structurally meaningful factor and will be indistinguishable from disorganization and cannot become a means for the transmission of meanings. It follows that "the abrogation of prohibitions" in the structure of a text does not mean their elimination. The system of abrogations is meaningful only against the background of the prohibitions and implies an awareness of them. When we say: "Derzhavin fought against Classicism" and "Nekrasov fought against the censorship," we have in view completely different meanings of the concept "fought." The complete abolition of censorship would have in no way affected the significance of Nekrasov's poetry. "Fight" here signifies an interest in total destruction. Derzhavin's artistic system is meaningful only in relation to those prohibitions that he violated with a boldness unheard of in his time. Therefore, his poetic system not only destroyed Classicism but also ceaselessly renewed the awareness of its norms. Without these norms, Derzhavin's bold innovation loses its meaning. A counterforce is indispensable as background and makes Derzhavin's new system of rules and prescriptions meaningful. For the reader knowing the norms of Classicism and acknowledging their cultural value, Derzhavin was a hero; for the reader who has lost touch with the cultural standard of the eighteenth century, who does not recognize its prohibitions as either valuable or meaningful, Derzhavin's boldness seems totally incomprehensible. It is instructive that for such poets it is precisely the total victory of their system, the destruction of the cultural value of those artistic structures against which they fought, that means the end of their own popularity. In this sense when we speak of the conflict of structural tendencies we are not dealing with the destruction of one and its replacement by another but with the appearance of formerly proscribed structural types which are artistically active only against the background of that preceding system formerly considered their antagonist.

Precisely these regularities have determined the dynamics of Russian classical verse and, subsequently, of twentieth century Russian poetry.

Originally meter was the sign of poetry as such. Tension arising in the text had the character of a contradiction between constructs of different levels: metrical recurrences created equivalent segments and the phonological and lexical content of these segments underlined their non-equivalence. Thus positionally identical vowels, if seen as a realization of a metrical model, could be identified ("both stressed" or "both unstressed" in identical structural positions) or contrasted, if viewed as different phonemes. The same may be said about the relationship of metrical segments to words.

Insofar as phonetic or lexical difference among metrically equated elements became a distinctive feature, it obtained heightened meaning. That which in natural language simply constituted systemically unconnected, diverse elements (e.g., different words) became synonymic or antonymic elements of unified systems.

Still another system of relationships is associated with structural tension and contradictions within the level of metrico-rhythmical repetitions. It is determined by the differentiation of a structure's metrical level into subclasses.

In the history of Russian classical verse there initially arose an opposition of two types of disyllabic meters, the iamb and the trochee. Later the opposition "disyllabic meter"—"trisyllabic meter" arose. It is significant that differentiation within the trisyllabic meters never had the structural weight of the opposition of iamb and trochee.

Inasmuch as different types of meters develop according to the law of the presumption of structural significance, people begin to ascribe meanings to them, identifying them with the most active cultural oppositions. The polemic between Lomonosov and Tredyakovsky about the relative meaning of the iamb and the trochee is instructive in this regard. Neither participant in the quarrel doubted that the meters *have* meanings. This is not even argued but simply assumed as an obvious truth. One need only establish what this meaning is. This is done as follows: the most meaningful oppositions in the literary system of a period are determined, e.g., "high-low," "state-personal," "heroic-intimate," "noble-vulgar." The correspondence between these concepts and types of meters is then established in a rather arbitrary fashion.

Subsequently when a more ramified system of genres is formed, some one work, especially memorable to its contemporaries, adorns a particular meter with its own intonation, its lexico-semantic system, and its structure of images. A tradition is thereby established associating a given type of meter with [certain types of] intonational and ideational artistic structures. This association is arbitrary as are all conventional relationships of the *signi-fie* and the *signifiant.* However, inasmuch as all conventional associations in art tend to function iconically, a persistent effort to *semanticize* meters, to ascribe fixed meanings to them arises. Thus, K. Taranovsky has most convincingly shown the rise of a tradition stemming from Lermontov's poem "Alone I come out on to the road" ("Vykhozhu odin ia na dorogu"), which lent the Russian five-foot trochee a fixed, extremely stable, ideational tonality.[50]

The antithesis "poetry/non-poetry" had already assumed a different character during this period. "Poetry" is not a single entity but a paradigmatic set of possible meters united by their common membership in the category "poetic language" and differentiated in their genre-stylistic aspects. The process, however, does not end here: rhythmic figures whose alternation within a single metric system was initially elicited for purely linguistic reasons and which was artistically seen as an inadequacy began to acquire an esthetic role. (It is significant that in 1741 Lomonosov had ninety-five percent fully stressed forms in his iambic tetrameter [almost perfect scansion!]; in 1743, seventy-one percent; and in 1745 a figure of thirty to thirty-five percent was established as a norm that remained valid for Pushkin's time.)

The function of rhythmic figures was two-fold: on the one hand, they were perceived against the metrical background as elements of de-automatization, of anomaly, that eliminated the monosemy of the rhythmic intonations, increasing the unpredictability of the poetic text. On the other hand, the rhythmic figures themselves very quickly came to be firmly associated with certain word sequences, with poetic lines. They became constants.

Not only a metrical intent but even a fixed rhythmic scheme already existed as an independent and meaningful artistic element in Pushkin's consciousness. There are convincingly attested cases where the poet, reworking a poem, replaced all of the words in a line but preserved its rhythmic figure. Thus, in the second stanza of the draft of "Two feelings are marvelously close to us..." ("Dva chuvstva divno blizki nam...") there originally was a line "The independence of man" ("Samostoián'e chelovéka"). It belongs to an extremely rare variety of iambic tetrameter, the so-called type VI (according to the Taranovsky terminology). In Pushkin's work of 1830-1833 (the fragment which interests us was written in 1830) it is met in 8.1 percent of the total number of lines in this meter. Pushkin rejected the entire stanza, but in its new variant the line reappeared as "A life-creating sanctuary" ("Zhivotvoriáshchaia sviatýnia") with the same rhythmical structure.

The automatization of rhythmic figures in disyllabic meters took place concurrently with the shift of interest to trisyllablic meters where the interplay with word boundaries created opportunities for that variability and unpredictability which had been already supplanted by standardized tonalities in disyllabic meters.

After Nekrasov, Fet, and A. K. Tolstoy, even within the confines of the trisyllabic meters, intonational constants became fixed for certain authors, genres, and topics by the consciousness of the readers. Thus, Russian classical verse attained that limit of development which within its own boundaries could create the unexpected only by means of parody. Actually, the parodic conflict between rhythm and tonality became one of the favorite devices for renewing the artistic experiencing of rhythm at the end of the nineteenth century.

This was not the only alternative. On the basis of the immense poetic culture of the nineteenth century, of an extensively elaborated system which had become classic and the norm, much bolder violations, even sharper deviations from the norms of poetic speech, became possible. The tradition of the nineteenth century played the same role for poetry of the twentieth century (in reference to the experiencing of rhythm) as had the fully stressed iambs of the early Lomonosov or the scansion in children's declamation had played for the eighteenth century. It gave the feel of a norm which was so deep and strong that even *dolniki* and *vers libre* could be unmistakably experienced as verse.

Thus rhythmico-metrical structure is not an isolated system, not a scheme for the distribution of stressed and unstressed syllables devoid of internal contradictions, but a conflict, a tension between different types of structure. The play of intersecting regularities gives rise to that "accidentalness in conditionedness" which guarantees poetry its high information content.

The Problem of Rhyme

The belletristic function of rhyme is in many ways similar to the function of rhythmic units. This is not surprising: the complex relationship of recurrence and non-recurrence is inherent to rhyme just as it is to rhythmic constructions. The basis of modern rhyme theory (in contrast to the phonetic school of poetics *[Ohrphilologie]*) was laid by V. M. Zhirmunsky in his 1923 book, *Rhyme, Its History and Theory (Rifma, ee istoriia i teoriia)* in which he saw rhyme not merely as the coincidence of sound but as a rhythmic phenomenon. Zhirmunsky wrote: "Every sound recurrence that has an organizing function in the metrical composition of poetry must be assigned to the concept of rhyme."[51] Zhirmunsky's formulation underlies all subsequent definitions of rhyme.

One must, however, note that this definition has in view the most widespread and indisputably most significant case, i.e., rhyme in verse, which is far from being the only possible one. The history of Russian verse attests that its association with poetic language is not the only possibility. Ancient Russian poetry (psalms, popular lyric, epic) not only did not know rhyme, but even excluded it. Poetry was associated with song and the relationship between song and rhyme was evidently that of complementarity. Rhyme was met only in spoken genres and could not be mixed with singing. Rhyme in this system was *a feature of prose,* ornamental prose that was structurally distinguished both from poetry and from non-belletristic language of all types. It was differentiated from both the commercial and conversational language that stood below art on the scale of medieval cultural values and also from the religious, sacred, governmental, and historical [chronicle] language that stood above it. This ornamental "entertainment" prose included, on the one hand, proverbs and trade fair buffoonery, and, on the other, the "weaving of words" style *[vitie sloves]*. (As D. S. Likhachev has shown, the style of "The Supplication of Daniil the Incarcerated" ("Molenie Daniila Zatochnika") was elaborated under the influence of the former.) Here we particularly see that mingling of trade fair and baroque culture which we have discussed elsewhere.[52] Rhyme was united with poetry and assumed an organizing metrical function only with the rise of spoken declamatory poetry. However, it preserved one essential aspect of prose: the tendency toward content.

Rhythmic recurrence is the recurrence of position. Given this fact, the phoneme as a unit of a certain linguistic level enters into a differentiating group of features. Thus, the element being activated belongs to the plane of expression.

The earliest rhymes were either grammatical or root rhymes. Most were of a flexional character.

> The Dutch doctor
> And the good druggist
>
> Gollandskii lek*ar'*
> I dobryi aptek*ar*
>
> To send off old women like young
> And in no way to harm their mind
>
> Starykh starukh molodymi perepravl*iati,*
> A uma ikh nichem ne povrezh*dati.*
>
> I have prepared my machine
> And readied my whole [in] strument.
> Come to me from all lands
> My art make renown.
>
> Ia mashinu sovsem izgot*ovil*
> I ves' svoi strument prigot*ovil.*
> So vsekh stran ko mne priezzh*aite.*
> Moiu nauku proslavli*aite.*[53]

Rhyme in the "word weaving" prose style is similar. We cite a text of Epiphanius Premudryi (d. 1420):

For I am most sinful and uncomprehending. . . weaving the word, fructifying the word and thinking to honor by the word, both coining and weaving together words of praise, I say anew: I call thee leader to those gone astray, discoverer to the perished, preceptor to the tempted, minister of the mind to the blinded, purifier to the defiled, punisher to the dissipated, guardian to warriors, consoler to the grieved, giver of nourishment to the hungry, deliverer to those in need, instructor to the unthinking, helper to the offended, warm prayer, true intercessor, savior to the heathen, curser of devils, smasher of idols, trampler of images, servant of God, zealot for wisdom, lover of philosophy, creator of truth, narrator of books, scribe of Permian literacy.

Da i az mnogogreshnyi i nerazumnyi. . . slovo plet*ushchii* i slovo plod-*iashchii* i slovom pochtiti mni*ashchii,* ot sloves pokhvaleniia i prio-br*etaia* i priplet*aia,* paki glagoliu: chto tia nareku vozha zablud*ivshim,* obret*atelia* pog*ibshim,* nastavnika prel'shch*ennym,* rukovod*itel'ia* umom oslepl*ennym,* chist*itelia* oskver*ennym,* vzyskat*elia* rastoch*ennym,* strazha ratn*ym,* uteshit*elia* pechal'n*ym,* kormit*elia* alch*ushchim,* poda-*telia* treb*uiushchim,* pokazat*elia* nesmysl*ennym,* pomoshchnik*a* obidi-m*ym,* molitvenn*ika* tepla, khodataia vern*a,* pogan*ym* spasit*elia,* bes*om* proklinat*elia,* kumir*om* potrebit*elia,* idol*om* popirat*elia,* bogu sluzhit-*elia,* mudrosti rachit*elia,* filosofii liubit*elia,* pravde tvorit*elia,* knigam skazat*elia,* gramote permstei spisat*elia.*"[54]

Flexional and root rhymes, being among the recurrences of the morphological and lexical levels, directly bear upon the area of semantics. Inasmuch as the elements on the plane of expression coincide and *meaning* becomes a distinctive feature, the connection of structure with content is laid bare.

The sound of a rhyme is directly linked to its unexpectedness, i.e., its character is not acoustic or phonetic but rather semantic. Comparing tautological rhymes with homonymic ones easily persuades one of this. In both cases the nature of the rhythmical-phonetic coincidence is identical. However, rhyme resounds richly only given non-coincidence and remoteness of meanings. (The juxtaposition is perceived as a surprise.) In cases of the recurrence of both sound and meaning, rhyme produces an impression of poverty and is recognized as rhyme only with difficulty.

Again we meet with the fact that recurrence also implies difference, that coincidence on one level only highlights non-coincidence on another. Rhyme is one of the most conflictive dialectical levels of poetic structure. It fulfills the function performed by semantic parallelisms in unrhymed popular and psalmic poetry. It juxtaposes lines in pairs, forcing us to perceive them not as a conjunction of two separate utterances, but as two modes of saying the same thing. Rhyme on the morphological-lexical level parallels the function of anaphora on the syntactic level.

That construction of content which constitutes the characteristic feature of poetry takes rhyme as its starting point. In this sense the principle of rhyme can also be pursued on higher structural levels. Rhyme belongs equally to the metrical, phonological, and semantic organization [of poetry]. That rhyme has been insufficiently studied in comparison with other poetic categories is closely connected with its complexity.

The question of the relationship of rhyme to other levels of textual organization has not been considered at all. For Russian poetry of the nineteenth and twentieth centuries it is evident, for example, that the "shattering" of prohibitions on rhythmic systems has almost always been supplemented by an increase in prohibitions on the concept of "good" rhyme. The more the rhythmic structures strive to imitate non-poetic language, the more marked rhyme becomes in verse. The weakening of metaphorism is, on the contrary, usually accompanied by a weakening of the structural mode of rhyme. Blank verse as a rule shuns tropes. Pushkin's poetry of the 1830's is a clear example.[55]

Words, which have nothing in common outside of a given text, create sound complex coincidences in rhyme. This contrastive comparison gives rise to unexpected sense effects. The fewer the intersections among the semantic, stylistic, and emotional fields of meaning of these words, the more unexpected their contact, and the intersecting structural level that permits us to join them becomes all the more meaningful in the textual construction.

Even
　　　a gray gelding
wants
　　　a life elegant
　　　　　　and pretty.
It twirls
　　　playfully
its tail and its mane.
It always twirls [them]
　　　　　　but especially ardently
if
　　　it meets
　　　　　a personage-mare.

　　　　　　—V. Maiakovskii, "Give Us an Elegant Life"

Dazhe
　　　merin sivyi
zhelaet
　　　zhizni iziashchnoi
　　　　　　　　i krasivoi.
Vertit
　　　igrivo
khvostom i grivoi.
Vertit vsegda,
　　　　　no osobo pylko—
esli　navstrechu
　　　　　　osoba-kobylka.

　　　—V. Maiakovskii, "Daiosh' iziashchnuiu zhizn' "

The juxtaposition "sivyi — "krasivyi" ("gray" — "pretty") immediately sets the basic semantic contradiction of the entire poem. The stylistic and semantic contradiction of these words in ordinary usage and in their traditional literary meanings forces us to assume that "krasivyi" will obtain a special meaning in the text such that it will elucidate "sivyi" which is a constituent part of the phraseologism "sivyi merin" whose meaning is completely fixed.[56] It is precisely by the unusualness of this second meaning, the resistance which all of our linguistic and cultural experience offers it, that the unexpectedness and efficacy of the text's semantic structure is determined. Other rhymes in the text also display this same phenomenon, e.g., "rach'ei" — "frach'ei" ("crab" — "cutaway").

The rhyme "osobo pylko"—"osoba-kobylka" ("especially ardently"— "personage-mare") creates still more complex relations. The stylistic contrast between the romantic "pylko" ("ardently") and the familiar "ko-bylka" ("mare") is supplemented by the juxtaposition of identical sound complexes ("osobo" and "osoba" are identical in pronunciation) and different grammatical functions. The reader experienced in questions of language and poetry will note one further effect here: the contradictions between the graphics and the phonetics of the verse. The heightened attention of the Futurists to the graphic aspect of the text must not be forgotten. "Igrivo" — "i grivoi" ("playfully" — "and with its mane") demonstrate yet another semantic aspect. In the cited excerpt, words of two semantic types are encountered: some belong to the human world, others to the world of horses. The elucidation of vulgar meanings through conventional poetic ones is supplemented by the same sort of elucidation of "equine" meanings via human ones. (This is possible in that words of one series are realized in other series as parts of words, and this, because of the meaningfulness of the entire area of expression in poetry, is transferred to the sphere of meanings.)

Recurrences on the Phonemic Level

It has long been noted that the recurrence of phonemes in poetry is subject to somewhat different laws than in non-belletristic language. If one views ordinary speech as unordered (that is, not taking into account the strictly linguistic regularities of its construction), then poetic language, including its phonemic level, shows itself to be ordered in a special way.

The most common situation (or more accurately, the most noticeable, thanks to its elementary nature) involves the selection of words so that certain phonemes are met more frequently or less frequently than in that linguistic norm that is difficult to formulate, but which is known intuitively to every native speaker. This norm is realized in a particular way without being observed. If we fail to notice some aspect of language, we may be certain that its construction is in accord with the norms of usage. A deliberate increase in the use of a given element makes it noticeable, structurally active. Diminished frequency may also be a mode of isolation. However, inasmuch as the linguistic norm on all levels shows a certain, sometimes significant, difference between the lower and upper boundaries of admissibility, and also because of the restricted length of literary texts (which means that the absence of a given element may be completely accidental), structural non-usage is more often elaborated in a different fashion. It is properly preceded by an organized, heightened frequency that creates a certain rhythmic inertia. Subsequently, in a place where a given element is expected, it is absent. Through this, we obtain an effect of frustration. Seeming disorganization, simplicity, and naturalness of the text are all imitated.

Apart from the frequency of the recurrence of the same phonemes, the recurrence of their positions is essential: at the beginning of words or of lines, in inflectional elements, under stress, in the recurrence of groups of phonemes in relation to each other, and so on. Recurrences of phonemes in verse have an artistic function. Phonemes are presented to the reader only in the constituency of lexical units. Phonemic ordering is transferred to words that are grouped in a certain fashion. To the natural semantic ties that organize language we add a "supra-organization," uniting words which are not interconnected in the language into new semantic groups. The phonological organization of the text has, thus, an immediate semantic significance. However, even in the system of sound recurrences we can discover two previously noted tendencies: firstly, one toward the establishment of a certain pattern of order, a certain automatism of structure, and, secondly, one toward its violation.

Let us give an example:

Persephone destroyed by the fruit!
The persisting purple of thy lips,
And thy eyelashes like notches,
And the golden tooth of a star.

—M. Tsvetaeva, "Poem of the Mountain"

Persefona zernom zagublennaia!
Gub uporstvuiushchii bagrets,
I resnitsy tvoi—zazubrinami,
I zvezdy zolotoi zubets.

—M. Tsvetaeva, "Poema gory"

The text includes several sequences of words that are completely natural from the standpoint of the laws of ordinary language: "Persephone destroyed by the fruit" and "Thy eyelashes like notches." However, alongside them we encounter sequences that produce a somewhat unusual impression. Such is the relationship of the second line to the first and of the fourth to the third. These unusual adjunctions are expressed differently however: some connection between the first and second lines is implied and perhaps even manifested intonationally (for example, comparison, equation, or causal-consequential subordination), but it is not expressed syntactically. The second and third, and also the third and fourth lines are united by a syntactic link, but it contradicts the content of the utterances included in the lines. One can easily be persuaded that where the usual linguistic associations are incomplete or unmotivated, phonological associations are especially concentrated. Conversely, in parts of the text where the morphological ordering is clear, the phonological aspect is weakened.

Let us examine the basic phonological associations of an excerpt from the above Tsvetaeva poem. In the first line we have the fixed alliterative conjunction:"zernom zagublennaia" ("by the fruit destroyed"). The confrontation of these two words and the association with the myth of Persephone activates in the word "zerno" ("fruit") the mythological theme: "eating the fruit (the symbol of love) is the cause of destruction." However, this association of "zerno" with amatory symbolism is fully revealed only by the phonological ties of the second line. If the coincidence of the initial "z" unites "zerno" and "zagublennaia," then the sharing of the group "gub" links the end of the first line with the second, and the meaning "destruction" is linked with the meaning of "guba" ("lip"). The second line is phonologically close-knit: "uporstvuiushchii" ("persisting") duplicates the vocalism of the first syllable ("ub-up"), and "bagrets" ("purple") repeats its consonantism ("gb-bg"). As a result, a semantic whole is formed that subsumes the intersection of the semantic fields of these three words.

62

This whole cycle of meanings is connected with Persephone who in this excerpt replaces the "I" of the poem's other chapters. The opposing "thou" ("ty") also has its own phonological "distribution." The modulation "z-zub—zv-zd—zlt—zub" in "zazubrinami" ("notches"), "zvezdy" ("star"), "zolotoi" ("golden"), "zubets" ("tooth") creates a connected series. The common semantic content arising at the intersection of the lexical meanings of these components is ascribed to "resnitsa" ("eyelash"). These two meanings producing the conflict of "I" and "thou" are brought closer and opposed by the sound correlations "zagublennaia"—"zazubrinamy" ("perished"—"notched") and "bagrets"—"zubets" ("purple"—"tooth").

Thus the text's phonological organization forms supra-linguistic associations that assume a semantic organizing character.

The view is widespread that the sound organization of the text is a construct comprised of several sounds specially selected by the poet. "Sounds" ("zvuchanie") are understood to be acoustic units of a certain physical nature. Consequently it is said that in studying sound organization one must focus not on the written text, but on its transcription. The question is actually considerably more complex. Organization is built on several levels: in some cases distinctive phonemic or allophonic features are ordered, as in modern Russian poetry:[57] in other cases—the phonemes themselves; in still others—morphological orderings are also included in the organization. Thus, the preposition "s" ("with") will be pronounced, in certain positions, as voiced, but because of communality of morphological function, it will be identified with voiceless pronunciations of this same preposition.

> **You with belches, I with books,**
> **With truffle, I with slate pencil,**
> **You with olives, I with rhymes,**
> **With a pickle, I with dactyl.**
>
> —M. Tsvetaeva, "The Table"

> **Vy—s otryzhkami, Ia—s knizhkami,**
> **S triufelem, Ia—s grifelem,**
> **Vy—s olivkami, Ia—s rifmami,**
> **S pikulem, Ia—s daktilem.**
>
> —M. Tsvetaeva, "Stol"

"S" is pronounced here first as "s" then as "z" ("z grifelem" and "z daktilem"), but their morphological (and orthographic) communality forces us to direct our attention to the indisputable unity of this element in the recurring structure of the text. In this case, the poem's usual orthography yields more than a transcription.

In ordinary non-belletristic languages the correlation among the levels of phoneme, distinctive features, graphemes, and morphemes is automatized and we perceive all of these aspects as a unity. In poetry, inasmuch as some of these levels in the text can be supplementarily ordered, and others not, there arises a freedom within their correlation that permits us to make the very system of correlations meaningful. Depending on what is maximally ordered in this complex, it may be useful to resort to an analysis of a transcription reflecting the actual pronunciation, or to a morphemic or graphic transcript.

A number of conclusions may be drawn from the above. Most important of these is that the so-called musicality of poetry is not of an acoustic nature. In this sense the opposition "musicality"/"content" is at best simply not true. The musicality of verse is born at the expense of that tension which arises when certain phonemes bear differing structural loads. The greater the extent of the non-coincidences (semantic, grammatical, intonational, etc.) falling upon coinciding phonemes, the more palpable the rupture between the recurrence on the phonemic level and the difference on the levels of any of its meanings, the more musical, the more sonorous, the text seems to the reader. It follows that the sonority of the text is not its absolute, purely physical property. For the listener who already knows the entire set of possible rhymes of a given poet or school, a clear perception of the text's phonological aspect is impossible. The aging of words, a well-known phenomenon in the history of poetry, is connected with this. Words "become a habit, they age like apparel" (Mayakovsky). Pushkin also wrote of "the aging of rhymes" as have many others since. However, the lexical composition of language does not change so rapidly and a rhyme "which has grown old" in one system, a type of sound organization forbidden by virtue of its banality, upon entering into a new cultural context, becomes unexpected, capable of bearing information. The sound of words may be "rejuvenated," although the words themselves remain unchanged in their phonetic constituency.

A firm understanding that the phoneme is not simply a sound of a certain physical nature, but a sound to which a certain structural significance is ascribed in the language of art, a sound meaningful on many levels, elucidates the problem of onomatopoeia in a special way. Usually the similarity of poetic sound texture to sounds of the real world is emphasized. But the similarity here is no greater than that between a real object and any mode of its depiction. The physical sound is recreated by the mechanism of the phonemes, that is, by systemic and meaningful sounds. The "naturalness" and "amorphousness" of these sounds is secondary and reminds one of those "wordless noises" that occur when the extra-linguistic sounds emitted by man, such as sneezing and coughing, are transmitted by phonemes; that is, by linguistic units. Here we are dealing not with exact reproduction but with a conventional correspondence as accepted in a given system. It is instructive that onomatopoeic interjections, which reproduce the cries of various animals *do not coincide in different languages.* The correspondence between onomatopoeic utterances and their referents exists only within the limits of a given language, although, of course, it is distinguished by a higher degree of iconicity than are ordinary words.

The question of trans-rational ("zaumnyi") language assumes another meaning in this context. The everyday idea of trans-rational language as nonsense is inaccurate because "senseless language," i.e., one devoid of meanings, is a contradiction in terms. The concept "language" implies a mechanism for the transmission of meanings. So-called "trans-rational words" are composed of the phonemes and also very frequently of the morphemes and root elements of a known language. They are words with unfixed lexical meaning. However, they are words inasmuch as they have the formal features of words and are found between word boundaries. Since they are words, it is to be assumed that they have meaning (there are no words without meanings), but that it is somehow unknown to the reader and sometimes even to the author. "I very much like this word, but cannot translate it" ("Liubliu ia ochen' eto slovo, no ne mogu perevesti"), Pushkin's lines in *Eugene Onegin* where the author cannot, or pretends he cannot, give the translation of a word is typologically close to trans-rational language.

Alexei E. Kruchenykh, introducing the concept of trans-rational language, had in view subjective, fluid, individualized meanings in opposition to the "frozen" ordinary language meanings of words. This interpretation was determined by his literary position and the logic of the polemic over the language of poetry. There is no longer any basis for regarding this definition as obligatory.

Long before the rise of the poetics of Futurism and apart from any connection with it, the use of words that were incomprehensible to the audience, words that were constituted on an *ad hoc* basis, words whose meanings were completely occasional and determined by the given context were encountered in folklore, in children's poetry and in the practice of many literary schools.

> **Our Automedons are spirited,**
> **Unwearying are our troikas.**
>
>   A. Pushkin, *Eugene Onegin*
>   • • •
>   • • •
> **Avtomedony nashi boiki,**
> **Neutomimy nashi troiki.**

That all of *Eugene Onegin's* readers knew the meaning of the name Automedon is doubtful.

The meaning of an unknown word is defined by its context. This is how people behave. They do not resort to the dictionary (if we are speaking about the living perception of language) but guess the meaning from the general contextual import of the situation. But context in poetry is first of all poetic structure. Therefore, the unknown word does not remain devoid of meanings but becomes a cluster of *structural meanings* for us. In the following case the major structural meaning is produced by the conflict between the words of the text and the objects designated by them.

> **Meanwhile like village Cyclopses**
> **Before a slow fire**
> **They treat with Russian hammer**
> **The light manufacture of Europe,**
> **Blessing the chuckholes**
> **And ruts of the Fatherland's earth.**
>
> **⋮ ⋮**
>
> **Mezh tem kak sel'skie tsiklopy**
> **Pered medlitel'nym ognem**
> **Rossiiskim lechat molotkom**
> **Izdel'e legkoe Evropy,**
> **Blagoslavliaia kolei**
> **I rvy otecheskoi zemli.**

The comic effect of the contradiction between the poeticism "village Cyclopses" and the actual visage of a village blacksmith[58] in the reader's mind affords the key to the entire passage.

Thus, tension develops between the extreme familiarity, the commonplaceness of the poetic referent and the extreme remoteness, the unusualness, the poetic quality of the words which designate it. Therefore, the fact that the reader does not know the meaning of the name Automedon does no harm: remoteness from the commonplace is only underscored. An unknown word always incorporates an element of exoticism. It is perceived as an *alien word,* secret, and therefore, not at all meaningless but rather especially significant. It is for this reason that translators often retain meaningful names and onomatopoeic words without translation, although it would not be difficult to decipher and translate them.

Incomprehensible words are perceived as evidence of the authenticity of the recreation of alien life. They lend it color. Thus, non-Japanese words in an original Japanese text become Japanese (i.e., alien) in the Russian translation:

> **"Await me by the bridge!**
> **Bakkara-fungoro—by the bridge!**
> **He asked. —Tell me, will you wait?"**
> **"Oh, I haven't brought my umbrella with me!**
> **Look, it's getting ready to rain!**
> **Bakkara-vakkara-fungoro,**
> **Bakkara-vakkara-fungoro."**
>
> —Chikatmatsu Monzaemon,
> *The Suicide of Lovers on the Isle of Heavenly Nets*
> (Trans. V. Markova)

"Podozhdi menia u mosta!
        Bakkara-fungoro—u mosta!—
"Prosil on. —Skazhi, podozhdesh?"
"Akh, ia s soboi ne vziala zonta!
Gliadi, sobiraetsia dozhd'!
        Bakkara-vakkara-fungoro,
        Bakkara-vakkara-fungoro!"

Other meanings may also be ascribed to the unknown word. These are determined, on the one hand, by the work's poetic structure and, on the other, by those functions which are assigned to an unknown word in that cultural system. Such words may be "exalted," "holy," "true," or possibly "hostile," "harmful," "unnecessary," and "offensive." When we define the meaning of an unknown word, the same mechanism functions as in hearing unintelligible speech in a foreign langue: we "translate" the sounds and words of the alien language ascribing to them those meanings which they have in our own languages.

We have defined the nature of recurrence in the belletristic structure and we have seen that all cases of recurrence can be reduced to operations of identity, of the contrastive-comparison of elements on a given structural level. It follows that elements of poetic structure form oppositional pairs that are inherent to a given structure and which are not properties of its building material, i.e., for literature—language. It also follows that the structural nature of this material is reckoned on certain levels and is generally not taken into account on more abstract levels. It is sufficient to establish a structure which is obligatory for all kinds of art, e.g., "Romanticism is art" (the usefulness of such a model is difficult to dispute) in order to understand that at such a high level of abstraction the structure of language as building matériel will no longer play a role.

These oppositional pairs will, realizing their own structural difference, isolate archi-units which in their turn form pairs of pairs isolating second order structural archi-units. It must be stressed that the hierarchy of levels in language is based on a unidirectional movement from the simplest elements (phonemes) to the more complex.

The hierarchy of the structural levels of a poetic work is built differently: it consists of the unity of the macro- and micro-systems which are above and below a fixed horizon. It is the word level that comprises the semantic basis of the whole system and which functions as such a horizon. Above the horizon we have the levels of elements larger than the word; below, elements which constitute words.

As we shall try to show, semantic units create the level of the lexicon, while all other units create those complex systems of oppositions that unite lexical units in oppositional pairs, (impossible apart from that particular structure) and which serve as the basis for the isolation of those semantic features and archi-elements of the semantic level (archisemes) constituting the specific character of that particular structure, i.e., that "coupling of ideas" which Tolstoy remarked.

The Graphic Image of Poetry

An important difference between poetic and non-poetic text is that for ordinary language the number of structural levels and their meaningful elements is restricted and known to the speaker in advance, whereas for the poetic text it remains for the reader or listener to establish the nature of the aggregate of code systems that regulate the text.

Therefore, any system of regularities can in principle be perceived as meaningful in poetry. For this the system must first be perceptibly regulated and differ in this from the unorganized textual background, and second, it must be disrupted in an internally consistent fashion. The set of possible disruptions provides a diversity of informational possibilities within a given type of organization.

Graphic regulation is an interesting example of this characteristic of poetic texts. It permits us to pursue certain general regularities of the relationship of poetic structure to ordinary language structure. In natural language, the graphic structure is neither a style nor a special system of expressiveness. It is merely a graphic equivalent of the oral form of language.

The poetic text with its general striving toward maximal ordering implies the presumption of the graphic ordering of the text. The combination of the graphic line and the verse line must first be noted. This essentially auxiliary circumstance assumes great significance in cases of striving for the maximum non-expressiveness of structural devices, their reduction to "minus devices." Here graphic spacing into lines may remain the sole signal that the text belongs to the category of poetry.

In the period of the birth of modern Russian written poetry the demands for the graphic formulation of verse were much more rigid than subsequently. Poetry of the Baroque period, having become free of its compulsory union with music, so completely merged with illustration that it was seen as a variety of representational art. The iconic principle was observed with naive consistency. The transfer of this iconicity to linguistic signs generally is a typical characteristic of such poetry. In Simeon Polotsky's verses, the graphic representation of the text is in a number of cases defined by the content. [59]

But even in the eighteenth century several kinds of typographical highlighting were used for poetry which, in application to prose text, gave an impression of excessive refinement, e.g., frames, vignettes, etc. Printed and manuscript album poetic text was organically combined with illustration while the novel was accompanied at best by a "crude picture" on the title page.

Toward the end of the eighteenth century insofar as the opposition of poetry and prose as two functionally distinct types of belletristic language was firmly fixed in the consciousness of readers and the need for its reinforcement diminished, the meaningfulness of the distinction was preserved only by the basic features of spacing into lines. On the other hand, different graphic styles within verse structure were revealed. Thus, Karamzin introduced a number of specifically poetic types of punctuation usage (the dash, dots). Zhukovsky began to utilize italics as an intonational device. At the same time a number of other graphically significant elements were introduced.

The numeration of the stanzas in *Eugene Onegin* affords an interesting example of how the successive introduction and disruption of a certain graphic ordering became a device for artistic expressiveness. Stanza numeration is encountered in European poetry of the Pushkin epoch. Inasmuch as numerical designation immediately established rigid ordering, its disruption was most unexpected and consequently capable of bearing considerable information. Pushkin widely utilized this eventuality. He not only omitted stanzas, giving only their numbers when he had excluded actually existing text, but also designated by number stanzas which never had existed for purely compositional, ideational-artistic reasons. Pushkin evidently wished to use an analogous device in the numeration of chapters. Having omitted the chapter devoted to Onegin's journey, he could not omit the number: this would have been equivalent to a self-accusation of having composed texts not acceptable to the censor. In the 1830s, Pushkin could not allow himself this in print, but he clearly gave the reader to understand that the *real* number of the following chapter was the ninth.

A special stage in the development of the graphic aspect of the poetic text comes in the twentieth century. Against the background of the poetic graphic norms which had become fixed in the nineteenth century, diverse individual graphic styles arise. (Andrei Bely was a pioneer in this process.) The graphic illustration of the poetic text typical of Mayakovsky, Khlebnikov, Tsvetaeva, Selvinsky, and many other poets can be mentioned. A secondary individualization of graphics, its emphasized traditionality, develops against this background (Pasternak, Bagritsky, and Tvardovsky).

The graphic structure of poetry is as yet almost unstudied.[60] By way of preliminary observation, one might single out the graphics of rhythmico-syntactic intonation (omissions, line arrangements) and the graphics of lexical tone (type fonts). These kinds of graphic expressiveness may only approximate graphic equivalents of non-graphic structural levels, but in a number of cases graphic organization in poetry forms an independent structural level which cannot be transmitted by any other means. Such, for example, in Mayakovsky's poem "150,000,000" is the reproduction of not only the text but also of a poster at the beginning of the text. The inclusion in the lyric poem *About This (Pro eto)* of the technical devices of newspaper layout in the arrangement of the chapters plays the same role. The character of the newspaper style in the arrangement of the columns plays no less a role than the frankly albumic and therefore ironic citation of the graphic euphemism:

The name	Imia
for this	etoi
theme:	teme: 61
....!	....!

These forms of the new synthesis of text and graphics that were created in the posters of Mayakovsky and Rodchenko and in S. Tretyakov's photo-montages and which essentially influenced the utilization of verbal text in Eizenshtein's montage system are almost unstudied.

Similar problems arise in the study of the combination of poetic text and illustration in children's poetry.

* * *

In nineteenth century poetry approximate rhyme won a firm place for itself. Under its influence it was shown that rhyme is not a graphic but an acoustic phenomenon. Simultaneously in linguistics ever greater interest was manifested in the sound aspect of language. Phonetics was isolated as an independent discipline and rapidly moved forward: its experimental character linked it with acoustics and its susceptibility to measurement gave the impression of a general spirit of scientific positivism. The "acoustic school" was formed in philology.

The poetry of Symbolism which saw in poetry "music above all" consolidated its triumph.[62] The idea that poetry is an auditive text, that poems are intended for auditory perception, became widespread. This seemed so evident that its verification appeared completely superfluous to many. We have already satisfied ourselves that the auditory character of verse is not of a phonetic but a phonological character, that is, it is connected with the discrimination of meaning. If this is so, then it can scarcely be that graphics, one of the varieties of a language text's organization, is of no interest for its structure. Of course, the meaning of the text's graphic organization is less important than its phonological organization by virtue of the subordinate role of the graphic form of the language. But is it possible completely to forego its consideration? Attempts to study a text's letter organization often encounter resistance from specialists who feel that only the phonematic structure reflects the reality of poetry.

Thus, from the viewpoint of Russian phonology, "iu" ("ю") does not exist: it is the iotated vowel "u" ("у") and in counting the vowels in a line "iu" must be added to occurrences of "u". However, poetic consciousness, for example, Lermontov's, is formed not only under the influence of pronunciation but also of the graphic aspect of language. (Such is the case for any educated person.) When Lermontov wrote:

I am wild about triple assonance
And moist rhymes, as in "iu," for example
• • •
Ia bez uma ot troistvennykh sozvuchii
I vlazhnykh rifm, kak, naprimer na "iu"...

"Iu" for him had its *own distinct* meaning, although it is only a grapheme. The letter "iu" could not merge with "u" in his consciousness notwithstanding the purely graphic character of the difference between them. Moreover, it is obvious that in the Russian literary language of the end of the nineteenth and the beginning of the twentieth century, the difference between the letter "e" and "iat" was merely graphic. Nonetheless, it can be shown that the unification of these signs changes the countenance of the text's organization in a number of cases. The non-discrimination of "e" and "iat" was a sign of illiteracy and in the linguistic thought of the cultured person they were not equivalent. The insistence with which Blok demanded that the collection of his works that had begun publication before the orthographic reform of 1918 all be printed according to the old system is instructive. The conversion of the text into the new graphic system significantly altered the text for the poet.

All this must be kept in mind insofar as it is precisely in graphics that the greatest editorial arbitrariness is tolerated due to a conviction that the text is auditory. Thus the modernization of graphics is not so inoffensive and painless a phenomenon for an author's text as is customarily thought.

Unusual authorial spellings should especially give one pause for thought. Vyazemsky insisted on his right to orthographic mistakes as an expression of his personality in the text. Blok insisted on the spelling "zholtyi" ("yellow") distinguishing it from the correct "zheltyi." Such examples can be multiplied.

In cases where we detect in the graphics an intentional organization we are justified in speaking of their poetic meaning in that everything that is organized in poetry becomes meaningful. But the graphic aspect is already organized in the general system of language. Is this organization meaningful? It may be assumed that in those cases where the graphic system coincides with the phonological system and they are both present in the mind of the native speaker as a single system, graphics more rarely become a bearer of poetic meaning. But in cases where the automatic character of their association is disrupted and a conflict is felt between these systems, the possibility of imbuing the graphics with poetic meaning arises.

Just as the oral existence of a belletristic text is regulated by its performance (declamation), a written text must have appropriate signs of organization. The graphic system performs this role.

The Level of Morphological and Grammatical Elements

Based on the foregoing and somewhat anticipating ourselves, the following conclusion may be formulated: in a poetic text all of the elements are mutually correlated and are correlated with their own unrealized alternatives; consequently, they are semantically loaded. Artistic structure manifests itself on all levels. Therefore, nothing is more mistaken than to divide the text of an artistic work into an "ordinary language part" that ostensibly lacks artistic significance and into a part having "artistic characteristics."

On the basis of the initial postulates underlying our approach to poetic structure, one may assume *a priori* that the morpho-grammatical level of the poetic text is not equivalent to the common language one.

The question of the poetic function of grammatical categories in belletristic text has been a subject of scholarly scrutiny in the works of R. Jakobson. Differentiating meanings that are "material," lexical, and "entirely grammatical, purely relational," Jakobson writes:

> Poetry in superimposing similarity on contiguity raises equivalency to a principle of the construction of combinations. Symmetrical recurrence and the contrast of grammatical meanings become artistic devices here.[63]

Actually grammatical meanings, thanks to the fact that their elemental unconscious use in language is replaced by the artist's meaningful construction of the text, can assume unaccustomed semantic expressiveness on being incorporated into unusual oppositions.

It is apparent that in rhymes of the following type we are dealing with different structural phenomena:

> It's time, my friend, it's time! the heart asks [respite] —
> Days fly after days, and each day bears away...
> • • •
> Pora, moi drug, pora! [pokoia] serdtse prosit—
> Letiat za dniami dni, i kazhdii den' unosit...

and

> As from a tree the betrayer pupil tore away
> The devil flew up, pressed up to his face...[64]
>
> Kak s dreva sorvalsia predatel' uchenik,
> Diiavol priletel, k licu ego prinik...[64]

If we divert our attention from the effect in the first example arising from the violation of the prohibition against verbal rhyme and from the formation of a negative structure that is perceived by the poet and the listener of his epoch as a rejection of the conventionalities of poetic structure in general, as a movement toward simplicity, toward non-poetry, then we cannot but note a difference between the types of rhyme under investigation.

In the first example in the pair "prosit—unosit" ("asks—bears away") not only the rhythmico-phonological aspects of the rhyme but also the morpho-grammatical ones coincide. The latter form the neutralized basis of the rhymed pair while the root part, the bearer of the lexico-semantic content, appears in a correlated-contrasting position. Incidentally, the interest of the mature Pushkin and the poets of the Realistic school in verbal and other grammatical rhymes was connected not only with the effect of the disruption of the canon and with the expansion of the boundaries of the very concept of rhyme (although that, of course, was taking place), but also with the attempt to transfer the focus to the physical objective semantic content, i.e., to the root-base of the word which R. Jakobson called "the material equipment of language."[65] In the rhymed pair "uchenik—prinik" ("pupil—pressed up") the situation is different: only the rhythmico-phonological aspect of the rhyme serves as the basis for analogy. The grammatical meanings are emphasized and enter into complex interrelations of equivalency.

In contrast to phonological elements of structure that obtain all of their meaning from lexical units, morphological (and other grammatical) elements of structure also have independent content. They express the relational meanings in poetry. They largely create the model of the poetic vision of the world, the structure of subjective-objective relations. It is clearly mistaken to reduce the specific nature of poetry to "imagery," rejecting that from which the poet constructs his model of the world. In the above-cited article, Jakobson has indicated the significance of pronouns in poetry. "Pronouns are clearly opposed to the remaining inflected parts of speech as entirely grammatical, purely relational words devoid of their own lexical material meaning."[66]

Relational meanings are also expressed by other grammatical classes. Most important in this regard are conjunctions:

> **In alarm motley and barren**
> **Of high society and court...**
> • • •
> **V trevoge pestroi i besplodnoi**
> **Bol'shogo sveta i dvora...**
>
> —A. Pushkin

Here in the form of an underscored parallelism the two occurrences of the conjunction "i" ("and"), two seemingly identical grammatical constructions are set side by side. However they are not identical but parallel, and their comparison only emphasizes the difference. In the second case the "and" unites such equal members that it even loses the character of being the means of conjoining them. The expression "bol'shoi svet i dvor" ("high society and the court") merges into a single phraseological whole whose individual components lose their independence. In the first case ("alarm motley and barren"), the conjunction unites not only different kinds of concepts but even concepts of different planes. Affirming their parallelness, it facilitates the isolation in their meanings of a common semantic field (an archiseme) while these concepts in their turn, insofar as a difference is clearly felt between the archiseme and each of them taken separately, lend a hint of adversative meaning to the semantics of the conjunction. This meaning of the relationship between the concepts of "motley" ("pestryi") and "barren" ("besplodnoi") might have passed by unnoticed had the first "and" not been parallel to the second in which this nuance is clearly absent. This meaning is made to stand out in the act of comparison. Such examples of the fact that grammatical elements assume special meaning in poetry could be given for all grammatical classes.

Jakobson's idea requires only one emendation in our view. Having become engrossed in the beautiful parallel of grammar and geometry, Jakobson is inclined to oppose grammatical, purely relational meanings to material lexical ones. In poetry the unconditional delimitation of these levels of poetic language is not possible, given the greater independence of elements on the lexico-grammatical level in comparison with those of the sound level of poetic language. This is extremely noticeable in the case of those pronouns whose relationships construct a model of a poetic world, while the structure of the content of this same pronoun is often dependent on the entire conceptual (lexico-semantic) structure of the work as a whole.

We shall clarify this idea with an example. Let us examine Lermontov's poem "Meditation" ("Duma") as one of the clearest illustrations in Russian poetry of the revelation of the author's basic idea via a system of subject-object relations which find their expression chiefly in the pronouns. This poem is also a vivid example of the connection between the purely relational and the material planes. Although not connected in the language as a whole, these planes are correlated in the poem in that both the subject ("I") ["ia"] and the object ("we") ["my"] have no ordinary language meaning but are modeled in the eyes of the reader.

The text of the poem is as follows.*

---

* Lotman does not give the text of the poem, apparently assuming it to be known or readily available to his Russian readers. Since the following discussion is difficult to follow without the text, I give it here (DBJ).

74

1. Sadly I gaze on our generation!
2. Its future is either empty or dark;
3. Meanwhile under the burden of knowledge and doubt,
4. In idleness it will age,
5. Rich are we, scarcely from the cradle,
6. In the errors of our fathers and their tardy wit,
7. And life wearies us like an even road without a goal,
8. Like a feast on an alien holiday.
9. To good and evil shamefully indifferent,
10. At the outset of our calling, we wither without a struggle,
11. Before danger shamefully timorous
12. And before power despised slaves.
13. Thus a meager fruit before-time ripened,
14. Neither our taste nor eyes rejoicing,
15. Hangs amidst the flowers, an orphaned stranger,
16. And the hour of their beauty is the hour of its fall!

17. We have desiccated our wit with barren learning,
18. Hiding enviously from near ones and friends
19. Our best hopes and noble voice
20. With the disbelief of mocked passions.
21. We have scarcely touched the cup of delight
22. But we did not conserve our youthful powers by this;
23. From each joy, fearing satiety,
24. We have extracted the best sap forever.
25. Dreams of poetry, of the creation of art
26. Do not stir our mind with sweet ecstasy;
27. We greedily guard in our breast a remnant of feeling—
28. A useless treasure buried by miserliness.
29. And we hate and we love by chance,
30. Sacrificing nothing either to malice or to love,
31. And a kind of secret cold reigns in the soul,
32. While a fire seethes in the blood.
33. The sumptuous amusements of our forefathers bore us,
34. Their goodhearted, childish dissipation;
35. And to the grave we hasten without happiness and without words,
36. Gazing mockingly back.

37. Like a sullen and soon forgotten crowd,
38. Over the world we shall pass without a noise or trace,
39. Having thrown to the centuries neither fruitful thought
40. Nor labor undertaken by genius.
41. And our ashes with the severity of judge and citizen,
42. Our progeny will scorn with despising verse,
43. With the deceived son's bitter mockery
44. Of the father who has squandered all.

∴

1. Pechal'no ia gliazhu na nashe pokolen'e!
2. Ego griadushchee—il' pusto, il' temno;
3. Mezh tem, pod bremenem poznan'ia i somnen'ia,
4. V bezdeistvii sostaritsia ono.

75

5. Bogaty my, edva iz kolybeli,
6. Oshibkami otsov i pozdnim ikh umom,
7. I zhizn' uzh nas tomit, kak rovnyi put' bez tseli,
8. Kak pir na prazdnike chuzhom.
9. K dobru i zlu postydno ravnodushny,
10. V nachale poprishcha my vianem bez bor'by,
11. Pered opasnost'iu pozorno-malodushny
12. I pered vlastiiu prezrennye raby.
13. Tak toshchii plod, do vremeni sozrelyi,
14. Ni vkusa nashego ne raduia, ni glaz,
15. Visit mezhdu tsvetov, prishlets osirotelyi,
16. I chas ikh krasoty—ego paden'ia chas!

17. My issushili um naukoiu besplodnoi,
18. Taia zavistlivo ot blizhnikh i druzei
19. Nadezhdy luchshie i golos blagorodnyi
20. Neveriem osmeiannykh strastei.
21. Edva kasalis' my do chashi naslazhden'ia
22. No iunykh sil my tem ne sberegli;
23. Iz kazhdoi radosti, boias' presyshchen'ia,
24. My luchshii sok naveki izvlekli.
25. Mechty poezii, sozdaniia iskusstva
26. Vostorgom sladostnym nash um ne sheveliat;
27. My zhadno berezhem v grudi ostatok chuvstva—
28. Zarytyi skupost'iu i bezpoleznyi klad.
29. I nenavidim my, i liubim my sluchaino,
30. Nichem ne zhertvuia ni zlobe, ni liubvi,
31. I tsarstvuet v dushe kakoi-to kholod tainyi,
32. Kogda ogon' kipit v krovi.
33. I predkov skuchny nam roskoshnye zabavy,
34. Ikh dobrosovestnyi, rebiacheskii razvrat;
35. I k grobu my speshim bez schast'ia i bez slavy,
36. Gliadia nasmeshlivo nazad.

37. Tolpoi ugriumoiu i skoro pozabytoi,
38. Nad mirom my proidem bez shuma i sleda,
39. Ne brosivshi vekam ni mysli plodovitoi,
40. Ni geniem nachatogo truda.
41. I prakh nash, s strogost'iu sud'i i grazhdanina,
42. Potomok oskorbit prezritel'nym stikhom,
43. Nasmeshkoi gor'koiu obmanutogo syna
44. Nad promotavshimsia ottsom!

The beginning of the poem proclaims the division of subject and
object. The subject is given in the form of the first person singular pronoun
"I" and the object in the form of the third person singular pronoun in the
expressions "it will age" ("sostaritsi ono"), "its future" ("ego griadushchee")
and directly in "generation" ("pokolen'e"). The arrangement of subject and
object according to the grammatical scheme subject-object with an inter-
vening predicate expressed by the transitive verb "gaze" ("gliazhu") sharply
divides them as two separate and opposed spheres, i.e., "I gaze on [our]

generation" ("Ia gliazhu na pokolen'e"). The action ("I gaze") has not only direction but an emotional coloration that is transmitted by the adverb "sadly" ("pechal'no") which further deepens the gulf between "I" and "it" ("our generation").

| I | ←——— gaze ———→
sadly | generation |

In this same stanza the appearance of "generation" ("pokolen'e") is also to be noted: *"its* future is empty or dark" ("ego griadushchego—il' pusto, il' temno"), "in idleness *it* will age" ("v bezdeistvii sostaritsa ono"). The structure of the fourth line is very important since it presents a grammatical parallel to the first. Only in these two lines of the first quatrain is the subject expressed by a pronoun. One need only lay bare the grammatical form of the text in order to see the parallelism of both the structure of the sentences and of the arrangement and character of their adverbial secondary members: "I gaze sadly..." "It will age in idleness..." One can represent the scheme of the sentence as follows:

Subject:	Predicate:
expressed by a singular personal pronoun	verb ↓ Circumstantial mode of action (adverb or noun functioning as an adverb)

This schema, however, only serves as a basis for the parallel (analogy) in order to make the difference an informationally loaded factor. Let us compare the verbs "gaze" and "will age."

The grammatical meaning of transitivity obtains a supplementary meaning in the poetic context. In the first case it is supported by the presence, and in the second, by the absence of an object to the verb. Appearing as a difference in the analogy, this feature is activated. However, this relational scheme is closely interwoven with the lexical one as an active countenance of the judging authorial "I" and the passive "it" ("ono"). The adverbial modifier "in idleness" ("v bezdeistvii") pertains to the verb, the designation of action! The rhyme "pokolen'e" ("generation")/"somnen'e" ("doubt") has great significance. We have already seen that rhyme relationships are always semantic. "Pokolen'e" is equated to "somnen'e" toward which the similar and phonetically associated "poznan'e" ("knowledge") strives.

The verb tense modulation is also of interest. The pair "Ia gliazhu" ("I gaze")—"ono sostaritsia" ("it will age") is differentiated not only by voice but by tense. The future tense in a discourse on a generation assumes a structural meaning in the poem all the more in that the lexical level denies the presence of a future for this generation, i.e., "Its future is either empty or dark" ("Ego griadushchee—il' pusto, il' temno"). The relational (grammatical) and material (lexical) constructs are correlated according to the principle of contrast.

However, in the first quatrain there already is an element that sharply contradicts the whole clearly expressed opposition of its subject-object poles. The generation is characterized as "ours" ("nashe") in the first line. But this carries over the entire system of relationships of the type "I" ("ia")—"our generation" ("nashe pokolen'e") to the relationship of the subject to the object (which, up to this time, we have seen as adversative in accord with the scheme "I"—"it"). The subject is included in the object as its part. All that is characteristic of the generation is likewise characteristic of the author and this makes its exposure especially bitter. Before us we see a system of grammatical relationships that creates a model of the world absolutely impossible for Romanticism. The Romantic "I" has devoured reality; the lyrical "I" of the poem is a part of his generation, of the milieu, of the objective world.

Having established this complex system of relations between "I" and "it" (generation), Lermontov in the following part of the poem drastically simplifies it by uniting subject and object in a single "we" ("my"). The complex dialectic of the merging and opposing of himself and his generation is resolved.[67]

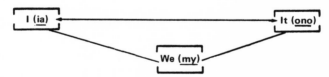

The opposition "I"—"It" is resolved in "We" and the remainder of the poem is built on its persistent repetition: "Rich are *we,* scarcely from the cradle...," "Life wearies *us,*" *"We* wither without a struggle...," "*we* have desiccated *our* wit...," "...do not stir *our* mind," etc. In the interval between the fifth line in which this new (in opposition to the initial line) first person plural pronoun appears for the first time, and the forty-first line in which it figures for the last time (37 lines), "we" figures fifteen times in various grammatical cases. It is especially important to note that the pronoun "we" in different forms plays the grammatical role of both subject and object in the sentence uniting both members of the relational pair "I"—"it."

Lines

5-6	We are rich in errors. . .
10	We wither. . .
17	We have desiccated. . .
21	We have scarcely touched. . .
22	We did not conserve. . .

78

24	We extracted...
27	We greedily guard...
29	We hate...
29	We love...
35	We hasten to the grave...
38	We shall pass over the world...

7	Life wearies us...
25-26	the Dreams of poetry... do not stir our mind...
33	Amusements bore us...

We are excluding from consideration the character of the pronouns in lines 13-16, following "Thus a meager fruit, before time ripened...," because they structurally represent a thematically inserted episode, a comparison, and genetically, an insertion of earlier lines from the poem "He was born for happiness, for hope..." ("on byl rozhden dlia schast'ia, dlia nadezhd...," 1830).

The conflict, constant for this part of the poem, between the grammatical and lexical structures is easily noted. The former implies the presence of activity and is built on the principle "subject ——→ action" or "action ——→ object." The latter rejects this with a whole set of verbs. Thus the basic semantic motif of this passage, i.e., idleness or empty false activity, stems from the correlation of the grammatical and lexical structure.

The relational ties of Lermontov's "we" with the surrounding world (which is built from the material of grammatical relations) are not fully revealed to us apart from the content of this "we" in whose construction elements of the lexical level take an active part.

The lexical structure of the central part of the poem is built on contrast and oxymora. Curious regularities may be traced here:

I	9	To good and to evil shamefully indifferent...
	29	... and we hate and we love by chance,
	30	Sacrificing nothing either to malice or to love,
II	31	And a kind of cold reigns in the soul,
	32	While a fire seethes in the blood.

I. The specific character of the construction of the "lexico-grammatical figure" of the first example is such that it mutually imposes the lexical opposition of the words "good" and "evil" on the full identity of their grammatical structures and of their syntactic position. The lexical antonyms are in a position of parallelism. The conjuction "and" only underlines their relational equality.

79

Thus, insofar as in poetry the grammatical level is projected against the semantic, "good" and "evil" are equated. This grammatical structure is supported by the lexical meaning of the word "indifferent." "Good" and "evil" form an archiseme that preserves their shared meaning and from which everything that comprises the specific character of each concept is excluded. If one isolates the shared essence in the concepts "good" and "evil", it can be formulated approximately as "a moral category which is devoid of meaning." Precisely such is the model of the *ethical* system of the "we"—the generation of Lermontov's poem "Meditation" ("Duma").

II. Here too we can apply the same system of judgments on the combination of lexical opposition and of grammatical identity that converts the concepts "we love" and "we hate" into mutual models. Here again they are neutralized in the archiseme "an emotion of any inclination whatsoever." This is how the *emotional* world of the "we" is modeled. A complex system of lexical oppositions is constructed in order to refute the basic meaning of all the pivotal words in order to introduce the reader into a world of valueless values. "Rich in errors," "life—wearies," "holiday—alien," "wit—barren," "treasure—useless," "sumptuous amusements—boring." The lexical meaning of the basic nouns that constitute the "inventory" of the world of the author's "generation" is composed of "minus concepts," not of concepts but of their negation; it is negative in essence. Insofar as good and evil, love and hate, cold and fire, are equated, it is in principle a world without values. Its evaluational capability has been replaced by a lexicon of the type: "indifferent" (to good and evil), "by chance" (we hate and love), etc.

Such are the outlines of the structure of that "we" which enveloped the whole middle section of the poem having gathered into itself the "I" and the "it" of the first part. However, having recognized himself as a part of his generation, of his time, having recognized its ailments as his own, having united the subjective and the objective, satire and lyric into a single construct, Lermontov, even in this section does not permit his "I" to disappear, to completely dissolve into the "we." Although not expressed in pronominal form, the "I" is present in the system of evaluational epithets sharply condemning the "we" and contrasting with its accentuated ethical indifference. "To good and evil—indifferent" ("K dobru i zlu—ravnodushny") gives the structure of the "we." The epithet "shamefully" introduces some subject clearly external to the "we." The lines "Before danger shamefully timorous / And before power despised slaves" also present a completely different structure of relations than the other lines. "We" here does not form a unique constructed world at all. It is contrasted with objective (and more sharply with political) reality:

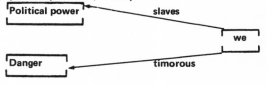

Having replaced the monistic world, this binomial system, completely filled by the "we" which is inherent to the structure of the other lines in this section, must be supplemented by a third unnamed but relationally determined member from whose viewpoint the relationship of "we" to reality is described as "shameful" and "despised." That this third member is not grammatically isolated is extremely important: the opposition "I"—"it" is removed by virtue of the peculiarities of Lermontov's artistic thought in these years while a foundation for another antithesis had not yet been found.

The basis of this antithesis is in the last four lines. The grammatical structure sharply changes. The "we" changes from subject to object. In order to understand the significance of this it suffices to compare "Amusements bore *us*. . ." ("Zabavy *nam* skuchny. . .") and "Dreams of poetry do not stir *our* mind" ("Mechty poezii. . .*nash* um ne sheveliat") from the middle part of the poem with the concluding "Our progeny will scorn *our* ashes" ("Potomok oskorbit *nash* prakh") in order to see a deep difference. Grammatically the constructions "Dreams do not stir our mind" and "Our progeny will scorn our ashes" are of the same type. But this is precisely what underscores the deep difference. On the plane of content the first sentence had but one character, "we," which was in the passive position of the direct object. The second sentence has two personal centers. Although the subject is not a pronoun, the acting personage is named—"progeny." It occupies the place of the third member unnamed in the central part. Evaluational epithets are clustered around him. His mood is "despising," his mockery is "bitter." The "we" has been transformed from subject into object, is seen from without, and submits to judgment.

The verbal tense of the poem's three sections is modulated in a most interesting way: the first section has the present tense for "I" and negation of the future ("minus-future") for "generation." The entire central section is in the present tense, which is especially noticeable thanks to its high degree of verbal saturation. The final quatrain carries the action into the future: "Our progeny will scorn." This is affirmed by the establishment of the age relationships of "our progeny" and "our generation," of the hierarchy of fathers, of "us" and of "our descendants."

> **With the bitter mockery of the deceived son**
> **Of the father who has squandered all.**
> • • •
> **Nasmeshkoi gor'koiu obmanutogo syna**
> **Nad promotavshimsia ottsom.**

The authorial "I" that was opposed to "generation" in the first section merges into it in the second, and in the third part functions in the name of the descendant as "judge and citizen." This is a true synthesis that does not exclude any of the parts. Notwithstanding the harshness of the judgment, it is not forgotten that the "I" was identified with the "we" and that a small part of the author is not only in the voice of the descendant but also in the ashes of his own "generation." The attribute "our" is not assigned to it without reason. The bitter evaluative epithets link the author and the descendant; the pronoun links the author and "our generation."

Pronouns in general are extremely important for demonstrating the influence of grammatical structure on the construction of poetic text. Let us pause on one further example: the thematic [siuzhetnyi] construction of a lyric poem.

In the final reckoning certain biographic situations underlie the theme [siuzhet] in a lyric poem. This is so far beyond dispute that direct reconstructions of actual relationships between the author and the people surrounding him have been frequently attempted on the basis of lyric poems. We are not speaking only of folklore studies where the reconstruction of family and social relationships on the basis of lyric materials is a very widespread research technique, but of such works as Academician A. M. Veselovsky's classic monograph on Zhukovsky.

It has already long been noted, however, that a coding system operates between biographic situations and the "lyric situations" of a poetic text that determines *how* certain phenomena of the real world are refracted in the structure of the text. By ignoring the laws of this transformation and assuming that we are dealing with an elementary "duplication of reality," we risk either repeating the mistakes of naive biographism or losing the specific character of an artistic recreation of the world.

The structure of artistic thinking and, on a higher level, the structure of the ideological models of a given society will obviously be one of the basic coding systems of this type. It is worthwhile comparing a novel and a lyric poem that belong to a single artistic and ideological system in order to see that completely different types of internal structure underlie their construction. The comparison should convince us that we do not know those intermediate codes that transform certain biographic materials into the thematic [siuzhetnyi] organization of lyric and narrational genres.

If thematic situations in narrational genres model actual episodes in the language of particular ideational-artistic structures, lyric poetry adds yet one more link, i.e., a system of pronouns that becomes a universal model of human relations. For example, such situations as the lover's rectangle, quite possible in non-lyric genres, are very rarely encountered in the lyric.[68] Compare the even more complex situation in Fonvizin's comedy "The Brigadier."

The fact that the heroes of a narrative work all belong to a single grammatical person, namely the third, attests that the category of person is generally not *meaningful* in such genres. (Its meaning becomes critical only in connection with the problem of *skaz*.)

The lyric is another matter. All lyric personages are categorized according to the pronominal scheme of first, second, and third person. By establishing the types of relations among these semantic centers, we can obtain the basic thematic [siuzhetnyi] schemes of the lyric. The thematic models thus obtained have an extremely general abstract character. Even if one considers that the lyric poetry of each cultural historical epoch or literary school provides a comparatively limited set of personages—considerably more limited than contemporaneous narrational and dramatic genres—an enumeration of its heroes will always be of a more concrete level than the corresponding scheme of pronominal relationships. Thus, for example, one can isolate a thematic scheme whose centers will be "I" and "thou." Their relationship will be structured in terms of the domination of the first center by the second and the dependence of the first on the second. In specific texts of particular epochs "thou" can be interpreted as "a beloved girl," "maiden," "God," "the motherland," "the people," or "the monarch." However, on some high level of abstraction a relationship of isomorphism can be established among these themes. At the same time it is evident that a plot with the identical personages arrayed, for example, not according to the scheme "I"—"thou," but in the relationship "I"—"he/she/it" is significantly modified.

Let us adduce an even clearer example. Let us try to compare two possible interpretations of the system "I"—"thou": I = Job, Thou = God, and also the reverse system (as in Lomonosov's work, for example). It is evident what great semantic possibilities lie in the *relationship* of the pronominal scheme to the personages that interpret its structure.

Obviously the meaning "to be in the first person," "to be in the second person," or "to be in the third person" incorporates in itself the elementary and simultaneously basic definition of the places of these persons and the construction of the collective. This formal grammatical scheme, having meaning in practical language only in determining the direction of speech and its relationship to the speaker, assumes a special meaning as soon as the text becomes a poetic *model of the world.* It is indicative that the higher the modeling role of the text, the more significant is the constructional function of the pronouns. In a sacred text or a lyric poem "the right to be in the first person" is a fully specified characterization that unambiguously predetermines the essence of the personage and his behavior. The more distinctly the text is directed toward depicting not the "speech" of reality but its "language," the more significant will be the role of pronouns in it.

The connection between lyric themes and the pronominal structure of a given language is evident, for example, in the translation from French into Russian of poems that contain an address to God. The French text uses the pronoun "Vous," which is equivalent neither to the Russian "Vy" ("you") nor to the Russian "Ty" ("thou"). The appearance in Russian translations of "Ty" actually constitutes a transformation of the text's theme [siuzhet] insofar as it permits contexts that are impossible for "Vous."

The Lexical Level of Verse

Poetry consists of words. Nothing could be more obvious. Nonetheless, taken by itself this assertion is capable of generating certain misunderstandings. The word in poetry is a word from the natural language, a unit of the lexicon, which can be found in a dictionary. Nonetheless it is not equivalent to itself. It is precisely this similarity, this coincidence of the poetic word with the "dictionary word" of a given language that makes the difference between these units so palpable; units that first draw apart and then near, but which are separated and contrasted.

The poetic text is organized language of a special form. This language breaks down into lexical units and regularly identifies them with words of the ordinary language inasmuch as this is the simplest and most inviting way of segmenting the text into meaningful units. However, several difficulties appear. As a text in some language, say, Russian, Estonian, or Czech a poem realizes only a part of that language's lexical elements. The words used are part of a more extended system that is only partially realized in the text.

If we regard a given poetic text as a special form of organized language then the latter will be fully realized in it. That which was a part of a system will be the *entire* system.[69] The latter circumstance is very important. Any "language of a culture," language as a kind of modeling system, pretends to universality, strives to cover the entire world and to identify itself with the world. If some portions of reality are not encompassed by this system (e.g., "crude nature" or the "vulgar lexicon" do not figure in the poetic world of high Classicism), they are proclaimed "non-existent" from its point of view. As a result, a system of language-models characterizing a given culture is formed. These models are in an isomorphic relationship mutually resembling each other as different models of a single object, i.e., *the entire world.*

In this sense a poem as an integral language resembles an *entire* natural language but not a part of it. The fact that the number of words in this language is reckoned in tens or hundreds and not hundreds of thousands changes the weight of the word as a meaningful segment of the text. The word in poetry is "larger" than this same word in a general language text. It is easily noted that the more concise the text, the weightier the word and the larger the portion of the universe it designates.

Having compiled a dictionary of a poem, we obtain, albeit approximately, the contours that shape the world from the viewpoint of the poet. In one of his poems Kiukhelbeker used the expression "He tended the flock of my head. . ." ("Pas stada glavy moei. . ."). Pushkin noted in the margin: "lice"? Why did Kiukhelbeker not notice the comic effect of this line, whereas it caught Pushkin's eye at once? The reason is that "lice" did not exist in Kiukhelbeker's poetic world or in that "higher reality" that was for him the only true one. They did not enter into his model of the world, being something extra-systemic and hence non-existent in the higher sense.

The vocabulary of a Pushkin poem, granted all of the inexactitude of this criterion, forms a different structure of the world:

> Now our roads are bad,
> Forgotten bridges rot,
> At the way-stations bedbugs and fleas
> Don't give a minute's sleep.
>
> —Eugene Onegin

> Teper' u nas dorogi plokhi,
> Mosty zabytye gniiut,
> Na stanciiakh klopy da blokhi
> Zasnut' minuty ne daiut...

Hence lines that were completely unambiguous in Kiukhelbeker's poetic system sound ambiguous to Pushkin. The glossary of a poetic text represents a first approximation of its universe, and the words constituting it, the population of this universe. Their relationship is perceived as the structure of the world.

The poetic world has thus not only its own vocabulary, but its own system of synonyms and antonyms. Thus, in some texts "love" can be a synonym of "life," whereas in others it is a synonym of "death." In a poetic text, "day" and "night," or "life" and "death" can be synonyms. Counter to this, a word in poetry may not equal itself and may even be its own antonym. Note Tsvetaeva's lines "Life—it's a place where one can't live." ("Zhizn'—eto mesto, gde zhit' nel'zia.") and "Home—so little home-like." ("Dom—tak malo domashnii").

Words, while obtaining special meanings in the poetic structure, also preserve their own dictionary meanings. Conflict, tension between these two types of meanings, is all the more palpable in that they are expressed in the text by a single sign, a given word.

AND COULD YOU?

> I immediately daubed a map of humdrum life,
> having splashed the paint from a glass;
> I showed on a dish of gelatin
> the oblique cheekbones of the ocean.

> On the scales of a tinny fish
> I read the summons of new lips.
> And could
> you
> play a nocturne

on a flute of plumbing pipes?

—V. Maiakovskii

• • •

A VY MOGLI BY?

Ia srazu smazal kartu budnia,
plesnuvshi krasku iz stakana;
ia pokazal na bliude studnia
kosye skuly okeana

Na cheshue zhestianoi ryby
prochel ia zovy novykh gub.
A vy
noktiurn sygrat'
mogli by
na fleite vodostochnykh trub?

Glossary of the Poem

I	map	oblique	daub	immediately	from	and
you	humdrum life	tinny	splash		on	
	paint	new	show			
	glass	plumbing	read			
	dish		play			
	gelatin		could			
	cheekbones					
	ocean					
	scale					
	fish					
	summons					
	lips					
	nocturne					
	flute					
	pipe					

First of all the nominal character of the glossary catches one's eye: the world of the text is defined by objects. The poem's nominal lexicon is easily divided into two groups: one consists of words with meanings of vividness, unusualness, and the non-mundane (paint, ocean, flute, nocturne); the other contains words from the everyday mundane, material, ordinary lexicon (a dish of gelatin, the scale of a tinny fish, plumbing pipes). Underlying each of these groups is the traditional literary antithesis: "poetic—non-poetic."

Insofar as the text is immediately assigned the opposition "I—you," the interpretation of this opposition presents itself for consideration:

I	—	You
poetry		everyday reality
vividness		banality

86

Mayakovsky's text first evokes this organizational system of the text's "world of words" in the reader's memory and then rejects it. In the first place, the entire verb system that links the noun-concepts in the poetic picture points not to the delimitation of the "mundane" and "poetic" semantic fields, but rather to their fusion. The verbs are those of contact, "to read," "to show," or of artistic activity such as "to play." For the "I" they reveal poetic meanings not outside of but in the midst of the mundane meanings. The ocean as a poetic symbol is found in "[fish] gelatin" and "the summons of new lips" is seen in a tinny fish scale. The poeticism "summons" and the epithet "new" that does not allow material reification forces us to perceive "lips" as a generalized poetic symbol.

This mundane reality has a characteristic feature. These words do not simply designate objects, but objects that are not mentioned in traditional poetry. They constitute the world of another art—painting. The mundane portion of the poem's lexicon constitutes the inventory of a still life and, more specifically, a still life of the Cézanne school. It is not by chance that mundane reality is associated with the purely pictorial verbs "to daub," "to splash paint." The everyday, that is, the actual world, is the world of prose, of reality and painting, while the conventionalized and false world is that of traditional poetry.

The poetic model of the world that builds the "I" while repulsing every possible "you" is a semantic system in which "[fish] gelatin" and "ocean" are synonyms while the opposition "poetry—prosaic reality" is neutralized. The following organizational scheme of the text's sense units presents itself:

I	$\langle\!\!-\!\!\rangle$	You
vividness		**banality**
fusion of poetry and		**opposition of poetry and**
mundane reality		**mundane reality**

Thus, in Mayakovsky's poem the text's semantic organization on the lexical level is structured as a conflict between the organizational system of the sense units in the individual structure of the text and the semantic structure of the words in natural language on the one hand and in traditional poetic models on the other.[70]

The Concept of Parallelism

In examining the role of repetition, the concept of parallelism should also be considered. It has frequently been scrutinized in connection with the principles of poetics. A. N. Veselovsky indicated the dialectical nature of parallelism in art:

> It is not a matter of the identification of human life with nature nor of a comparison that presupposes an awareness of the separateness of the compared objects, but of comparison in terms of some feature of an activity.[71]

Thus, in parallelism, analogy rather than identity or separateness is stressed. A recent investigator, R. Austerlitz, defines parallelism as follows: "Two segments (lines) may be considered parallel if they are identical with the exception of some part that occupies the same relative position in both segments."[72] Further: "Parallelism can be viewed as an incomplete repetition."[73]

These properties of parallelism may be defined in the following fashion: parallelism is a binomial wherein one of its members is known through a second one that functions as an analogue in relation to the first. This second member is neither identical to the first nor is it separate from it. It is in a state of analogy having those common features which are isolated in the recognition of the first member. Recalling that the first and second members are not identical, we equate them in some particular aspect and consider the first in terms of the properties and behavior of the second member of the parallel. Such, for example, is the parallelism in:

> **Rise, rise, sun, rise higher than the forest,**
> **Come, come, brother, visit [my] sister. . .**
> • • •
> **Vzoidi, vzoidi, solntse, vzoidi vyshe lesu**
> **Pridi, pridi, bratets, ko sestritse v gosti. . .**

An analogy is established between the actions of the sun and a brother ("rise, rise"—"come, come"), while the sun's image serves as an analogue for the concept "brother." The sun is something known; the concept "brother" is modeled in analogy with it.

However, still another more complex case of parallelism occurs when both parts of the binomial mutually model each other, isolating in each something analogous to the other.

Sad and gay I enter, sculptor, into thy studio. . .

Grusten i vesel vkhozhu, viaitel', v tvoiu masterskuiu. . .

—A. Pushkin

The short form adjectives "grusten" ("sad") and "vesel" ("gay") are in the same syntactic position and are expressed by the same grammatical forms. A relationship of parallelism which does not permit an interpretation of the text in which the author is simultaneously in two different unrelated mental states is established between these states. (This would be quite possible in a non-belletristic text.) In an artistic text both members are perceived as mutually analogous. The concepts "grusten" ("sad") and "vesel" ("gay") constitute a mutually correlated complex structure.

Where we are dealing with parallelism on the level of words and word combinations a trope relationship arises between the object-member and the model-member, since so-called "transferred meaning" is the establishment of analogy between two concepts. This is the source of that "imagery" traditionally considered a basic property of poetry, but which, as we have seen, constitutes only a manifestation of a more general regularity in a comparatively limited sphere. In fact, it might be said that poetry is a structure all of whose elements on all levels are in a state of mutual parallelism and which, consequently, bear a particular semantic load.

This brings us to yet another important difference between belletristic and non-belletristic structure. Language possesses high redundancy. Identical meanings can be expressed variously. In the structure of the belletristic text, redundancy declines. The cause of this phenomenon is that, although the phonetic shape of a word is essentially neutral from the standpoint of content transmission, this same acoustic form of a word in art is inescapably in a state of parallelism with that of some other word resulting in the establishment of a relationship of analogy between them.

The redundancy of language is a useful and necessary property. In particular it assures the stability of language with regard to mistakes and arbitrary, subjective perception. The reduced level of redundancy in poetry means that adequacy of perception is never so absolute as it is in ordinary language. On the other hand, poetic structure is semantically incomparably more highly saturated and is better suited for the transmission of complex semantic structures not generally communicable by ordinary language.

The system of connections among all elements and levels of elements gives the poetic work a certain independence after its creation and permits it to function not as a simple sign system but as a complex autonomously developing structure significantly outstripping all of the feedback systems thus far created by man and in some ways even approximating those of living organisms: the artistic work is in a state of regenerative coupling [i.e., feedback (DBJ)] with its environment and changes shape under its influence. Inasmuch as ancient dialecticians already understood that one can not cross the same river twice, then the assertion that we no longer have the "same" *Eugene Onegin* that its first readers and the author himself knew, should not perplex modern dialecticians. Those extra-textual structures of Pushkin's time in relation to which the text functioned are not recoverable. For their resurrection one not only would have to know everything that Pushkin knew, but also to forget everything Pushkin did not know, i.e., all that constitutes the basis of our own esthetic perception. (The historian can and must approximate this knowledge of an epoch's basic structural elements but he unfortunately cannot hope to resurrect all of the intersections of the interblended structures of the concrete phenomena of those years.) This task is beyond fulfillment. Being included, as is the consciousness of the perceiver, in the objective course of history, an artistic work lives the life of history. Therefore, the Pushkinian perception of *Eugene Onegin,* lost as a living reader's feeling, may yield completely to a scholar's reconstruction. Reading Pushkin, we cannot forget the historical and literary events of the succeeding epochs, but we can completely reconstruct the consciousness to which these events were unknown. Of course, this will be an approximate model.

The belletristic work establishes a feedback relationship with its consumer. Such features of art as its exceptional longevity and its capability, within certain limits, of giving different information to different users in different epochs (and also to different concurrent users) are also obviously connected with this type of relationship.

The Line as a Unity

Rhyme is the line boundary. In one of Akhmatova's poems, rhymes are called "signal bells" referring to the bell that marks the end of a line when typing. The marked character of the boundary makes the line akin to the word and the pause at the end of the line to the spaces between words.

The following contradiction among the basic constructional principles of the poetic text should be noted. Each significant element strives to function as a *sign* having independent meaning. The textual whole functions as a kind of phrase, a syntagmatic chain of a unified construction. Simultaneously, this same element has a tendency to act only as *part of a sign,* while the whole assumes the features of a unified sign having a general and unanalyzable meaning.

If we can say that each phoneme in the line behaves like a word, then we can view the line, then the stanza, and finally the entire text as specially constructed words. In this sense, the line is a special *ad hoc* word having a unified and indivisible content. Its relationship to other lines is syntagmatic in the narrational structure and paradigmatic in all cases of poetic parallelism.

The unity of the line manifests itself on the metrical, intonational, syntactic and semantic levels. It can be supplemented by a unity of phonological organization which often forms firm local associations within the line.

The semantic unity of the line is manifested in what Iu. N. Tynyanov called "the closeness of the poetic sequence." The lexical meaning of the words within a line induces in neighboring words supra-meanings impossible outside of the given poetic context. This frequently leads, on the one hand, to the isolation of the semantic centers that dominate in the line and, on the other, to the isolation of words that are reduced to the role of copula and particles of a prefixal-suffixal character.

The fact that the line is simultaneously both a sequence of words and *a word* whose meaning is far from equal to the mechanical sum of the meanings of its components (insofar as the syntagmatics of individual sign meanings and the construction of sign meanings from functionally different ingredients are completely different operations) gives the line a two-fold character. We encounter this situation, one extremely important for any art, when a text allows more than one interpretation. The interpretation of a model on a more concrete level yields a set of mutually equivalent meanings rather than an unambiguous recoding.

The line preserves the entire meaning inherent to that text as a non-belletristic communication and, simultaneously, assumes an integrated supra-meaning. The tension between these meanings creates that relationship of text to meaning that is specific to poetry. Whether we take P. Vasilev's line "The fields smelling of absinth" ("Pakhuchie polia polyni") or M. Dudin's "To hang rubies on rowan trees" ("Rubiny veshat' na riabiny") we see that the line's rhythmico-phonological unity creates the indivisibility of its semantic unity.

Divergence between the general language meaning and the integral meaning of the line can be null in two extreme cases: (1) given full equivalency of the meaning of the poetic line to its prose retelling, i.e., in the extreme case of the conversion of poetry into prose, and (2) given the total destruction of the general language meaning, i.e., in the creation of poetry of the glossolalic type. Firstly, such cases are possible only as exceptions against the backdrop of a standardized poetic culture, as its negation, but are impossible as independent systems for the construction of poetic meanings. Secondly, the relationship of the two systems, even if one of them is an empty class, is not structurally identical to prose uncorrelated with poetry.

The unity of the line as a semantic whole exists on several structural levels. We can note an initial tendency toward the maximum realization of all systemic prohibitions, and, subsequently, to their relaxation which creates auxiliary semantic possibilities.

The original singling out of the line as a unified and basic feature of poetry implied the obligatory presence of a unity of metrico-rhythmic, syntactic, and intonational series. In the initial stage of the history of post-Lomonosov Russian verse, the presence of isocola and phonological recurrences was seen as a facultative feature. Thus isocola were typical of rhetorical poetry, but were far from being a feature of all poetry.

In this period "to be verse" meant both a certain rhythmic structure that gravitated toward unification (one meter had to prevail and become, as it were, a symbol of poetry in general; for Russian verse this was historically iambic tetrameter) and a certain "poetic" tone that was realized both through a special declamatory style and via a particular system of "high style" orthoepic norm. Insofar as poetry was thought of as a special language (in the eighteenth century the expression "the language of the gods" was the commonplace for its definition[74]), its non-identity with everyday speech was regarded as a signal that a text belonged to the category of poetry.

Basic textual meanings were determined by the feature "belonging to poetry" or "not belonging to poetry." These categories did not as yet observe any internal differentiation within poetry.[75]

Subsequently, the possibilities of divergence between metrical completeness and syntactic incompleteness were discovered, i.e., "enjambment." Poetic intonation was differentiated into rhythmic and lexical tonality (tonality definable by the arrangement of prosodic elements, and tonality associated with the structure of the lexicon). and possible conflict between them was revealed. Thus, for example, in A. K. Tolstoy's poem "The impious killer plunged the dagger. . ." ("Vonzil kinzhal ubiitsa nechestivyi. . ."), conflict arises between the ballad intonation of the rhyme and the everyday conversational tonality of its lexical realization.

> Across your shoulder they'll drape the order of Stanislav
> > As an example to others
> I have the right to give counsel to the authorities:
> > I am a chamberlain!
>
> Do you wish to get engaged to my daughter Dunya?
> > And I for that
> Will count off with wet thumb for you
> > A hundred thousand in banknotes.
>
> • • •
> • • •
>
> Cherez plexho dadut vam Stanislava
> > Drugim v primer
> Ia dat' sovet vlastiam imeiu pravo:
> > Ia kamerger!
>
> Khotite doch' moiu, prosvatat' Duniu?
> > A ia za to
> Kreditnymi biletami otsliuniu
> > Vam tysiach sto

In A. Vvedensky's[76] "Elegy" conflict arises between the major tonality of the rhythm that distinctly evokes in the reader's consciousness Lermontov's "Borodino" and the tragic tonality of the lexical level with its lowly everyday elements which in another context might sound comic.

Only when a structural layer ceases to be automatically connected with the concept of the line and can be present in one of two aspects, realization or non-realization, does it become a bearer of independent artistic meanings. The complete coincidence of all elements, as we also saw in "meter-rhythm" problem, has moved to the level of an idealized structure in relation to which the real text is perceived.

Simultaneously another process has been taking place. We have observed that the historical development is subject to a law involving the introduction of maximal restrictions and their subsequent "shattering." However, it must be emphasized that this is accurate only for artificially isolated structural levels, e.g., "the development of the rhythmic system of Russian poetry," "the history of poetic style," etc. In the actual development of texts the maximal "shattering" of prohibitions on one level is accompanied by their maximal observation on another. Obligatory features become facultative and it appears that all normative rules have been abolished. But simultaneously facultative features are elevated to the rank of obligatory ones. Thus, for example, in twentieth century poetic culture a high degree of phonological organization has become obligatory for certain poetic schools, namely, those that have permitted maximum freedom of rhythmic patterning. In like fashion, the Romantics removed all of the seeming prohibitions on genres, language and "high" and "low" styles but introduced new prohibitions against the non-individual, the banal and the traditional, on the level of content and language.

The Stanza as a Unity

While the *line* and the *entire text* are obligatory entities within the poetic work,[77] the division into stanzas is facultative. It is parallel to the division of a prose text into paragraphs and chapters and often accompanies the introduction of the narrative principle into poetry. In a text divided into stanzas, the stanzas are related to lines as lines are to words. In this sense it can be said that stanzas constitute semantic unities just as "words" do. This is quite evident, for example, in *Eugene Onegin,* where each stanza has its own integrated meaning, its compositionally determined semantic center (its semantic "root"), i.e., the first quatrain and the "suffixal" and syntagmatic "flexional" meanings that are concentrated in the following lines. The fact that a certain percent of the stanzas represent violations of this inertia and that there are divergences between the stanzaic and syntactic structures, between the stanzaic and lexical tonalities, etc., need not surprise us. We recall that it is precisely this freedom of the use or non-use of these structural elements that determines its artistic significance.

The simplest type of stanza is the couplet. One of the basic laws of rhyme is manifested in it—binarism.[78] It is not only a matter of the quantitative non-expansibility of the stanza, but of its structural elementariness. Lines entering into a stanza are structurally of equal value and are not arranged into a hierarchy, according to the feature of meaningfulness.

> I gaze like a madman at the black shawl,
> And grief tears at my cold soul.
> • • •
> Gliazhu kak bezumnyi, na chernuiu shal',
> I khladnuiu dushu terzaet pechal'.
>
> —A. Pushkin, "The Black Shawl"

True, even within the limits of the couplet, a tendency for the domination of one line (as a rule the first) over the other may be manifested:

> We were two brothers—we grew up together—
> And passed our wretched youth in need. . .
> • • •
> Nas bylo dva brata—my vmeste rosli—
> I zhalkuiu mladost' v nuzhde proveli. . .
>
> —A. Pushkin, rough draft for "The Robber-Brothers"[79]

In certain complex types of the stanza a meaningful and consecutively realizable hierarchy of dominant and subordinate lines is formed. Thus, in Baratynsky's poem "Fall" ("Osen' ") the stanza is constructed according to a clear logical scheme: thesis—four lines, antithesis—four lines, and synthesis—two lines. But within each of the quatrains, the odd lines with masculine rhymes semantically dominate and the synthesis consists of two lines ending in masculine rhymes, which, against the preceding background, are concise and succinct, assuring them the intonation of a conclusion, a maxim.

> **But if a cry of indignation,**
> > **But if a wail of great anguish**
> **From the vital depth arose**
> > **Completely triumphant and savage,—**
> **In its bones amidst its amusements**
> > **Capricious youth would quake,**
> **The playing infant, having burst out sobbing,**
> > **Would drop the toy, and joy**
> **Would forsake his brow forever,**
> **And the man in him would die alive!**
> > • • •
> > • • •
> **No esli by negodovan'ia krik,**
> > **No esli b vopl' toski velikoi**
> **Iz glubiny serdechnyia voznik**
> > **Vpolne torzhestvennyi i dikoi,—**
> **Kostiami by sredi svoikh zabav**
> > **Sodroglas' vetrenaia mladost',**
> **Igraiushchii mladenets, zarydav**
> > **Igrushku b vyronil, i radost'**
> **Pokinula b chelo ego na vek,**
> **I zazhivo v nem umer chelovek!**

Diverse deviations are imposed on this pattern that continues throughout all sixteen stanzas of the text and it is only thanks to them that the poem is transformed from a dead logical scheme into the living phenomenon of an artistic structure. In the first quatrain, the even lines complement, in the full sense of the word, the odd lines, so that they can be omitted without disruption of the sense, e.g., "But if a cry of indignation. . . " ("No esli by negodovan'ia krik"), "From the vital depth arose. . ." ("Iz glubiny serdechnyia voznik. . ."). The even lines are semantic parallels of the odd lines. But their stylistic originality stands out all the more. The lines that semantically dominate are sustained within the limits of the elevated lexicon of the eighteenth century. Their semantic doublets provide a *Romantic* high-flown lexicon within which "triumphant" and "savage" are synonyms and can be combined as equal members while "a cry of indigation" is transformed into "a wail of great anguish." The relationship of the first line to the third can be defined by the norms of logico-syntactic associations.

The second quatrain is constructed differently. The main members of the sentence are located both in the even and the odd lines and each of the two parts of this portion of the stanza is a syntactic and semantic unity. On the other hand, both parts are in a state of semantic parallelism with each other. The seventh and eighth lines only repeat the general sense of the fifth and sixth. However, the recurrence only activates a difference. Poetic cliches are purposely clustered ("to quake in one's bones," "amidst amusements," "capricious youth") in the earlier lines. The later lines create a naturalistic picture in that it is not only terrible but ordinary, something impossible for the norms of Romantic poetics. This recoding of a Romantic cliche in the picture of a child who wailingly dropped a toy because he has already died while living produces a special effect precisely by the co-location of these stylistic series.

On the boundary of the eighth and ninth lines there is a new conflict. Formally, syntactically, the sentence does not end at the end of the eighth line. The last two lines are syntactically a continuation of the sentence, but semantically relate to the image of the crying child. This is emphasized in that an enjambment occurs on the boundary of the eighth and ninth lines. It is the only one in the stanza and they are generally rare in the text.

Nonetheless, the inertia of the stanza's construction is so great that the last lines are perceived as a maxim, a synthesis of the stanza, and not as the ending of one of its scenes. The fact that these two lines are included in a series with the preceding couplets (the first two) and with the following synthetic couplets also of course plays a role:

> The caustic irresistible shame
> Of the wrongs and deceits of thy soul!
>
> Alone with an anguish whose mortal groan
> Scarcely muffled by thy proudness.
>
> Sit alone and mourn
> For the earthly joys of thy soul!
> • • •
> • • •
> Iazvitel'nyi, neotrazimyi styd
> Dushi tvoei obmanov i obid!
>
> Odin s toskoi, kotoroi smertnyi ston
> Edva tvoei gordynei zadushen.
>
> Sadis' odin i triznu sovershi
> Po radostiam zemnym tvoei dushi!

The numerous intersections of realizations and non-realizations of structural systems of different levels form the stanza as an integral unified sign with a certain indivisible content.

But if this is the nature of the stanza in relation to the lines that constitute it, the stanza remains merely a component in regard to the integral unity of the text. Thus, in Baratynsky's "Fall," the stanzas enter into the unified text construction that is subordinated to the same logical scheme: thesis—antithesis—synthesis. The thesis affirms the fruitfulness of work applied to nature; the antithesis—the sterility of the poet's labor, labor directed toward mankind. The opposition of nature's joyous and tranquil autumn and the barren "autumn of the days" of the poet arises. The synthesis removes this contradiction by its affirmation of tragedy as a cosmic law, whereas Baratynsky, with boldness unheard of in the Romantic era, asserts not only the indifference of nature but its banality ("poshlost' ") even in such lofty phenomena, sacred for the Romantic, as storm, hurricane or cosmic catastrophe:

> Now the hurricane violently rushes,
>   And the forest raises its noisy voice,
> And the ocean surges and foams,
>   And the frenzied wave beats on the shore;
> Thus sometimes the lazy mind of the crowd
>   Is roused from its slumber by
> A voice, a banal voice, a prophet of commonplaces,
>   And finds ringing response in it,
> But that word will not find a response,
> That has surpassed the impassioned earthly.
>   • • •
>   • • •
> Vot buistvenno nesetsia uragan,
>   I les pod'emlet govor shumnoi,
> I penitsia, i khodit okean,
>   I v bereg b'et volnoi bezumnoi;
> Tak inogda tolpy lenivyi um
>   Iz uspleniia vyvodit
> Glas, poshlyi glas, veshchatel' obshchikh dum,
>   I zvuchnyi otzyv v nei nakhodit,
> No ne naidet otzyva tot glagol,
> Chto strastnoe zemnoe prevzoshel.

Fruitful activity, responsiveness, that is, in the final reckoning, the ability to establish contact is peculiar to the banal world. A complex semantic structure arises in which a single characteristic of the poet, the impossibility of total self-expression, is realized both as a deep flaw and as a high achievement.

The stanza enters into this integral semantic structure only as an element. The meaning of the poem is connected both with the sequence of stanzas as semantic units and with the integral construction of a unified text-sign, to which an indissoluble unity of content corresponds. The stanza is a structure built on the comparison of at least two poetic units. Having a certain mechanism, like any other level of poetry, the stanza is a semantic construct.

We have already discussed the semantic role of rhyme. However, one must not forget that the rhyming word, granting its significance in the line, does not exist in the real poetic texture outside of the line. Thus, everything that we have said about the comparison and opposition of concepts in rhyme must be transferred to the correlation of the structural pair, i.e., two lines conjoined by rhyme. This gives us the elementary form of the stanza.

If each line is a certain integration of meanings, a semantic whole, the stanza is a contrastive comparison *[so-protivopostavlenie]* of these elementary semantic units of the line and a creation of a higher level of semiotic structure.

> **The son did not forget his own mother;**
> **The son returned to die.**
> • • •
> **Syn ne zabyl rodnuiu mat';**
> **Syn vorotilsia umirat'.**

> > —A. Blok, "Son and Mother"

If one examines only those semantic associations arising within this couplet, one must note the semantic structure which stems from the combination of these lines and which is absent in each of them taken separately.

The uniform intonation, metric and syntactic, is reinforced by a pair rhyme. This type of stanza is met in this poem only at the beginning and at the end, making it especially expressive. However, the semantic parallelism of the lines is most strongly emphasized lexically. The anaphora "son" ("syn") is combined with the isosemantic complexes "did not forget his own mother" ("ne zabyl rodnuiu mat' ") and "returned" ("vorotilsia"). The lines are almost identical in content. But the semantic significance of the verb "to die" ("umirat' ") stands out all the more. However, "to die" does not exist in and of itself: it is part of the line "the son returned to die" ("Syn vorotilsia umirat' "). The meaning of the verb, "to die" ("umirat' ") is distributed along the line in a direction opposite to that of the reading and converts the entire line into an antithesis to the first line. All of this is already largely familiar to us. What is new, what attracts our attention, is the peculiar semantic nature of the rhyme. If one accepts the final words of the lines, i.e., "mat' " ("mother") and "umirat' " ("to die") as the rhyme, then we may feel that there is no semantic correlation here at all. It seems that what we have said about rhyme is not justified in the present case. But let us examine the semantic groups that constitute each line:

> **Syn + ne zabyl rodnuiu mat';**
> **Syn + vorotilsia umirat'.**
> • • •
> **The son + did not forget his own mother;**
> **The son + has returned to die.**

If we direct our attention to both of the verb phrases, we shall discover all of the properties of rhyme. And each of these phrases forms a particular semantic combination with the word "syn" ("son"). Thus, rhyme is a device for the semantic correlation not so much of end words but rather of lines as a whole. It is natural that simple stanzaic structure corresponds only to elementary sign construction.

Insofar as the character of the connection among the words within the line and between lines is different, we may speak of that specific characteristic of the line formed by the relationship of the integrating intra-line associations and the relational inter-line associations. We can alter this situation by introducing internal rhyme and by equating, according to the relational principle, as it were, the hemistiches to lines, and thereby increasing the number of associations of the interlineal type. The same effect is achieved by shortening the metrical length of line. And, conversely, given the metrical expansion of the line, the degree of relative saturation of interlineal connections decreases.

The opposition of two types of supra-linguistic associations in the poetic text, the integrating and the relational, is highly conventional. On the one hand, these are only different aspects of one process, and a single poetic phenomenon may manifest first its integrating and then its relational associations in relation to various units. On the other hand, both of these types are mutually alternative and, consequently, form a certain diversity of association. At the same time both together are alternative to linguistic associations insofar as they form a meaning according to a different synthetic principle and are not analyzable into the mechanical sum of meaningful units. By virtue of the fact that this series of meanings does not abolish linguistic meanings but co-exists with them forming a mutually correlated pair, we are dealing here with an increase of diversity. If we provisionally define the intra-lineal associations as associations within the syntagm, the couplet is differentiated from all other forms of the stanza by its maximal syntactic conciseness. It is not by chance that the couplet often plays the role of the ending as in the above cited fragment of the poem, "Syn i mat'." The semantic integration of a line in some degree implies syntactic completeness. A line extracted from a poetic construct frequently displays a certain semantic and syntactic completeness. Therefore, the typical line of a couplet cannot be overly short. Enjambment is encountered as an exception and only when the couplet constitutes a linked two-line narrative:

(Water understands this entire locality,
Since in spring the village swims

Like Venice.) Old Mazai
Loves dearly his low-lying region.

(Vsiu etu mestnost' voda ponimaet,
Tak chto derevnia vesnoiu vsplyvaet,

Slovno Venetsiia.) Staryi Mazai
Liubit do strasti svoi nizmennyi krai.

—N. Nekrasov

The first part of the poem "Grandfather Mazai and the Hares" ("Dedushka Mazai i zaitsy") in which the stanzaic division into couplets is especially clear, has thirty-five stanzas. Here we find two enjambments within a stanza and four, still more heavily emphasized, between stanzas. However, in this case we are clearly dealing with a secondary phenomenon, with a conscious deformation of the structural norm. In Pushkin's "Black Shawl," there is not a single enjambment in its sixteen stanzas.

Making an integrated idea more complex may lead to the impossibility of its expression within the limits of a line. Each of the lines of a couplet has its continuation in the form of an auxiliary line which in its turn is connected with the following rhyme. Thus arises the quatrain. The fact that the second and fourth lines most frequently constitute a development of the first and third permits a shortening of the line and the linking of the compared pair not as two but as four rhymes. All this sharply increases the relative weight of the relational associations.

The stanzaic articulation of the text repeats the intra-lineal relationships on a higher level. Just as the rise of the line gives birth to two kinds of associations, intra-lineal and inter-lineal, the rise of the stanza engenders intra-stanzaic and inter-stanzaic associations. Their nature is not identical. Inter-stanzaic associations repeat semantic constructional comparisons among lines on another level; intra-stanzaic associations determine the rise within the stanza of certain integrational associations among its lines that are parallel to the relationship of words.

This view is affirmed by a curious detail in the history of poetry. The rise of a stanza more complex than the couplet was accompanied in many national cultures (in oral poetry and, under its influence, also in written poetry) by the isolation of the refrain. This, according to Ibn Khaldun, is what happened in the transformation of the classic Arabic *qastdah* into the folk *zajal.* In the *zajal,* the refrain becomes an introductory verse and the poem starts with it. Subsequently, it is repeated after each tercet stanza each time obtaining some semantic nuance.[80] The refrain is not an independent structural unit standing between two stanzas, but is always related to the stanza that it follows. This is affirmed by the fact that, for example, in the old Provencal ballad the refrain is united with the last line of the stanza by a common rhyme. If one looks at the stanza as a homomorphic (similar) line, the refrain is assimilated to the rhyme.

The recurrence of the refrain plays the same role as the element of recurrence in rhyme. On the one hand, each time difference is revealed in sameness and, on the other, different stanzas are contrastively compared and mutually projected upon each other forming a complex semantic whole. The stanza figures on a higher level in the function of the line, while the refrain functions in the role of rhyme. Simultaneously, as we have already noted, integrational associations that have a certain semantic meaning arise within the stanza. Let us examine stanzaic intonation as an example of such stanzaic construction (a purely melodic "musical" case, as it were).

The division of an extended narrative poetic text into fixed stanzaic units, much less into complex stanzas (e.g., octaves, "the Onegin stanza," etc.), creates a certain inertia of intonation that, as it were, reduces the specific gravity of the semantic element and increases the musical element (if these can be opposed in poetry). There is at first glance a strange paradox: it is precisely these stanzaic structures, with their fixed intonation, that are the most suitable for speech, for deliberately "non-musical," genres. Pushkin did not resort to stanzas of this type in his Romantic poems but selected them for *Eugene Onegin* and *The Little House in Kolomna (Domik v Kolomne);* Lermontov made use of them in *Sashka* and *A Fairy Tale for Children (Skazka dlia detei).* This obviously is not by chance: the monotone quality of the stanzaic intonation serves as a background against which the abundance of prosaic intonations, extremely unusual for poetry, stand out. These intonations come about due to the diversity of syntactic structures.[81] Conversational intonations obtain their antithesis in stanzaic structures and are therefore felt more sharply than in ordinary speech. This is a paradoxical phenomenon well-known to anyone who has read *Eugene Onegin.* The animated ease of his poetic language ("chatter," according to Pushkin's definition) is especially keenly felt here. But if a narrative is constructed in the vocabulary and the syntactic structures of Pushkin's novel, it will sound more literary in terms of its language texture. The effect of unusual "conversationality" will be lost.

The Problem of Poetic Plot

The problem of thematic composition *[siuzhetoslozhenie]* cannot be fully examined herein inasmuch as the general laws of thematic construction apply both to poetry and to prose and, moreover, are manifested more clearly and consistently in the latter. Additionally, the subject matter *[siuzhet]* in prose and in poetry is not identical. Poetry and prose are not separated by an impassable border, but for a number of reasons, prose structure may greatly influence poetic works in certain periods. This influence is especially strongly felt in the area of subject matter. Penetration of the subject matter of the sketch, the romance or the novel into poetry is well-known in the history of poetry. The resolution of the resulting theoretical problems would demand too much of an excursus into the theory of prose. Therefore, we shall examine only those aspects of thematics that are specifically poetic.

Poetic themes *[siuzhety]* significantly differ from prose themes in their greater degree of generality. The poetic theme does not aspire to be a narrative about some one event among many, but rather a story about The Event, monumental and unique, about the essence of the lyrical world. In this sense poetry is closer to the myth than to the novel. Consequently, investigations utilizing lyric poetry as documentary material for biographic reconstruction recreate merely a mythologized image of the poet. Even A. N. Veselovsky's remarkable monograph on Zhukovsky errs in this regard. Biographical facts can become poetic subject matter only after having been appropriately transformed.

Let us give an example. If we did not know of Pushkin's exile to the south but were guided only by his poetry, we might well wonder: "Was Pushkin exiled?" The word "exile" virtually does not appear in his poems of the southern period although *flight,* voluntary exile, is mentioned many times:

> **A seeker of new impressions,**
> **I fled from you, paternal lands. . .**
> *—Extinguished is the day's luminary...*

> **Iskatel' novykh vpechatlenii,**
> **Ia vas bezhal, otecheski kraia. . .**
> *—Pogaslo dnevnoe svetilo...*
> • • •

> **Self-willed exile,**
> **Dissatisfied with the world, himself and life. . .**
> *—To Ovid.*

Izgnannik samovol'nyi,
I svetom i soboi i zhizn'iu nedovol'nyi. . .
        —K Ovidiiu

Also note the clearly autobiographical lines from *The Caucasian Prisoner:*

Apostate of the world, friend of nature,
He abandoned his native bounds
And to a region remote he flew
With the merry phantom of freedom.
            • • •
Otstupnik sveta, drug prirody,
Pokinul on rodnoi predel
I v krai dalekii poletel
S veselym prizrakom svobody.

Pushkin was proud of his exile and it is not by chance that he named it among the events of his life which he could proudly compare to the incarceration of V. F. Raevsky:

                    . . . by persecution
I became renown among people. . .

            —To V. F. Raevsky
                • • •
                    . . . gonen'em
Ia stal izvesten mezh liudei. . .

            —V. F. Raevskomu

There is insufficient evidence to see in this image, in the image of the fugitive, the voluntary exile, merely a censorship-inspired substitute for the figure of the exile since Pushkin mentions both "ostracism" and "exile" in other poems and in still others, "cage" and "cell."

To understand the meaning of the transformation of the image of the exile into the fugitive, we must pause for an examination of this standard Romantic "myth" which inspired themes of this type. High satire of the Enlightenment created a theme which elevated an entire complex of the epoch's social and philosophical ideas to the level of a standard "mythological" model. The world was divided into two spheres: the domain of slavery, of the power of prejudice and money, e.g., "the city," "the court," "Rome"; and the province of freedom, simplicity, labor, and natural patriarchal morals, e.g., "the village," "the cottage," and "the family penates." The plot *[siuzhet]* lay in the hero's divorcement from the former world and his voluntary flight into the latter. It was utilized by Derzhavin, Milonov, Vyazemsky, and Pushkin.[82]

Texts of this type represent a realization of the theme in the following format: the world of slavery—the flight of the hero—the world of freedom.

It is important that "the world of slavery" and "the world of freedom" be on the same level of concreteness: if one is "Rome," then the other is "paternal Penates"; if one is "The City," then the other is "The Village." They are opposed politically and morally but not in their degree of concreteness. In Radishchev's poem the geographical location of the place of exile is actually specified.

The analogous theme [siuzhet] in works of Romanticism is handled differently. The universe of Romantic poetry is divided not into two closed, opposed worlds, slave and free, but into a circumscribed static sphere of slavery and the boundless extra-spatial world of freedom that lies without. The Enlightenment treatment of the theme involved a transition from one state into another and had an initial and a terminal point. The Romantic theme of liberation is not a transition but a departure. It has a point of origin and a *direction* rather than a final destination. In principle it is open in that movement from one fixed point to another is a symbol of immobility for Romanticism. Movement (being equivalent to liberation whence the standard Romantic theme "banishment equals emancipation") is understood only as a ceaseless migration. Therefore, exile without right of departure can be transformed in Romantic works into "poetic flight," "eternal banishment" or into "ostracism" but it cannot be depicted as imprisonment in Ilimsk or exile to Kishinev or to Odessa.

Thus, the poetic theme implies extreme generality, the reduction of conflict to a certain set of elementary models which are characteristic of a particular belletristic conception. Subsequently, a poem's plot [siuzhet] may become more concrete, consciously being brought nearer to more immediate life situations. These situations are then taken as confirmations or rejections of an initial lyrical model but never outside of correlation with it.

Pushkin's poem "She" ("Ona") (1817) ends: "I am not *he* for *her*" ("Ia ei ne on"). Also compare:

> "He" and "she" is my ballad.
> It's not terrible that I'm the new one.
> What's terrible is
>   that "he" *is* I
> and that "she"
> is mine.
>
>   —V. Mayakovsky, *About This*

> "On" i "ona"—ballada moia.
> Ne strashno nov ia.
> Strashno to,
>   chto "on"—eto ia
> i to, chto "ona"—
>   moia.
>   —*Pro eto*

Correlation with traditional lyrical schemes gives rise in these cases to different semantic effects, but it is always filled with meaning. The transformation of the entire abundance of life's situations into a fixed, comparatively small set of lyrical themes is a characteristic feature of poetry. The character of these sets depends on several various models of human relationships and their transformation under the influence of the standard models of the culture.

Another distinguishing property of the poetic theme is the presence of a kind of rhythm, of recurrences, parallelisms. In some cases it is possible to speak of "situational rhymes." This principle may also penetrate into prose (the recurrence of details, of situations, and attitudes) as it has filtered into cinematography. But in these cases, critics, on feeling the intrusion of poetic structural principles, speak of "poetic cinematography" or of the "non-prosaic" structure of a prose theme as in A. Bely's *Symphonies* or his *St. Petersburg* as well as in many other works of the 1920s.

"The Alien Word" in the Poetic Text

The relations between text and system in poetry are specially constructed. In ordinary language usage the receiver of communication reconstructs
the text and deciphers it with the aid of the code system of the appropriate
language. However, knowledge of the language itself and also of the fact that
the communicated text is in that language is provided the hearer by some
initial convention which precedes the communicational act.

The perception of a poetic text is differently structured. The poetic
text exists in the field of intersection of many semantic systems, many
"languages." Information about the *language*[83] of a communication, its
reconstruction by the hearer, the "schooling" of the hearer in a type of
belletristic modeling new to him often constitutes the text's basic information. Whenever a listener encounters a poetic text that does not conform
to his structural expectations, a text impossible within the limits of the
standard language and which consequently constitutes a fragment of another
text, a text in some other language, he attempts, sometimes rather arbitrarily,
to reconstruct that language. The relationship, sometimes one of proximity
and compatibility, sometimes of remoteness and incompatibility, between
these two ideational, cultural, belletristic languages becomes the source of
a new type of artistic effect on the reader. Thus, for example, it is widely
known that Pushkin's poem *Ruslan and Liudmila* seemed indecent to critics
of the 1820s. Now, it is almost impossible for us to feel the "indecency" of
this work. But were the readers of Pushkin's epoch really so squeamish? Can
it be that readers who knew "The Dangerous Neighbor" and Voltaire's "La
Pucelle d'Orléans" or Parny's erotic poems and Bogdanovich's *Dushenka,*
readers who on a firsthand basis knew Ovid's *Ars Amatoria,* and the bold ex-
plicitness of the descriptions of Petronius or Juvenal, readers who were
familiar with Apuleius and Boccaccio, could they really have been offended
by a few ambiguous lines and wayward scenes? We should not forget that
Pushkin's poem appeared in a censored edition in an epoch when morality
was prescribed in no less a degree than political reliability. If the text had
actually contained anything offensive to the generally accepted sense of
decency of that era, the poem indisputably would have been withheld by
the censor. The poem's indecency was of another sort—literary.

The work opens with the lines:

Deeds of long bygone days,
Traditions of deep ancientry.

Dela davno minuvshikh deni,
Predan'ia stariny glubokoi.

This was a citation well-known to readers of the time. Its presence was intended to draw the audience into a particular system of ideo-cultural associations, into the proper mode of experiencing of the text, i.e., as exalted, heroic. This system implied certain situations and their admissible combinations. Thus, for example, heroic episodes could be combined with elegaic ones but not with gay, erotic or fantastic episodes. (It is known that Mac-Pherson, composing his "Ossian" on the basis of original bardic texts, painstakingly removed the fantastic episodes as did the first German and Russian translators of *Macbeth* when they excised the scenes with the witches. The fantastic element in *The Tempest* and in *A Midsummer Night's Dream,* on the other hand, was not disturbing since the heroic was not intermingled in it.) The "Ossianic" key to Pushkin's text was not accidental. Later episodes such as that of Ruslan on the field of battle as well as other images and epithets bring it to mind.

However, the subsequent portions of the text were composed in accord with a system which completely proscribed any combination with "Ossianic" elements. Another type of belletristic organization was introduced, i.e., that of the humorous "bogatyr' " type of poem. It too had been well-known to the reader since the last third of the eighteenth century and was to be recognized by a small set of features such as the conventionalized "bogatyr' " names familiar from the works of Popov, Chulkov, and Levshin, or in terms of a typical theme such as that of the abduction of the bride. However, these two types of artistic organization were mutually incompatible. Thus, for example, the "Ossian" type implied lyrical reflection and psychologism, while the "bogatyr' " type focused on the plot and fantastic adventure episodes. It is not by accident that Karamzin abandoned his poem about Ilya Muromets for he had failed to successfully combine the style of a "bogatyr' " poem with one focusing on psychologism and irony.

The combination of the non-combinable structures of "Ossianism" and "bogatyr' " poems did not exhaust the constructional dissonances of *Ruslan and Liudmila.* Elegant eroticism in the spirit of Bogdanovich or Batyushkov[84] and "sumptuous" lines such as of the type "Jealous clothing shall fall/ On Contantinople carpets. . ." ("Padut revnivye odezhdy/ Na tsaregradskie kovry. . .")[85] were combined with the naturalism of lines on the cock whose beloved was stolen by a kite or "Voltairian" judgments on Chernomor's physical abilities or the platonic nature of the relationship between the two protagonists.

The mention by name of the artist Orlovsky in the poem incorporates the text into the system of ultra-Romantic experiences which were then novel and therefore especially keenly felt. However the reference to Zhukovsky's ballads evokes the belletristic language of Romanticism only in order to subject it to coarse mockery. The poem's text freely and with contrived casualness switches from one system to another, bringing the two into conflict so that the reader cannot find a single unified "language" for the entire text in his own cultural arsenal. The text speaks in many voices and the artistic effect stems from their co-location, their seeming incompatibility notwithstanding.

This is how the structural meaning of the "alien word" is determined. Just as an alien body falling into a supersaturated solution causes the precipitation of crystals, i.e., reveals the true structure of the dissolved substance, the "alien word" by its incompatibility with the structure of the text activates that structure. This is the meaning of those "specks of dust" which only make the water more pure according to Tolstoy's often cited observation. Structure is intangible until it is contrasted with another structure or until it is disturbed. These two modes of activation constitute the very essence of the belletristic text.

M. Bakhtin was the first to study the problem of the "alien word" and its artistic function.[86] The connection between the problems of the "alien word" and the dialogization of belletristic language has also been noted in his works.

> Relations analogous to those of dialogic utterance and response are established via the absolute interplay between the alien speech and the author's context. In this way the author stands alongside the hero and their relationship becomes dialogic.[87]

This idea is extremely important in such works as *Eugene Onegin* where the abundance of citations, literary, mundane, ideo-political and philosophical results in the inclusion of numerous contexts and disrupts the monologic character of the text.

All this reveals still another important conflict inherent in the structure of poetry. In accord with its construction as speech of a certain type, poetry linguistically gravitates toward monologue. Since any formal artistic structure tends to become a bearer of content, the monologism of poetry assumes constructional significance, being interpreted in some systems as lyricism and others as a lyrical-epic element depending on who is regarded as the center of the poetic world.

The principle of monologism enters into conflict with the constant displacement of semantic units in the general field of the construction of meanings. In a text a polylogue of different systems is constantly taking place; different modes of the explanation and systematization of the world, different pictures of the world, come into conflict. The poetic (belletristic) text is in principle polyphonic.

It would be too simple to show the internal multilingualism of the text in parodic poetry or in cases of the poet's overt usage of diverse intonations or of contradictory styles. Let us see how this principle is realized in the deliberately monologic, consciously self-contained and meticulously created poetic world of a poet such as Innokenty Annensky. Let us examine the poem below from this point of view.

There Will Still Be Lillies

When under black wings
I bow my weary head
And death silently snuffs out the flame
In my gold icon lamp. . .

If, smiling upon new life,
And from earthly existence
My soul, having burst its fetters,
Bears off an atom of being,—

I shall not take the memories
Of past delights of love,
Nor of the eyes of a woman, nor the fairy tales of my nurse,
Nor the poetry of golden dreams,

Having forgotten the ephemeral beauty
Of the flowers of my turbulent dream,
From a lone snow-white lily
I shall take over into a better world
Both the aroma and tender contour.

• • •

Eshche lillii

Kogda pod chernymi krylami
Sklonius' ustaloi golovoi
I molcha smert' pogasit plamia
V moei lampade zolotoi. . .

Kol', ulybaias' zhizni novoi,
I iz zemnogo zhitiia
Dusha, porvavshaia okovy,
Unosit atom bytiia,—

Ia ne voz'mu vospominanii,
Utekh liubvi perezhitykh,
Ni glaz zheny, ni skazok niani,
Ni snov poezii zlatykh,

Tsvetov mechty moei miatezhnoi
Zabyv minutnuiu krasku,
Odnoi lilei belosnezhnoi
Ia v luchshii mir perenesu
I aromat, i abris nezhnyi.

The poem strikes one by the unity of its lyric tone, a unity intuitively felt by the reader. The feeling of unity here is stronger than that, say, in a chemistry textbook in that it arises in conflict with the heterosystemicity of the text's

110

elements. If we attempt to isolate the common element of the text's different stylistic orders, then perhaps only one can be indicated, i.e., literariness. The text is demonstrably and obviously built on literary associations. Although there are no direct citations, the reader is nonetheless referred to certain everyday and literary milieus outside of whose context the poem cannot be understood. The words of the text are secondary signals of certain systems that lie outside it. This accentuated "culturedness," the bookishness of the text, sharply opposes it to works whose authors subjectively attempt to break through the limits of "words" as for example in the mature Lermontov, in Mayakovsky and Tsvetaeva.

This unity is more than conventional, however. The first two lines already involve *different* literary associations. "Black wings" evokes the poetry of demonism, or, more accurately, those of its features which in the popular mind were associated with Lermontov and with Byronism. (See N. Kotliarevsky's monograph which exhaustively defined this cultural cliche.) The expression "my weary head" involves associations with popular poetry of the 1880s and 90s, such as that of Apukhtin and Nadson, e.g., "See how weak we are, see how tired we are, How helpless are we in the tormenting struggle" ("Vzgliani, kak slaby my, vzgliani, kak my ustali, Kak my bespomoshchny v muchitel'noi bor'be") and also with Chaikovsky's romances and the vocabulary of the intelligentsia of the period.[88] It is not by chance that the word "kryla" ("wings") is in a poetic lexical variant (i.e., not the usual form "kryl'ia"), and that "golova" ("head") is given in a contrasting everyday form. Had the more exotic variant "glava" ("head") been used, it would have signified a more elevated style, cf.,

> **Wearied, on the bosom of a new friendship,**
> **I with a tremble nestled my caressing head**
>
> **Ia s trepetom na lono druzhby novoi,**
> **Ustav, prinik laskaiushchei** *glavoi. . .*
>
> —A. Pushkin, October 19, 1825

The poetry of the eighties was directly in the Nekrasov tradition and entailed an everyday concreteness in the treatment of the lyric's subject.

In the context of the entire stanza, the "gold icon lamp" ("zolotaia lampada") is perceived as a metaphor (death will extinguish the lamp) while the epithet "gold" ("zolotoi") which is in structural antithesis to "black" is not felt to be associated with concrete material meanings. But further on, we encounter the line "Nor the poetry of golden dreams" ("Ni snov poezii zlatykh"). In comparison the "gold icon lamp" (cf., the antithesis "gold—golden" ("zolotoi—zlatoi") assumes features of materiality and is correlated with the already completely specific *object,* i.e., the lamp standing before the icon. But the image of the lamp going out may have two different kinds of meanings: the conventional literary ones, e.g., "burnest thou, our lamp?," or "extinguished in the name of divine love" and those meanings associated with Christianity, e.g.,

> **And he was snuffed out like a candle**
> **Waxen, before an icon. . .**
>
> —N. Nekrasov, "Orina, a Soldier's Mother"
>
> • • •
>
> **I pogas on, slovno svechen'ka**
> **Voskovaia, predykonnaia. . .**
>
> —"Orina, mat' soldatskaia"

Initially we have the conventional literary system of semantic associations; then the realization of the icon lamp as an object activates the second system, the religious one.

The second stanza is constructed in terms of that body of Christian religious meanings so familiar to the readers of the time. An antithesis develops between "a new life" (a synonym of "death" and "the black wings" of the first stanza), and "earthly life." The image of the soul parting from earthly bondage with a smile was completely in order in this regard. But the last line is unexpected. The word "atom" has no place in the semantic universe of the preceding lines. The subsequent word "existence" ("bytie") fits quite naturally into the circle of cultural meanings which it evokes and brings to mind the world of scientific and philosophical vocabulary and [related] semantic associations.

The following stanza begins with the word "recollections" as a textual signal. Different systems of poetic texts have different content for the concept "recollection." Here it does not designate a psychological activity but serves as a cultural symbol. A whole array of interpretations of this concept may be found in the stanza. The delights of love and the golden dreams of poetry sound like straightforward citations drawn from that Pushkinian poetic tradition which in Annensky's cultural world was perceived not as one of the varieties of poetry, but as poetry itself. "The fairy tales of my nurse" refers to two types of extra-textual associations: non-literary, everyday ones, the world of childhood in opposition to the world of books and, simultaneously, the literary tradition of the recreation of the world of childhood. "The fairy tales of my nurse" in poetry of the end of the nineteenth century was a cultural sign of the non-symbolic, the child's world. Against this backdrop the expression "the eyes of a woman" is "an alien, non-literary phrase" which is perceived as the voice of life in a polyphonic choir of literary associations, i.e., "eyes" ("glaza") but not "orbs" ("ochi"), "women" ("zheny") and not "maidens" ("devy").

The poem's first three stanzas establish a certain compositional inertia: each consists of three lines sustained in a certain conventional literary style, and of one that diverges from that style. The first two stanzas also establish the position of that line as stanza final. Subsequently, infringements occur and in the third stanza the "disruptive" line is shifted to the penultimate position. The structural dissonance in the final stanza, however, is even more pronounced. Four of the five lines are markedly literary in terms of their vocabulary and central theme and must be perceived against the background of the entire poetic tradition of the nineteenth century. It is not by chance that the word "lilies" in the title is stressed on the first syllable while in the third line of the last stanza "From a lone snow-white lily" ("Odnoi lilei belosnezhnoi") the stress is on the second syllable in accordance with the norms of poetic speech at the beginning of the nineteenth century. The name of the flower is converted into a poetic association. Unexpectedly, counter to the rhythmic inertia of the entire text, a fifth line is added to this final stanza: "Both the aroma and tender contour" ("I aromat, i abris nezhnyi"). This line is opposed to the entire text in its materiality and its isolation from the world of literary associations. Thus, on the one hand, the poem renders both the earthly and unearthly worlds in their literary countenances, and, on the other, non-literary reality. But this reality is not a thing, not an object (in this, it is distinct from the expression "the eyes of a woman") but a form of an object. "Snow-white" ("belosnezhnyi") in conjunction with "lily" ("lilei") is a floral banality which even in poetry of the eighteenth century could be counted by the dozen. But for the idea "outlines," a unique word was found, "contour" ("abris"). Reality as an aggregate of abstract forms is an Aristotelian world largely restricted to and characteristic of Innokenty Annensky. It is not by chance that the last line also provides the only alliteration in the poem. The unification of "aromat" ("aroma") and "abris" ("contour"), which are both rhythmically and phonologically parallel, into one archiseme is possible only in one meaning, i.e., "form," "entelechy." In this way the voice of still another culture, that of ancient Classicism in its most organic semantogenic associations, is introduced into the text.

Thus emerges the tension in the text's semantic structure: monologue proves to be polylogue and the polyphony of various voices speaking in the different languages of the culture forms a unity. Other than in poetry, such a structure would fill many pages.

The Text as a Whole:
The Composition of the Poem

Any poem admits two points of view. As a text in a *natural language,* it presents a sequence of separate signs (words) which are conjoined in accord with the syntagmatic rules of a certain level of a given language; as a poetic text, it can be viewed as a unified sign, as a representative of a unified integrated meaning.

There is a contradiction in this assertion. A work of art (i.e., a good work of art, a text that most effectively and durably fulfills an artistic function in the text system of one or more cultures) is in principle unique. The contradiction stems from the fact that the very concept of the sign implies repetition. This contradiction, however, is only apparent. Let us initially note the minimal unit of recurrence—two. To be capable of performing the function of a sign, a signal must be repeated at least once. However, the meaning of this minimal figure for repetition is different for conventional and iconic signs. The conventional sign must repeat itself at least once; an iconic sign must repeat the object replaced by it at least once. *The resemblance of sign and object constitutes the minimal act of repetition.* Artistic texts (literary, pictorial, and even musical) are built according to the iconic principle. The tension between the conventional nature of signs in ordinary language and the iconic nature of signs in poetry is one of the basic structural contradictions of the poetic text.

The question cannot be reduced to this, however. The poetic sign which is non-repeatable on the level of the text is constituted from numerous intersections of different recurrences on the lower levels and is incorporated into genre, stylistic, epochal, and other recurrences on the supratextual level. The very non-repeatability of the text, i.e., its uniqueness, is an individual modality inherent to the text and comprised of the intersection of numerous recurrences.

Thus, a text which is created as a result of artistic improvisation may, for example, be considered a model of non-repeatability. It is no accident that the Romantics saw improvisation as the highest manifestation of art, opposing it to the "pedantry" of poetic labor which stifles the originality of poetic creation. Whatever form of improvisation we might take, be it Russian folk laments or the Italian commedia dell'arte, we can easily view improvised text as an inspired montage of numerous common formulae, ready-made plot ploys, images, and rhythmico-intonational devices instantly synthesized in the creator's consciousness. The craft of the actor in the commedia dell'arte demanded the mastering of many thousands of poetic lines, the possession of a repertoire of poses, gestures, and of costume. This huge arsenal of recurrent ploys did not confine the individual creativity of the improviser but, on the contrary, gave him freedom of artistic self-expression.

The greater the number of non-individual associations in a given artistic text, the more individual it will seem to the audience.

The unity of the text as an indivisible sign is assured by all levels of its organization but particularly by its composition. The composition of the poetic text always has a dual nature. In one sense, it is a sequence of the various segments of the text. Insofar as the largest segments are implied, it should be possible to define composition as the supra-phrasal and supra-lineal syntagmatics of the poetic text. However, these same segments are somehow equated and constitute a set of unambiguous unities in fixed relationships. Not only adjoining, but also in a state of contrastive comparison [so-protivo-postavlenie] , they form a structural paradigm both on the supra-phrasal and supra-lineal levels, and for texts in stanza form, on the supra-stanzaic level as well.

We shall now examine the composition of Pushkin's poem, "When I wander out of town, pensive. . ." ("Kogda za gorodom, zadumchiv, ia brozhu. . .).

> When I wander out of town, pensive,
> And stop by the public cemetery,
> Lattices, columns, elegant tombs,
> Beneath which decay all the corpses of the capital,
> In a bog crowded together in a row anyhow,
> Like greedy guests at a beggars' table,
> The mausolea of deceased merchants and officials,
> The ridiculous embellishments of the cheap chisel,
> Over them, inscriptions both in prose and verse
> Of virtues, employment, and ranks;
> The love plaint of a widow for her old cuckolded mate,
> Urns screwed off their columns by thieves,
> Slimy graves, which also here
> Gapingly await their inhabitants come morning—
> All this brings me such troubled thoughts
> That an evil despondency falls over me.
> You want to spit and run. . .
>   But how pleasant for me
> In the autumn, in the evening quiet
> To visit my ancestral cemetery in the country,
> Where the dead doze in solemn peace.
> There, there is space for the unadorned graves;
> The pale thief does not creep to them at night;
> Near the ancient stones, covered with yellow moss,
> Passes the villager with a prayer and a sigh;
> Instead of empty urns and petty pyramids,
> Instead of noseless geniuses and slovenly Graces
> Stands an oak spreading over the stately graves,
> Fluttering and rustling. . .

Kogda za gorodom, zadumchiv, ia brozhu
I na publichnoe kladbishche zakhozhu,
Reshetki, stolbiki, nariadnye grobnitsy,
Pod koimi gniiut vse mertvetsy stolitsy,
V bolote koe-kak stesnennye riadkom,
Kak gosti zhadnye za nishchenskim stolom,
Kuptsov, chinovnikov usopshikh mavzolei,
Deshevogo reztsa nelepye zatei,
Nad nimi nadpisi i v proze i v stikhakh
O dobrodeteliakh, o sluzhbe i chinakh;
Po starom rogache vdovitsy plach amurnyi,
Vorami so stolbov otvinchennye urny,
Mogily sklizkie, kotory takzhe tut
Zevaiuchi zhil'tsov k sebe na utro zhdut,—
Takie smutnye mne mysli vse navodit,
Chto zloe na menia unynie nakhodit.
Khot' pliunut', d bezhat'. . .

                                    No kak zhe liubo mne
Osenneiu poroi, v vechernei tishine,
V derevne poseshchat' kladbishche rodovoe,
Gde dremliut mertvye v torzhestvennom pokoe.
Tam neukrashennym mogilam est' prostor;
K nim noch'iu temnoiu ne lezet blednyi vor;
Bliz kamnei vekovykh, pokrytykh zheltym mokhom,
Prokhodit selianin s molitvoi i so vzdokhom;
Na mesto prazdnykh urn, i melkikh piramid,
Beznosykh geniev, rastrepannykh kharit
Stoit shiroko dub nad vazhnymi grobami,
Koleblias' i shumia...

The poem is obviously divided both graphically and thematically into halves whose sequence defines the syntactic structure of the text: a city graveyard—a country graveyard.

The first half of the text has its own distinct principle of internal organization. Pairs of words are combined according to the principle of the oxymoron: a word is conjoined with another word which is semantically least combinable with it with the result that impossible combinations are realized:

elegant	—	tombs
corpses	—	capitals
mausolea	—	merchants, officials
the deceased	—	officials
cheap	—	chisel
plaint	—	amorous

The description of the city cemetery in the second part of the text is constructed according to the same principle:

empty	—	urns

trivial	—	pyramids
noseless	—	geniuses
slovenly	—	graces

The principles of the semantic incompatibility of these pairs differ: "elegant" and "tombs" unite the meanings of vanity and adornment with the concept of eternity, of death. "Elegant" is here set against the background of the word "splendid" which is unrealized in the text but possible in the context. The semantic difference between these words becomes its dominant meaning in the line. "Corpses" and "capitals" yield a pair whose incompatibility is considerably more covert. (Different degrees of incompatibility create supplementary play in the text.) "Capital" in the lexicon of the Pushkin epoch is not simply a synonym of the concept "city." It is a city with its administrative aspect emphasized, the city as a clustering of society's political and civil structures, and finally, in administrative officialese and street-lackey jargon, it is a substitute for the word "Petersburg." Note the lackey's song:

> What a glorious capital
> Merry Petersburg!
> • • •
> Chto za slavnaia stolitsa
> Razveselyi Peterburg!

As in Bunin's story "The Gentleman from San Francisco," this whole cluster of meanings is not to be linked with the concept "corpse." The luxurious ocean liner or the fashionable hotel are not concordant with the idea of a corpse and conceal or hide it because the very possibility of death turns them into a mirage and an absurdity.

"Mausolea" and "merchants" taken in conjuction have an ironic ring, just as do "deceased officials" or "cheap chisel." The replacement of "sculptor" by "chisel" gives the text a poetic quality and solemnity which is immediately refuted by the context. "Petty pyramids" is a spatial incongruity while "empty urns" is a semantic absurdity. Note the definition: "Urn—a receptacle for ashes": urns containing nothing and devoid of those culturally meaningful associations connected with the word "urns."

This principle of revealing the absurdity of a scene by projecting it against some semantically "correct" background, the principle of contrasting each word with its unrealized double underlies the construction of the first part of the text. Thus "slimy" ("sklizkie") functions against the background of "slippery" ("skol'zkie"). Pushkin in one of his prose texts cites the word "sklizkie" as an example of attractive folk speech. However it has another function here. The entire text is built on the stylistic dissonance between the solemnity of several of the text's key words (tombs, chisel, virtue, urns, etc.) and the unceremoniousness of words such as "slimy" and "gapingly." Such dissonances, especially in conjunction with stylistic bureaucratisms such

117

as "beneath which" ("pod koimi") impart a complex character to the text. It sounds like a text retold by an author (immersed in the author's language) in the governmentalese of the capital city.

Stylistic dissonances are also manifested in other elements of its construction. Thus the enumerative intonation and the syntactic homogeny of the members equate "virtues" to "service" and "ranks." The last example is especially instructive. The impossibility of combining the combined pairs depicts an impossible world. It is organized according to the laws of a lie ("the love plaint") or of an absurdity, a mirage. But it exists. And simultaneously a point of view is formulated in which such combinations are possible and do not seem surprising. It is the point of view that equates "virtues" and "ranks" and "service" and that permits the conjoining of "public" and "cemetery." It is the point of view of the official, the "capital," St. Petersburg, set in the framework of the author's unambiguous straightforward evaluation. Such evaluations as "ridiculous embellishment," "an evil despondency falls on me" are rare in Pushkin's work.

The second half of the text is not merely *another* scene joined to the first. It is simultaneously a transformation of that *same* picture and is to be perceived in relation to it and against its background.

The interrupted line yields not only two polarities of mood "spit/ pleasant" ("pliunut'/liubo") but also the significant sound parallelism: *p l iu/l iu b*. The active character of the opposition *p/b* is also revealed against the background "spit—run" ("pliunut'—bezhat' ").

Comparison of the first and second halves of the text reveals several new ideas: at the center of each part taken separately, we see the theme of the cemetery, of death. But in the following juxtaposition the feature "cemetery" is set outside of brackets [and serves] as the basis for the comparison.

The poem's basic semantic differentiation rests on this foundation but is encompassed in the *structure of life* rather than in the "cemetery" opposition. Henceforth, and this is typical for Pushkin, the opposition is that of a life constructed according to an order necessary and worthy of man and of a life resting on false and deceitful foundations. Life and death do not constitute a basis of contrast: they are leveled in an indivisible concept of being— either worthy or deceitful. From this point of view the semantic opposition of the first and second parts may be seen in terms of yet another feature. Transience is characteristic of the "city": even a corpse is merely a guest of the grave. It is not by chance that in the poem's first half the word "guest" is used twice, oftener than any other word.

The naturalness and simplicity stressed in the second part are synonyms of eternity. In the opposition "noseless geniuses"—"the oak over the graves" a whole series of semantic features is activated: "artificiality—naturalness," "insignificance—grandeur." However, still another element must be isolated: the tree (especially an "eternal" tree, an oak) is a stable mythological and cultural symbol of life. It introduces both the symbolism of eternity as a sign of existence (not death) and the world of antiquity, of mythology, and the idea, important for Pushkin, of the present as a link between past and future.

The text's unity, however, is due not only to intra-comparison among its parts but also to its non-singularity in the system of texts known to us. The poem is perceived by us as a whole because we know other poems and involuntarily project it upon this background. This is what defines the meaning of the concluding couplet. Our acquaintance with numerous poetic texts establishes a stereotype of the finished poem. Seen against the background of our idea of the obligatory features of completeness, the detached final line "Fluttering and rustling. . ." is filled with numerous meanings, i.e., incompleteness, the impossibility of verbally expressing the depth of life, infiniteness of life's flow. The inescapable subjectiveness of these interpretations enters into the structure of the text and is foreseen in it. The images of the poet and of the oak, the symbol of life that rises above the graves, frame the contrasted scenes of the two cemeteries. Death figures as an ambivalent element. Repulsive as a social phenomenon, it can be beautiful. As a manifestation of eternity, it is a synonym rather than an antonym to life in its natural course.

Thus, the unity of the text's structure reveals content that enters into conflict with its purely linguistic meanings: an account of a place of death, a cemetery, and an account concerning the proper order of life, about existence, enter into mutual tension creating in its totality the "non-repeatability," i.e., the uniqueness, of the text's meaning.

Text and System

The regularities which we have examined permit us to ascertain the internal structure of the text and to determine its dominant associations and orderings. Apart from those constructional principles which are peculiar to a given text, semantic organization does not exist. However, the system is not the text. It organizes the text and functions as a deciphering code, but cannot and must not replace it as an object esthetically perceived by the reader. In this sense, criticism of any given system of textual analysis is based on a misunderstanding because it does not replace the direct esthetic impression of the work of art. As a matter of principle, science cannot replace practical activity and is not called upon to do so. It analyzes it.

The relationship of system to text in a work of art is significantly more complex than in non-artistic sign systems. In natural language the system describes the text. The text is a concrete expression of the system. Extra-systemic elements in the text are not bearers of meanings and remain unnoticed by the reader. Thus for example, without special training we do not notice misprints and slips of the pen in a text unless new meanings are accidentally formed. Similarly we fail to notice the book's typeface or paper unless this information is incorporated into some sort of sign system. If the paper for a book were to be selected from a set of possibilities (not less than two) and this set itself bears information about the book's price, quality, potential readership and the status of the publisher or the epoch of printing, we, of course, would regard this aspect of the book differently than in a case where a publisher has no choice or this choice is purely random. Deviations from the system in non-belletristic texts are perceived as mistakes subject to removal. Should a new meaning spontaneously appear as for example, in a misprint which results in a new word, the need for its elimination is all the more pressing. Thus, in the transmission of textual information from author to reader, it is precisely the mechanism of systematicity that functions.

In an artistic work the situation is different in principle and the wholly specific nature of the organization of a work of art as a sign system is connected with this fact. In a work of art *deviations* from the structural organization can be as meaningful as the realization of the latter. Recognition of this circumstance does not, however, force us to concede the correctness of those who, stressing the richness, the multi-facetedness and the living plasticity of the artistic text, make this a pretext for claiming the unsuitability of structural, and, more generally, of scientific methods for the analysis of works of art and describing them as somehow "desiccating" and incapable of catching the vital richness of art.

Even an extremely schematic description of a text's most general structural regularities does more to facilitate an understanding of its unique originality than any number of statements about the uniqueness of the text in that the a-normative, the extra-systemic, exists as an artistic fact only against the background of some norm and in relation to it. Where there are no rules there can be no violation of these rules, i.e., no individual originality. This is true regardless of whether we are speaking of an artistic work, the behavior of a person, or any other semiotic text. Thus jaywalking becomes a fact of individual behavior only against the background of certain proscriptive rules which regulate human behavior. When we say that only the popular literature of a period allows us to properly evaluate the genius of a great author, we essentially have the following in view: in reading writers of a given epoch, we unconsciously assimilate the obligatory norms of art in that period. In a given case, it is irrelevant whether we obtain this knowledge from the normative works of theoreticians of the art of the period, from descriptions by modern scholars, or directly from reading texts themselves. In any case, an established *norm* for the belletristic texts of a given historical epoch will be present in our consciousness. This is comparable to the way in which one may learn a living language, i.e., either by utilizing descriptions of it or simply by practicing, listening to ordinary language usage. As a result, when complete mastery of the language is achieved a *norm* of correct usage will be present in the consciousness of the speaker whether it is expressed in a formalized grammatical rule system or as some aggregate of language usage. Knowing the artistic norm of an epoch tells us what is individual in the work of one of its writers. Those who argue that the essence of an artistic work does not lend itself to exact description, when investigating a text, necessarily single out certain constructional tendencies felt to be typical of the epoch and the genre. Thanks to the absence of any carefully elaborated methodology, the subjectivity of the approach, and the incompleteness of the material examined, typical phenomena of belletristic language are often seen as "uniquely individual" and vice versa.

Thus, in a belletristic text, meaning arises not only as a result of the observation of certain structural rules but also as a result of their violation. Why is this possible? Questioning this assertion is not inappropriate because it seemingly contradicts the most fundamental assumptions of information theory. Indeed, what is meant when we speak of decoding a text as a communication? The process can very roughly be visualized as follows: our sense organs receive a non-discrete (continuous) stream of stimuli (i.e., a certain acoustic reality which is defined by purely physical parameters) upon which the decoding consciousness imposes a grid of structural oppositions that permits us to identify certain acoustic segments with meaningful elements of language on various levels, i.e., phonemes, morphemes, lexemes, and so on. Portions not coinciding with fixed structural positions (e.g., a sound located *between* two phonemes of a given language) do not form a new structural position such as, for example, a new phoneme previously nonexistent in that language although quite possible in others. A sound falling into an intermediate position in relation to the phonemic grid of a given language will either be drawn into the orbit of an existing phoneme as its variant with the difference being declared unimportant or it will be categorized as noise and be declared non-existent. All this will strictly conform to the fundaments of the decoding process. The situation in which deviation from a certain norm creates new meanings is so usual in artistic practice that it constitutes a paradox from the standpoint of information theory and requires supplementary explanation.

The contradiction between artistic communication and the general rules for the correlation of text and code in a given case is not a real one. First of all, not every deviation from the norms of structural expectation generates new meanings. Some deviations behave as in the corresponding cases in non-belletristic texts. Why is there such a difference between those deviations from expected norms which are perceived as textual deficiencies, as mechanical impairment, and those in which the reader sees new meaning? Why for example, in some cases is a completed work perceived as an excerpt and in others an excerpt as a complete work?

Such fundamental characteristics of artistic works as that of multiplicity of interpretation are obviously connected with these properties of the artistic text. A scientific text gravitates toward monosemy, i.e., its content can be evaluated as true or false. An artistic text creates a field of possible interpretations, sometimes a very wide one. The more meaningful, the deeper the work, the greater its tenure in the memory of humanity, the greater will be the range of possible interpretations and also of those historically realized by the reader and criticism.

Manifesting such flexibility on the one hand, the artistic text reveals extraordinary stability on the other: it is capable of resisting mechanical impairment and of attracting into its field meanings which undoubtedly were not intended. The missing arms of Venus di Milo, the time-darkened colors of a painting, the use of archaic words in poetry are clear examples of the onset of informational entropy, of noise in the communication channel between the addressor and the addressee. These simultaneously become techniques for the creation of new artistic information which is sometimes so essential that in a sense restoration may seem a cultural violation of the monument and become a variety of entropy. Historically, restorations have frequently resulted in the destruction of objects of great cultural value. One must distinguish restoration from conservation, the preservation of the monument. This is not, of course, true of all restoration which is a basically necessary albeit dangerous way of preserving the cultural heritage.

A well-known example from *Anna Karenina* involves an accidental spot on his canvas which suggests to the artist the placement of a figure and becomes a means of esthetic expressiveness.

An artistic text's ability to draw the surrounding world into its own sphere and make it a bearer of information is truly astounding. The artistic text reacts with (sometimes completely accidentally) co-located texts and enters into semantic relations with them. This phenomenon may be seen in the composition of assemblages ranging from an anthology, an almanac or an album, all seen as structural unities to the relationship of various pictures in an exhibition or buildings in an architectural ensemble. Special laws of creolization or incompatibility come into play: in some cases different texts "willingly" enter into relationships forming a structural whole, while in others, they "do not notice one another," as it were, and are capable only of mutual disruption. In this sense, any city which has existed for a long time offers an extremely interesting text for observation. In Prague, for example, sometimes even in the confines of a single building, one can observe how the Gothic, the Renaissance and the Baroque organically blend into a structural whole. One can also cite examples of twentieth century architecture that in some cases "react" with the context and in others, disrupt it.

These "mysterious" peculiarities of the artistic text by no means attest its principled non-correlation with structural orderings of a general type; quite the contrary. In contradistinction to non-belletristic texts, a work of art is correlated not with one but with several deciphering codes. That which is individual in an artistic text is not the extra-systemic but the multi-systemic. The greater the number of deciphering structures that one or another constructional bundle of the text simultaneously enters into, the more individual its meaning. Entering into the different "languages" of a culture, a text is seen from different aspects. That which is extra-systemic becomes systemic and vice versa. This, however, does not indicate unlimited arbitrariness, that boundless subjectivity in which the specific nature of art is sometimes seen. The set of possible deciphering systems constitutes a dimension characteristic of a given epoch or culture and can and must be an object of study and description.

The presence of at least two different belletristic languages which decipher a single work of art and the resulting semantic tension (whose sharpness stems from the bifurcation of the single unified text that underlies it) constitute the minimal condition for regarding a text as artistic. A single text interpretable by two modes is seen as not being equal to itself and its two meanings become poles of conflict. However, in an actual work of art we find, as a rule, a more complex pluralistic paradigm of codes giving life to the text via the "interplay" of numerous meanings. Thus the relationship of text and system in an artistic work is not the automatic realization of an abstract structure in concrete form, but is always a relationship of struggle, tension, and conflict.

The situation in which the whole text is, so to speak, uniformly switched into another system is far from being the only source of internal structural tension underlying the life of the work. No less important is another sort of case where separate portions of a single text are constituted according to different structural laws and a possible paradigm of codes is realized in the different portions of the work in varying degrees of intensiveness. Thus, B. A. Uspensky in analyzing the structure of the icon has irrefutably established that different types of artistic perspective function in the center and at the edges of the painted text and that the nature of the artistic phenomenon of a figure in an icon is determined by its position relative to such indices as the axis of construction or the edge of the picture. The observation that the "central" and "peripheral" heroes in a literary work are, in some cases, constructed according to the rules of more than one artistic system must also be credited to Uspensky. Cinematographic theory affords numerous examples of the *replacement* of constructional principles as the basis of the text's artistic composition. The text with the aid of a series of signals evokes in the consciousness of the reader or the hearer a code system which functioning successfully thereby reveals the text's meaning.

At a certain place in a work we begin to notice that the correspondence of text and code has been disrupted: the code ceases to operate and the work is no longer decipherable. The reader, guided by the new signal indicators, must evoke from his own cultural resources a new system or even independently synthesize a code hitherto unknown to him. In this latter case covert indications of how this is to be done are incorporated into the text. As a result, the text is deciphered not by some synchronic code or codes but by *a sequence of codes* whose interrelations create a supplementary semantic effect. To some extent such a sequence can be established in advance. In poetic collections of the eighteenth and early nineteenth centuries the sections devoted to the "ode," the "elegy," the "epistle," and other [genres] each implied a certain system against which the text was to be projected but the collection as a whole admitted only certain types of these sequences. Together with this there also could be free sequences that permitted the rearrangment of types of structural organizations, of parts of the text in conformity to its individual construction.

The shift of structural organizational principles is a powerful technique for reducing the redundancy of an artistic text: just as the reader settles on a certain expectation and builds for himself a certain system of predication for the as-yet-unread part of the text, its structural principle changes, deceiving his expectation. The redundant portions assume informational content in the light of the new structure. This conflict between the structures of different parts of the text sharply increases the information content of artistic works in comparison with all other texts.

Diversity of a text's artistic organization is one of the most general laws of art. Although it is variously manifested in different historical epochs and within the limits of different styles and genres, the principle almost always makes itself felt in some form. Thus, for example, in reading Pushkin's *Poltava* one is immediately struck by the presence of two parts quite completely different in their construction: everything associated with the plot line of the love of Mazepa and Maria is, as G. A. Gukovsky has pointed out, connected with the artistic tradition of the Russian Romantic poem, whereas the battle scenes and the artistic treatment of Peter reflect the stylistic standards of the Lomonosovian ode, and more generally of Lomonosovian culture. (The text's reflection of the influence of Lomonosov's mosaics has also been noted by researchers.) G. A. Gukovsky's well-known work *Pushkin and Problems of the Realistic Style (Pushkin i problemy realisticheskogo stilia)* has shown that this stylistic conflict was premeditated. For our purposes it is important to stress that the clash of the heroes and of the ideological tendencies expressed by them is constructed as a conflict of two artistic structures, each of which is contrastively isolated against the background of the other. The new stylistic manner disrupts the previously constituted inertia of the reader's expectation and sharply curtails the text's redundancy.

In *War and Peace* the different groups of protagonists each have their own characteristic worlds, their own systems of authorial relationship and their own special principles of artistic typification. However, Tolstoy structures the composition so that these parallel plot lines merge into one. The reader arrays the different scenes into a single chain so that pictures of battle action are supplanted by domestic scenes, staff episodes by front line episodes, or capital scenes by country ones. Scenes with one or two persons alternate with crowd scenes and the relationship of the author to the scale of his depiction is sharply altered. In the language of the film this would be expressed by foreshortening and foreground effects.

A given type of construction is frequently not supplanted by its polar opposite. Much more commonly it is simply *something else.* However, this constant replacement of the most diverse elements of belletristic language entails a high level of meaningfulness. That which would be automatized in a uniform structure is shown to be not the only possible type of structure but the one consciously selected by the author. Consequently, it is significant.

Analogous phenomenon may also be observed in lyric poetry although they are differently manifested. Thus, for example, in Victor Hugo's book, *L'Année Terrible,* there is a poem called "Our Corpses." The author divides the text by a blank space between the poem's two parts: in the first part, there are twenty-three lines preceding the space, the graphic sign of a pause; in the second, one line. The first section is a horrible and repellent description of the rotting corpses of dead soldiers: "Their blood forms a ghastly swamp," "repulsive hawks dig into their ruptured stomachs," "horrible, twisted, black," "skulls resembling blind stones," etc. Each new line strengthens the expectation of the repellent, that which inspires disgust and loathing, horror and pity. However, when this impression has been so firmly inculcated that the reader feels he understands the author's scheme and can predict what follows, Hugo pauses and continues "I envy you, cut down for the fatherland." The last line is built on a completely different system of relationships: "I" and "they," and "low" and "high" have changed places. This forces us once again to consciously return to the first part and reread it in a different light. A dual conflict develops: initially it is between the different semantic structures of the first and second parts, and then later between different possible interpretations, between the two readings of the poem's first part.

The alternation between the comic and tragic in Shakespeare, the complex replacement of types of artistic organization in the various scenes of *Boris Godunov,* the change of meters within a single text which after Katenin became entrenched as one of the expressive devices of Russian poetry, these, and still other types of transition from one set of structure-forming principles to others within a single work, are merely different manifestations of a single tendency, i.e., the tendency of the artistic text toward maximal information content.

On "Bad" and "Good" Poetry

The concept of "bad" and "good" poetry is among the most personal and subjective of categories and, consequently, is the most disputed. It is not by chance that the theoreticians of the eighteenth century introduced the concept of "taste," a complex combination of knowledge, of ability and intuition, and of innate talent.

How does the concept of good and bad poetry appear from the viewpoint of the structural semiotic approach? First of all, the functionalism and historical circumscription of these definitions must be stressed: what is "good" from some historical perspectives may seem "bad" in another epoch and from another point of view. The young Turgenev, a person of highly developed poetic sensibility, was enraptured by Benediktov; Chernyshevsky considered Fet, one of Tolstoy's favorite poets, a model of nonsense, assuming that only Lobachevsky's geometry could compare in degree of absurdity. Cases where poetry is considered "good" from one standpoint and "bad" from another are so numerous that they must be considered the rule rather than the exception.

By what is this conditioned? To understand this the following point must be kept in mind: we have been examining poetry as a semiotic system, defining it as a kind of secondary language. However, there is a vital difference between belletristic languages and primary natural language: to speak Russian well means to speak it "correctly," that is, to speak in accordance with certain rules. To compose poems "well" and to compose them "correctly" are different things, sometimes similar and sometimes extremely divergent. We already know the reason: natural language is a device for the transmission of information but does not itself bear such information. In speaking Russian we can recognize an infinite amount of new information, but the Russian language is so taken for granted that we cease to notice it. There cannot be linguistic surprises in the normal act of speaking. In poetry this is not true. Its very structure is informational and must be experienced as non-automatic at all times. This comes about because, as we have attempted to show, each poetic level is "two-layered"; it is simultaneously subordinate to not less than two non-coinciding systems of rules and the observation of some rules inescapably means the violation of others. To write poetry well is to write both correctly and incorrectly at the same time.

Bad poems are poems that do not bear information or bear it in insufficient amounts. Information is present only when a text cannot be guessed in advance. Consequently, the poet cannot play "give-away" [i.e., backwards checkers] with the reader: the relationship "poet—reader" is always one of tension and conflict. The more intense the conflict, the more the reader will win from his struggle. The reader armed with a set of artistic and non-artistic ideas approaches the reading of a poem. He begins with expectations provided by his earlier artistic and biographical experience, by the name of the poet, the name of the book, and, sometimes, by its cover or its publisher.

The writer accepts the terms of battle. He considers the readers' expectations and sometimes consciously arouses them. When we know two facts and the principle of their organization we immediately begin to form suppositions about the third, the fourth, and so on. The poet gives us rhythmic series[89] on various levels and in doing so determines the character of our expectations. Lacking this the text cannot serve as a bridge from the writer to the reader and cannot perform a communicative function. But if our expectations are realized one after the other, the text will seem devoid of information.

From this we conclude that good poems, i.e., those that bear poetic information, are poems in which all of the elements are simultaneously both expected and unexpected. Violation of the first principle makes the text senseless; violation of the second renders it trivial.

Let us look at two parodies that illustrate the infringement of both principles. P. A. Vyazemsky's fable "Gluttony" ("Obzhorstvo") violates the first principle. Vyazemsky's parody of D. I. Khostov's lines is a talented recreation of bad poetry and is, consequently, in a certain sense, a "good" poem. But we are now interested not in how these lines are good but in how Vyazemsky recreates the mechanism of bad poetry:

> A Frenchman
> Was chewing a watermelon:
> The Frenchman, even though a French marquis,
> But he favors Russian taste
> And is far from slow to gulp down sweets.
> A muzhik having lept upon an aspen,
> Guzzled a rowan berry for all he was worth
> Or, speaking bluntly, a Russian prune:
> He was, it seems, unhappy in love!
> An ass seeing this, peels his ass's eyes
> And brays: "Thieves, thieves!"
> But our Frenchman was not born a coward.
> Nor was our muzhik a pawn,
> And no nut tree fell the ass's lot.
> Here in parable is revealed a little bundle to taste:
> That Mrs. Ass,
> Even having strained herself braying, will
> never be a vixen.

Odin frantsuz
Zheval arbuz:
Frantsuz, khot' i markiz frantsuzskii,
No zhaluet vkus russkii
I sladkoe glotat' on ne ves'ma leniv.
Muzhik, vskochivsi na osinu,
Za obe shcheki dral riabinu
Il', poprostu skazat', rossiiskii chernosliv:
Znat' on v liubvi byl neschastliv!
Osel, uvidia to, osliny lupit vzory
I laet: "Vory, vory!"
No nash frantsuz
S rozhden'ia byl ne trus.
Muzhik zhe tozh ne peshka,
I na oslinu chast' ne vypal oreshka.
Zdes' v pritche kroetsia tolikii uzl na vkus:
Chto gospozha oslitsa,
Khot' s laiu nadorvis', ne budet vvek
lisitsa.

From Vyazemsky's point of view, this poem is "bad" (not as a parody) since it is "senseless." Its lack of sense lies in the non-agreement of the parts, in the fact that every element not only fails to predict the following ones but rejects it. Further, each pair fails to form a series with its own inertia. Above all we have a string of semantic absurdities; the muzhik leapt upon an *aspen*, but, contrary to all logical expectation, he tore off a *rowan berry*, and subsequently *nut trees* are mentioned. No regular connection is established among the personages: the "Frenchman," the "muzhik," or the "ass" who turns out to be a "she ass" and a "Mrs." in the bargain. The plot becomes an anti-plot. It is impossible to establish a "correct" relationship between the plot and the moral by means of the author's evaluation which reports that the "muzhik guzzled rowan berries for all he was worth," accompanying this with the explanation that "or speaking bluntly, the Russian prune" ("bluntly" and "prune" are also an unexpected combination; why should a "prune" be more blunt than a "rowan berry"?), the author concludes: "he was, it seems, unhappy in love." The moral concluding the fable is also unpredictable.

Stylistically, the text is equally "disjointed": "he flogs" ("lupit") and "gazes" ("vzory") do not form a series. A situation is mimicked wherein conflict with the rhyme causes such difficulty for the author that all remaining orderings are violated: "the ass brays" ("osel laet") and the vulgar lexicon is conjoined with the archaic "a little bundle to taste" ("tolikii uzl na vkus"). If one removes the secondary order which stems from the fact that this is a parody, "a conversation on the language of Khvostov," then the text is chaotic.

A second parody reproduces a poem meeting all the norms of the reader's expectations by having converted them into a set of cliches. This is a poem of Kozma Prutkov:

To My Portrait
(Which will shortly be issued in my complete collected works)

When in a crowd you meet a person
   Who is naked;[90]
Whose forehead is gloomier than foggy Mt. Kazbek,
   Whose step is unsteady;
Whose hair is dishevelled,
   Who, clamouring,
Already trembles in a nervous fit—
   Know—it is I!

Whom they mock with malice, eternally new
   From kith to kin;
From whom the crowd his laurel wreath
   Silently tears;
Who bends his supple back to no one,—
   Know—it is I!
On my lips, a quiet smile,
   In my breast—a serpent!. .

Moemu Portretu
(Kotoryi budet izdan vskore pri polnom sobranii moikh sochinenii)

Kogda v tolpe ty vstretish' cheloveka,
   Kotoryi nag;[90]
Chei lob mrachnei tumannogo Kazbeka,
   Neroven shag;
Kogo vlasy pod'iaty v besporiadke,
   Kto vopiia,
Vsegda drozhit v nervicheskom pripadke,—
   Znai—eto ia!

Kogo iazviat so zlostiu, vechno novoi
   Iz roda v rod;
S kogo tolpa, venets ego lavrovyi
   Bezumno rvet;
Kto ni pred kem spiny ne klonit gibkoi,—
   Znai—eto ia!
V moikh ustakh spokoinaia ulybka,
   V grudi—zmeia!. .

The poem is assembled from cliches of the Romantic poetry widely known in that epoch and imitates that pseudo-meaningful, thoroughly overworked and trite system. The basic oppositions "I" (the poet)—"the crowd," "the wilderness and strangeness of the poet—the banality of the crowd, its hostility" were already all semantic stock phrases. These are supplemented by an ostentatious set of cliches on the levels of phraseology, the stanza, and the meter. The inertia is set and is nowhere violated: the text (as an original artistic work) is devoid of information. The parodistic content is attained by indicating the relationship of the text to extra-textual reality. The "mad poet" in the text turns out to be a prudent civil servant in real life. The proof lies in the two variants of a single line: in the text we have "Who is naked" ("Kotoryi nag") while in the footnote, the alternate "Who wears a frock-coat." The more cliche-ridden the text, the richer in content is the evidence of its real life meaning. But this is already the information of the parody and not of the object parodied in it.

Thus, performing the function of "good poems" in a cultural system is the prerogative of only those texts which are highly informative for that culture. This implies a conflict with the reader's expectation, tension, struggle, and in the final reckoning, forces the reader to accept an artistic system that is more meaningful than his usual one. But in convincing the reader, the writer takes upon himself the obligation to go further. The conquered novelty is converted into a cliche and loses its informativeness. Novelty is not always in the invention of the new. Novelty has a meaningful relationship to tradition in being simultaneously the resurrection of its memory and non-coincidence with it.

Insofar as good poems are always poems in no less than two dimensions, their artificial reproduction, ranging from parody to the creation of generative models, is always difficult. When we say "good poems are those which bear information (of all types), i.e., those that can not be guessed in advance," we are affirming that "good poems are those whose synthetic generation is at present beyond our capability and for which the very possibility of such generation remains to be demonstrated."

Some Conclusions

Poetic structure is a supple and complexly constituted artistic mechanism. In it the diverse possibilities for the storage and transmission of information attain such complexity and perfection that nothing else created by the hand of man can compare with it.

As we have seen, poetic structure falls into many particular types of organization. Information storage is possible only due to the diversity which arises from the difference between substructures, and also because each of the substructures does not operate automatically but falls into at least two lower level substructures which, in intersecting, deautomatize the text by introducing elements of chance into it. Insofar as that which is accidental for one substructure is systemic for another, [poetic structure] can be both systemic and simultaneously non-predictable so that practically inexhaustible informational possibilities are created.

Simultaneously the poetic world is a model of the real world but is correlated with it in an exceedingly complex fashion. The poetic text is a powerful and deeply dialectical mechanism of the search for truth, for understanding the surrounding world and our orientation in it.

What sort of relationship prevails between poetic language and everyday language? At the beginning of the 1920s theoreticians of the Formalist school began to speak of the conflict of device and language and of the resistance of linguistic material which constitutes both the essence and the measure of esthetic effect. In counterbalance to this at the end of the twenties and the beginning of the thirties a theory of the complete correspondence of conversational language and poetry and of the natural birth of poetry from the speech element was advanced. This was a renewal of the theory of poetry as an emphatic style of ordinary speech put forward by French literary theoreticians at the end of the nineteenth century. Statements by the theoreticians of the twenties suffered from one-sidedness although they directed attention toward the real aspect of the relationship between poetry and language. Apart from this, relying on twentieth century Russian poetic practice, they naturally generalized the new regularities which were revealed to them.

The aim of poetry, of course, is not "devices" but a knowledge of the world and the relationship among people, self-knowledge, and the development of the human personality in the process of learning and social communication. In the final summing up, the goal of poetry coincides with the goal of culture as a whole. But poetry realizes this goal specifically and an understanding of its specific character is impossible if one ignores its mechanism, its internal structure. This mechanism actually is more readily revealed when it enters into conflict with the automatism of language. However, as we have seen, not only the retreat from the natural norms of language but also their approximation can be a source of artistic effect. Poetry introduces freedom into the world of linguistic automatism, those structural regularities lacking alternatives in natural language. Originally this freedom is manifested in structures which are impossible or unused in the language. Then a growing approximation to the norm of ordinary speech is possible up to the point of full coincidence. But insofar as this coincidence will not be a result of linguistic automatism but a consequence of the selection of one of a number of possibilities, it will become a bearer of artistic information.

Natural synonymy in the lexicon and parallel forms on all other levels constitute a reservoir of artistic meanings in language itself. Affording the possibility of selection, they are a source of stylistic meaning. The essence of poetic structure is that it obviously uses non-synonymic and non-equivalent units as synonyms and equivalents. Language is converted into the building material of diverse models and the proper structure of language in its turn exerts an influence on them. Thus, whatever character is assumed by the relationship of the system of poetic language to the system of everyday speech, whether of extreme coincidence or extreme divergence, these are particular cases. It is important that there be no automatic unambiguous dependence between these systems, so that the relationship can become a bearer of meanings.

Apart from natural language man has at least two biologically given (and therefore tacit) but nonetheless very powerful modeling systems which actively form his consciousness. These are the system of "common sense," of everyday ordinary knowledge and that of man's spatio-visual picture of the world.

Art introduces freedom into the automatism of both of these worlds by disrupting the unambiguousness of their prevailing associations and thus broadening the boundaries of knowledge. When Gogol tells us that an official's nose ran off, he is violating both the system of ordinary associations and the relationship between the visual representations (a nose the height of a man). But precisely the disruption of the automatism of the associations makes them an object of knowledge. After Gogol, a time of the rejection of the fantastic set in. Writers depicted the world as everyday experience recognizes it in its mundane outlines. But this was a conscious selection of a certain type of representation against the possibility of other types. In this case the observation of the norms of probability is just as informative as their violation. This area of human consciousness had already become a sphere of conscious and free knowledge. However, these aspects of the construction of the poetic world are common both to poetry and prose and must be specially examined.

part 2

Introductory Comments

In the final reckoning all investigative analysis rests upon the reader's direct perception. This perception underlies that intuition which enables the scholar to avoid sifting through all the logically possible combinations of structural elements and immediately to set aside a certain minimum number for further consideration. Consequently, the absence of a reader's direct reaction, as when, for example, the object of study is from a remote epoch or an alien culture, drastically reduces the economy of the investigation. Very frequently a conception whose refutation would be most difficult can be rejected out of hand for the simple reason that it sharply diverges from a direct experiencing of the text. Also connected with this general phenomenon are those difficulties, common in the history of scholarship, which often arise when an investigator richly endowed with erudition is deprived of intuitive contact with the text and of the capability to perceive it directly.

However, the reader's feeling that constitutes the basis of scientific knowledge can also be a source of error; within certain limits surmounting it is just as much a necessity as adherence to it. The reader's feeling and the investigator's analysis are two principally different types of activity. They come into contact in no greater degree than do the "common sense" of everyday experience and the principles of contemporary physics. Meanwhile the reader's perception aggressively and partially gauges the truth of scientific conclusions by their coincidence with its own ideas. No matter how conditional or relative the judgment stemming from the reader's impression, their formulators are most frequently inclined to accept them as absolute truth. If scientific thinking is critical, the reader's is "mythological," that is, it gravitates toward the creation of "myths" and regards their criticism with extreme irritation.

Another distinction between the reader's approach to a text and a scholarly approach is that the former is synthetic. The reader perceives all of a work's aspects in their unity. Indeed, he must not perceive them otherwise for the author reckons on just such an attitude. The danger comes when the reader, seeing analysis as the "murder" of art and an infringement on its organic integrity, begins to demand such a synthetic view on the part of the investigator. However, the integrity of a work cannot be conveyed in an investigative study given that feeling of direct unanalyzable integration which remains both the superiority and inadequacy of the reader's perception. Science attains its goals through *preliminary analysis* and *subsequent synthesis*.

One must note still one further important difference in the approaches of a reader and a scholar to a text: they make different demands with regard to the exhaustiveness of the conclusions. The reader prefers definitive conclusions even if doubtful; the scholar, conclusions that submit to scientific verification even if incomplete. Each of these positions is completely justified so long as it remains within the limits set aside for it in the general scheme of the culture. To replace the reader by the researcher would be ruinous for literature just as would be the replacement of the investigator by the reader.

The disarticulation of a problem into operations and the positing of a series of restricted cognitive tasks are the basis of scientific understanding. Accordingly, the following monographs do not address themselves to a multilateral analysis of the works under study. Of the three possible areas for study, the internal examination of the text, the inspection of the relationship among texts, and the relationship of the texts to their external social structures—only the first is singled out as primary. This primacy is to be understood in a purely heuristic sense, i.e., as a convenient initial stage from the standpoint of the sequence of scientific operations.

The selection of texts for analysis in the remaining part of the book is not arbitrary. Although correct scientific method must possess universality and, in principle, "work" on any material, the structure of the analyzed text strongly influences the selection and combination of the most expedient investigative techniques. The texts analyzed here are not intended to give the reader a *history* of Russian poetry "in models." Historical study presupposes a different methodology. Therefore, the chronological arrangement of the texts is a compositional convention. In principle *all* of the analytic techniques offered for the reader's consideration could be demonstrated on the texts of a single poet or even on some one text. However, the use of diverse poetic texts affords certain conveniences: it permits the selection of works in which the analyzed level of structural organization is expressed most clearly and dominates over the other levels. It is this attempt to demonstrate analytic investigative techniques on poetic text rather than any intent to present, even in the most schematic form, the historical development of Russian verse that has determined our selection of texts. Therefore the author must reject in advance any reproach of incompleteness (from the historical point of view) in the choice of the texts here used.

The Batyushkov poem "Thou awakest, O Baiae, from the tomb" ("Ty probuzhdaesh'sia, o Baiia, iz grobnitsy") was chosen for demonstration of the phonological-metrical level as dominant in the general structure of a text. The Pushkin poem which follows it aptly demonstrates another feature: the poetic epistle, "To F. N. Glinka," enables us to explicate the mechanism of poetic displacement of meanings, while the following poem "They sound retreat. . . from my hands" ("Zoriu b'iut. . . iz ruk moikh") is typical of Pushkin's construction of the "denuded" text, a structure built on the realization of "minus devices." This aspect—the analysis of style, of semantic displacement and poetic phraseologisms—is similar to that shown for the Nekrasov poem "Last Elegies" ("Poslednie elegii"). In the Nekrasov text the clash of poeticisms and prosaisms make the phraseological level the most active one. The problem of genre meaning is incidentally activated in the process.

The subsequent textual analyses touch upon composition, the dynamics of stanzaic construction, the progression of the lyric theme, and the general structure of the lyric text as a whole. Lermontov's poem "We have parted but thy portrait. . ." ("Rasstalis' my; no tvoi portret. . .") allows us to demonstrate the connection of the text's grammatical structure (the pronominal system) with the poet's model of the world and of human relationships. Tyutchev's "Two Voices" ("Dva golosa") illustrates dialogic construction in the text of a lyric poem. This analysis enables us to delve into the nature of dialogue construction as one of the basic laws of lyric narration. Another example of dialogue, this time covert, is illustrated in Blok's poem "To Anna Akhmatova" ("Anne Akhmatovoi"). This last text is also suitable for the examination of another problem: the complexly mediated construal of the author's point of view.

The analyses of Tyutchev's "On the Eve on the Anniversary of August 4, 1864" ("Nakanune godovshchiny 4 avgusta 1864 goda"), Tsvetaeva's "Vainly with my eye, as with a nail" ("Naprasno glazom, kak gvozdem. . .") and Zabolotsky's "Passerby" ("Prokhozhii") focus on the reconstruction of more general models of the authorial world view in conjunction with the structure of the lower levels of the poetic text. Here we attempt a study of the poem's spatial relations and through them, the philosophical construction of the text.

The specific nature of the construction of satiric poetry demands singling out of texts of this type. A. K. Tolstoy's "He sits beneath the canopy. . ." ("Sidit pod baldakhinom. . .") and Mayakovsky's "Scheme of Laughter" ("Skhema smekh") permit us to analyse the distinctive characteristics of the semantic construction of a satiric poetic text.

The proffered analyses are monographic studies of the *internal* structure of the texts. The following must be kept in view: analysis of the internal structure of the poetic text in principle requires complete description of all of the work's levels from the lowest, the metrico-rhythmic and phonological, to the very highest, the levels of plot and composition. However in the absence of preliminary reference works such as poetry frequency dictionaries, reference books on rhythm, dictionaries of rhyme, etc., a *full* description would unavoidably be unwieldy. To avoid this we shall draw into our analysis only the dominant levels rather than all of the material relating to intra-textual associations. Inasmuch as the elucidation of what, in a given case, belongs to the dominant elements of structure and what does not is essentially an intuitive matter, important elements of imprecision are introduced into the analysis. The author concedes this but argues its necessity for reasons of expositional compactness. For demonstrational purposes extra-textual associations are introduced into the analysis in individual cases.

For the same reason still another departure from the canon of exhaustive description must be allowed. The artistic activeness of a text is determined not so much by the presence of certain elements as by their action within the system of the given artistic whole. Therefore the description of a text is not an enumeration of these elements but of a system of functions. Practically speaking, two descriptions of a single text are necessary for the explication of a system of functions: one description should present it as the realization of a certain system of rules (both common ones for all levels and rules specifically organizing various levels), and the other, as the violation of that system. Rule violations can be described as the realization of certain other norms. The poetic text with all the wealth of its individual meanings thrives in the *field of tension* that arises among these systems. Only having presented each structural element of the poetic text simultaneously both as the fulfillment and the non-fulfillment of a certain normative system of poetic organization shall we obtain a functional description which reveals the artistic meaning of the work. In the present exposition we have, however, adopted a somewhat more abbreviated approach: we admit only the dominant cases and the clearest examples both of the establishment of structural inertias and also of their violation.

K. N. Batyushkov

Thou awakest, o Baiae, from the tomb
At the appearance of Aurora's rays,
But the purple dawn will not return to thee
   The radiance of bygone days,
Nor will it bring back the refuges of coolness
   Where luxuriated swarms of beauties,
And never will thy porphyry colonnades
   Arise from the abyss of the blue waters.

Ty probuzhdaesh'sia, o Baiia, iz grobnitsy
Pri poiavlenii Avrorinykh luchei,
No ne otdast tebe bagrianaia dennitsa
   Siianiia protekshikh dnei,
Ne vozratit ubezhishchei prokhlady,
   Gde nezhilis' roi krasot.
I nikogda tvoi porfirny kolonnady
   So dna ne vstanut sinikh vod.

The poem "Thou awakest, o Baiae, from the tomb. . ." is among Batyushkov's last and most mature works, having been written in Italy in 1819. It is of particular interest in that Batyushkov's characteristic mastery of the text's sound organization becomes a technique for the construction and transmittal of profound content. Taken separately from the immanent structure of the text, the poem's meaning might seem trivial. It would be impossible to single it out in the flood of meditations "on ruins and tombs" seen "in the light of the rising sun," that inundated European literature after Ossian, Young, and particularly Volney's "Les Ruines" with its hundreds of imitations.

The lowest levels, the phonological and metrical, are the dominant, most actively functioning ones. Each in its way forms an organized structure while the lexico-semantic level functions as their interpretation. The correlation of phonological meanings with rhythmic ones takes place through the latter level. The dependence is bilateral and is determined by the iconicity of signs in art and by the presumption of meaningfulness for the structural elements of a belletristic text: the semantic units and their relationship in a given text interpret the meanings of the elements of the lowest levels. But there is also a reverse dependency: the correlation of phonemes generates semantic convergencies and antitheses on the highest levels, i.e., the phonological structure interprets the semantic.

The first line "Thou awakest, o Baiae, from the tomb" creates a semantic conflict: the primary meaning of "Baiae awakes" indicates first transition, a change of state, and second, a particular transition—from sleep to waking. Both of these states are part of life and the transition from one to the other involves nothing difficult or impossible in the usual contexts of the concepts. Adjoining the adverbial "from the tomb" to the nucleus of the sentence, Batyushkov decisively displaces the entire semantic plane. "Awakening" is a synonym for resurrection. Instead of an ordinary change of state *within life,* the transition is *from death to life.* The poem begins with a declaration of the possibility of this transition, although simultaneously the extraordinariness, the unusualness of this situation is revealed to us, i.e., the awakening is not from sleep, not in bed, but from death, from the tomb.

The presence of two semantic centers in the line and the conflict between them is distinctly retraced on the phonological level which is organized in a particularly interesting way in the poem. The reader's intuition attests to the complexity and richness of the text's organization. However, the technique of sound analysis usual in investigative practice such as the search for onomatopoeia and alliteration yields nothing. The real structure of the correlation of the text's phonemes is not captured by these techniques. On the other hand, if we reject the identification of such phenomena with sound organization as a whole and concede that any significant contrast of phonemes in a poetic text is not accidental, then an interesting picture opens before us.

The opposition of the two stressed vowels corresponds to the two semantic centers of the first line of the Russian text, i.e., a ←——→ i. The entire poem is characterized by three strong stressed vowels per line excluding the last where there are four. Their distribution by line is as follows:

```
1.    a ——— a ——— i
2.    e ——— o ——— e
3.    a ——— a ——— i
4.    a ——— e ——— e
5.    i ——— e ——— a
6.    e ——— i ——— o
7.    a ——— i ——— a
8.    a ——— a ——— i ——— o
```

The simplicity of the skeletal structure displayed by the vowel phonemes immediately strikes the eye. Only four phonemes participate in the structure and these are easily generalized into two groups: *a/o* and *e/i.* The opposition fronto-lingual/non-fronto-lingual is activated.

In the first line the meaning "awakening" ("probuzhdenie") is attached to the phoneme "a," and that of "tomb" ("grobnitsa"), to "i."

However, the austerity, even parsimoniousness, of the text's supporting vocalic system contradicts our intuitive feeling of the richness of the sound texture. This intuition reflects an interesting aspect of the text's vocalism.

In examining the relationship of the stressed to the unstressed vowels in the first line, the following picture is obtained. The first stressed vowel "a" is set against the background of an almost full set of Russian vowels in this first line (i.e., *i, e, a, o, u*), and enters into the oppositions:

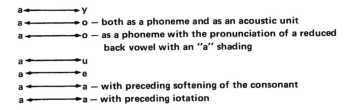

The differential features of the phoneme /a/ which are activated in each of these oppositions will constitute its real sound content in the first line.

The second central phoneme /i/ is given in a significantly narrower circle of oppositions:

i ⟷ o
i ⟷ y

In /i/, fronto-linguality and the capability to soften the preceding consonant are manifested.

The opposition /a/⟵/i/ thus assumes the character of the opposition of an element rich in sound content to one poor in sound content. Richness, beauty, and plentitude of meaning are assigned to /a/ as its structural-semantic attribute.

The underlying opposition in the first line is further supported by two consonantal oppositions: the "a" group is set against the background of the stops "t — p — b — d" that taken together with the "i" (which is geminated between the two "a's" in the word "Baiia" ["Baiae"]) stands in opposition to the significantly less articulationally tense environment of "i."

Simultaneously singled out is the opposition of the sound groups *prob — grob (prob*uzhdaesh'sia ["awake"] — *grob*nitsy ["tomb"]). The differential element *p — g* obtains the meaning of revival, of life, on the one side, and of the grave, of death, on the other.

The first line thus incorporates a structural contradiction: lexically it affirms the removal of the opposition between life and death, i.e., resurrection, while phonologically, it emphasizes the separateness, the irreconcilability of the two semantico-structural centers.

The second line is an organic continuation of the first and together they constitute a single syntagm. The connection of the lines is supported by sound parallels: *pro — pri — po:* the first line begins with the group of vowels *y —e — u* while the second ends in *y — u — e.* However, it also introduces something new: "awakening" (resurrection) is linked with the appearance of the dawn, with light. The word "rays" is the semantic center of the second line. But the merger of the images of resurrected Baiae and of the tomb occurs here not only on the lexico-semantic level in the image of the dawn but also on the phonological level.

The skeletal structure provided by the second line's vocalism assumes the following appearance:

$$e \text{———} o \text{———} e$$

That the 2:1 ratio has here changed to the advantage of the front vowels is especially significant. There are only two such cases in the seven lines having three support vowels while the eighth line is still more instructive in that there are three back vowels and one front. Equally significant is that the "a" in this function is replaced by an "o"—the only case in the text. Another matter is of cardinal import here, however: owing to the absence of any semantic opposition on the lexico-semantic level, the difference among the support vowels loses the character of an opposition. Moreover if we examine the relationship of the stressed vowel and of the unstressed vocalism group which gravitates toward it (confined between the pauses of the word divisions), we shall see that the feature of background richness is here assigned to both "o" and "e." The vowel "e" is given in contrast with "i," "o," "a" with preceding iotation) and in the third group with "u." Such a set activates a significantly greater number of differential features and makes the front vowel much richer in content associations than in the first line. The "o" is set against the backdrop $a - i - y$ also fully revealing the internal phonological structure.

The following two lines introduce a new opposition: "But the purple dawn will not return to thee,/ The radiance of bygone days. . ." The radiance of the dawn is not the radiance of bygone days and the awakening is not a real resurrection. If "Aurora's rays" ("Avroriny luchi") and "tomb" ("grobnitsy") were opposed in the first two lines, "the purple dawn" ("bagrianaia dennitsa") now draws near to "tomb" ("grobnitsa"). Their phonological parallelism on the consonantal level stands out distinctly: *grbnc — bgrnc.* It might also be noted that the combination "gr" is met in the poem only in these two words and that its meaning has already been established in the antithesis "prob" — "grob."

The contrast is reinforced by two local oppositions: "bagrianaia" ("purple")—"siianiia" ("radiance") and "dennitsa" ("dawn")—"dnei" ("days"). The basic opposition of the text on the level of the vowel phonemes is greatly strengthened. "Bagrianaia—siianiia" lays bare the opposition "aiaaia—iiaiia" where "ia" (iotated "a") serves as the basis for comparison of the groups and the doubled "a" and "i" as differential features. However, the semantic interpretation of these differentials has changed.

144

The "a" sound was initially connected with the meaning "awakening" and was opposed to "i" which expressed the meaning of "death." Subsequently this opposition was cancelled in the group of words with the meaning "dawn." Now when "dennitsa" (dawn) is opposed as an unreal light to a real "siianiia" (radiance), "i" has become the sense discriminating vowel of the "real light" group (front vowels decisively predominate in this line), while "a" has remained in the group of words characterizing the impossibility of rebirth. It is not by chance that in the group "bagrianaia dennitsa" ("purple dawn"), the basic phonemes of the words "Baiia" and "grobnitsa" ("tomb") are merged. On the other hand, the element "pr," whose antithetical relationship to "gr" has already been discussed and which was initially associated with the meaning "awakening" is transferred to the group consisting of "protekshii" ("bygone"), "prokhlada" ("coolness"), and "porfira" ("porphyry"). The meaning of the front vowels is now determined by the fact that, on the one hand, words of the group of lost plentitude and of the richness of life are connected with them, i.e., "siianiia" ("radiance"), "protekshii" ("bygone"), "dnei" ("days"), "ubezhichshei" ("refuges"), "nezhilis' " ("luxuriated"), "roi" ("swarms") and, on the other hand, words of negation, for example, the phonological isolation of "e" in the chain o—e—o "no ne otdast. . ." ("but will not return. . .").

The poem's overall composition is extremely interesting. The underlying idea of the impossibility of resurrecting lost beauty is already structurally complete at the end of the first quatrain. The poem appears to be already exhausted at the midpoint. Actually, the following four lines are a development of the first stanza's concluding couplet. As can be shown, they do not have independent meaning. However, the rhythmic structure contradicts this idea. Let us examine this structure closely.

1. U–U⌣U–U⌣U–U⌣U
2. U–U⌣U–U⌣U–U⌣
3. U–U⌣U⌣U⌣U–U⌣U
4.   U⌣U–U⌣U⌣
5. U–U⌣U⌣U–U⌣U
6.   U⌣U–U⌣U⌣
7. U–U⌣U⌣U⌣U–U⌣U
8.   U⌣U⌣U⌣U⌣

In the first three lines, the six foot iamb displays stably regulated pyrrhics on the odd feet actually being transformed into a three stressed line. This is a very rare meter in Russian poetry and all the more so in Batyushkov's epoch. The unusualness of this rhythmic inertia, on the one hand, and its careful sustainment, on the other, make it highly palpable. Accordingly the fourth line assumes heightened significance. Isolated both phonologically and metrically, it becomes an antithesis to the preceding three lines: the radiance of the past is opposed to both the "tomb" and "Aurora's rays" of today.

The following stanza sharply alters the metrical structure: that which was a violation of the rhythmic system in the first quatrain becomes a law of composition. The odd lines reproduce the structure of the basic rhythmic inertia while the even ones interrupt it, reproducing the rhythmic scheme of the fourth line. Thus a rhythmic synthesis of the two scenes is created—that of the radiant lost past and of the ruined present. However, no sooner is this new structure established as a norm in the reader's consciousness than a new violation ensues. The poem concludes with a unique (for it) tetratonic line which by this very fact assumes special summational meaning. The rhythmic structure is formulated as a dynamic combination of both the affirmation and violation of the norms. In the process a conflict arises between the rhythmic and the lexico-syntactic structures. The rhythmic structure affirms the summational character of the fourth line in relation to the first three; that of the second quatrain in relation to the first; and, finally, that of the last line, in relation to the second quatrain and to the entire poem. The intonation of a conclusion, a maxim, swells toward the end and triumphs in the last line which, indisputably, must be read slowly and meaningfully as the conclusion of the entire text. The entire rhythmico-syntactic structure attests to this.

Meanwhile the lexico-syntactic level is constructed in just the opposite fashion. The image of the past is given in the following sequence: "the radiance of bygone days," "the refuges of coolness," "where swarms of beauties luxuriated" and "porphyry colonnades" beneath the "blue waters." The concreteness, particularity, and substantiality of the text's nouns increase. At first the generalized image is of "bygone days" although it is supplied with the visually metaphoric "radiance"; next a more concrete scene is indicated—the palaces and their female inhabitants. But both substantive nouns are replaced by paraphrases: the palaces become "refuges of coolness" and their residents, "swarms of beauties." Only in the last two lines do concrete tangible objects appear, the substantiality of which is emphasized by the "materializing" epithets "porphyry" and "blue." Thus there where the maxim might be expected intonationally, a detail is given in the lexicon. Not only does a growth of materiality occur but also a narrowing of the field of vision. If the chain of images were translated into the language of the cinema, then we would see a distinct transition from a long shot, to a medium shot and, finally, to a close-up, i.e., the columns on the bottom of the sea. In this case, as in cinema language, the detail assumes added, transferred significance and is perceived as a trope. The more significant the detail, the more substantial and spatially enlarged it becomes. The porphyry columns and the blue waters while preserving all of the concreteness of individual objects become textual symbols concentrating in themselves an involved complex of ideas—beauties, ruins, the impossibility of recovering that which is lost, and eternity.

146

Our concept of the structure of Batyushkov's poem would be incomplete if we did not indicate one further significant contradiction in the text. We saw that the text's entire structure creates a tragic image of the destruction of beauty and of the impossibility of its resurrection. However, this idea, expressed by the poem's entire construction, contradicts the feeling of eternity and of the indestructability of beauty which arises from the very same text. This feeling arises from the *richness* of the sound organization and is attained exclusively by phonological means. The secret of Batyushkov's instrumentation is in the diversity of phoneme combinations. It was precisely this principle which underlay the text's sound organization in the work of Derzhavin, the most skillful master of sound organization up to Batyushkov. If in the repetition of certain phonemes the phoneme itself is isolated as the meaningful, structurally tangible unit, then in the combination of different phonemes, its elements, the differential features, become structurally meaningful. The phoneme in different combinations becomes not equal to itself. Its real content becomes fluid and many meanings may be assumed. Alongside this in Batyushkov's work combinations of phonemic repetitions and contrasts are widely encountered. Thus in the words "siianiia" ("radiance"), the "s" and the "n" obtain independence and meaning against the background of the two "iia" groups in relationship to which each phoneme reveals the specific nature of its content. As a whole the text creates a feeling of acoustic supersaturation, of a richness that generates a complex conflict with its melancholy content. The general conception of the text's meaning is generated only in the unity of these disparate structures.

A. S. Pushkin

When midst the orgies of bustling life
I was censured by ostracism,
I saw the senseless crowd's
Despised, timid egoism.
Without tears I sorely forsook
The garlands of feasts and the glitter of Athens,
But thy voice was a joy to me,
Magnanimous Citizen!
Even if Fate has destined
Dread persecutions for me anew,
Even if friendship has betrayed me,
As love often betrayed me,
In my banishment I shall forget
The injustice of their insults:
They are paltry—if I shall be
Vindicated by thee, Aristides.

Kogda sred' orgii zhizni shumnoi
Menia postignul ostrakizm,
Uvidel ia tolpy bezumnoi
Prezrennyi, robkii egoizm.
Bez slez ostavil ia s dosadoi
Venki pirov i blesk Afin,
No golos tvoi mne byl otradoi,
Velikodushnyi grazhdanin!
Puskai Sud'ba opredelila
Gonen'ia groznye mne vnov',
Puskai mne druzhba izmenila,
Kak izmeniala mne liubov',
V moiem izgnan'ie pozabudu
Nespravedlivost' ikh obid:
Oni nichtozhny—esli budu
Toboi opravdan, Aristid.

The poetics of this 1822 poem is built on metaphorism. However, the metaphorism here is of a special kind. Identical existential content can, in this type of poetics, be transmitted by various techniques and each of them forms a closed system, i.e., a style. Stylistic unity may be achieved via a system of explicit (expressed) rules such as those characteristic of Classicism or, on the other hand, it may be implicit, i.e., unexpressed. In the latter case, the author and the reader must identify the system directly on the basis of their previous artistic experience and verify that assumption by their feeling of dissonance arising from the introduction of a word not in conformity with that stylistic unity.[91]

The poetics of the eighteenth century canonized the hierarchy of three stylistic systems. By the time of the above Pushkin poem, only a heightened sense of stylistic unity remained. The set of styles was significantly more variegated and did not form a unified system: it revolved around certain genre, ideo-thematic, or personal areas, e.g., "the elegiac style," "the Ossian, Northern style," "the Zhukovsky style," etc.

Within the general semantic field of the Russian lexicon these styles do not form a universal all-embracing system with mutually exclusive layers like that of Lomonosov, but rather a set of local orders wherein a word might enter into several stylistic systems obtaining particular supplementary meanings each time. A special sort of metaphorism arose in this process: the retelling of events within the limits of a particular style was similar to translation into another language, to switching to another system of coding. Thus, in the periphrastic poetics of the eighteenth century "luminary of the day" ("svetilo dnia"), designated the sun, while "to be aflame" or "to be aflame in one's soul," ("pylat' dushoiu") meant "to love." Such encipherment was recognized not only as an appurtenance of Classicism but as a feature of poetry in general, particularly the bardic "Ossian style of poetry" which was perceived as consonant with Romantic contemporaneity. A. Rikhter, the author of the brochure *On Bards, Skalds, and Poets of the Middle Ages (O bardakh, skal'dakh i stikhotvortsakh srednikh vekov)* wrote:

Mythology has formed a new type of poetic language rich in form and vigorous in expression. The sky is called "the skull of the giant Ymer," the rivers—"blood of the valley," the rainbow—"the bridge of the gods," or "the pathway of the sky," and gold—"Freyia's tears."[92]

In this process, insofar as any given stylistic order (if it were to be regarded as "poetic" in opposition to non-belletristic "prose") generally had to be built on semantic shifts or metaphorism, a dual metaphorism arose: this dual metaphorism was within a given style, (i.e., the syntagmatic relationship of the different units of a given system) and was a result of the assignment of the semantic bundles of a given style to corresponding units of everyday reality and to ordinary language units identifiable with it. Thus, ". . .the orgies of bustling life" ("orgii zhizni shumnoi") in the first line of the missive to F. N. Glinka constitutes a metaphor to the extent that the intersection of the meanings of "orgy" and "life" produces a semantic effect. But this metaphor, functioning within the limits of the poetic text, obtains a secondary meaning insofar as it is unambiguously related to the extra-textual situation, i.e., meaning "sojourn in Saint Petersburg."

The presence of a series of local semantic orders within the general language system and the possibility of their utilization as different styles still did not mean, however, that the poetic text had become merely a new type of linguistic expression whose content was the same event retold by means of ordinary language. Telling of his exile in a style that the reader would feel to be "Classical," Pushkin created a special thematic model in which the countenance of the participants, the situation surrounding them, and their feelings were unequivocally predetermined. The very possibility of such a thematic modeling (in this case, his own biography and the character of his friend) already constitutes a certain interpretation. There is a definite freedom in the relationship between the event described and the style selected. (Pushkin might have described his banishment in joking ironic fashion, equating it to the voluntary exile of Childe Harold, etc.) But *the very selection of the style* bore significant belletristic information, especially in comparison to the eighteenth century where it was categorically attached to theme and genre.

It must be emphasized that the stylistic-semantic orders which we are discussing here do not fully coincide with the usual concept of style. Being incorporated into those extensive stylistic layers which most frequently attract the attention of the investigator, they are considerably more local. In the final reckoning it may be a system of relationships established by some one *single* text, if it is sufficiently significant to occupy an independent place in the form of a separate modeling system in the consciousness of the reader or in the cultural model of the epoch. Such local orders can theoretically be divided into semantic and stylistic ones but in the actual cultural functioning of the texts, these two aspects are so closely knit that their separation would be difficult and even useless in studying the text's functioning.

The missive to F. N. Glinka is sustained within the limits of the "Classical" style. Indicating this, as well as the fact that such a style lay within the limits of the "poetic" and "exalted," does not go beyond the most obvious observations. However, the semantico-stylistic construction of "Classicism" could be concretized for the reader of the Pushkin era in several ways. Iu. N. Tynyanov made an extremely cogent observation on this aspect of the text: "The word 'egoism' is, of course, a 'barbarism' in Pushkin's lexicon with a striking prose coloration." Note the following two lines in evidence of the role of such words: ". . . Such is my *organism,/ Please deign to forgive me the needless prosaism.*" (". . .Takov moi organizm,/ Izvol'te mne prostit' nenuzhnyi prozaizm'.") The word "ostracism" ("ostrakizm") which precedes "egoism" is lexically vivid not as a prosaism but as a "Grecism." This is felt not only in the lexical material aspect of the word but also in the formal one: "ism," precisely because of the lexical vividness of its material aspect is recognized as a suffixal "Grecism." The word "ostracism" is the first member in the rhyme "ostracism—egoism" ("ostrakizm—egoizm") where the rhyme element is provided by the formal part of the word. The "Greek" suffix of the word "ostracism" evokes an identical lexical coloration in the suffix of the word "egoism" which re-colors the entire word anew: "egoism" is transformed from a "prosaism" into a "Grecism."[93]

"Grecism" in the sense used by Tynyanov is not equivalent to "Classicism." It represents the "archeological" tendency in reference to Classical culture that was associated with the names of Barthelemy, Winkelmann, Foss, and Gnedich[94] and was based on the opposition between the conventional antiquity of Classicism, the world of Classical realia and of actual ancient everyday life, coarsely primitive, free and heroic. An awareness of the opposition of the conventionalized "antiquity" of Classicism and "Grecism" as two stylistic decisions guided Pushkin when he, working on his missive to Delvig in 1830, replaced the line "We both appeared early on Parnassus. . ."[95] ("My oba rano na Parnase. . .") with "We both appeared early/ At the hippodrome but not at the marketplace"[96] ("Iavilisia my oba rano/ Na ippodrom, a ne na torg. . ."). The associations elicited by the words "Parnassus" and "hippodrome" are, of course, of a fundamentally different nature and activate different types of semantico-stylistic orders. It might be incidentally noted that in their environment even "marketplace" acquires traits of being a "Grecism."

Not everything in the Tynyanov quotation is beyond dispute: outside of the given context "egoism" is scarcely to be viewed as "prosaism." We note in passing that even "organism" represents a prosaism only in the oft-cited Pushkin lines and not as an independent dictionary entity: the explanation of its relationship to nature in terms of the physiological properties of an organism constitutes an inadmissible prosaism. "Egoism" as a term from the philosophical lexicon of the eighteenth century could, in Pushkin's time, enter into a whole series of semantic subsystems insofar as the attitude toward personal interest was one of the fundamental indices in the distribution of the epoch's modeling systems. In Pushkin's creative work we meet the word "egoism" in contexts that direct us to the most diverse systems of semantic orders. Thus, the well-known passage in *Eugene Onegin,* where "hopeless egoism" ("beznadezhnyi egoizm") is rhymed with "doleful Romanticism" ("unylyi romantizm") animates the Romantic system of concepts which, however, is no longer a universal model but a system marking a certain stage in the chain of historically possible systems and one which is to be externally evaluated as transitional and limited.

In Pushkin's publicistic writings we find an identification of egoism with the personal element in the spirit of eighteenth century publicistic writings, e.g., "France, *the focal point of Europe,* is the spokeswoman for public life, a life at once egoistic and popular."[97] However, the word can also be included in another, hedonistic, model that sets egoism beyond moral evaluation. This also goes back to the eighteenth century but to a considerably more private tradition. "Remind that kind, forgetful egoist that there exists a certain A. Pushkin, also an egoist. . ."[98]

In what semantic system is the "egoism" of the missive to Glinka to be set? Its sharply negative appraisal, i.e., "despised, timid," as opposed to "the magnanimous citizen," provides grounds for judgment. Let us, however, make one prefatory semantic reconstruction. The poem is built on a system of paired antitheses which characterize, on the one hand, the negative, egoistic world which banished the poet, and, on the other, the high ideals of civic spirit. Both worlds spatially coincide with ancient Greece. The negative world is geographically specified as Athens. Its antithesis is left without concretization and we shall see that this is not accidental. The omission can easily be reconstructed. It is, of course, Sparta. "The Spartan," the citizen of Sparta, functions in Pushkin's vocabulary of 1822 as a synonym of "the magnanimous citizen," the austere hero. According to I. P. Liprandi's memoirs, Pushkin, having read V. F. Raevsky's "Singer in the Dungeon" ("Pevets v temnitse"), said "No one has hitherto depicted a tyrant so powerfully. . ." and added, sighing, "After such lines we shall not see this Spartan soon again."[99]

The reconstruction of the second member of the opposition permits us to reconstitute that semantic field which the text requires for itself.

Athens (region of luxury, feasts, art and slavery)		Sparta (land of austere civic spirit and heroism)	
egoism	(egoizm)	heroism	(geroizm)
wealth	(bogatstvo)	poverty	(bednost')
effeteness	(iznezhennost')	stoicism	(stoicism)
feasts	(piry)	persecution	(gonenie)
slavery	(rabstvo)	freedom	(svoboda)
paltriness	(nichtozhestvo)	grandeur	(velichie)

This interpretation of Classical heroism constitutes a restricted although very wide-spread system of meanings. It goes back to Mably and, in some measure, Rousseau, and defines the Jacobin treatment and also Schiller's conception. This semantic construct is opposed to another stemming from Helvetius and the French materialists of the eighteenth century and is also widely represented in Pushkin. According to the Helvetian model, happiness, freedom, and civic spirit were synonyms and the citizen was endowed not with features of austere asceticism but with a striving toward repleteness of life and with uniqueness of personality in contrast to the narrowness and monotony of the life of slaves and tyrants. "Ostracism" and "egoism" belong to two different semantic orders which, however, are within the limits of a single more general type.

These semantic orders are not, however, the only "cultural languages" necessary for the decipherment of the text: an entire system of Romantic oppositions is activated in the text in connection with the opposition "I" vs. "the crowd." Although the "civic" semantic model included the unification of tyrants and slaves,[100] identifying slavery with a certain conventionalized geographical area ("Athens," "Rome") and anti-despotic protest with *departure,* flight and voluntary exile (cf., "To Licinius"), the analysed texts also contain features clearly directed toward the activation in the reader's consciousness of the Romantic model. "Tyrant" and "slaves" are not equated but *directly merged* into the single concept of "the crowd." Stylizing the facts of his own autobiography, Pushkin terms his exile "ostracism," i.e., banishment by the will of the people. The reference to betrayals in love and friendship led directly to the cliches of Romantic elegies.

The coincidence of the "civic" and the "Romantic" codes is also manifested in the absence of an antithesis to Athens. Representing revolt as departure, civic poetry of the early nineteenth century invariably outlined a spatial scheme in which both the world of slavery and the opposing region of freedom were concretized. Most frequently, it was the city (Rome, Athens) and the countryside. In the Romantic system the place departed from was not concretized: "poetic flight," the path, movement were opposed to the motionless space of slavery. The point of departure was invariably indicated but not the goal.

Thus the text is projected against various semantic structures. Although it obtains a specific meaning in relation to each structure, all these systems are compatible and on a higher level of organization can be reduced to a single lexico-stylistic structure.

As a result, the intersection of several semantic systems belonging to the culture of that epoch as a whole constitutes the text's ideological individuality. The semantic systems enumerated above (and many others) come to constitute a single stylistic emotional organization which might be defined as "heroic," a particular variety of "classical heroism." On this level, in reference to the Russian civic Romanticism so well described by G. A. Gukovsky,[101] the maximum activeness of words is manifested not in the coupling of their lexical meanings but in that emotional aureole ascribed to them by their cultural context. Words are not of equal meaning in this regard. Some determine the text's emotional countenance by "charging" the entire poetic series; others obtain their emotional tone from their proximity to *the first,* "being infected" with a coloration not characteristic of them in other contexts; members of a third group are in principle incapable of undergoing adaptation and are present in the text only as elements of *another style.*

The unity of the analyzed text is determined by the absence of words of the third type.

Words of the first group possess an unconditional property: they cannot be found (at least in the literary texts of a given epoch) in contexts of any other emotional coloration. Their emotional charge is provided not by that text which they "infect" but outside of it: it is determined by the general cultural context of the epoch. This need is best met by proper names and barbarisms. They can play their role of emotional ferments with all the greater success in that their lexical meaning is ultimately clear to the reader. This is one of the poetic functions of proper names. In the present text, these include "ostracism," "Athens," and "Aristides." It is not by chance that all are in key positions in the composition of the text, i.e., in the rhymes and endings.

Words with civic, heroic meaning, which are understood as specifically "Greek" in connection with the highlighting function of the first group constitute the second set. One must also assign to this category the poem's conventional everyday lexicon such as "garlands," "feasts" and "orgies" which are also possible in other completely non-"Greek" contexts, but which here obtain such meaning owing to their proximity to words of the first group.

Due to the text's poetic structure, words selected from these stylistic categories enter into special relationships, obtaining from their environments and couplings a specific occasional meaning. This sytem of associations forms a special level.

The unity of the emotional-stylistic layer still more sharply reveals the semantic disjunctions that give the entire conceptual level its character of metaphorism, the unification of contrasting meanings. The text of the poem breaks down into two compositional parts with parallel content: each begins with a description of persecutions and exile and is concluded as by a refrain with an appeal for the approval of "the magnanimous citizen":

> But thy voice was a joy to me,
> Magnanimous Citizen.
> * * *
> They are paltry—if I shall be
> Vindicated by thee, Aristides.

Parallelism of content is merely the basis for the isolation of constructional differences. The tri-partite scheme of each of the parts, i.e., 1) Pursuit, 2) My relationship to it, 3) Evaluation, is resolved in each case by special lexico-semantic, grammatical and phonological devices as a result of which the repetition acquires not an absolute, but a structural-relative meaning and thereby creates that thematic movement which we shall discuss subsequently.

On the lexico-semantic level, the world from which the poet is exiled in the first part of the poem is assigned a particular spatial characterization although conceding all the poetic conventionalism of this geography. It is Athens. In this connection, exile, "ostracism" acquires features of spatial locomotion, *wandering.* This is not to deny that the geographic concretization continues to be perceived as imaginary and purely poetic. Its meaning fluctuates between the concrete material image of a scene from classical times and the view that the scene is not at all real but is merely a poetic equivalent of the concept of persecutions in the modern *prosaic* world, and ultimately is a projection against the biographical circumstances of the author's exile from St. Petersburg.

This semantic "glitter" obtains special significance in that the gross meaning of all three interpretations is identical. All three are expressions of approximately the same content. The difference among them lies in the degree of abstraction. This interplay of meanings which permits us to see simultaneously in a single utterance three degrees of generality ranging from the extremely personal to the universal-historic constitutes the semantic richness of the poem.

This concrete material abstractness and transparent poetic concreteness underlies the semantic construction of the first half of the text. The abstract nouns "gaiety," "love," "passions" are replaced by the concrete nouns "orgies" and "garlands" which bear the double imprint of "Grecism" and "materiality." The appearance of action with its fixity of external expression, of being a visible act, is attributed to the relationship of the author to his "persecutions," e.g., "Without tears I sorely forsook/ The garlands of feasts and the glitter of Athens. . ." In the second half of the poem the theme of persecutions is freed from semantic embellishment and appears in a bared, abstract form, e.g., "Even if Fate has destined/ Dread persecutions for me anew. . ." The paraphrases "orgies of life," "garlands of feasts," are replaced by the personifications "Fate," "Friendship," "Love."

This change of the principle of semantic construction is underlined by the fact that in the "refrain" there is an exchange of places: the first part concludes with the abstract, allegorical "Magnanimous Citizen," and the second, with the "multi-planed" Aristides, referring both to the Classical political figure and to the conventional schematic image associated with this name in eighteenth century literature and also to F. Glinka.[102].

Thematic parallelism and the difference between the semantic constructs of the first and second parts becomes obvious on consecutive comparison:

I	1) When midst the orgies of bustling life 2) I was censured by ostracism. . .	exile
II	9) Even if Fate has destined 10) Dread persecutions for me anew. . .	
I	3) I saw the senseless crowd's 4) Despised, timid egoism. . .	betrayals
II	11) Even if friendship has betrayed me, 12) As love often betrayed me. . .	
I	5) Without tears I sorely forsook 6) The garlands of feasts and the glitter of Athens. . .	contempt for persecutors
II	13) In my banishment I shall forget 14) The injustice of their insults. . .	
I	7) But thy voice was a joy to me, 8) Magnanimous Citizen!	benediction of "the Citizens"
II	15) They are paltry—if I shall be 16) Vindicated by Thee, Aristides.	

155

Thematic parallelism isolates the contrast of grammatical structures: the opposition of the temporal (with a causal nuance) "when" ("kogda") and the concessive restrictive "even if" ("puskai"); the opposition of past and future and of reality and conditionality ("if I shall") of action. Such is the general structural field in which the poem's plot *[siuzhet]* is developed.

The text is organized by two constructional centers: "they" and "thou."

"They"	"Thou"
senseless crowd	magnanimous citizen
friendship	Aristides
love	
their insults	

The development of the poetic narrative scheme *[siuzhet]* involves the movement of the "I" from the first center to the second. The poetic "I" initially is found "amidst orgies"; the world of "the senseless crowd" is its world. It is also a festive world, a world of feasts and glitter. But exile and "betrayals" reveal to the "I" the paltriness of this life and the "egoism" of "the crowd," but the voice of the Citizen reveals to the "I" the possibility of another, heroic, mode of existence. The "I" successively stands before us in the guise of a participant at feasts, as a disenchanted exile, and as a disciple striving to approximate its master. One must keep in view that for people of Glinka's type, connected both with the Masonic tradition and with the Decembrist conspiracy, the poetry of voluntary discipleship, of submission to an ideal moral norm incarnate in a Master was familiar and immediate. That the "I" does not merge with the "thou" as its equal in degree of moral perfection but *approaches* it attests Pushkin's deep insight into the essence of how the idea of social education was understood in the circles of the Union of Prosperity.

The flow of the narrative scheme *[siuzhet]* is subtly correlated with the verbal system. A set of lines showing consecutive progression of the verbal meanings forms the central part of the first half of the text. At the beginning, the relationship of the "I" and "the crowd" is one of identity. The "I" is submerged in the life surrounding it. Simultaneously, the words exert their influences upon each other. Those contexts that are not congruent with the preceding "orgies" and the subsequent "bustling" are immediately excluded from the possible contexts of the word "life." Thus, the actual meaning of "life" is sharply narrowed in relation to its potential. The relationship of these two semantic possibilities determines the meaning of the word in the line. For the action "censured," the "I" is not the subject, but the object. But insofar as in its own meaning it is directed only toward the "I" and not toward "the crowd" among which the "I" has been found up to

156

this point, the possibility of a division arises. The poet saw "the egoism of the crowd"; the "I" is converted into the subject, and "the crowd" into the object of the action. This action is so far only the realization of a difference, but the evaluative epithets "despised" and "timid" show the nature of this difference. The concepts of "honor" and "boldness" are respectively opposed to those of "despisedness" and "timidity." This is the basis of the moral opposition of the "I" and "the crowd" while the prefix "u-" of "uvidel" ("saw") emphasizes the moment of the realization of this difference.

A new group of meanings is isolated in the verb pair "saw-forsook": the features of action, severance and spatial movement become more tangible in the second verb by virtue of its contrast with the meaning of the first. The character of the object of the action also changes. That which was presented initially as intoxicatingly attractive and subsequently as repulsive now has a *double* meaning. On the one hand, the description of the forsaken world emphasizes its attractiveness: "orgies" are replaced by "garlands of feasts" and its "bustle" by "glitter." But the adverbial modifiers "without tears" and "sorely" that characterize the action, show this attractiveness to be superficial.

In counterbalance to this chain of active verbs, the phrase "was a joy to me" ("mne byl otradoi") stands out as functionally parallel to the form "befell me" ("menia postignul").[103] Semantically, however, it is opposed to it giving not the initial point of the movement but the limit toward which it strives.

We previously observed that the second half of the poem repeats the thematic movement of the first. However, against the background of this repetition we see a difference that gives the theme [siuzhet] the character of its development: all the participants of the conflict are extremely generalized. "The persecutors" are generalized to the level of Fate; betrayal is represented not by the despised crowd but by higher values—love and friendship. Thus, persecution is exalted into the essence of life rather than being merely an episode from life. And the fact that all this is nothing in the face of Aristide's approval incomparably elevates this image both above the author and above the entire text.

The opposition of the concrete and of the abstract aspect of the first and second parts of the text is most interestingly adduced on the level of the phonological organization. The phonological continuity of the text is of a very high order. The following facts indicate the large number of sound repetitions: the total number of phonemes per line varies from 19 to 25 while the number of different phonemes excluding softness and velarity accordingly varies from 1 to 16. Consequently, repetitions account for more than a third of the phonological constituency of each line. However, this fact in and of itself does not say a great deal. Thus the high degree of repetition of the phoneme /o/ (in all its pronunciational variants) probably should be assigned to the linguistic background phenomena of the poem.

"Puskai mne druzhba izmenila" ("Even if friendship has betrayed me") is the only line in the text without an /o/ and is the sole exception to our statement.

The significance of the consonantal structure is considerably more overt. The same relatively small group of consonants, *z, s, r, t, m, n,* is repeated in many semantically exceedingly diverse words. If the combination "mn" immediately obtains vivid lexical coloration in connection with the word "menia," then the remaining occurrences of "me" (subsequently the dative form "mne" ["to me"] occurs four times and the prepositional form of the possessive pronoun "moem" ["my"] once) acquire a special and sometimes contradictory semantic characterization. This play of meanings lends great depth to the content of the text. Thus, the word "ostrakizm" ("ostracism") is formed from the phonemes of the first line but is opposed to its lexical content in that it designates an attack against the life of the "I" described in that line. Very characteristic is the opposition "zn-zm" in the antonymic pair "zhizn—ostrakizm" ("life—ostracism"). Subsequently the same combination is concatenated in connection with the image of the crowd: "tolpy bezumnoi/ Prezrennyi, robkii egoizm. . ." ("the senseless crowd's/ Despised, timid egoism"). The acoustic antonym of this combination is subtly developed in the following line. The combinations "zn" and "zm" make the voiced quality of the /z/ stand out. The following line which provides a sharp contrast of content to its predecessor is built on the antithetic voiceless sounds: "Bez slez ostavil ia s dosadoi" ("Without tears I sorely forsook") which gives two "z" 's (one of which is devoiced) and four (!) "s" 's (of which one is voiced). The number of "s" 's here is absolutely unique. To show this we adduce the following table:

Line No:	1	2	3	4	5	6	7	8	9	10	11	12	13	14	15	16
No. of "s":	1	2	0	0	4	1	1	0	2	0	1	0	0	2	1	1

In the lines 7 through 9, "z" is not met, but in 10 through 13 it again plays a large role. The lexical group with the meaning persecutions and betrayal is in significant degree organized by this phoneme, e.g., "groznye" ("dread"), "izmenila" ("betrayed"), "izmeniala" ("[often] betrayed") and "izgnan'e" ("banishment").

The constant combination of "z" with "m" and "n" is noteworthy all the more in that in the combinations "mne izmenila" ("betrayed me") and "izmeniala mne" ("[often] betrayed me"), the "mn" is clearly saturated with the meaning of the first person pronoun while the entire lexical meaning of betrayal is focused on the "z." But the "z" in conjunction with the "b" of "pozabudu" ("I shall forget") both lexically and compositionally constitutes an antonym to this entire series. The group "zb" in its opposition to "zm" and "zn" becomes the bearer of this antithesis. What actually happens

158

is that the opposition "stop—fricative" which is generally highly significant in the text's phonological structure is activated. In lines 14-16, the "z" is not encountered again.

The opposition of the first and second halves of the text creates the thematic [siuzhetnoe] movement. Some interesting observations may be made on the lines "Puskai mne druzhba izmenila/ Kak izmeniala mne liubov. . ." ("Even if friendship has betrayed me/ As love often betrayed me. . ."). The transposition of the word order and the opposition of the verb aspects ("izmenila—izmeniala" ["has betrayed—often betrayed"]) creates the basis for a whole series of semantic interpretations: the betrayal of friendship refers to Fate's new "persecutions." This, together with the aspectual difference, permits us to assign disenchantment in love to the epoch of "Athens" which creates the temporal development of the theme. Simultaneously, the fact that the betrayal of love is given as an iterative action in opposition to the one-time betrayal of friendship lends the first personification a much more concrete character than the second. In a text which would seem to be uniform in its degree of abstractness we find gradations whose relationship creates supplementary semantic movement.

Thus, the text's constructional idea becomes the poet's movement toward *a high yet unattained goal* incarnate in the person of the Citizen.

It is characteristic that in 1828 when Pushkin was preparing the text of the poem for publication, the very concept of on-going perfectivization as a drive toward the overcoming of all encumbrances on the path to stoic citizenship evidently seemed too exaltedly jejune. He revised the text, replacing the dynamic conception with a static one.

> Long ago I sorely forsook
> The garlands of feasts and the glitter of Athens,
> Where thy voice was a joy to me,
> Magnanimous Citizen.
> Even if Glory has betrayed me
> As love often betrayed me—
> Even if Fate has destined
> For me dark persecutions anew—
> Like a cool cynic I shall forget
> The injustice of their insults:
> They are paltry—if I shall be
> Vindicated by Thee, Aristides.[104]

> Davno ostavil ia s dosadoi
> Venki pirov i blesk Afin,
> Gde golos tvoi mne byl otradoi,
> Velikodushnyi grazhdanin.
> Puskai mne Slava izmenila
> Kak izmeniala mne liubov'—
> Puskai Sud'ba opredelila
> Mne temnye gonen'ia vnov'—

Kak khladnyi kinik ia zabudu
Nespravedlivost' ikh obid
Oni nichtozhny—esli budu
Toboi opravdan Aristid.[104]

The changes in the text may appear to be insignificant, but they are extremely characteristic in that they lay bare the structural dominant of the early text. The voice of the "magnanimous citizen" is transferred to Athens. Therefore the departure from that city ceases to be understood as the beginning of an approximation to an ideal. Instead of movement, we find a long since completed transition from one state (youthful illusions) to another (disenchantment). The replacement of heroic stoicism by "the cold cynic" is instructive. "Grecisms" flourish but the text's Romantic dynamic is destroyed. The replacement of "Friendship" by "Glory" has the same meaning.[105] The excision of the first four lines plays a different role, however. In addition to their previously discussed semantic function, one must note that the word "When" at the beginning of Pushkin's four-footed iambic line always created a special dynamic rhythmic inertia. Note the following examples: "Kogda vladyka assiriiskii. . ." ("When the Assyrian sovereign. . ."); "Kogda po gradu Konstantina" ("When about Constantine's city") from "Olegov shchit" ("Oleg's shield"); "Kogda k mechtatel'nomu miru. . ." ("When toward a dreamy world. . .") from "To Zhukovskii"; "Kogda poroi vospominan'e" ("When sometimes a memory. . .") and "Kogda tvoi mladye leta. . ." ("When the young years. . .") etc.

The complex interweaving of diverse semantic elements against the background of stylistic unity creates the intense semantic meaning characteristic of Pushkin's text.

A. S. Pushkin

Reveille sounds[106]. . . from my hands
Olden Dante falls,
On my lips the begun line
Not read to the end, has died away.
The spirit afar flies,
Sound accustomed, sound alive,
How often thou resounded
There, where quietly matured
I in remote times.

* * *
* * *

Zoriu b'iut. . . iz ruk moikh
Vetkhii Dante vypadaiet,
Na ustakh nachatyi stikh
Nedochitannyi zatikh.
Dukh daleche uletaiet.
Zvuk privychnyi, zvuk zhivoi,
Skol' ty chasto razdavalsia
Tam gde tikho razvivalsia
Ia davnishneiu poroi.

1829

Pushkin's poems are extremely difficult to analyze by traditional means owing to their "bareness" which is manifested by the absence of thematic [siuzhetnyi] elements, on the one hand, and the usual forms of "images," such as metaphors and epithets, on the other. Feeling the significance and richness of a text's poetic content, the investigator is powerless to explain the mechanism of the poem's effect. Why do these lines, so much resembling ordinary prose, contain so much meaning that non-belletristic language is powerless to convey?

The text is a *narrative* and the difficulties of its analysis are in large measure those of working with narrative material in the face of an insufficiently elaborated linguistic apparatus for the analysis of supra-phrasal structures. It is the theory of cinematography that has amassed the greatest experience in the study of the narrative text, its parsing into segments, and in the analysis of the structure of their correlations. Experience in the analysis of film may prove to be exceedingly useful in working with narrative verbal texts.

Having isolated the large narrative chunks of the text, we can examine the *relationship among them* being governed by principles of montage theory in cinematography. Formulating the essence of montage, Iu. N. Tynyanov wrote: "The visible world is presented on film not as it is but in its semiotic interdependence." And further:

The montage is not an association of frames. It is a differential succession of frames, but frames can be altered precisely because there is some correlation among them.[107]

The analysis of a narrational text into segments can be performed by parsing which is expressed on the plane of expression in the external structure of the text, i.e., in the breakdown into stanzas, chapters, and so on. In the example at hand, we are dealing with a more complex case: the text is parsed on the basis of a division in the plane of content which completely lacks external expression.

The unified narrative-monologue is broken down into two parts in terms of content: the first ends with the line "The spirit afar flies" ("Dukh daleche uletaet") while the second begins with the line "Sound accustomed, sound alive" ("Zvuk privychnyi, zvuk zhivoi"). In terms of content the two portions of the text can be opposed as the description of a real action and an imaginary action, i.e., a recollection.

The division of the text into two correlated parts raises the question of the type of connection between them. Strictly speaking, this connection may remain unexpressed and be reduced to simple colocation analogous to adjunction in phrasal syntax. However, the expressed connection (which in its turn may by analogy with grammatical government and agreement be separated into single or double directed) and the unexpressed connection will be distinguished by the degree (by the strength) of their correlatedness. The unexpressed connection may be called *weak* and the expressed, *strong* correlation.

Strong correlation implies the presence of some common member in both elements of the syntagmatic whole.

Very frequently the co-occurrence rules for units can be reduced to the requirement that certain constituent parts of these units be repeated. Thus, the formal structure of the line is based, in particular, on the repetition of similar sounding syllables as, for example, in the agreement of a noun with an adjective which shares identical features of gender, number, and case; the combinability of phonemes often is expressed in a rule that one and the same meaning of some differential feature must be repeated in adjacent phonemes. The coherence of the text in the paragraph is largely based on the repetition of identical semantic elements in adjacent phrases.[108]

An analogous principle is also observed in film montage: the common detail, visual or aural, parallelism of poses, and identical movement, unite two assembled frames. Thus,

. . .in the film "The Cranes Are Flying" ("Letiat zhuravli") the similarity of movements and the accompanying sounds justify the transition from Mark's feet walking among the crunching glass fragments in the apartment after the bombardment to Boris' feet slogging along in the mud on the road near the front, or in the film "The Outskirts" ("Okraina"), the boot of a dead soldier thrown out of a trench and the boot thrown by the shoemaker into a heap of footwear.[109]

In the above text the sound image "zoriu b'iut" ("reveille sounds") plays a similar role of linkage. This phrase, both compositionally and psychologically, unites both parts of the poem. The semantic community of the first and sixth lines is supported by their phonological parallelism:

(1)   zru———zru
(6)   zvu———zvu

The rhythmic picture is no less expressive: the parallelism of the first and sixth lines is sharply isolated against the background of the text's general structure:

1) ´u–´u–´u–´
2) ´u–´u–u–´u
3) –u–´u–u–´
4) –u–´u–u–´
5) ´u–´u–u–´u
6) ´u–´u–´u–´
7) ´u–´u–u–´u
8) ´u–u–u–´u
9) ´u–´u–u–´

The two parts of the text are opposed in all of their basic structural indices. If "light" syllables characterize the first half, then the second, apart from the concluding line, displays a larger role for the "heavy" syllables. This is evident from a count of the number of letters per line. (For the sake of convenience we shall use the graphic unit.)

Line no.:	1	2	3	4	5	6	7	8	9
No. of letters	17	19	18	17	16	22	22	20	15

This relationship is the result of a concentration of consonants in the syllables of the sixth through the eighth lines. Given the constant number of vowels (7-8), these lines show a notable increase in the number of consonants. However it is not only a matter of quantity. The poem produces an impression of extreme simplicity. To retell the "content" of this poem so that it does not completely lose its charm is impossible. Its "idea" becomes utterly flat in the retelling. But it is precisely this which proves that its simplicity is not unstructured and that outside of the given construct the simplicity of its poeticness and its profound meaning is transformed into the simplicity of a truism.

How is this text constructed?

First of all one must note the text's high degree of sound continuity. Let us examine the consonantal structure of the first five lines. [In the following transcriptions *i* represents the Russian phoneme *j*. DBJ.]

1) zr' b'it zrk mkh
2) v'tkh'i dnt vpdit
3) nstkh nch'ti st'khi
4) n'dch' tni zt' kh
5) dkh dl'ch' l'tit

The dominance of certain phonemes strikes the eye. In the first line—"zr"; in the second, "vtkh," the consonantal basis of the first word "vetkhii" ("olden") and of the second, "dnt" ("Dante"), is synthesized in the third, i.e., the "vdt" of "vypadaiet" ("falls"). In the third line there is a reverse dependency: "nstkh" isolates from itself "nch't" and "st'kh." The fourth line is a phonological variant of the third: *nch'ti/n'dch'tni* and *st'kh/zt'kh*. The fifth line forms two interimposed consonantal chains *d—dl—l* and *x—ch—t—t* wherein the second chain links the line with the support phonemes of the preceding lines.

The repetition of the same phonemes constitutes only a sound skeleton against whose background differences are all the more evident. Sound differences are obtained both through the alternation of the features of softness/hardness—"r" is repeated as "r'," "t" as "t'," "v" as "v',"; voice/voiceless—"st'kh" alternates with "zt'kh"; and also by means of the combination of one consonant with different vowels. Thus a picture of *organized diversity* is obtained.

This feature acquires particular meaning against the background of the organization of the text's last lines. Notwithstanding the fact that the deep rhyme "razdavalsia-razvivalsia" ("resounded-matured") and the repetition of the word "zvuk" ("sound") in the sixth line create a phonological ordering, the second half of the poem as a whole evinces significantly less consonantal reduplication. This is all the more noteworthy in that the number of consonants increases and, consequently, the probability of accidental repetition is higher.

The consonant structures of the second half of the text are built differently: it is not separate sounds that constitute the basis of the repetition but sequences of two adjacent consonants.

6) *zv———zv*
7) *sk———zd*
8) *———zv*
9) *vn———shn—*

It is easily noted that the differential elements of the phoneme under-lie the poem's sound organization rather than the phoneme, as was the case in single repetitions. The opposition of the combinations "zv," "zv"—"sk," "zd" can be reduced to the opposition "fricative—fricative/fricative—plosive." The following features are activated: 1) fricativeness—plosiveness, and 2) the feature of transition. In the first case the combination is uniform and the transition is manifested as a zero feature; in the second, the transition is from the feature to its opposite. Finally, in the opposition "sk—zd," two oppositions are activated: voiced/voiceless and dorso-lingual/fronto-lingual.

The establishment of the principle difference in types of sound organi-zation in the first and second halves of the text does not in and of itself af-ford a basis for substantive conclusions. The higher levels carry the inter-pretation of the phonological structure. Let us examine the grammatical organization of the text.

The verb is one of the most active elements of the poem's grammatical structure. It is not by chance that five of the nine lines end in verbs.

First of all it strikes one that in the first half of the text, the verbs are in the present tense. "Zatikh" ("has died away"), which we subsequently discuss, is an exception. The second half fully incorporates only the form of the past tense. Both halves of the poem (with the exception of "zatikh") utilize only imperfective aspectual forms. Now, let us direct our attention to the verb "zatikh." Formally, it is opposed to the verbs surrounding it. It is, however, worthwhile examining it in context in order to ascertain the character of the similarity.

> the begun line,
> Not read to the end, has died away. . .

> nachatyi stikh
> Nedochitannyi zatikh. . .

In the context "nachatyi—nedochitannyi" ("begun—not read to the end") even this perfective verb assumes the meaning of an incomplete, i.e., im-perfective action. The basic opposition in the verbal meaning of both halves of the text is also revealed at this point, i.e., "actions with marked begin-ning—actions with marked ending." A table of verbal meanings is obtained:

First half of text	Second half of text
Present tense	Past tense
Protracted action	Protracted action
Action with marked beginning	Action with marked ending

An adverbial-prepositional construction is layed over the verbal one. The opposition of the poem's parts as "here," which is unexpressed but clearly implied in the text, and "there," obtains a special meaning in that for "there," spatial features such as "daleche" ("afar") and temporal ones such as "davnishniaia pora" ("remote times") are synonyms. Speaking of the grammatical level, still another peculiarity must be noted: the system of prefixes, i.e., *vy-, na-, nedo-, raz-,* creates a meaning of incompleteness of action, of its duration. Therefore, the first part of the poem is built on the meaning of *transition.* An image of a moving, evolving mental world is created. In this process the durativeness of the action assumes a different meaning in the first and second halves of the poem. In the first half, there is a transition into another, as yet unknown state, i.e., "vypadaet" ("falls out"), "nachatyi" ("begun"), "nedochitannyi" ("not read through") "uletaet" ("fly away"). In the second half, there is a continuing action which is closed in on itself as exemplified by the medial verbs "razdavalsia" ("resounded") and "razvivalsia" ("matured"). This antithesis is created both lexically and grammatically by the opposition of the active voice to the medial.

The phonological and grammatical contrasts obtain substantive interpretation only in relationship to the lexico-semantic level of the text. Thus, for example, the line "Dukh daleche uletaet" ("The spirit flies afar") presents certain phonological sequences:

d——dl——lt
u——aee——ueae.

On the basis of these observations it may be concluded that the text's high degree of phonological continuity overcomes the division of the line into separate units. However these units are words and have independent dictionary meanings. The modeling of the phonological repetitions molds them into a certain unity. But the presumption of correspondence in the line between expression and content forces us to assume that even the meaning of the three words which constitute the line merges into some sort of semantic unity. See Pasternak's poem of this theme "Into a word are welded words" ("V slovo spaiany slova").

If one examines the line as a *word* then certain semantic factors are actualized and others are suppressed. Thus, "dukh" ("spirit") obtains new supplementary meanings. The meanings of lightness of movement directed far away, i.e., flight, are activated in this new word which arises from the unification of the line's lexical units. "Dukh" in the meaning of "soul" or "thought" obtains additional supplementary meaning from its more remote meanings and etymological associations, i.e., "dukh" ("breath") and "dykhanie" ("breathing, odor, air movement"). The combining of "daleche" ("afar") with a verb having a prefix meaning "departure" (*"u-*letaet" "fly *off*") creates the meaning of inclusion "from—to," the combining of the near and the far. Thus arises the meaning of the *unification* of the text's first and second parts and the "here" and the "afar" of reality and of recollection. Insofar as the grammatically meaningful "u-" ("off, away from")

166

phonologically repeats the "u" of "dukh" ("spirit") while the remaining vocalic system of "uletaet" duplicates that of "daleche," the latter word assumes semantic features of the first two. The transposition only deautomatizes the feeling of dissimilarity.

If one similarly examines all the text's lexeme sequences and isolates the basic common hypermeanings for the entire poem, the presence of two extremely general and active meanings becomes evident:

1) Semantic features of *sound.* The basic set of nouns is sonorous. The feature of sonority unites "zaria" ("dawn" or "dusk") and "poeziia" ("poetry"): the poem obtains a sound characterization—both mundane (reading the lines aloud) and generalized (poetry as the art of sound). The rhyme "stikh/zatikh" ("line—died away") is interesting in this regard. The pair "na ustakh—stikh" ("on my lips—line") both semantically and acoustically has already attributed the feature of articulation, of sonorous speech to poetry. "Zatikh" ("to fall silent, die away") yields a new semantic nuance in relationship to this group. According to its dictionary meaning it could be assigned to "tishina" ("silence"), i.e., not to the "zvuk" ("sound") group but to its antonym. However in the text the phoneme "z" is distinctly semanticized in connection with the meaning of sound. It is met in the text predominantly in words of this group: "zoriu" ("reveille"), "zvuk" ("sound"). In this connection "za-tikh" ("fell silent") is perceived as a secondarily bi-radical word which includes in itself the feature of sound and the feature of the silence that supplants it. The meanings of transition, movement, and time are simultaneously activated. This blending of the meaning of "zvuk" ("sound") with the meaning "movement" is especially palpable in the second half of the text.

In the first half of the poem the traditional lyric dyad "I—thou" is absent. The "I" of the text is not even named but only implied and the "thou" is entirely absent. They appear in the second half. "Zvuk" ("sound") functions as the "thou." A relationship of parallelism is established between both centers of the text.

| ty—chasto razdavalsia | thou—often resounded |
| ia—tikho razvivalsia | I   —quietly matured |

It is interesting to note that "tikho razvivalsia" is semantically isomorphic with "zatikh" ("fell silent, died away"): it incorporates the meaning of silence (a "sound" meaning is negatively attributed to "maturing") and "ra-zv-ivalsia" ("matured") is not only joined by rhyme to the resonant "razdavalsia" but also contains the group "zv" which recurs in the poem only in the word "zv-uk" ("sound").

Thus, sound is not merely the link between reality and recollection. Its features are attributed to poetry in the first part of the text and to youth in the second part.

2) The semantic feature of time which also figures here as a synonym of movement, transition, and fluidity. This relates not only to the meaning of the verbs. Almost all of the nouns have some relationship to time also. The following groups may be distinguished: "Vetkhii Dante" ("Olden Dante") is olden times; "davnishniaia pora" ("a remote time") is the time of recollections, and the present is represented by ". . .nachatyi stikh/ Nedochitannyi zatikh" (". . .the begun line,/ Not read to the end, has died away"). The groups are molded into one by the sound of "zaria" ("reveille") which itself is a temporal designation. All this establishes a unity, i.e., a nonce synonym of the meaning of *sound* and of *time.*

These two meanings are, however, directly cancelled out in a single archiseme: "Zvuk privychnyi, zvuk zhivoi. . ." ("Sound accustomed, sound alive. . ."). In its way, this line is the semantic focus of the text. "Zvuk privychnyi" ("Sound accustomed") is united with the concept of time in that the word "privychnyi" ("accustomed") gathers together the phonemes of the entire temporal series: "nachatyi" ("begun"), "nedochitannyi" ("not read through"), "daleche" ("afar"), "chasto" ("often") *(y—ch).* But still more significant is the second part of the line "zvuk zhivoi" ("sound alive"). "Zh" is met in the text only once as part of the combination of "zhv"— "zhivoi" ("alive"). It is the clear correlate of "zv," the basic bearer of the meaning "zvuk" ("sound"). This simultaneously equates "zvuk" and "zhizn' " ("sound" and "life") and places the word "zhivoi" ("alive") in an extremely strong semantic position.

Thus, the unity of the moving and the sonorous world also constitutes its life.

The lexico-semantic level interprets the structures of the lower levels of organization. However, it too is subject to interpretation. In any text, and particularly in a belletristic text, it is interpreted by its extra-textual associations, i.e., by its genre, cultural, daily life and biographical contexts. The meaning of these contexts can be so great that the text itself, as often happens in Romantic poetry, for example, plays the role of an external signal which activates fixed semantic constructs that are present in the consciousness of the reader.

In the text at hand, and this is characterisitc of Pushkin's late lyrics, the contextual level is *not filled in.* The text is consciously constructed so that it allows a certain set of different extra-textual substitutions. Thus the text does not specify whether morning reveille or evening retreat is being sounded. The reader can equally well imagine two scenes: the poet having spent the night reading Dante recalls his youth at the sound of morning reveille, or, having read all day, the poet is distracted by the sound of taps which carries him off into the world of his early recollections. Or yet another possibility: we well know (or, more accurately, we think we know well) Pushkin's biography and confidently interpret the text after having introduced the image of the poet in its first part and his Lycee in the second part.

The better informed reader may introduce, let's say, the Pushkin of 1829; the less well informed—some collective "adult" Pushkin, e.g., the Pushkin of Kiprensky's portrait. But none of this is in the text. And the reader, having become engrossed in the reading of the lines and having in childhood heard reveille or retreat sounded might introduce his own person rather than that of Pushkin into the poem. In Pushkin's time this sound was known to every reader, and even now the signal is familiar to many although it is associated not with the drum but with the bugle. In the final reckoning, it is not obligatory even to hear "reveille or retreat." It is sufficient to recollect any morning or evening sound that evokes memories.

This freedom of the text with regard to extra-textual associations is deliberate, and in it lies the principal difference between Realistic and Romantic reticence. The Romantic fragmentation of a text is created against the background of an unambiguously fixed system; the Realistic system gives a unified, non-fragmented text, but allows its incorporation into various contexts. Contrary to widespread impression, a realistic text always has a greater number of meanings.

All this enables a poem that strikes one by its simplicity and that produces an impression of "disorganization" and "artlessness" to embody in itself a high concentration of meanings.

Pushkin initially intended to write the poem in iambs:

> **Hark! They sound reveille. . .from my hands**
> **My olden Dante falls—**
> **And unread through is the gloomy line**
> **And the heart forgets.**[110]
> • • •
> Chu! zoriu b'iut. . .iz ruk moikh
> Moi vetkhii Dante upadaet—
> I nedochitan mrachnyi stikh
> I serdtse zabyvaet.

The meaning of the conversion of the iambic text into a trochaic one becomes clear if one summarizes Pushkin's trochaic verse of those years. First, we separate out the epigrams which are thematically clearly independent: "Luk zvenit, strela trepeshchet. . ." ("The bow twangs, the arrow quivers. . ."), "Kak satiroi bezymiannyi. . ." ("How by satire anonymous. . ."); also set aside are the ballads "Utoplennik" ("The drowned man"), "Voron k voronu letit. . ." ("Raven to raven flies. . ."), "Zhil na svete rytsar' bednyi. . ." ("There lived in the world a poor knight"); here also go the stylized "Kobylitsa molodaia. . ." ("The young filly. . .") and "Iz Gafiza" ("From Hafiz"), "Ne pleniaisia brannoi slavoi. . ." ("Be not captivated by martial glory"). Having done this, we obtain, within the poetry of the years 1826-1830, an appreciable group of lyric poems, which indisputably constituted some kind of unity in Pushkin's consciousness: "Zimniaia doroga" ("A winter road"), "Ek. N. Ushakovoi" ("To Ek. N. Ushakova") "V otdalenii ot vas"

("Far away from you. . ."), "Dar naprasnyi, dar sluchainyi. . ." ("A gift vain, a gift accidental. . ."), "Predchuvstvie" ("Presentiment") "Snova tuchi nado mnoi. . ." ("Anew the storm clouds above me. . ."), "Rifma, zvuchnaia podruga. . ." ("Rhyme, resounding friend. . ."), "Gorod pyshnyi, gorod bednyi. . ." ("Town magnificent, town poor. . ."), "Strekotun'ia beloboka..." ("Grasshopper whitesided. . ."). The description of all these poems *as a single text* against the background of the iambic tradition would permit a more precise explication of the meaning of the trochee in Pushkin's lyric poetry between the years 1826 and 1830.

Given the thematic diversity of these texts, they possess an essential feature in common: all contain a transition from a real mood to forms of the unreal, the optative, the exhortative, the hypothetical, etc. The replacement of the real by the unreal, that which would be done in cinematography by flux (desire, memory, the transition from the real to the imaginary), is associated with the four-foot trochee in Pushkin's works of these years. The iamb is persistently linked with the indicative and with the modal consistency of the entire text.

Thus time and memory become the organizing ideas of the poem. Time is organized, notwithstanding the grammatical categories of the Russian language, into a chain: the remote past—the past—the present. This unification of time and memory sets forth Pushkin's thoughts on culture and history as the accumulation of spiritual experience and on the respect of the individual for himself, for his own internal richness as the basis of culture—thoughts extremely important for the Pushkin of those years. Note in this context Pushkin's poem "They teach me an important lesson—to respect myself" ("Oni menia nauke glavnoi uchat—chtit' samogo sebia").

The need to link the present with the past becomes the foundation of Pushkin's historicism.

M. Iu. Lermontov

We parted; but thy portrait
I preserve on my breast:
As a pale specter of better years,
It rejoices my soul.

And devoted to new passions
I cannot fall out of love with it:
Thus a temple forsaken is all the same a temple,
An idol overthrown is all the same a god!
* * *
* * *
Rasstalis' my; no tvoi portret
Ia na grudi moei khraniu:
Kak blednyi prizrak luchshikh let,
On dushu raduet moiu.

I novym predanyi strastiam
Ia razliubit' ego ne mog:
Tak khram ostavlennyi vse khram,
Kumir poverzhennyi vse bog!

1837

The semantic structure of the poem is quite distinctive notwithstanding its apparent simplicity. The Romantic system and, more narrowly, the particular relationship of the "I" and the "thou" as the two semantic centers in the lyric poetry of this system forms a backdrop against which the individual originality of the conceptual couplings of Lermontov's text, its ideational belletristic language, is created.

The Romantic conception of man proceeds from the representation of his singularity, his isolation and his divorcement from all earthly ties. The immemorial isolation of the lyric "I" (and equally of the hero of Romanticism's narrative works) function simultaneously both as the reward for exclusiveness, for "non-banality" and also as the curse condemning him to banishment and lack of understanding on the one hand, and malice and egoism on the other.

The thematic tension always lies in the contradiction between attempts to break through to another "I," between the striving for understanding, love, friendship, human contact, and an appeal to posterity and the *impossibility* of such contact inasmuch as it would mean the loss of exclusivity for the "I" i.e., the removal of the basic opposition that organizes a given type of culture. All the aforementioned strivings are, on a certain level, merely variants of some invariant model of contact between the "I" and the world of other people which lies outside.

Of the diverse semantic models generated by this initial presupposition, let us examine only one. The Romantic model of love is that of the impossibility of contact: love always figures as deceit, lack of understanding, and betrayal.

> In friends—deceit, in love—loss of faith
> And poison in all that the heart treasures. . .
>   • • •
> V druz'iakh obman, v liubvi razuvereniia
> I iad vo vsem, chem serdtse dorozhit. . .
>
> —A. Del'vig

That love always figures as *severance* is characteristic of the Russian Romantic tradition from Lermontov to Tsvetaeva. However, another conception was also widely represented in the texts: the impossibility in love of breaking through the lack of understanding created alongside tragic, *real* love, an ideal "love-striving" in which the love object could in no way be endowed with the features of an independent personality. This was not another "I" but a complement to my "I," i.e., an "anti-I." It was endowed with features opposed to those of the "I." The lyric "I" is tragic and fragmented while the object ʻ of its love is harmonious; the "I" is evil and egotistic while "she" is good; "I" is ugly—"she" is beautiful; "I" is a demon—"she" is an angel, a peri, a pure maiden.

Being totally opposed to the "I," this image is, as it were, composed of different letters from the same alphabet as the "I." It is my complement, my ideal other-existence, opposed but connected. It is not a person but the tendency of my movement. Therefore, love here is completely freed from any tinge of man's physical attraction to woman. This explains Lermontov's complete indifference to the fact that in his translation of Heine's poem "Ein Fichtenbaum steht einsam" the opposition of the grammatical genders of the words "pine" and "palm" which is so important to the original is lost. The attempts of Tiutchev and Maikov to preserve this antithesis in their own translations as an opposition of a *cedar* to a palm is of particular interest in this regard.[111]

The ideal of union is possible only *in abstracto,* and therefore real love is always a contradiction between the striving toward the ideal other-existence of "my" spirit, a merging with which would mean a breakthrough beyond the limits of individuality, from a world of fragmented ties into one of universal understanding, and a final earthly embodiment of this ideal in the earthly object of the poet's passion.[112]

Thus arises the Romantic interpretation of the considerably older cultural motif of *substitution:* in loving his beloved, the poet loves something other in her. It is precisely the act of substitution that is functionally active here. That you love not the one you love is the important assertion. The concrete functional elements of the substitution can be altered. It may be the replacement of one woman by another woman, of a real woman by an impossible dream, by the illusions of bygone years, or of the replacement of a woman by her gift or her portrait, etc.

In Russian poetry one of the earliest images of "substitution" in love was Pushkin's poem "Dorida"[113]:

> . . .In her embraces I drank in languor with my soul;
> Swift ecstasies were succeeded by ecstasies,
> Desires suddenly died away and flared anew;
> I melted; but amidst flickering darkness
> Other dear features appeared to me,
> And I was full of secret sorrow,
> And my lips whispered an alien name.
>
> • • •
>
> . . .V ee ob"iatiiakh ia negu pil dushoi;
> Vostorgi bystrye vostorgami smenialis',
> Zhelan'ia gasli vdrug i snova razgoralis';
> Ia taial; no sredi nevernoi temnoty
> Drugie milye mne videlis' cherty,
> I ves' ia polon byl tainstvennoi pechali,
> I imia chuzhdoe usta moi sheptali.

This theme, having gained wide currency in Russian Romantic poetry, was especially significant for Lermontov, for whom real love was very frequently merely a substitute for another, an impossible feeling:

1

> No, it is not thou that I love so ardently,
> Not for me is the shining of thy beauty:
> I love in thee my past suffering
> And my perished youth.

2

> When at times I look on you,
> Penetrating into thy eyes with long gaze:
> I am engaged in a secret conversation,
> But it is not with thee that I speak in my heart.

3

> I speak with a woman of my youthful days;
> In thy features I seek other features;
> In thy lips alive, lips long mute,
> In thy eyes, the fire of extinguished orbs.
>
> • • •
> • • •

1

> Net, ne tebia tak pylko ia liubliu,
> Ne dlia menia krasy tvoei blistan'e:
> Liubliu v tebe ia proshloe stradan'e

173

I molodost' pogibshuiu moiu.

2

Kogda poroi ia na tebia smotriu,
V tvoi glaza vnikaia dolgim vzorom:
Tainstvennym ia zaniat razgovorom,
No ne s toboi ia serdtsem govoriu.

3

Ia govoriu s podrugoi iunykh dnei;
V tvoikh chertakh ishchu cherty drugie;
V ustakh zhivykh usta davno nemye,
V glazakh ogon' ugasnuvshikh ochei.

Substitution is the organizing constructional idea of this text. The basic schema of the typical lyric text is:

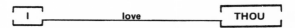

This basic scheme is here subjected to a decided transformation. The poem begins with a denial and the reader, perceiving this as a signal of a violation of the customary lyric model, transforms it in his consciousness into its simplest opposite:

However this schema is disputed by the text. Love is not only not rejected but, on the contrary, is affirmed in a form more intense than in the usual scheme i.e., "so ardently do I love." The negation is transferred to the lyric "thou" and this immediately creates the text's unexpected duality: "thou" is preserved as the object, the second person of the speech text, but is denied as the object of feeling.

Such a "schema of referral" is confirmed by the second line in which the same relationship is preserved with the successive replacement of the "thou" in the first position by "me," and the "I" in the second position by "thy." In the second line there is a phenomenon characteristic of Lermontov. The grammatical meaning is deliberately unclear and can be interpreted either as "It is not you I love" or as "You love not me." The choice is clarified only in regard to the remaining text thus increasing the specific gravity of the occasional meaning.[114]

The following two lines complete the semantic model by entering into a new conflict, this time with concepts already formulated after the

174

reading of the first two lines. The "not thou" that constituted the object of "my" feeling is in a state of logical inclusion in relation to the object of the speech text. It is subsumed in the "thou":

The object of "my" love which is included in the "thou" is characterized by the first person pronoun:

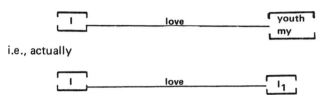

i.e., actually

where "I_1" is "I," but in another, *earlier,* temporal phase. Thus the final mode of the first stanza is:

Transformed into the object of love, the "I_1" is endowed with the features of the past, i.e., "past suffering" and "past youth" are lexically and grammatically isolated against the background of the stanza's present tense verbs. Being identified with "perished youth," the "I_1" in relation to the "I" activates the features of non-existence (already having perished) and, possibly, of certain positive qualities (i.e., spiritual wholeness, freshness of feeling, etc.) which have now been lost.

The second stanza which at first glance does not contain important semantic differences from the first actually does essentially modify its semantic grouping. On the one hand, the verbal cupola which characterizes the relationships of subject and object and which is expressed extremely laconically in the first stanza here branches out into a whole system of actions all of which are conveyed by verbs of contact, as acts of communication, i.e., "smotriu" ("look"), "vnikaia" ("penetrating"), "zaniat razgovorom" ("engaged in conversation"), "govoriu" ("speak").[115] On the other hand, although the indication of the falsity of the contact with the "thou" is retained, mention of the "I_1" disappears from the text. Pairs stand out: "I look—I speak," "with long gaze—engaged in conversation." Here, on one hand, verbs of seeing are equated with verbs of speaking revealing that the problem of communication is central. But, on the other hand, in calling the conversation "secret" Lermontov stresses the special extra-textual character of this communication. This is "a conversation with the heart." A dual scheme is created: an external contact expressed by the "I see" whose object is "thou," and an internal contact manifested in the "secret conver-

175

sation," "the conversation of the heart" whose object cannot be "thou."

The first line of the third stanza provides still another semantic break, forcing us to reject our previously formulated models of the text.

I speak with a woman friend of my youthful days.
•
Ia govoriu s podrugoi iunykh dnei.

The subject and predicate which connect him with the object of communication are as before. On the other hand, its object has drastically changed. Instead of the modification of the "I" (that is, instead of the "I_1"), we have a modification of the "thou," who is, of course, the "woman friend." Subsequently an emphatic parallelism is established: "thy lips—her lips," "thy eyes—her eyes."

The "$thou_1$" is distinguished from the "thou" in the same way as the "I_1" is from the "I." It is remote from it in time, thus constituting the opposition "woman friend of past days—woman friend of present days." But the difference is also explained by the fact that the "I" and the "I_1" are *one and the same "I" in different temporal segments,* whereas the "thou" and the "$thou_1$" are *different* "thou's" *at different times.* It is because of this that one of the "thou's" can be a surrogate for the other. Examine the two antitheses "lips alive—lips mute" and "eyes—the fire of extinguished orbs." In the first case, the "thou" is opposed to the "$thou_1$" as something living to something dead, but in the second case the "thou" stands out both as more poetic ("orbs" not "eyes") and also as more vivid in its own time, i.e., a fire, albeit one already extinguished.

Thus, insofar as the "I_1" and the "$thou_1$" functionally occupy the same place, they are equivalent in an archiseme of a higher level while isolating the following indispensable qualities in the love object: it must be divided into a substitute that constitutes the object of merely external affection and that which is substituted. That which is substituted, being equal to me in my highest essence, constitutes another form-of-being of my "I" in its best and most basic manifestations. It is for this reason that on this level the distribution of grammatical genders between object and subject cannot be semantically meaningful.

The poem which we have just examined was written in 1841, four years after "We parted; but thy portrait. . .". However, the two poems interest us not as a unified consecutively unfolding text but as a certain system in which each of the components appears in relationship to the other on the purely synchronic plane. Therefore we can examine the 1837 text against the background of the 1841 text without posing the question of their actual historical order. The entire sense structure of the poem "We parted; but thy portrait. . ." is built on the semantics of substitution and has its own unique metonymic structure; the major constructional principle is that of the replacement of the whole by a part. Not another woman, but a portrait performs the function of the substitute. We are speaking here of the portrait not of a dead woman but of a forsaken one. (The portrait of a dead loved one which replaces the deceased for the living is in this sense analogous to the substitution in "No, it is not thou. . .") The conflict "I"–"thou"–"substitute" is resolved here quite originally: the "I" and "thou" are immediately equated and reduced to a single "we." But the meaning of the pronoun that *unites* both centers is opposed to the *disjunctive* meaning of the verb, i.e., "We parted. . ." ("Rasstalis' my. . ."). However, the continuation again jolts us with unexpected features: the paired opposition in which the "we" separates proves to be not "I" and "thou," but "my" and "thy" with their meaning of partialness which is revealed against the background of our expectation. They designate not the personalities of the text's two lyric centers but bear a certain partial meaning in relation to them: "thy portrait" ("tvoi portret") and "my breast" ("moia grud' "). But even here the unexpected features are not exhausted: if the "I" and "thou" are in a state of divorcement then their substitutes which appear in the text are united:

> We parted; but thy portrait
> . . . I preserve on my breast.

> Rasstalis' my; no tvoi portret
> . . . na grudi moei khraniu.

In the third and fourth lines the meaning again becomes complex: the portrait is united not with "my breast" but with "my soul." The formal grammatical concept of the partitive is preserved even here (note that the poetic text's grammatical categories obtain a substantive realization), but "my soul" in the full measure of its content designates, of course, not a part of the "I." Thus, a synthesis of the two meanings takes place affirming that the part ("my") and the whole ("I") are synonymic. In consequence, the contradiction between this local semantic structure and the meaning of the two last lines as a whole stands out all the more vividly:

> Like a pale specter of better years,
> It rejoices my soul.

> Kak blednyi prizrak luchshikh let,
> On dushu raduet moiu.

"My soul," a part of the "I," is equated with it but this only emphasizes that *thy* portrait is not an adequate substitute for "thou." It is "a pale specter of better years." We note in passing that the initial substitution was of "thou" by "thy portrait" and subsequently by the pronoun "it." However, the fact that both semantic centers of the lyric poem are expressed by masculine pronouns remains completely unremarked owing to the system of substitutions which serve as the basis of the semantic construction.

A substitution also occurs in the second stanza: the "I" belonging to the world of the whole and the "it" of the world of parts are equated as components of a single level. The parallelism between the second lines of the first and second stanzas is interesting in this regard. The mutual equivalency of these lines is emphasized structurally. Let us adduce the rhythmic scheme of the poem.

(1)	u–́u–́u–́u–́
(2)	u—u–́u–̀u–́
(3)	u–́u–́u–́u–́
(4)	u–́u–́u—u–́
(5)	u–́u–́u—u–́
(6)	u—u–́u–̀u–́
(7)	u–́u–́u—u–̀
(8)	u–́u–́u—u–́

Without pausing to comment on the rhythmic structure of the text as a whole, we shall note only the parallelism of lines 2 and 6 which sharply stand out against the general background. Their syntactic parallelism, their anaphora, is no less evident. But this is precisely what creates the basis for the isolation of their differences which, as a result, acquires a heavy semantic load. In the first stanza the "I" is not set directly in opposition to the portrait but remains on a different plane. In the second stanza, the "on my breast," which assigns the portrait not to the "I" but to its part, is no longer mentioned. The replacement of "I preserve" ("khraniu"), a verb lacking obligatory equality in specifying the relationship between subject and object, by "to fall out of love" ("razliubit" (derived from "liubit' " ["to love"]) as a designation of the feeling of *one person for another* creates a relationship of equality between the pronouns "I" and "it" [ego], but the "it" is equated in capacity and opposed in content to the "thou": having fallen out of love with *thee,* I cannot fall out of love with *it.* The last two lines reinforce this interpretation. The third line completely equates the surrogate and that which is being replaced, i.e., "a temple forsaken is all the same a temple," while the fourth line "An idol overthrown is all the same a god!" creates a certain evaluative and emotional heightening. Against the background of "a temple forsaken is all the same a temple" where the assertion of the preservation of a value is transmitted by the repetition of the same word at the beginning and the end of the line, one might expect a construction of the type "an idol forsaken is all the same an idol." But the replacement of the second "idol" by "god" is not at all the same from the semantic point of

178

view.

The general grouping of the semantic units creates the basic scheme of meaning. However, this semantic skeleton is significantly complicated by the construction of the lower levels. First of all both stanzas can be examined not only paradigmatically as realizations of a unified system of meaning but also syntagmatically as two independent compositional parts of the text. Examined as two parts of a narrative, the stanzas display certain supplementary constructional features. The rhythmic scheme shows us that the first line has already posed not only the basic theme while introducing all three of the text's main components ("we — I," "thou" and "portrait"), but also the rhythmic dominant, i.e., an absolutely correct iambic tetrameter. Repeated in the third line, it comes to be perceived as the organizing norm while deviations become variants of the general pattern.

The first stanza sees in the portrait only an inadequate substitute, "a pale specter of better years"; the second, a more solid attachment than the already forsaken loved one. This semantic difference between the two stanzas requires a compositional link, a common element. The fourth line of the first stanza functions as such a link: semantically contradicting the stanza as a whole, it speaks of affection for the portrait; rhythmically, it manifests a pyrrhic third foot. In the context of the first stanza, both are perceived as extra-systemic variants, but in the second, they both become the norm forming a new systemic inertia.

Structural conflicts can also be found on other levels and particularly on the rhythmico-syntactic level. As a whole, the poem presents a sustained model of syntactic parallelism: each stanza breaks down into two syntagmas while the boundary between the parts is fixed, i.e., the end of the second line. The causal-resultative relationship of the first syntagm to the second is marked in both cases by a colon. Against this background the differing tonality of the concluding lines (expressed by the relationship of the period to the exclamation point) is all the more sharply etched. However, another matter is of still greater interest: the odd and even lines taken in pairs form a structural whole which is brought together in a syntagmatic unity. (Only the two last lines form separate and mutually parallel syntagmas.) This is reflected in a curious constructional peculiarity: the odd lines both graphically and aurally are opposed to the even lines as longer to shorter. In stanzaic structure this alternation of long and short lines usually stems from the different number of feet in the lines or from the alternation of masculine and feminine rhymes or both together. In the poem under analysis, however, both the long and the short lines have an identical number of feet and the entire poem is in masculine rhymes.

The inequality of the lines has another source: if one counts the number of phonemes per line, the following figures are obtained:

| Stanza I | 23 | 20 | 26 | 17 |
| Stanza II | 22 | 19 | 24 | 21 |

The greater length of the odd lines is connected with the fact that heavy syllables of three or more phonemes dominate, while in the even lines, light syllables of one or two phonemes are predominate. This shows the significantly greater consonantism of the odd lines. An analysis of the poem's consonantism shows no striking phoneme repetition. However, if one examines the text's consonants from the point of view of the *structure of their elements,* the following conclusion may be drawn: neither the sounds' point of articulation nor the opposition "voiceless-voiced" or "soft-hard" give a picture of consistent ordering for the text as a whole.

On the other hand, the opposition "plosive—non-plosive" organizes the text in a most striking way. If one counts sonorants and fricatives together (and insofar as it is the plosive that is marked we have a right to do this), we obtain the scheme shown below. Plosives are designated by a plus sign; non-plosives by a minus sign.

Line No.		Total No. of consonants	Plosive consonants
1)	− − + − − − − + − − + − + − +	15	5
2)	− − + − + − − − − − −	11	2
3)	+ + + − + − − + − − − + − +/− − − − +	18	8
4)	− + − − + + − −	8	3
5)	− − − + − + − − − + − − + −	14	4
6)	− − − − + + − − − −	11	2
7)	+ + − − − − + − − − − − − −	16	3
8)	+ − − + − − − − − − − + −	13	3

It is quite obvious that there is a certain ordering in the distribution of plosive and non-plosive consonants. In a poetic context such an ordering inescapably comes to be understood as intentional and becomes a bearer of meaning. The clustering of plosives indisputably facilitates the singling out of certain places in the text. If one replaces the above plus signs with the appropriate words, we obtain: "tvoi portret" ("thy portrait"), "na grudi" ("on my breast"), "blednyi prizrak" ("pale specter"), "predannyi strastiam" ("devoted to passions"), "razliubit' ego" ("to fall out of love with it") and "bog" ("god"). "Portret," as the first cluster, is especially emphasized as is the final "bog" ("god"). It is characteristic that in the first part of the parallel, "vse khram" ("all the same a temple"), there is not a single plosive; against this backdrop the semantic significance of the last word "bog" is particularly emphasized. It is striking that *all* of the isolated words which constitute the text's semantic motif relate to portrait and, on another level, repeat the basic semantic construction of the text. The first stanza stresses that the portrait, while serving as a replacement, is merely a shadow of that which is replaced:

Thy portrait—on [my] breast—pale specter.
Tvoi portret—na grudi—blednyi prizrak.

The second, on the contrary, asserts the higher value of the substitute:

devoted to passions—cannot fall out of love with it.
predannyi strastiam—razliubit' ego ne mog.

The final "god" ("bog") is inevitably perceived as the apotheosis of the portrait. The fourth line of the first stanza "rejoices my soul" functions as a semantic transition to the second stanza.

The opposition of plosive and non-plosive consonants creates a series of other relationships in the text. Thus, the first line (which finds a mirror image in the third) creates a scheme of *transition* from non-plosive to plosive. In this connection, the combination "st" becomes, as it were, the implicit constructional program of one semantic center of the text (the schema "— +"), and "tv," "pr," "gr," "bl" (the schema "+ —"), of the second. Accordingly, two lexical poles are sharply distinguished:

"st" (— +)		"pr and others" (+ —)	
rasstalis	parted	*tvoi portret*	thy portrait
strastiam	to passions	*na grudi*	on [my] breast
ostavlennyi	forsaken	*blednyi prizrak*	pale specter

If we remember that the "passions" of the first group are new feelings reinforcing the separation, then it is evident that this entire column is devoted to the meaning of separation, to the relationship of the "I" and the "thou," and the second column, to the portrait. The structure of the stressed word "portret" ("+ — + — +") is significant.

The text also contains a series of supplementary orderings, e.g., the pair "khram" ("temple")—"khranit" ("to preserve"). These serve to concretize the basic semantic construction.

F. I. Tiutchev

Two Voices

I

Be manly, O friends, fight steadfastly,
Although the battle be unequal, the struggle hopeless!
Above you the luminaries are silent on high,
Beneath you are graves—and silent are they.

Let on lofty Olympus be blissful the gods:
Their immortality is alien to toil and alarm;
Alarm and toil are only for mortal hearts. . .
For them there is no victory, for them there is an end.

II

Be manly, fight, O brave friends,
However cruel be the battle, however stubborn the struggle!
Above you are the soundless starry circles,
Beneath you are mute muffled graves.

Let the Olympians with envious orb
Look on the struggle of austere hearts.
He who falls fighting is conquered only by Fate,
He tears from their hands the victory garland.

. . .
. . .

Dva Golosa

I

Muzhaites', o drugi, borites' prilezhno,
Khot' boi i neraven, bor'ba beznadezhna!
Nad vami svetila molchat v vyshine,
Pod vami mogily—molchat i one.

Pust' v gornem Olimpe blazhenstvuiut bogi:
Bessmert'e ikh chuzhdo truda i trevogi;
Trevoga i trud lish' dlia smertnykh serdets. . .
Dlia nikh net pobedy, dlia nikh est' konets.

II

Muzhaites', borites', o khrabrye drugi,
Kak boi ni zhestok, ni uporna bor'ba!
Nad vami bezmolvnye zvezdnye krugi,
Pod vami nemye, glukhie groba.

Puskai Olimpiitsy zavistlivym okom
Gliadiat na bor'bu nepreklonnykh serdets.

Kto, ratuia, pal, pobezhdennyi lish' Rokom,
Tot vyrval iz ruk ikh pobednyi venets.

The poem is constructed so that its text is distinctly divisible into segments: the two large compositional units of two stanzas each are correlated by their numeration and by their syntactic and semantic parallelism. Their equivalency is also asserted by the title "Two Voices." The poem is built so that each element of the text's "first voice" is, as it were, reflected in a corresponding element of the second. Each "voice" is broken down into stanzas while the lines are divided by a caesura which falls on the sixth and, in individual cases, on the fifth syllable at the hemistich.

Thus, the segmentation of the text is basically provided on the sublexical level by rhythmico-phonological parallelism and, on the supralexical level, by rhythmico-syntactic parallelism. For subsequent analysis it is necessary to ascertain whether we are dealing with the unification of different segments, or with a set of semantic equivalencies, i.e., whether the syntagmatic or the paradigmatic axis dominates. The question is resolved by attending to the lexico-semantic level of organization. In the case at hand we are indisputably dealing with the domination of the paradigmatic axis: both the title and the general composition convincingly demonstrate that the two voices are speaking of *a single thing in different ways,* giving possible interpretations of a single view of the world which is born of their correlation.

The first line "Be manly, o friends, fight steadfastly" ("Muzhaites', o drugi, borites' prilezhno"), is divided into two hemistichs with a pause at the caesura and with rhythmico-intonational parallelism. This construction forces us to view "muzhaites' " ("be manly") and "borites' " ("fight") as synonyms by isolating their common semantic nucleus. However, outside of this context these words are far from always synonymic. "Muzhat'sia" is not obligatorily connected with behavior in battle in the language of Tiutchev's epoch. Belonging to the "elevated" lexicon, this word still vividly preserved that meaning which it had in numerous church texts current in the cultural usage of the time. Thus, Petr Alekseev's dictionary[116] in defining the word "muzhatisia" as "to behave in a manly fashion," gives only a single example: "Stand fast in the faith, quit you like men, be strong," from Paul's Epistle to the Corinthians (16:13).

It is of interest that subsequently in the Epistle we find: "Let all good things be done with charity." It is instructive that in the works of Pushkin, whose language served as a norm for Tiutchev, the imperative of the verb "muzhat'sia" is never used in a military sense: "Muzhaisia, kniaz'!/ V obratnyi put'/ Stupai so spiashcheiu Liudmiloi" ("Be manly, Prince!/ On the return road/ Tread with the sleeping Liudmila") *(Ruslan and Liudmila);* "Muzhaitesia, bezvinnye stradal'tsy" ("Be manly, innocent sufferers") *(Boris Godunov);* "Muzhaites' i vnemlite" ("Be manly and pay heed") ("The Ode 'Freedom' " ["Oda 'Vol'nost' ' "]); "Muzhaisia zh, prezirai obman,/ Stezeiu

183

pravdy bodro sledui" ("Be manly, despise deceit,/ Pursue boldly the foot-path of truth" ("An Imitation of the Koran" ["Podrazhanie Koranu"]). In all these cases, "muzhaisia" means "be firm amidst misfortunes." This may be supplemented by a citation from Lomonosov's "Ode Drawn from Job" ("Oda izbrannaia iz Iova") in a letter from Pushkin to Bestuzhev-Marlinsky: "Muzhaisia—give your answer more quickly, as the god of Job or Lomonosov says."[117] Thus, a common semantic nucleus with the meaning of steadfast in difficult circumstances is isolated in the pair "muzhaites'—borites' " ("be manly—fight"). The differential feature is that of energetic, i.e., military, activity. However, a complication arises: rhythmico-intonational parallelism isolates "muzhaites' " and "borites' " as two nonce synonyms while activating in the first the feature of struggle and in the second that of steadfastness. However, the same construction forces a false parallelism between "O friends" and "steadfastly," although there is no equivalency on the semantic level. "O friends" pertains to the entire line while "steadfastly" ("prilezhno") is a semantic characterization inseparable from "fight" ("borites' "). Thus, "borites' " ("fight") as a synonym for "muzhaites' " ("be manly") and "bor-ites' " ("fight") as part of "borites' prilezhno" ("fight steadfastly") enter into a certain relationship. As is often the case in poetry, the word is not equal to itself.

The semantic relationship that arises here is extremely interesting. We saw that in contrast to "muzhaites' " ("to be manly") the feature of activeness was contrastively isolated in "borites' " ("fight"). But it is this feature that makes impossible the combination of "borites' " with "prilezhno" ("stead-fastly") which implies stubbornness, a passive characteristic. (Ushakov's dictionary defines "prilezhno" as "zealous, diligent".) Additionally "borites' " and "prilezhno" have different meaning in relation to duration of action, as will be especially clear in the second line.

Although the battle be unequal, the struggle—hopeless!

Khot' boi i neraven, bor'ba beznadezhna!

The parallelism "battle—struggle" and "unequal—hopeless" ("boi/ bor'ba" and "neraven/ beznadezhna," respectively) is an obvious one but it neatly emphasizes the semantic distinction. "Battle" possesses the feature of tempo-ral limitation while "struggle" characterizes a state involving the feature of extended duration. (Blok's oxymoron "eternal battle" stresses the meaning of temporal restriction.) Thus, the feature of time inscribed in the opposition "short term—long term" is activated over the common semantic core. "Un-equal" and "hopeless" also being mutually projected against each other reveal the semantic difference. "Unequal battle" is a hard battle, but not necessarily one excluding victory. (Compare, for example, Pushkin's line "And equal was the unequal dispute.") "Hopeless" excludes victory. The feature of hopelessness is so forcefully revealed in the word "hopeless" because the word "unequal" ("neraven") which is semantically very similar but which lacks the meaning of being doomed stands alongside it in a position of equivalency.

Thus, the first line displays the differential semantic elements of steadfastness in an active and passive form. (This should be taken in conjunction with the verbal meaning of the imperative, which stands out sharply against the background of the absence of verbality in the lines devoted to the battlers, and of the indicative mood of the verbs relating to stars, graves and Olympians.) The second line reveals the elements of the hopelessness of both brief and eternal battle. Their unification by the concessive conjunction "although"("khot' ") creates a unique semantic relationship. This link does not have a direct correspondent in mathematical logic although the so-called domination of the first variable most closely approaches it. We are not, however, discussing the truthfulness of the first utternace given any meaning of the second (either true or false), but the truth of the first *notwithstanding* the truth of the second and *notwithstanding* their incompatibility. Although the simultaneous truthfulness of both utterances is excluded by their content they nonetheless both function as true. Truth is presented not as a synthesis of mutually contradictory positions but as their *relationship.*

The third line does not break down syntactically into two parts. It appears as a whole in relation to the preceding lines, although in comparison with the fourth line which is obviously parallel to it and which simultaneously breaks at the hemistich, it is perceived as being composed of two structural halves. The oppositions "Above you—Beneath you" and "luminaries—graves" are simultaneously isolated. The world of the warriors which up to this time has been regarded as spatially single now seems pressed "between a double abyss." The spatial opposition "above and below" which is posed in the antithesis "the *light* of luminaries, the *darkness* of graves" is emphasized in this way. But immediately the common characterization "silent" equates them in common indifference to the "warriors" assigning to the first two lines an auxiliary meaning of solitude, of forsakenness in the boundless world above and below.

The second stanza transfers the action spatially upward, to "lofty Olympus," separating it from the world of warriors. Three lexical groups connected by sound repetitions catch the eye: 1) "blazhenstvuiut" ("be blissful"), "bogi" ("gods"), "bessmert'e" ("immortality"); 2) "trud" ("toil"), "trevoga" ("alarm"); 3) "smertnye" ("mortal"), "serdtsa" ("hearts"). The second group is repeated. Instead of the tripartite division of the world in the first stanza with an equated above and below in their common antithesis to an earthly battle, a bipartite scheme stands out: above (gods) and below (people). The gods are endowed with *immortality (bessmert'e)* and people are designated as "mortal hearts" ("smertnye serdtsa"). "Alarm" and "toil" ("trevoga" and "trud") are repeated to affirm that this is the lot, not of the gods, but of men. (The constant insertion of differences in similarity is attained here by the change of word order.) The apotheosis of the bliss of the gods is crowned by the contrasting opposition of victory (an outcome impossible for men) and death (as the only possibility).

The system of semantic associations which creates the world of the "first voice" is still not the structure of the author's thought, however. It is only one of its constituents. The "second voice" is heard against the background of the "first voice" and in relation to it. The emphatic parallelism of constructions forces us to regard each line in the second part as another variant of the communication already received. Thus, it is not a new communication which is being formulated but a new *attitude* to what has already been said, i.e., a new *point of view*. Antitheses are created which are seen in the text as antonyms although outside it they are not, e.g., "the battle is unequal—the battle is cruel": "the struggle is hopeless—the struggle is stubborn"; and even "friends—brave friends." In the first case the semantic feature of the severity of the battle only for "friends" is replaced by an assertion of reciprocity; in the second, doom is replaced by severity and the characterization of friends as brave makes the result, i.e., death or victory, ambivalent by denying the significance of the opposition itself.[118] The replacement of "luminaries" by "starry circles" expands the universe, while the replacement of "silent graves" by "mute muffled graves" accentuates solitariness. (Silence does not necessarily exclude communication but merely states its absence at a given moment.) Deafness and muteness exclude communication. Not only the spatial opposition "above and below," but also the opposition "cosmos and history," i.e., the history of past generations corresponds to the antithesis "starry circles — graves." But both of these are also deaf and mute for man.

Against this emphasized background of solitude the change of the correlation of men and gods is sharply isolated. The verb "to be blissful" refers to an action enclosed within its subject, i.e., the gods. Instead of the former disjunction of these worlds, there is now a connection although it is unidirectional, i.e., the gods gaze on earth. The replacement of "they are blissful" by "they gave with envious orb" is characteristic. "Alarm" and "toil" have been transformed into "struggle" and "mortal hearts" into "austere" ones.

Two concluding lines crown the second section. The first voice confirms the antithesis "victory or death" by proving the exclusive possibility of the second. The second voice removes this opposition which is basic for the first voice. Instead of "victory or death" we have "victory and death." Instead of "He who *fell* fighting. . .," we find "he tears from their hands the *victory* garland." "Conquered only by Fate" obtains special significance in that it does not have a correspondent in the first part and, consequently, sharply stands out from the general structure of the poem.

Fate enters as a third member into the bipartite world of the last lines of both sections. At this point the possibility arises of establishing a parallel between the first tri-nomial, i.e., cosmos—man—history (luminaries—friends—graves) and the second, i.e., freedom—struggle—causality (gods—people—Fate). Tragic conflict inescapably finds distinct expression in the poem's structure which, on the one hand, constantly prescribes the regularities of the text's construction by means of strict parallelism, and which, on the other hand, wages constant conflict with these regularities, disputing their power with an entire arsenal of transpositions and variations that create a picture of rich diversity against the background of recurrences. Most important is that the poem's ultimate semantic construction is created not by the victory of one of the voices but by their correlation. The voices provide semantic boundaries that accommodate a field of possible interpretations which depend on the declamatory interpretation and a number of other factors falling into the reader's domain. The text does not provide a final interpretation; it only *indicates* the limits of the picture of the world drawn by it.

Thus, the analysis of this poem enables us to pursue the mechanism of the text's polyphonic construction.[119] The meaning is provided not by the words or the text's segments but by the relationship among the points of view. In the case at hand the system of semantic relations is distinguished by its great complexity, each of the voices, as we have seen, gives its own (emotional, ethical, spatial) point of view. Simultaneously both voices adhere to the specifically Classical view that is also reflected in the lexicon and in that coloration of "heroic pessimism" which attaches to the poem. That the conception of tragic heroism which would have been expressed in other terms in Tiutchev's own ethical system is here given by the voice of antiquity which lends itself to emotional translation, creates a supplementary polyphonism between the text and its reader.

F. I. Tiutchev

On the Eve of the Anniversary of August 4, 1864

Now I wander along the highroad
In the quiet light of the dying day.
Wretched am I, stock-still are my feet. . .
My dear friend, dost thou see me?

Ever darker, darker over the earth—
Off has flown the last reflection of the day. . .
Here is that world, where we lived with thee,
Angel mine, dost thou see me?

Tomorrow is the day of prayer and sorrow,
Tomorrow is the commemoration of the fateful day. . .
Angel mine, where e'er souls may hover,
Angel mine, dost thou see me?

Nakanune godovshchiny 4 avgusta 1864 g.

Vot bredu ia vdol' bol'shoi dorogi
V tikhom svete gasnushchego dnia.
Tiazhelo mne, zamiraiut nogi. . .
Drug moi milyi, vidish' li menia?

Vse temnei, temnee nad zemleiu—
Uletel poslednii otblesk dnia. . .
Vot tot mir, gde zhili my s toboiu,
Angel moi, ty vidish' li menia?

Zavtra den' molitvy i pechali,
Zavtra pamiat' rokovogo dnia. . .
Angel moi, gde b dushi ni vitali,
Angel moi, ty vidish' li menia?

This poem, which was written on the eve of the first anniversary of D. A. Deniseva's death occupies an extremely significant place in the "Deniseva cycle." Biographical commentary is an absolute prerequisite to understanding the text and has frequently been given in the Tiutchev literature. Nevertheless, it must be emphasized that if we imagine two readers, one of whom knows nothing of the relationship of the poet and E. A. Deniseva but who perceives the text as a work of art, and a second reader who examines the poem only as a document among others, belletristic, epistolary, diary, etc., all throwing light on an episode from Tiutchev's biography, the second reader, even given the wealth of his information, will, of course, be farther from understanding the meaning of this work. It is appropriate to refer here to Tiuchev himself who wrote ". . .you know how I have always abhorred those pseudo-poetic profanations of internal feeling, the shameful exhibition of one's heartfelt sores. . . my God, my God! For what is there in common between poetry, prose, literature, the whole external world and that. . . terrible inexpressibly unendurable emotion that exists in my soul at this very minute. . ."[120]

Let us examine how Tiutchev's idea is embodied in the text of the poem. Like "Two Voices," the text breaks down clearly into parallel segments. The compositional and semantic parallelism of its three constituent stanzas is evident and constitues the intuitive data of the reader. The repetition of the last line of each stanza, the repetition of the lexical units in analogous positions, and the parallelism of intonation permit examination of the three stanzas as three paradigmatic forms of a single unified semantic construct. If this is so, then the lexicon of these stanzas must form correlated closed cycles. Each text has its own world and its lexicon is a crude but adequate copy of that world. An enumeration of the lexemes of a text is an enumeration of the objects of its poetic world. The montage of the lexemes creates a specifically poetic picture of the world.

Let us attempt to compile a micro-dictionary of the stanzas. Having arranged the words of each stanza in parallel columns we shall make a few observations on the lexicon of the text.

I		II		III	
bredu	(I) wander	angel	angel	angel	angel (2)
bol'shoi	high (great)			b*	—e'e
v	in				
vdol'	along				
videt'	see	videt'	see	videt'	see
				vitat'	hover
vot	here (now)	vot	here		
		vse	ever		
gasnushchii	dying				
		gde	where	gde	where
den'	day	den'	day	den'	day (2)
doroga	road				
drug	friend				
				dusha	soul
		zhit'	live		
		zavtra	tomorrow	zavtra	tomorrow (2)
zamirat'	stop	zemlia	earth		
	stock-still				
				i	and
li	dost?	li	dost?	li	dost?
milyi	dear	mir	world		
moi	mine	moi	mine	moi	mine (2)
				molitva	prayer
		my	we		

189

		nad	over	ni*	ever
nogi	feet	oblesk	reflection		
				pamiat'	commemoration
				pechal'	sorrow
		poslednii	last	rokovoi	fateful
		s	with		
svet	world				
		temnee	darker (2)		
tikhii	quiet				
		tot	that		
		ty	thou (2)	ty	thou
tiazhelo	wretched				
		uletet'	fly off		
ia	I (3)	ia	I	ia	I

* The two Russian words marked with the asterisk *(b, ni)* are conveyed by the single English meaning "ever" (e'er).

A stable group of the recurrent lexicon is isolated wherein a majority of the words are met more than one time so that there is a very high degree of redundancy for such a short list. "I," "thou" (with its nonce synonyms "angel" "my dear friend"), "to see," "day" and "tomorrow" are repeated. Thus the invariant structural schema is isolated: the two semantic centers, the "I" and "thou" and the two possible types of relationship between them, i.e., separation, "Tomorrow is the day of prayer and sorrow" or, meeting, "Dost thou see me?" All the remaining lexicon constitutes the "environment" of these personages and their meeting-separation. However, this general schema is varied in each stanza. First of all, the character of the environment changes. In the first stanza, it is a real, earthly landscape: the highroad and the dying day. A *road,* a part of the earth's surface is found at the center of the scene as space accessible to the vision of the author. The extent of the scene corresponds to a man's ordinary perception. Other nouns such as "earth" and "world" define the spatiality of the second stanza. In the third stanza, spatial indicators disappear entirely, the poetic world has a null spatial characterization; it falls outside of this category. The meaning of the word "day" changes in this connection. The "dying day" in the first stanza is a completely real sunset; in the second stanza, the reflection of the day dims "over the earth" and the play of darkness and light assumes a cosmic character; in the third stanza, "day" is generally devoid of any connection with the opposition "light—darkness" and functions quite abstractly as a synonym of the concepts "date" and "time."

Thus, the spatiality of these poetic worlds is successively broadened, initially including the everyday environment, then cosmic space and, finally, the universe which being *everything* is so expansive that it no longer has spatial features.

The aspect of the personages and their correlation changes with the environment. In the first stanza, the "I" is a small part of earthly space. The terrestrial road (the dual meaning of this image is obvious) seems to him incommensurably huge and exhausting. His movement along the road is characterized by the verb "wander" and the road's vastness for the "me" is conveyed by exhaustion from movement (Wretched am I, stock-still are my feet). Given this spatial structuring, the "my dear friend" to which the "I" addresses himself in the fourth line must be found outside of this expanse. The "dear friend" is evidently above and the question "Dost thou see me?" implies a view from above to below.

The second stanza in generalizing the spatiality of the "earth" and the "world," excludes the speaker from it. The particle "vot" ("here") against the background of the first stanza's exhortative particle "vot" ("now"), which has a completely different meaning, reveals its demonstrative nature by spatially separating the indicator from the indicated. That the world is characterized by the demonstrative pronoun "that" ("tot") and not "this" ("etot") is connected with this fact.[121] The bearing off of the poetic "I" into superterrestrial space accords with the characteristic change of the verbs in the first stanza. The verbs designating concrete actions and states are markedly "earth-bound" and concrete in their meanings: "I wander" and (my feet) "are stock-still" are replaced by the more general verb "to live." Another matter is of still greater interest: the verbs in the first stanza are in the present tense; the second stanza separates the "I" and the "world" in which it lived in the past. This is achieved by the temporal separation of the actor from the action via the use of the past tense, i.e., "Here is that world where we lived. . .' ("Vot tot mir, gde zhili my. . ."). The approximation of the "I" to the "thou" is parallel to the separation of the "I" from the world. The line "Here is that world where we lived *with thee*" ("Vot tot mir, gde zhili my *s toboiu"*) ascribes to the "I" and the "thou" a common *external* point of view in relation to the "world."

The final lines of each stanza have a special structural function. They shatter that construction of the world which the three preceding lines create. As the topic of the first three lines of each stanza they are maximally unimplied and cannot be unified with the preceding stanza into a single structural picture of the world. Thus, the last line of the first stanza owing to the linear movement in it ("I wander along. . . the road") structurally breaks out of that two-valued world whose image is created by the three preceding lines.

The fourth line of the second stanza is also constructed according to this same "explosive" principle. The entire text affirms the spatial unity, the coincidence, of the points of view of the "I" and the "thou" (right up to the construal of the "I" which "lived," i.e., *no longer lives*). It would seem that now there is no hindrance to contact. But the last line destroys

191

the impression of contact in that against the background of the stanza as a whole its interrogatory intonation sounds like a negation. The "I" does not see the "thou" and it is unknown whether or not the "thou" sees the "I."

Yet another peculiarity merits notice. The first stanza in declaring the spatial divorcement between the "I" and the "thou" isolates their identical nature (the "thou" is a friend, a being of one nature with the "I." Only separation hinders them from seeing each other). The second stanza spatially unites the "I" and the "thou," but changes the nature of the "thou": the "thou" has changed from a "friend" to an angel for the "I." In the contrast "friend — angel" one can isolate a second degree of emotional experiencing of the same meaning. (The twice-repeated "angel mine" in the third stanza yields the superlative degree.) The meanings are not at all uniform, however: appeals to the loved one of the type "my friend," "my heart," "angel mine," "goddess" provide certain sense shifts within the limits of general synonymy, especially in a poetic text where there is a tendency toward the semantization of formal elements. "Friend mine" shows a relationship of equality, nearness, of the oneness of the "I" and "thou"; "heart mine" suggests partialness ("thou" is part of "I") and inclusivity (the "thou" is in the "I"). (Compare Pasternak's use of the Shakespearean image "I hide you in the heart of my heart.") "Angel mine" and "goddess" bear in themselves the meaning of the substantial inequality of the "I" and the "thou" and of their spatial distribution, i.e., the "thou" is higher than the "I" in the general model of the world. Thus, the use of "angel mine" instead of "friend mine" introduces a meaning contradictory to the entire stanza of the divorcement between the "I" and the "thou" and makes the doubt which is expressed well-founded.

The third stanza, in responding to the doubtful possibility of meeting on earth and above the earth, breaks with the earth of *any* spatiality and is transferred into non-space. Simultaneously the tense structure changes. In the first stanza, the time of the text is earthly time. In the second, earthly events are in the past and unearthly ones are in the present. In the third stanza, we have earthly events which are *yet to be* realized, e.g., "Tomorrow is the day of prayer and sorrow" and conditional action is introduced which is opposed to the indicative mood of the preceding verbs. This conditional usage has the meaning of universality, e.g., "where e'er souls might hover." (Note also the semantic ladder of the meaning of universality: "to wander" —"to live"— "to hover").

The fourth line again brings the unexpected: a return to the initial verbal form, the present tense indicative, the structural separation of the image in the "hovering" soul from the "I" and, consequently, a return to the initial, earthly experience of the individual. And if the entire last stanza creates the image of a meeting outside of space and time, then the last line presents a hopeless ultimatum to it: the meeting must take place on earth. Thus, a model of the necessity of the impossible is constructed. This model constitutes the semantic basis for the construction of the text. Insofar as each fourth line simultaneously functions as the stanza rhyme and by referring the reader back to the preceding text supports the previously noted sense structures in his memory, there arises before us not a single picture of the world, but three different pictures casting light through each other, as it were. The change of the images of the world (expansion and self-denial) and the movement of the poetic "I" within this world imparts to the text that dynamism, which, in the opinion of investigators, is characteristic of Tiutchev's lyric poetry.[122] However, the results thus far leave much to be said about the poem's content structure. One can also proceed from the level we have just examined to a lower one to describe the rhythmic and phonological structures. These we shall omit for the sake of brevity. One may also turn to higher levels.

The poem can be examined as a communication in some specially organized belletristic language. Until now we have interpreted this language from the data of the text itself. However, such an interpretation remains incomplete. Naturally not all language elements are manifested in a text that is always equally a realization of some and a non-realization of other, potentially possible, structural components. By considering only what is physically present in a given text, we never reveal the cases of *non-usage.* Semantically these are no less active than cases of actual usage.[123]

To understand more fully an author's belletristic language, one must go beyond the limits of the text. To accomplish this would require colossal effort. Tiutchev's text can be examined as a materialization of such abstract systems as "the Russian lyric of the mid-nineteenth century," "Russian philosophical poetry," "the European lyric of the last century" and many others. The building of such functional structures is indisputably a goal of science, but one must concede the considerable extent to which it remains a remote goal. Let us pose a narrower question. We shall take only two types of extra-textual connections: 1) the connection of the text with the tradition of the Russian trochaic pentameter and 2) its relationship to other contemporaneous Tiutchev poems of the "Deniseva cycle." We shall determine what new semantic relationships the text obtains against their background.

I. Tiutchev's poem is written in trochaic pentameter. This meter is comparatively rare in Russian poetry. The author of a special monograph devoted to this question, Kirill Taranovsky, observes that "up to the 40s of the nineteenth century trochaic pentameter is extremely rare in Russian poetry."[124] The author associates its spread with the influence of Lermontov's poetry and convincingly argues this thesis by means of almost exhaustive poetic material. He assigns special significance here to Lermontov's last poem "I go out alone onto the road" ("Vykhozhu odin ia na dorogu") which, according to his assertion, enjoyed exceptionally wide popularity.[125] It was set to music, probably by P. P. Bulakhov, and entered popular circulation as a song, not only in urban but also in peasant settings and still continues to enjoy wide popularity. It evoked not only a whole series of "variations on the theme" in which *the dynamic motif of the road* is opposed to *the static motif of life,* but also a whole series of poetic reflections on life and death, on the immediate contact of the lone individual with indifferent nature.[126]

Enumerating the poetic reflexes of the Lermontov text, K. Taranovsky also mentions the above Tiutchev poem:

> The sole Tiutchev poem written in trochaic pentameter, "On the Eve of the Anniversary of 4 August 1864," i.e., the day of E. A. Deniseva's death, is already a direct variation on the Lermontovian theme.[127]

Thus, both for the author and for the reader, the widely-known Lermontov poem has, by its structure, established a certain private language, a tradition, a certain system of expectation in relation to which Tiutchev's text was perceived.

Let us examine the general structure of the Lermontov poem, allowing ourselves, however, only that degree of detail necessary for our subsequent goals.

I go out alone onto the road

Vykhozhu odin ia na dorogu

Lermontov's poem introduces us to a clear-cut semantic system whose basic opposition is that of the conjunct to the disjunct.[128] Concrete manifestations of this basic opposition include the ability to communicate vs. the inability to make contact, "togetherness vs. solitude," "movement vs. immobility," "fullness vs. diminution" and "life vs. death." The poem's first line already indicates a wide circle of problems. In essence each word is a token of certain ideational structures well-known to the readers of Lermontov's time from their preceding cultural experience. However, a complication arises in that the semantic structures which are activated in the text are mutually exclusive: the first line already sets the reader the task of making the incompatible compatible.

"I go out" and "onto the road" give the idea of movement and of movement directed afar. "Road" and "going" are cultural symbols of general significance. In classical and medieval literature they were already associated with the idea of contact: "going" is either the wanderer who observes the life and customs of people, i.e., contact with the surrounding world, or, the pilgrim seeking salvation and truth, i.e., contact with God. Going along the *road* he advances toward a *goal.* In this he is distinguished from the "wanderer," a person who has entrusted his fate to unknown powers. The association of movement with contact is revealed in Tiutchev's poem "The Wanderer" ("Strannik").[129] The divorce from people means here not the breaking off of contacts but a transition to other, significantly more valuable relationships such as those with nature and with God.

> From domestic hearths an exile,
> He became a guest of beneficent gods!...
>
> Through villages, cities and fields,
> Brightening, spreads the road,—
> To him the whole earth is open,
> He sees all—and glorifies God!...
>
> Domashnikh ochagov izgnannik,
> On gostem stal blagikh bogov!..
>
> Chrez vesi, grady i polia,
> Svetleia, steletsia doroga,—
> Emu otversta vsia zemlia,
> On vidit vse—i slavit boga! ...

Lermontov's "The Prophet" ("Prorok") which is obviously synchronic with "Vykhozhu odin ia na dorogu..." is also built according to this same scheme. The divorcement from people as exemplified in the lines "At me all my near ones/ Were furiously throwing stones" ("V menia ia vse blizhnie moi/ Brosali besheno kamen'ia") is the price for unity with that world which in its lexical characterization almost verbatim coincides with the world of the text which interests us.

> And now in the wilderness I live...
> The testament of the everlasting preserving,
> To me earthly creation is obedient;
>
> And the stars heed me,
> With their rays joyously playing.
>
> I vot v pustyne ia zhivu...
> Zavet predvechnogo khrania,
> Mne tvar' pokorna tam zemnaia;
>
> I zvezdy slushaiut menia,
> Luchami radostno igraia.

We encounter the identical conceptual scheme in A. K. Tolstoy's "Ioann Damaskin" and in a series of other texts. Obviously, it corresponded to a certain model cultural standard which most probably had as its immediate predecessor "Profession de foi du vicaire savoyard" from Rousseau's *Emile*.

However, the image of "going" also suggests another set idea: movement in space is not only a sign of contact but also a sign of internal change. In that very wide circle of texts which created a backdrop for Lermontov, the moving hero is one who is either being regenerated or who is perishing. Insofar as his every step is a change of his internal state, he is always given *in relationship* to the past and to the future. *The road is inseparable from movement in time.* As we shall see, the Lermontov text gives not a model of movement but a schema of its denial. If, as we have already noted, "I go out" ("vykhozhu") and the "road" ("doroga") afford semantic stereotypes of movement, then immediately the emphasized "I alone" contradicts the state of contact associated with movement. This is especially so, as is subsequently explained, inasmuch as solitude in the midst of people is not compensated for by unity with nature, but, on the contrary, serves only as a manifestation of one's total isolation from the entire world.

But another thing is no less essential: the text's lyric "I" is not included in the stream of temporal development. It rejects both the past and the future.

> I no longer expect anything of life,
> And regret the past not at all. . .
>
> Uzh ne zhdu ot zhizni nichego ia,
> I ne zhal' mne proshlogo nichut'. . .

Detachment from the chain of changes sets the hero outside of time. Note the following lines:

> My future is in fog,
> The past full of torments and evil. . .
> Why not later or not earlier
> Did nature create me?
>
> Moe griadushchee v tumane,
> Byloe polno muk i zla. . .
> Zachem ne pozzhe il' ne rane
> Menia priroda sozdala?

This basically resolves the question of development and also eliminates the problem of movement. The Lermontov text introduces what K. Taranovsky calls "the dynamic motif of the road" only in order to reject movement as its hero's mode of existence.[130]

The sound repetition is palindromic:

> alone I on to the road   odin ia na dorogu
> one—must—   odna—nado—

This reinforces the antithesis: the road is not in my world but in my anti-world. A complex semantic relationship of an analogous type arises: just as the kinship of the "I" and the "road" was initially posited and then rejected, so here the approximation of the "I" and the "wilderness" is to be remarked. It is reinforced by the phonological parallelism $o-d-i-n-ia-u-t-y-n-ia$,[131] and by the etymology of the word "pustynia" ("wilderness"—etymologically "an empty place") which suggests a semantic similarity to the concept of solitude. Compare the word "pustynnik" ("wilderness dweller") with the meaning "monk."[132] But "wilderness" is in a state of contact, "it heeds God"; it, like the road, is included in that world from which the "I" is excluded. The world which is open on all sides, i.e., length (the road), width (the wilderness), height (the heavens) is opposed to the "I" which constitutes a special isolated microcosm. The world is permeated with connections. The *shining* road draws together the near and the far. The above is connected with the below: the wilderness *heeds* God and the earth is flooded with "a blue radiance." The vastness of space is no hindrance to contact for "star speaks with star." The *expanded* world is interconnected and the *compressed* world is torn free of its connections. The cosmic world is endowed with the features of life: it "sleeps," "heeds," and "speaks." As for the "I," its relationship to the opposition "life—death" is extremely complex.[133]

The opposition "solemn and wonderful"—"painful and burdensome" creates a contrast between a world unified and replete, and by virtue of this repletion without external goals, sojourning but not moving,[134] and a world deficient and seeking a goal outside of itself. From this arises the idea, strange for Lermontov, of life as a *motionless* plenitude characterized by *internal peace*. This is unusual because of Lermontov's constant identification of life with struggle, with striving and with movement. The "I" of the poem tends from external movement to internal. Note the "I go out" ("vykhozhu") at the beginning of the poem versus the "I seek" ("Ia ishchu") in the third stanza where movement has immobility as its goal:

> I seek for freedom and peace!
> I would like to find oblivion and to fall asleep!
>
> Ia ishchu—svobody i pokoia!
> Ia b khotel—zabyt'sia i zasnut'!

The "I," leading a life resembling death, dreams of a death resembling life. This will be a state having neither past nor future, devoid of memory ("to find oblivion" ["zabyt'sia"]) and excised from the chain of events of earthly life. "Freedom and peace" ("Svoboda i pokoi") is a paraphrase of Pushkin's "peace and liberty" ("pokoi i volia"). This will also be a death ("to fall asleep forever" ["naveki. . .zasnut' "]), but one which does not destroy the plenitude of inner life ("in my breast might slumber the forces of life" ["v grudi dremali zhizni sily"]) or of inner movement ("my breast would quietly rise in breathing" ["dysha, vzdymalas' tikho grud' "]). It is precisely this abundance of inner life striving toward itself that will convert the "I" in a simulacrum of the world rather than into a body alien to it and that will endow it with the prime attribute of nature, i.e., the ability to establish contact. It is here that the author introduces the voice singing of love (the "I" "heeds" it like the wilderness heeds God)[135] and the symbol of immortality, i.e., the oak which unites the microcosm—the grave—with the universe. Thus, the poem initially states the incompatibility of the "I" and of the living world, then the obliteration of the "I" and an ideal resurrection in a new form of inner plenitude and organicity resembling the world and therefore capable of entering into contact with it.

In having constructed a model for surmounting tragic alienation, Lermontov has created a text that is sharply differentiated from that picture of the world which arises from the majority of his poems. If one regards "I go out alone onto the road" ("Vykhozhu odin ia na dorogu") as that cultural background against which Tiutchev's text as projected, certain features of Tiutchev's poem become clear.

First, one must note the marked irreducibility of the poem to a harmonic whole: it ends with an unanswerable question. Made from diverse semantic structures, it affirms the impossibility of bringing them into unity. Precisely in the light of this tradition, it is clear that Tiutchev's world is not that of Romantic divorcement *[razorvannost']* built on the conjunction of contrasts of a single plane[136] but is rather of entities that cannot be combined within a single rational system. In this, Tiutchev's world is closer to that of twentieth century poetics. Moreover the poet does not propose any models that would "negate" this impossibility. Let us cite only two examples:

I

The evening is hazy and foul. . .
Hark, is it not the lark's voice?. .
Is it thou, beautiful guest of the morning,
At this late, dead hour?
Supple, sportive, clear-toned,
At this dead, late hour,
Like the terrible laugh of madness,
It shakes my whole soul!

Vecher mglistyi i nenastyi. . .
Chu, ne zhavoronka l' glas?. .
Ty li, utra gost' prekrasnyi,
V etot pozdnii, mertvyi chas?
Gibkii, rezvyi, zvuchno-iasnyi,
V etot mertvyi, pozdnii chas,
Kak bezum'ia smekh uzhasnyi,
On vsiu dushu mne potrias!

II

Half-asleep I hear—and can not
Imagine such a combination,
And I hear the whistle of runners on snow
And the twittering of a spring swallow.

198

Vprosonkakh slyshu ia—i ne mogu
Voobrazit' takoe sochetan'e,
A slyshu svist poloz'ev na snegu
I lastochki vesennei shchebetan'e.

The first poem was written in 1836 and the second in 1871, but in neither does Tuitchev explain how such a combination may be conceived. He simply contrasts the incompatible.

The almost full coincidence of the first stanzas of Tiutchev's and Lermontov's poems establishes, as it were, their communality of semantic structures and immediately affirms that the one text must be perceived in relation to the second.

Lermontov

I go out alone onto the road;
Through the mist the stony way glistens;
The night is still, the wilderness heeds God,
And star speaks with star.
. . .
Vykhozhu odin ia na dorogu;
Skvoz' tuman kremnistyi put' blestit;
Noch' tikha, pustynia vnemlet bogu,
I zvezda s zvezdoiu govorit.

Tiutchev

Now I wander along the highroad
In the quiet light of the dying day.
Wretched am I, stock-still are my feet. . .
My dear friend, dost thou see me?
. .
Vot bredu ia vdol' bolshoi dorogi
V tikhom svete gasnushchego dnia.
Tiazhelo mne, zamiraiut nogi. . .
Drug moi milyi, vidish' li menia?

If one compares "I wander" ("bredu") against the background of "I go out" ("vykhozhu") or "the highroad" ("bol'shaia doroga") against "the road," and also "along" ("vdol' ") against "onto" ("na"), the latter appear much more earthbound, substantive, and real. This intensification of "reality," taken in conjunction with the clear indication of the advanced age of the "I" as opposed to its non-indication in the Lermontov poem, is also reflected in the replacement of "The night is still" ("Noch' tikha") for "Wretched am I" ("Tiazhelo mne").

Insofar as the general appearance of the world surrounding the "I" is described in similar features, i.e.,

Through the fog the stony way glistens
. . .Skvoz' tuman kremnistyi put' blestit. . .

versus

> ...In the quiet light of the dying day,
> ...V tikhom svete gasnushchego dnia...

it may be assumed that the prime obstacle to a meeting is the material earthly guise of the "I." But then, following the Lermontov scheme the tragic element of the first stanza must be gradually removed: contact between the poet and the person of his beloved who has merged with the cosmos will become possible when he surmounts his deathly solitude and, having become imbued with shared life, acquires the ability to hear her voice.

The second stanza of the Tiutchev poem corresponds to the second and third stanzas of the Lermontov text but provides a completely different line of thought: severance from the earthly "I" does not bring harmony. As a result we have the tragic final stanza instead of the two reconciling ones at the end of the Lermontov poem.[137]

The Tiutchev poem is built as a rejection of the hope of harmony. Therefore the thrice-repeated concluding question intensifies doubt. The questions are constructed so that they demand a compression of intonation which, given the coincidence of their common linguistic meaning, becomes a fundamental sense-discriminating element. If the replacement in the second stanza of "friend" by "angel," apart from the previously noted semantic difference, bears with it a heightening of emotion, then the final repetition involves not only an emphatic doubling but also a deliberate violation of logical syntax to the point of consciously eclipsing the rational meaning of the last two lines. It might be noted in support of the above that "angel" is a point on a scale from "friend," with its completely real semantic content, toward an interjection. As we have already remarked, repetition of the type "far, far away" ("daleko-daleko") is perceived as an intensification of the degree of quality.

Against the background of the Lermontov text still another differentia is evident in the Tiutchev poem. One that is all the more remarkable because Lermontov and Tiutchev, as it were, change places in that the above poems, taken in isolation from their other works generally, fail to coincide with the "standard" view of the artistic position of these poets. The very concept of contact in the contrasted texts is fundamentally different. In Lermontov, it is contact with nature which is more nearly a "Tiutchevian theme" and in Tiutchev's poem, it is a matter of contact with a human being, a question more typical of Lermontov. In Lermontov's case, merger with nature replaces the impossible contact with another person while in Tiutchev's work, earthly human closeness is irreplaceable.[138]

II. Other aspects of the poem are revealed by examining it in the context of the whole of Tiutchev's lyric poetry. While not pretending to elaborate even the most approximate model of Tiutchev's lyric work, we shall indicate those aspects important for understanding the text at hand. Granted the diversity of Tiutchev's conception of the world, it does include several reasonably stable constructs. Thus we have the very important oppositions:

banal vulgarity	(poshlost')	poetry	(poeziia)
the crowd	(tolpa)	I	(ia)
day	(den')	night	(noch')
noise	(shum)	silence	(tishina, molchanie)
human society	(chelovecheskoe obshchestvo)	nature	(priroda)

These are organized on the axis "below—above" so that the path from "banal vulgarity" to "poetry," from "the crowd" to the "I," etc., is modeled as an ascending path.

It is characteristic that in a number of texts the movement is from below to above, i.e., a shift from day to night.[139] Thus in the poem under study darkness becomes more intense as the author's point of view shifts upward.

In the poem "My soul would like to be a star. . ." ("Dusha khotela b byt' zvezdoi. . ."), it is the earthly day that makes the night reigning on high invisible. In the poem "Finished is the feast, fallen silent the choirs. . ." ("Konchen pir, umolkli khory. . .") not only "the bright hall" and "the dimly glowing lighting" but also "noise" are found below while night and silence are above.

Wherever a similar spatial scheme occurs, the narrative development is constructed as *a movement from below to above* or tending in this direction. The impossibility of ascension is perceived as the tragic power of vulgar banality over the poet.

> O, how then from *the earthly sphere*
> In soul toward the immortal *we shall fly*. . .
> . . .As if like ether's stream
> *Through our veins the sky flowed.*
> But, ah, not for us was it predestined;
> We soon tire in the sky,—
> And it is not given to paltry dust
> To breathe the divine fire.
> . . .Anew *we fall*. . .
>   —"Awakening"

> O, kak togda s *zemnogo kruga*
> Dushoi k bessmertnomu *letim*. . .
> . . .Kak by efirnoiu strueiu
> *Po zhilam nebo proteklo.*
> No, akh ne nam ego sudili;
> My v nebe skoro ustaem,—
> I ne dano nichtozhnoi pyli
> Dyshat' bozhestvennym ognem.
> . . .Vnov' upadaem. . .
>   —"Probuzhdenie"

Tiutchev's basic scheme is as follows:

  A. Landscape. Insofar as it functions here as "below" and is, conse-
     quently, isomorphic (similar) not to nature but to the crowd,
     motleyness, importunity, noise, and brightness are all stressed
     in it.
  B. Flight (a bird).
  C. The "I" (the impossibility of flight). The "I" strives toward "B"
     but sojourns in "A."

Let us cite two texts the second of which belongs to the "Deniseva
cycle" and chronologically immediately precedes "On the Eve of. . . August
4, 1864," while the first was written in 1836. The chronological interval attests to the stability of the above spatial model in Tiutchev's lyric work.

I

From the glade the kite rises,
High toward the sky he soars;
Ever higher, farther he spirals,
And now he has gone beyond the horizon.

Mother Nature gave him
Two mighty, two living wings—
While I am here covered with sweat and dust,
I, Tsar of the earth, am rooted to the earth!..

S poliany korshun podnialsia,
Vysoko k nebu on vzyilsia;
Vse vyshe, dale v'etsia on,
I vot ushel za nebosklon,

Priroda-mat' emu dala
Dva moshchnykh, dva zhivykh kryla—
A ia zdes' v pote i v pyli,
Ia, tsar' zemli, priros k zemli! . .

II

O, this South! O this Nice! ..
O, how their brilliance troubles me!..
Life, like a wounded bird,
Wishes to rise—and can not. ..

No, neither flight, nor sweep,
The broken wings hang,
And it, having pressed itself to the dust,
Trembles from pain and impotence...

O, etot yug! o, eta Nitstsa! ..
O, kak ikh blesk menia trevozhit! ..

202

Zhizn', kak podstrelennaia ptitsa,
Podniat'sia khochet—i ne mozhet. . .

Net ni poleta, ni razmakhu,
Visiat polomannye kryl'ia,
I vsia ona, prizhavshis' k prakhu,
Drozhit ot boli i bessil'ia. . .

Ignoring much of interest in these poems (particularly that unique quality created by the grammatico-phonological level), and restricting our attention to the matter at hand we cannot but note that "up" and "distant" function as synonyms in the lyric movement that organizes both texts, e.g., "Ever higher, farther he spirals. . ." ("Vse vyshe, dale v'etsia on. . .") and "No, neither flight nor sweep. . ." ("Net ni poleta, ni razmakhu. . ."). The movement from below to above is from an area of restricted boundaries into a sphere of their expansion.

"South," "Nice," and the "brilliance" are synonyms of "the earth"; the glade—of sweat and dust. Tiutchev's persistent location of the more highly valued "higher" in lyrical space is connected with a scheme of this sort. Banal vulgarity's aggression occurs in one space; victory over it—in another.

In "To what prayest thou with love. . ." ("Chemu molilas' ty s liubov'iu. . .") the struggle of the "she" and "the crowd" is tragically crowned by the victory of the latter in that the two combatant forces are located on the level of the earth, of the "crowd's idle chatter" ("liudskoe sueslovie"), i.e., "The crowd entered, the crowd broke in. . ." ("Tolpa voshla, tolpa vlomilas'. . ."). Victory is possible only in "flight";

Ah, if the living wings[140]
Of the soul, *soaring above the crowd,*
Might have saved her from the violence
Of the crowd's immortal banality!

Akh, esli by zhivye kryl'ia
Dushi, *pariashchei nad tolpoi,*
Ee spasali ot nasil'ia
Bessmertnoi poshlosti liudskoi!

The poem "She was sitting on the floor" ("Ona sidela na polu") is most interesting in this regard. Initially, the level of the text's heroine is given as below that of "the text's horizon," i.e., "She *was sitting on the floor*" ("Ona *sidela na polu*"). Then the heroine's viewpoint is borne upward, above her physical point of view: she looks at everything that is taking place and *at her self from outside and from above.*

As souls look from on high
At the body discarded by them. . .

> Kak dushi smotriat s vysoty
> Na imi broshennoe telo. . .

After this the viewpoint of the author (the text's horizon), who was initially perceived as *standing* before the *heroine who is sitting on the floor, drops downward,* emphasizing the measureless elevation of the "her" over the "I."

> I *stood* silently on the side
> And was ready to fall to my knees.
> • • •
> *Stoial* ia molcha v storone
> I past' gotov byl na koleni.

Finally, his beloved moves into the supraearthly world of shadows, leaving the poet in earthly space. (The poem was written during Deniseva's lifetime.)

Another spatial model which is also characteristic of Tiutchev's work is no less important for our text. Here we encounter expansion rather than displacement within the spatial construct of the world. The point of view of the text, the ideal, desired position of the lyric "I" is static, but the world around it expands limitlessly.

The opposition "top—bottom" is replaced by another one, i.e., "limited—limitless" wherein the "limited" world is spatially in the middle. It is the earthly world surrounded on all sides by an overturned abyss.

> The heavenly vault burning with starry glory
> Secretly gazes from the depths,—
> And we swim, by a blazing abyss
> On all sides surrounded.
> • • •
> Nebesnyi svod, goriashchii slavoi zvezdnoi
> Tainstvenno gliadit iz glubiny,—
> I my plyvem, pylaiushcheiu bezdnoi
> So vsekh storon okruzheny.

The typical Tiutchevian scene of night on the sea with a double reflection is also connected with this:

> And again a star dives
> Into the light swell of the Neva's waves.
> • • •
> I opiat' zvezda nyriaet
> V legkoi zybi nevskikh voln.

Thus, if the hero's worth in the first model is fixed by his proximity to the "above," then in the second we are dealing with the limits of the surrounding world. The hierarchy of expanding spaces from the most compact to the most limitless corresponds to the hierarchy of the heroes. The poem "The Swan" ("Lebed' ") is characteristic in that both of the characterized spatial models are consciously contrasted. The Eagle, the creature of the "above," is opposed to the Swan, the hero of an infinitely opened world.

The Swan

Let the eagle beyond the clouds
Meet the lightening's flight
And with motionless eyes
Into himself imbibe the sun's light.

But there is no lot more enviable,
O pure swan, than thine.
And with a pure element, like thou thyself,
Hath divinity clothed thee.

She, between the dual abyss,
Cherishes thy all-seeing dream—
And by the full glory of the starry firmament
Thou art from all sides surrounded.
. . .
. . .
Lebed'

Puskai orel za oblakami
Vstrechaet molnii polet
I nepodvizhnymi ochami
V sebia vpivaet solntsa svet.

No net zavidnee udela,
O lebed' chistyi, tvoego.
I chistoi, kak ty sam, odelo
Tebia stikhiei bozhestvo.

Ona, mezhdu dvoinoiu bezdnoi,
Leleet tvoi vsezriashchii son—
I polnoi slavoi tverdi zvezdnoi
Ty otovsiudu okruzhen.

It is instructive that in such a contrast the "eagle" is coincident with day and the "swan" with night. The feeling of contact as a blending or dissolving of the lesser into the greater arises in connection with the idea that heroes of a single level are co-occurrent in a single type of space.

How she instilled her whole soul,
How she transfused herself into me.
. . .
Kak dushu vsiu svoiu ona vdokhnula,
Kak vsiu sebia perelila v menia.

As we see, both spatial models are represented in the text:

I (below)————————————Thou (above)
I and thou (limitless space)————the earthly world (restricted space)

But both models which are serially affirmed by the text are neutralized by its interrogative ending which is perceived as a craving for a "simple," non-theoretical, real and ordinary meeting in earthly space. Both of these spaces are "banal" and "restricted" from the standpoint of both models.

Thus, the text speaks in the language of the systems of the Tiutchevian lyric but realizes an "anti-system" which destroys this language. It bares a double tragedy: the failure of "poorly constructed" theories in the face of "simple life," and the poor structuring of this "simple life" which excludes happiness.

N. A. Nekrasov

Last Elegies

I

My soul is gloomy, my dreams despondent,
The future is silhouetted darkly,
Habits, formerly sweet, are repellent,
And bitter is the smoke of my cigar. It is decided!
Thou art not bitter, beloved friend
Of nocturnal labors and solitary thoughts—
My lot is bitter. The ailment of thirst
I have not evaded. My mind is still lucid,
Still in stupid and obedient hope
It does not seek craven joy,
I see all. . . But early death approaches,
And life is tormentingly grievous. I am young,
Now there are fewer trivial worries,
And more rarely does hunger knock on my door:
Now I might do something:
But it is too late!. . I am like a reckless traveler,
Having set out on a far long journey,
Not having measured my strength against the hard road
Around all is strange, there is nowhere to rest,
He stands, pale, midst the highroad.
No one took pity on him, nor gave him a ride:
A troika rushed by, a wagon train creaked on—
Everything past, past! . . His legs buckled,
And he fell . . . Then around him in a crowd
People will gather—troubled, despondent,
They honor him with a needless tear
And willingly give him a ride—to the grave. . .

II

I rose early, not long were my preparations,
I went out to the road when the dawn had barely broken:
Walked I over abysses and mountains,
Swam I across rivers and seas;
Struggled I, alone and unarmed,
With a throng of enemies; I did not lose heart in disaster
And did not grumble. But I came to need rest—
And I did not find shelter anywhere!
Often, having fallen face down on the damp ground,
In despair, hungry, I repeated:
"Is it in my strength, O Lord! to undertake this labor?"
And I went anew, having gathered the remnant of my strength.
Ever nearer and more familiar is the road,

And past is all that is difficult on the road!
The cupolas of the churches shine ahead—
It is not far to the paternal threshold!
Derisively bending and groaning
Under weight of his holey bag,
Hungry labor, my sly fellow-traveler
Goes away: now we have a smooth road,
Forward, forward! But my strength has betrayed me—
I come to on the edge of the grave. . .

There is no one to pray to and nothing to pray!
Morning will come—the sun will light
My soulless corpse: all will have been decided!
And in the whole world only one heart—
And that but scarcely—will notice my death. . .

III

Magnificent in flood is the proud river,
Boats ply, swaying majestically,
Tarred are their black sides,
Above them the flag, on the flag an inscription: Glory!
Crowds of people run along the bank,
Having fixed their idle attention on them,
And, waving their hats, the sailors send
To their native shore a farewell,—
And in an instant it is taken up by the crowd,
And in friendly fashion the entire shore answers it.
But here, if overturned by a wave,
A bark perishes—who will even notice it?
And if a wild groan resounds
On the shore—unexpected, solitary,
It will not be heard above the shouts
And will not reach the bottom of the deep river. . .
Friend of my dark lot!
Forsake more quickly the shore, illuminated
By the hot glitter of the sun's rays
And by the motley crowd animated,—
The brighter the sun, the merrier the people,
The more pain for a crushed heart!

. . .
. . .

Poslednie Elegii

I

Dusha mrachna, mechty moi unyly,
Griadushchee risuetsia temno,
Privychki, prezhda milye, postyly,
I gorek dym sigary. Resheno!
Ne ty gor'ka, liubimaia podruga
Nochnykh trudov i odinokikh dum—
Moi zhrebii gorek. Zhadnogo neduga
Ia ne izbeg. Eshche moi svetel um,

208

Eshche v nadezhde glupoi i poslushnoi,
Ne ishchet on otrady malodushnoi,
Ia vizhu vse. . . A rano smert' idet,
I zhizni zhal' muchitel'no. Ia molod,
Teper' pomen'she melochnykh zabot,
I rezhe v dver' moiu stuchitsia golod:
Teper' by mog ia sdelat' chto-nibud.
No pozdno! . . Ia kak putnik bezrassudnyi,
Pustivshiisia v dalekii, dolgii put',
Ne sorazmeriv sil s dorogoi trudnoi:
Krugom vse chuzhdo, negde otdokhnut',
Stoit on, blednyi, sred' bol'shoi dorogi.
Nikto ego ne prizrel, ne podvez:
Promchalas' troika, proskripel oboz—
Vse mimo, mimo! podkosilis' nogi,
I on upal . . . Togda k nemu tolpoi
Soidutsia liudi—smushcheny, unyly,
Pochtiat ego nenuzhnoiu slezoi
I podvezut okhotno—do mogily. . .

II

Ia rano vstal, ne dolgi byli sbory,
Ia vyshel v put', chut' zanialas' zaria;
Perekhodil ia propasti i gory,
Pereplyval ia reki i moria;
Borolsia ia, odin i bezoruzhen,
S tolpoi vragov; ne unyval v bede
I ne roptal. No stal mne otdykh nuzhen—
I ne nashel priiuta ia nigde!
Ne raz, upav litsom v syruiu zemliu
S otchaian'em, golodny, ia tverdil:
"Po silam li, o bozhe! trud pod"emliu?"
I snova shel, sobrav ostatok sil.
Vse blizhe i znakomee doroga,
I proideno vse trudnoe v puti!
Glavy tserkvei siiaiut vperedi—
Ne daleko do otchego poroga!
Nasmeshlivo sgibaias' i kriakhtia
Pod tiazhest'iu sumy svoei dyriavoi,
Golodnyi trud, poputchik moi lukavoi,
Uzh proch' idet: teper' nam rovnyi put'.
Vpered, vpered! No izmenili sily—

I nekomu i nechem pomianut'!
Nastanet utro—solnyshko osvetit
Bezdushnyi trup: vse budet resheno!
I v tselom mire serdtse lish' odno—
I to edva li—smert' moiu zametit . . .

III

Pyshna v razlive gordaia reka,
Plyvut suda, koleblias' velichavo,

209

Prosmoleny ikh chernye boka,
Nad nimi flag, na flage nadpis': slava!
Tolpy naroda beregom begut,
K nim prikovav dosuzhee vniman'e,
I, shliapami razmakhivaia, shliut
Plovtsy rodnomu beregu proshchan'e,—
I v mig ono podkhvacheno tolpoi,
I druzhno bereg ves' emu otvetit.
No tut zhe, oprokinutyi volnoi,
Pogibni cheln—i kto ego zametit?
A esli i razdastsia dikii ston
Na beregu—vnezapnyi, odinokii,
Za krikami ne budet slyshen on
I ne doidet na dno reki glubokoi. . .
Podruga temnoi uchasti moei!
Ostav' skoree bereg, ozarennyi
Goriachim bleskom solnechnykh luchei
I pestroiu tolpoiu ozhivlennyi,—
Chem solntse iarche, liudi veselei,
Tem serdtsu sokrushennomu bol'nei!

This poetic cycle of three elegies is in many ways characteristic of Nekrasov's poetry.

The reader's immediate perception of Nekrasov's style is inseparately connected with a feeling of its simplicity, its conversational quality, its "prose-like" character. That the poet's work has maintained such a reputation in the consciousness of many generations cannot be by chance; it reflects a deliberate attempt by the author, the striving of the poet, to elaborate a style which would be perceived as something immediate containing the living intonations of conversational speech.

The success with which Nekrasov accomplished this task has given rise to an illusory idea about the "unstructuredness," the artistic amorphousness, of his text. A characteristic misunderstanding arose: prosaic conversational speech, its everyday intonations, were for Nekrasov *an object of representation.* The naive conclusion has frequently been drawn, that Nekrasov, as it were, directly carried over into poetry *actual speech in its conversational forms.* In fact, Nekrasov's style is distinguished by great complexity. Its seeming simplicity arose as a particular artistic effect and had nothing in common with any fundamental amorphism of the text. His "Last Elegies" are suitable for a study of the organization of the stylistic level of the text. We shall restrict our examination to precisely this area.

As early as 1922, B. M. Eikhenbaum demonstrated in Nekrasov's poetry the author's conscious non-acceptance of the norms of the "high style" poetry of the preceding period:

Frequently Nekrasov directly displayed his method of deviation, contrastively opposing his own "crude" words to the system of old poetic cliches or emphasizing the prosiac nature of his themes and images.[141]

Still earlier Iu. N. Tynyanov established a connection between the rhythmico-syntactic forms of Zhukovsky, Pushkin and Lermontov on the one hand, and Nekrasov on the other.[142] Subsequently this question also attracted the attention of K. Simkevich, V. V. Gippius, and K. I. Chukovsky.[143]

These investigators have elucidated the structural complexity of Nekrasov's style. Nekrasov's poetry was intended for the reader who keenly felt the poetic norms of the "Romantic" Pushkinian and post-Pushkinian styles against whose background stylistic layers that had not been incorporated into poetry prior to Nekrasov became esthetically active.

The reservation must be made that the scholarly literature often emphasizes the parodistic, unmasking character of the inclusion in Nekrasov's texts of Romantic cliches (sometimes in the form of direct quotations). However, it must not be forgotten that parody and direct discreditation of the "poetic" word represents only an extreme case of the relationship of "poetry" and "prose" within Nekrasov's style. Other correlations are possible. Still another feature is constant and basic: the presence within a single stylistic system of two diverse substructures and the effect of their correlation. In order that this effect be stylistically meaningful, each of these subsystems must be active, alive in the consciousness of the reader, and directly experienced by him as esthetically valuable. The reader, having lost his perception of early nineteenth century Russian Romantic poetry as an artistic value, would not perceive the novelty of Nekrasov. Therefore, Nekrasov's style not only "parodies," "unmasks," or otherwise discredits the pre-existing poetic tradition but also constantly appeals to it, evoking its norms and recreating new artistic values within its system. The presence of two incompatible systems, each of which is internally completely organic and their combination, in spite of everything, in different stylistico-semantic relationships constitutes the specific character of Nekrasov's stylistic structure.

The "Last Elegies" are three formally independent poems basically devoted to a single theme, i.e., the death of the poet just when he has surmounted his hungry and solitary youth and the crowd's indifference. The unity of the rhythmico-syntactic structure of these pieces and their communality of stylistic resolution also reinforces our view of the cycle as a single text. The common title and their sequential numeration further supports this assumption. Let us initially look at each elegy separately.

The first elegy breaks down into two parts in terms of its principles of semantic organization: up to the middle of the sixteenth line it is a direct description of the author's spiritual state and words are used almost exclusively in their direct "ordinary language" sense. From the words "I am like a reckless traveler. . ." the text constitutes an extended comparison, each of whose elements has two meanings: an ordinary language one proper to the given lexeme and a second one that is contextual-poetic.

Such an opposition normally disposes the reader to anticipate certain stylistic devices: the allegorical scene "life is a road," which belongs to the most traditional literary images, disposes one to expect "literariness," while the description of the poet's experiences in this regard is neutral; it leaves the author freedom of choice and can be resolved either by conventionalized poetic or by "prosaic" means. Against the background of the "poetic character" of the second part, this freedom is perceived as a *simplification* of the artistic system.

The expectation is not realized, however. The second part, in its turn, is divided into three diversely organized lexico-semantic segments. The first contains images of the road, which are expressed by lexical means that confirm the inertia of his literary allegorical perception in the reader's mind. These phraseologisms are widely encountered in the poetic tradition of the eighteenth through the nineteenth centuries and go back to the moral allegorical prose of biblical imagery. The second segment includes words and phraseologisms that are colored in a distinctly mundane tone and are connected with the idea of an actual Russian road well-known to the reader:

First Segment	Second Segment
reckless traveler *(putnik bezrassudnyi)*	highway *(bol'shaia doroga)*
long journey *(dolgii put')*	no one gave him a ride *(nikto ne podvez)*
hard road *(trudnaia doroga)*	a troika rushed past *(promchalas' troika)*
around all is strange *(krugom vse chuzhdo)*	a wagon train creaks by *(proskripel oboz)*

The established inertia of stylistic expectation is disrupted by the everyday character of the scene and by the fact that its individual details such as "the troika rushed past" or "the wagon train creaked by" are generally devoid of a second plane of meaning and do not lend themselves to allegorical decipherment. It is worthwhile, however, for the reader to adopt the position that the expectation is false and that the text does not lend itself to interpretation in the spirit of conventional literary allegory. This second expectation also turns out to be false and the text returns the reader to the initial stylistic inertia.

The final line, which constitues the third segment, introduces an image of the road ending in the grave, i.e., it returns the entire scene to the semantics of allegory: "And they willingly give him a ride—to the grave. . ." ("I podvezut okhotno—do mogily. . ."). The conventional poetic lexicon in the spirit of the first segment ("the grave") and the everyday road lexicon of the second ("they willingly give him a ride") are synthesized here. Thus, the dual semantic planarity of the text's second part is created in a conflicting structure which affirms in the reader's consciousness both a certain structural expectation and the *non-fulfillment* of that expectation. This also applies to the entire second part as a whole: instead of the expected conventional allegory, the everyday scene dominates here.

On the other hand, the first part, which is given as an antithesis to the "poetic" second part is, counter to all expectation, built from the very beginning as an emphatic assemblage of poetic cliches: "[my] soul is gloomy" ("dusha mrachna") (cf. Lermontov's "My soul is gloomy" ("Dusha moia mrachna"), "dreams despondent"("mechty unyly") (cf. Pushkin's "Despondent dreaming" ("Unylye mechtan'ia"); "my future is dark" ("griadushchee temno"—a quote from Lermontov's "Meditation" ("Duma"), and Pushkin's "sweet habit" ("privychka milaia") from Onegin's letter to Tatiana.[144]

As we see, Nekrasov begins the poem with a string of blatant poetic cliches which are associated with many texts well-known to the reader. On closer inspection, however, it becomes clear that this chain of literary cliches is forged from functionally diverse links. "My soul is gloomy" ("Dusha mrachna") and "[my] dreams are despondent" ("mechty unyly") create a wholly traditional stylistic inertia. "The future is silhouetted darkly" ("Griadushchee temno") stands out against this background as somewhat more individualized. Lermontov's line "the future is either empty or dark" ("griadushchee il' pusto, il' temno") does not imply any visual realization of the metaphor. The addition of "is silhouetted" ("risuetsia") functionally changes the line's entire basis: the future which is barely perceptible in the darkness implies the *visual concretization* of the cliche and in doing so removes it from the category of totally automatized phraseologisms. "Habits, formerly sweet, are repellent" ("Privychki, prezhde milye, postyli") is another type of cliche de-automatization. In the phrase used by Pushkin "I did not give reign to sweet habit" ("Privychke miloi ne dal khodu"), "sweet habit" is a gallant replacement of the fixed phraseologism "the science of tender passion" and as such is not reducible to its constituent lexemes. In Nekrasov's work "habits" designates "habits," and "sweet" means "sweet." This makes the word combination simultaneously both a poetic cliche and a violation of the cliche. The entire series is crowned by the word "cigar" which absolutely cannot by introduced into the chain of poeticisms either as an *object,* a thing, or as a detail of the extra-poetic world. (Both poverty and wealth can be objects of poetization whereas comfort lies entirely outside the sphere of art.) The fact that Romantic cliches are found at one end of the chain and a "cigar," an item of everyday realia with certain social implications at the other, reveals the relativity of the organizational principle underlying the semantics along the axis "poeticism—prosaism."

The directionality of the semantic structure reverses itself at this point: the cigar, the beloved friend of his nocturnal labors and solitary thoughts —bitter fate—thirsty ailment. "Beloved friend" refers the reader to the Pushkin lines:

> **Friend of idle meditation**
> **my inkwell. . .**

213

Podruga dumy prazdnoi,
Chernil'nitsa moia. . .

These lines were a sharp violation of tradition for Pushkin's epoch in that the reality of the poet was being introduced into the category of poetic "reality." For Nekrasov's epoch, however, they had already become the stylistic norm, while "cigar" was still looked upon as an uncanonized item of poetic "reality." The chain ends with a high poeticism wherein the contrast "bitter is the smoke of my cigar" and "bitter is my lot" reveal the antithesis "poetic-mundane."

The five central lines in which poeticisms and prosaisms are functionally equated follow. In the lines "Now there are fewer trivial worries,/ And more rarely does hunger knock on my door" ("Teper' pomen'she melochnykh zabot,/ I rezhe v dver' moiu stuchitsia golod"), the ordinary language and the poetic content coincide in a certain regard. (If one restates the lines by the formula "need no longer hinder serious work," then both lines figure as synonyms realizing the same idea by different means.) The "poetic" and the "prosaic" types of style function as two interrelated methods of recreating a certain reality. It is impossible to say here that the "poetic" is an object of parody or unmasking. The same reality may be realized both in the form of everyday prose and also as the actual content of poetic formulas. Here is the root difference between the poetics of Nekrasov and that of the Romantic tradition. From the latter point of view, the poetic system of expressions creates a *special* world which is separate from everyday reality and which is not translatable into its language. (Every such case of "translation" gives rise to comic effect.) For Nekrasov the poetic and anti-poetic formulas are but two countenances of a single reality.

The relationship of the text to reality becomes an artistically registered fact. Such a relationship must not be automatically given. Only when a given artistic system permits *several* types of semantic correlations of a constructed text and of the extra-textual reality related to it, can this correlation be artistically significant. The present text is interesting precisely because each of the cycle's sections realizes its own special semantic model and their mutual correlation lays bare the principles of its semantic structure. Nekrasov's poetics implies a multitude of semantic structural types.

All three of the analyzed texts relate to a single biographical fact: during the creation of the cycle Nekrasov was ill and thought his illness mortal. For readers who knew Nekrasov personally, the text was indisputably correlated with the author's biography. For readers not familiar with Nekrasov's biography, the author's personality and the poetic text jointly created an image of the poet-pauper broken by his labors and deprivations and doomed to an untimely end. This image lay outside of the texts and arose partially on their basis and partially as a generalization of the biographies of many poets and literary men of non-gentle birth and, perhaps, even the reader's own biography. It might appear a rejection of the traditional Romantic ideal of the hounded poet but might also be perceived as its *content*. This extra-textual construct of the poet's personality is the key to the individual texts.[145]

The second elegy is closely connected with the first both by the "life is a road" image and by the extra-textual situation. The principle of the text's semantic organization here is different however: while the poem as a whole is directed toward a concrete situation, the same cannot be said about a segment of its text. The literary cliches are selected here so that their immediate *visualization* by the reader is excluded. They remain markedly bookish turns of phrase which are recoded (owing to a cultural tradition familiar to the reader) into a particular biographical situation, but which are not recoded into visual images represented by certain lexemes in the language. Any attempt to picture the author with a *cigar in his hands*, as he is depicted in the preceding text, while *crossing over "abysses and mountains"* or *swimming across "rivers and seas"* can only create a comic effect. Commenting on this aspect of Nekrasov's style, K. I. Chukovsky wrote "In order to say that in some person's *breast* a *throne* is found, one must abstract oneself from the actual meaning of these words."[146] In this sense, a comparison of the second and third elegies is essential. It may seem that they are similarly constructed from the stylistico-semantic point of view. Both realize the same traditional metaphor, i.e., "life is a road"; both draw widely on phraseologisms affirmed by literary usage; and both relate to the same biographical situation. Their serial disposition is not accidental, however. Neither text in any way tautologically repeats the other: while the second elegy is constructed so that its words are correlated with a certain syntagmatic stylistic structure and with the extra-textual biography of the poet, the third elegy provides still another correlation for each word. It is the visual image of the object indicated by it.

The traditional, consciously banal examples of metaphorism such as "on the flag an inscription: Glory!" support the reader's feeling of the conventionalism of the entire scene. But the clustering of *visible* details which are completely absent in the second elegy changes the very nature of the metaphorism, laying bare one of the most important elements of Nekrasov's style, i.e., the unique creation of an organized *visible* series which constitutes a second level of structure lying between the level of the text and of reality. In this sense not one of the poets of the nineteenth century (perhaps excluding Fet) approached the poetics of film and visual montage as closely as Nekrasov. In such poems as "Morning" ("Utro"), a montage of visual images represented in the diversity of foreshortenings and planes is displayed; the poem is constructed according to the laws of the cinematographer's scenario. But the creation of this style could be realized only in works such as "Last Elegies" with their complex correlation of various types of textual constructions and extra-textual structures of varying depth.

The principle of the alternation of planes is purely cinematic. Thus, in the poem "Morning" a series of scenes unfolds before us forming montage series wherein not only the content but also the plane shifts: "The distance covered with blue fog" ("Dal', sokrytaia sinim tumanom") is a long shot; "The wet sleepy jackdaws that sit on the top of the haystack" ("Mokrye, sonnie galki, chto sidiat na vershine stoga") is a close-up; "From the fort thunder the cannons! Flooding threatens the capital" ("Iz kreposti grianuli pushki! Navodnen'e stolitse grozit") is a medium take, "The janitor stabs the thief—he is caught!" ("Dvornik vora kolotit—popalsia!")—a medium shot and "Someone has died: on a red pillow lies an Anna of the First Degree" ("Kto-to umer: na krasnoi podushke Pervoi stepeni Anna lezhit")— a close-up, and so on.

The existence in Nekrasov's poetry, between text and reality, of still another series reminiscent of cinemagraphic montage is shown in a characteristic example: in Nekrasov's lyrics, as in the cinema, the plane is perceived as a correlate of metaphor (or of metonymy) in a verbal series. Details given in the close-up are perceived as especially meaningful, symbolic, or suggestive and are related not only to their immediate denotatum, i.e., to the actual object designated by these words. In a verbal series, the "jackdaws" or the "order on the red pillow" are not only not metaphors, but, in accord with the principle of semantic organization, completely fail to stand out against the general background. The fact that the visual images elicited by them are *enlarged* (and that, by virture of the contrasting alternation in the series, this enlargement is noticeable and meaningful) gives them special meaningfulness, while the fact that the separate "frames" in the visual series possess different degrees of suggestiveness creates supplementary possibilities for the transmission of meanings.

The "Last Elegies" from the standpoint of stylistic structure constitute an experimental work. Nekrasov's achievement was the creation of "poetic popular speech" not as a result of the simple casting off of a rejected tradition (popular speech could not become an esthetic fact in this case) but by its inclusion as one of the elements of style and by the creation of contrastive effects based on the correlation of formerly incompatible structures.

This course was also that of all subsequent Russian poetry. Not rejection of cliched, traditional, and banalized stylistic forms, but their bold use as a contrastive background (not merely with the aim of mockery or parody) came to be the basis of the new style. For Romanticism the banal and poetic excluded each other. The Nekrasovian style exposed the banality of poetic cliches but did not reject them, choosing rather to reveal *the poetic in the banal*. Precisely this aspect of Nekrasov's style is subsequently important for Blok.

The "Last Elegies" provoked Dobroliubov's famous parody "Having scorned people and the world and having prayed to God. . ." ("Prezrev liudei i mir i pomolivshis' bogu. . .") Although in his parody Dobroliubov, of course, had in view the theme of the poem he also exposed the very basis of Nekrasov's style and, in particular, the abundance of poetic cliches. The idea of the hopelessness and pointlessness of life's struggle, of poetic exhaustion, did not satisfy him. Given this, it is all the more interesting to note the effect of Nekrasov's stylistic structure on the poetic system of Dobroliubov's lyric.

Let us cite one example. The poem "Let me die—there is little grief. . ." ("Puskai umru pechali malo. . .") is seen as a direct expression of Dobroliubov's bitter reflections on the eve of his death. First of all, the simplicity, directness, and "non-literariness" of the poem catches the reader's eye. On closer inspection, however, two contrasting stylistic layers in the poem are easily isolated:

1) Phraseologisms and cliches of a distinctly literary origin, e.g., "sick mind" ("um bol'noi"), "cold corpse" ("kholodnyi trup"), "burning tears" ("goriachie slezy"), "selfless friends" ("beskorystnye druz'ia"), "sepulchral earth" ("mogil'naia zemlia"), "headstone" ("grobovaia doska"), "smiled comfortingly" ("otradno ulybnulsia"), "avidly wish" ("zhadno zhelat"). It is characteristic that the "cliche quality" pertains not only to particular lexemes and phraseologisms but also to certain grammatico-syntactic structures. Thus, for example, the combination "noun—epithet" in Dobroliubov's text can only be a cliche.

2) Speech figures that were regarded as "antipoeticisms" in Dobroliubov's time, e.g., "there is little grief" ("pechali malo"), "to play a joke" ("razygrat' shutku"), "stupid zeal" ("glupoe userd'e"). To this category one assigns the concrete material lexicon deliberately purified of "symbolism," e.g., bringing flowers to the grave is stupid because it is a symbol; only the living require things, the dead need nothing. Compare also the phraseologism "object of love" ("predmet liubvi") drawn from the poeticisms of the Pushkinian epoch which had crossed over into the lower middle class "gallant style." Note, for example, in Pushkin's story "The Blizzard" ("Metel") the use of the phrase "the object chosen by her was a poor army ensign" which reflects the stylistic coincidence of the viewpoints of the author and the heroine, i.e., "ensign" equals "object." In the Dobroliubov text the "object of love" is no longer a poeticism but an ironic reference to the conversational language of a certain—not high—social sphere.

The various correlations of these stylistic layers form the fabric of the poem. Examine, for example, the following stanza:

> I fear lest over my cold body
> Hot tears be shed,
> Lest some one in stupid zeal
> Bring flowers to my grave.
>
> Boius', chtob nad kholodnym trupom
> Ne prolilos' goriachikh slez,

Chtob kto-nibud' v userd'e glupom
Na grob tsvetov mne ne prines—

These lines contain not only the development of a certain thought ("I fear that there may be tears over my grave and that someone might bring flowers"), but also represent a conjoining of two modes of expressing an idea. From the standpoint of ordinary language content, two different ideas, i.e., fear of tears + fear of flowers, are here united into a single chain. The mode of their expression is not activated. It is worthwhile, however, formulating the idea more generally ("the fear of unnecessary tokens of attention to the dead person") as the stanza breaks down into two parallel synonymic halves. The *mode of expression* of the idea is activated. In the first two lines not only the concentration of poetic vocabulary, but also the rhetorical antithesis "cold body—hot tears" is to be seen. In the second part of the stanza its deliberate conversational character and amorphousness stand out against this background as a structurally active fact. In passing it should be remarked that "in stupid zeal" ("v userd'e glupom") is obviously a rephrasing of "in stupid hope" ("v nadezhde glupoi") from "Last Elegies." What is of interest is that the textual element performing the function of "anti-litera-ture" is the citation, but one from a different kind of source. The influence of the Nekrasovian principle is evident here.

Thus analysis even on a single lexico-semantic plane provides a stylistic characterization and enables us to designate the landmarks of the traditional [literary] succession.

218

A. K. Tolstoy

There sits beneath a canopy
The Chinaman Tsu-Kin-Tsyn[147]
And says to the mandarins;
"I am the chief mandarin!

The ruler of the region has ordered
For me to ask your advice:
Why is it we have in China
No order up to now?"

The Chinamen all squatted down,
Shook their behinds and
Said: "Because up 'til now
There is no order on earth,

For we are very young, you know,
We are only five thousand years and some:
Because we have not the inclination,
Because there is no order!

We swear by various teas,
Both yellow and plain,
We promise much
And we shall accomplish much!"

"Your speeches are pleasing to me,—
Answered Tsu-Kin-Tsyn,—
I am convinced by the strength
Of such clear reasons.

Just think: five thousand,
Only five thousand years."
And he ordered flogged
Without delay the entire council.

$$\cdots$$
$$\cdots$$

Sidit pod baldakhinom
Kitaets Tsu-Kin-Tsyn
I molvit mandarinam;
"Ia glavnyi mandarin!

Velel vladyko kraia
Mne vash sprosit' sovet:
Zachem u nas v Kitae
Dosel' poriadka net?"

Kitaitsy vse priseli,
Zadamy potriasli,
Glasiat: "Zatem dosele
Poriadka net v zemli,

Chto my ved' ochen' mlady,
Nam tysiach piat' lish' let;
Zatem u nas net skladu,
Zatem poriadku net!

Klianemsia raznym chaem,
I zeltym i prostym,
My mnogo obeshchaem
I mnogo sovershim!"

"Mne vashi rechi mily,
Otvetil Tsu-Kin-Tsyn,
Ia ubezhdaius' siloi
Stol' iavstvennykh prichin.

Podumaesh': piat' tysiach,
Piat' tysiach tol'ko let."
I prikazal on vysech'
Nemedlia ves' sovet.

A. K. Tolstoy's satire, which was written in 1869, can be subjected to various sorts of commentary. First of all one must indicate the possibilities for a semantic interpretation hidden in extra-textual comparisons. Thus, for example, correlations of the text with the extra-textual political reality of A. K. Tolstoy's epoch are possible, as are its relationship with other texts:

I. The non-belletristic—various approaches are possible here:

A. Comparisons with the historical and philosophic ideas which were widespread in Russian publicistic writing, philosophy, and historical study in the years 1840 through 1860 stemming from Belinsky and Hertzen; specifically the ideas that serfdom and the autocratic bureaucracy were an "Eastern" element, a static element in Russian national life opposed to the idea of progress. Belinsky and other publicistic writers on China depicting it as a country in which standing-in-place had supplanted both history and social life, a country opposed to the historical dynamism of Europe, could be cited.

B. Comparisons with the historical conception of A. K. Tolstoy himself, who approximated Kievan Rus' with the knightly chivalrousness of Europe and who saw "Asiaticness" and "Sinicism" as features imposed by the rule of the Mongols in subsequent Russian history.

C. A. K. Tolstoy's closeness to Slavophil thought in its various manifestations and his rejection of it.

D. Many aspects of A. K. Tolstoy's historico-philosophical views are amazingly close to those of A. V. Sukhovo-Kobylin. Comparison of their texts might yield tangible results.

E. The establishment of the historical roots of A. K. Tolstoy's ideas and their subsequent fate. The theme "N. M. Karamzin and A. K. Tolstoy" suggests itself initially. Another such topic might be A. K. Tolstoy and VI. Solov'ev; "The Satiric Tradition of Twentieth Century Poetry" and so on.

II. Belletristic:

    A. Comparison of the text with A. K. Tolstoy's other satiric works.

    B. Comparison with Tolstoy's non-satiric works written at approximately the same time. These include "Tugar's Serpent" ("Zmei Tugarin"), "The song of Harold and Iaroslavna" ("Pesnia o Garol'de i Iaroslavne"), and "Three Bloody Battles" ("Tri poboishcha"), etc.

    C. Comparison of the text with satiric and historical poetry of the 1860s.

These latter methods of analysis might be called contextual: the work is included in various contexts, comparisons, and oppositions; the structurings of the invariant schemes permit us to uncover the text's specific structural character.

We shall, however, set ourselves a significantly less ambitious task by restricting our attention to an analysis of intra-textual associations. We shall examine only those structural relations that can be disclosed by an analysis of the *given* text. Even this undertaking is still quite broad. Further restricting it we shall confine ourselves to the supra-lexical levels, i.e., to those poetic hyper-meanings that arise in a given text on those levels for which the word functions as the elementary unit.

So formulated, the problem can also be defined as an analysis of the lexico-stylistic mechanism of the satire. It must be emphasized that satire is created here by the internal structure of the text and is not determined, for example, by the genre as it is in the fable.[148]

The semantic structure of the text is built on non-correspondences. These semantic non-correspondences become the chief bearers of meanings, the basic principle underlying the work's artistic semantic construction. In the poem we encounter several stylistic and semantic constructions whose colocation within the limits of a single work may seem unexpected to the reader.

The first layer of meanings can be provisionally called "Chinese." It is consciously oriented toward "China", not as a geographic and historical reality but as a complex of certain markedly trivial concepts that were signals of standard literary ideas about China which were widespread in A. K. Tolstoy's time. Notwithstanding all the conventionalism of the characterizations, the address to the reader is given in full-blown fashion. Let us cite the list of text words which can only be associated with the China theme:

canopy	*baldakhin*
Chinaman	*kitaets*

China	Kitai
mandarin	mandarin
tea	chai

If two descriptions of "customs" are added: "all squatted" and "they shook their behinds" and the proper name Tsu-Kin-Tsyn, then the list of "Sinicisms" is complete. They account for eight of the ninety-five words in the poem. As is evident from the list, they all belong simultaneously both to the most trivial and to the most obvious features of that conventionalized literary world which A. K. Tolstoy strives to evoke in the reader's consciousness. Some interesting observations on the distribution of these words in the text can also be made.

Stanza No.	No. of Lexical "Sinicisms"
1	5
2	1
3	1
4	–
5	1
6	1
7	–

These data clearly demonstrate that the "Chinese" lexicon is evoked only to give the text a certain semantic key. Subsequently it is reduced to nought. All the "Sinicisms" are represented by names. "Exoticisms" pertaining to actions are on the phraseological level. These include the combinations "all squatted" and "shook their behinds" which is intended to infuse an element of puppetry into the text.[149] The comic conventionalism of the vow sworn "by various teas" is shown by the introduction into the oath formula of the grades of tea current in Russian commerce of those years.

Another basic semantic layer of the text leads to the images, ideological and cultural, of ancient Kievan Rus'. "Old Rusisms" are given for effect and their stylistic activeness reckons on the feeling of the incompatibility of these layers. The "Old Rusisms" are also distributed unevenly. They are especially clustered in the second, third, and fourth stanzas. They too are represented in their most prosaic and trivial manifestations. This is especially obvious against the background of the general structure of "Old Rusisms" in A. K. Tolstoy's poetry. In his historical ballads, such words set the stylistic coloration by virtue of their rarity, e.g., "doni," "dub" (in the meaning of "boat"), "gumentsy" ("Borivoi"); "kut," "drom," "koty iz aksamita," "bertsa," "obor," "kryzhatyi mech" ("Svatovstvo"), and others. Their effect stems from the fact that being clearly unknown to the reader they are used as if generally comprehensible without any explanations or interpreting contexts. This leads the reader into a world unknown to him and simultaneously presents this world as being ordinary for him. But even in political satire of the time, for example, "In the merry month of May" ("Poroi veseloi maia. . ."), A. K. Tolstoy deliberately selects the least trivial in utilizing archaisms.

In "He sits beneath a canopy. . ." the archaisms are reduced to the most generally used Slavonicisms in stylized poetry. There are three in all: "to say" ("molvit' "), "to say" ("glasit' "), and "young" ("mladoi"). Here also belong the grammatical Slavonicism "on the earth" ("v zemli"), the archaism "ruler" ("vladyko"), and the colloquialisms which functionally play the role of "Rusisms": "up to now" ("dosel"), "turn" ("sklad"), "just think" ("podu-maesh' "). The basic "Old Russian" coloration is provided by the expression "till now there is no order" ("dosel' poriadka net") which is a quote from a very famous part of "The Chronicle of Bygone Years." In 1868 A. K. Tolstoy converted it into the refrain of his "A History of the Russian State from Gostomysl to Timashev" ("Istoriia godsudarstva Rossiiskogo ot Gostomysla do Timasheva"). As an epigraph to this poem he put "Our entire land is great and abundant, but there is no order in it" ("Vsia zemlia nasha velika i obil'na, a nariada v nei net") (Nestor, Chronicle, p. 8).

It may be concluded from the above that neither the quoted "Sinicisms" nor the "Rusisms" in and of themselves exceed the boundaries of deliberate triviality and, taken separately, cannot possess significant artistic activity. It is their *combination* that is significant. The impossibility of combining these semantic layers into any sort of structural expectation antedating the text makes such a combination especially rich in meaning. The proper name Tsu-Kin-Tsyn, a name in which the blending of layers assumes the character of a pun, is the focus of this combination of the uncombinable.

What ideational and artistic function does this mixture of stylistic and semantic layers have? If the text is to be perceived as "correct," (i.e., as "a correct text in the Russian language") it must satisfy certain norms of language use. However, a phrase of the type "the sun rises in the west" which is correct in a linguistic sense is seen as "incorrect" in terms of content because it contradicts everyday experience. One of the forms of comprehensibility that enables us to perceive a text as "correct" is its logicality, its combination of concepts in accord with the norms of logic, experience and common sense. However, it is possible to construct a text in which the poet combines not the most but the least probable sequences of words or word groups. Here are some examples, again from A. K. Tolstoy:

A. The text is built according to the laws of absurdity. Notwithstanding observation of the norms of grammatical syntactic construction, the text is semantically ungrammatical: each word represents an independent segment on the basis of which prediction of the following segment is almost impossible. The rhymes possess the greatest degree of predictability here. It is not by chance that the text approximates a joking imitation of *bouts-rimés,* i.e., amateur poetry set on given rhymes in which the semantic links give way to rhyming consonances:

223

The coffee-pot chanced
With the fork in the grove to stroll.
They came upon an anthill;
The fork jabbed it.

—"The coffee-pot chanced..."

• • •

Ugorazdilo kofeinik
S vilkoi v roshche poguliat'.
Nabreli na muraveinik;
Vilka nu ego pyriat'!

B. The text is divided into segments equal to the syntagmas. Each is internally grammatical from the logico-semantic point of view but the combination of segments blatantly ignores the rules of logic:

The ungodly killer plunged his dagger
   Into the breast of Delarue.
The latter, having removed his hat, told him politely,
   "Thank you."
Now into his left side the terrible dagger
   The evildoer drove.
And Delarue said, "What a beautiful
   Dagger you have there!"

• • •

Vonzil kinzhal ubiitsa nechestivyi
   V grud' Deliariu.
Tot, shliapu sniav, skazal emu uchtivo;
   "Blagodariu."
Tot v levyi bok emu kinzhal uzhasnyi
   Zlodei vognal.
A Deliariu skazal: "Kakoi prekrasnyi
   U vas kinzhal!"

The violation of logical associations is one of the well-tried techniques of such modeling. Let us recall that the analysis of aphasia was a great step in the theoretical study of language. Also relevant here is the long known and important role of "word play" ("perevertysha") and nonsense poetry in the formation of logical recognition habits among children.[150]
Precisely the possibility of a disruption of those or other associations in the usual picture of the world as dictated by common sense and everyday experience makes these associations bearers of information. A-logicality in children's poetry and the fantastic in fairy tale plots, notwithstanding doubts expressed in the 1920s by the Russian Proletarian Writers' Association and by vulgarized pedagogy, in no way disorient a child (or more generally, a reader), who does not equate the text with life. He knows "life as it is" apart from fairy tales and does not seek direct descriptions of reality in them. High information content, the capability of significant communication, is to be found in fairy tales or in a-logical texts precisely because they

involved the unexpected: no element in the consecutive chain that constitues the text fully predicts the following one. This very unexpectedness
arises on the foundation of a previously formulated picture of the world
with "correct" semantic associations. When the hero of Ostrovsky's play
"Poverty Is No Sin" takes up the joking song "A bear was flying through
the heavens. . ." ("Letal medved' po podnebes'iu. . .") the listeners do not
perceive the text as information about the beast's place of residence. The
reservations of those who fear that fantasy disorients the reader, especially
the young one, are completely unfounded. The text is perceived as *humorous*
and the basis of the laughter is precisely in the divergency of the customary
"correct" picture of the world and its description in the song. Thus a-logical
or fantastic texts neither impair nor destroy an initial picture of associations
but are deposited over and uniquely strengthen it insofar as the semantic
effect is formed precisely by the difference, that is by *the relationship* of
these two models of the world. But the possibility of divergency makes the
unspecified, "correct" association not only non-automatic but one of two
possibilities and, consequently, a bearer of information. Note, for example,
the folk song "The huge mosquito bruised the giant shoulder" ("Zashib
komarishche plechishche"). The combination of a lexeme designating a
small insect ("komar") with a suffix bearing the meaning of hugeness
(-ishche) makes manifest the feature of small size in the customary use of the
word. Apart from this antithesis, the feature of the mosquito's small size
is given automatically and is not noticed.

In Tolstoy's poem *the logicality* of the associations is the disrupted
link. The fact that the customary correlations of objects and concepts are
simultaneously also logical correlations is revealed to us only when the
poet introduces us into a world in which the associations that are obligatory
and automatically functioning within the sphere of logic are repealed. In A.
K. Tolstoy's world, the absurd lies between cause and consequence. The
characters' actions are devoid of meaning: their habits are nonsensical.

> **The Chinamen all squatted,**
> **Shook their behinds. . .**
>
> **Kitaitsy vse priseli,**
> **Zadami potriasli. . .**

Their oaths and obligations which "the ruler of the region" is evidently preparing to rely upon are devoid of real meaning, etc.

The a-logicality of this world is emphasized by the fact that an assertion
which is logically absurd is submitted and accepted as evidence: it is cloaked
in a quasi-logical form. The reason that "up 'til now/ There is no order on
earth" is formulated as:

> **. . .for we are very young,**
> **you know,**

> We are only five thousand
> years and some. . .

> . . .My ved' ochen' mlady,
> Nam tysiach piat' lish'
> let. . .

The unification of the concepts of youth and of five thousand years is perceived by the reader as absurd. But for Tsu-Kin-Tsyn this is not only a truth but even logical proof:

> I am convinced by the strength
> Of such clear reasons.

> Ia ubezhdaius' siloi
> Stol' iavstvennykh prichin.

Thus the reader is supposed to assume that there is a special "Tsu-Kin-Tsyn logic," whose absurdity is obvious against the background of our usual ideas of cause and effect. The character of this "logic" is revealed in the final stanza:

> Just think: five thousand
> Only five thousand years."
> And he ordered flogged
> Without delay the entire council.
> • • •
> Podumaesh': piat' tysiach,
> Piat' tysiach tol'ko let!"
> I prikazal on vysech'
> Nemedlia ves' sovet.

The lines "I am convinced by the strength. . ." and "And he ordered flogged. . ." are given as parallel. Only in them do we find the rhythmic schema "u—u—́u—́u" which is sharply felt against the rhythmic configurations of the other lines. The combination of the ideas and intonations of these two lines creates that structure of absurd combinations upon which the text is built.

In the general picture of absurd conjunctions and displacements, the non-correspondences of grammatical expression and content occupy a special place. In the line "And he ordered flogged. . ." the initial "And" which links the two fragments with the dominant meanings "he heard—he ordered" must have not only a coordinate but also a causal-resultative character. It mimics that co-ordinative copula in the Old Russian Historical Chronicle that in modern Russian translations is rendered by subordinate constructions of cause, consequence, or purpose. One can say with assurance that in the scheme "the ruler appeals to a council of high officials for aid—the council gives its recommendations—the ruler agrees—the ruler orders. . .," the continuation that "the council be flogged" is the least predictable on the basis of the preceding textual sequence. It immediately forces us to assume that we are dealing with a completely different world, one in which our idea that governmental orders should be distinguished by wisdom and significance and that governmental councils be accorded acknowledgment of their merit does not function just as the rules of logic and the norms of common sense do not apply.

There is still another peculiarity in this world; time stands still and there is, consequently, no historical experience in it. This is also expressed in the fact that numbers which seem large ("five thousand years") are used as small ("Just think!"). Another point of interest is that three grammatical tenses are used in the poem: the present ("sits, swears"), past ("they squatted, he answered, etc."), and the future ("we shall accomplish"). However all of them designate *a simultaneous state* in the plane of content. The action actually proceeds outside of time.

It must be noted that while the text may be divided into two non-combinable layers on the lexico-semantic level, they nevertheless function as one in relation to logic and common sense. The apparent contrast is false and is neutralized on a higher level.

Thus, the lexico-semantic and stylistic types of the text's construction create a satire, an artistic model of that bureaucratic absurdity and "Sinicism" seen by A. K. Tolstoy in the Russian autocracy.

A. A. Blok

To Anna Akhmatova

"Your beauty is terrible"—they will tell you —
You will throw lazily
A Spanish shawl on your shoulders,
A red rose is in your hair.

"Your beauty is simple"—they will tell you —
With a multi-colored shawl awkwardly
You will cover up your child,
The red rose is on the floor.

But, distractedly heeding
All the words sounding round,
You sadly sink into thought
And repeat to yourself:

"Neither terrible nor simple am I;
I am not so terrible that I might simply
Be killed; nor so simple am I
That I do not know how terrible is life."

—December 1913

• • •
• • •

Anne Akhmatovoi

"Krasota strashna"—Vam skazhut,—
Vy nakinete lenivo
Shal' ispanskuiu na plechi,
Krasnyi rozan—v volosakh.

"Krasota prosta"—Vam skazhut,—
Pestroi shal'iu neumelo
Vy ukroete rebenka,
Krasnyi rozan—na polu.

No, rasseianno vnimaia
Vsem slovam, krugom zvuchashchim,
Vy zadumaetes' grustno
I tverdite pro sebia:

"Ne strashna i ne prosta ia;
Ia ne tak strashna, chtob prosto
Ubivat'; ne tak prosta ia,
Chtob ne znat', kak zhizn' strashna."

In the analysis of this poem we deliberately eschew extra-textual associations, i.e., the explication of the history of Blok's and Akhmatova's acquaintance, biographical commentary on the text, and also its comparison with Akhmatova's poem "I came to visit the poet. . ." ("Ia prishla k poetu v gosti. . ."), which Blok answers in the above work. All of these aspects including the most abstract, i.e., Blok's relationship to Acmeism which was then being born and to the young poets who belonged to this movement, are absolutely indispensable for a full understanding of the text. In order to be incorporated in a complex system of external associations however, a work must be a text, i.e., have its own specific internal organization which can and must be an object of completely independent analysis. This analysis constitutes our task.

The plot [siuzhetnyi] basis of a lyric poem is formulated as a translation of the entire diversity of biographical situations into a specific artistic language in which the entire wealth of potential elements is reduced to three basic possibilities:

1) The one who speaks—the "I" (Ia)

2) The one who is addressed—the "Thou" (Ty)

3) The one who is neither the first nor the second—the "He" (On).

Insofar as each of these elements can be used in the singular or the plural we have before us the personal pronoun system. Lyric plots are biographical situations translated into the pronominal system of a natural language.[151]

The traditional lyric scheme "I—thou" is considerably distorted in Blok's text. The authorial "I" is generally not set forth as the clear center of the text's organization. It is present, however, in a covert form being revealed initially in that the second semantic center is given in the form of the second person pronoun, i.e., the person being addressed. This implies the presence of an addressor, i.e., of another center in the construction of the text that occupies the position of the "I." The second person pronoun is given not in the form "thou" ("ty") which is traditional for the lyric and therefore neutral, but in the specifically "polite" form "you" ("Vy").[152] This immediately establishes the type of relationship between the structural centers of the text. If the formula "I—thou" transfers the plot into an abstract lyric space in which the dramatis personae are sublimated figures, then the address to the "you" combines the lyrical world with the everyday one (more narrowly, the everyday world which actually existed in Blok's epoch and in his circle) and gives the entire text an unexpected congruency with everyday and biographical systems. But the fact that they are set in a structural position in a lyric poem gives them a more generalized meaning: they do not copy everyday relations but model them.

The work is constructed so that the author's "I," although clearly functioning as the bearer of the point of view, is not the bearer of the text. It represents itself as "a persona without dialogue." This is emphasized by the fact that the dialogue is conducted not between the "I" and the "you," but between the "you" and some extremely generalized and featureless

229

third person hidden in the impersonal phrases "they will tell you" and in the reference "words sounding round."

The two first stanzas which are devoted to the utterances of this "third person" and to the "you" 's reaction to them are constructed in a demonstrably parallel fashion.

"Your beauty is terrible"—they will tell you—
You will throw lazily
A Spanish shawl on your shoulders,
A red rose is in your hair.

"Your beauty is simple"—they will tell you—
With a multi-colored shawl awkwardly
You will cover up your child,
The red rose is on the floor.

• • •

"Krasota strashna"—Vam skazhut,—
Vy nakinete lenivo
Shal' ispanskuiu na plechi,
Krasnyi rozan—v volosakh.

"Krasota prosta"—Vam skazhut,—
Pestroi shal'iu neumelo
Vy ukroete rebenka,
Krasnyi rozan—na polu.

In these parallel stanzas the "they" say opposing things and the heroine of the poem, whom Blok described in a draft as "submissive to rumor"[153] ("pokornaia molve"), by her silence expresses agreement with both of "their" evaluations, each of which completely transforms the entire picture.

If "beauty is terrible" ("krasota strashna"), then "shawl" ("shal' ") becomes "Spanish" ("ispanskaia"), but if "beauty is simple" ("krasota prosta"), then the shawl is "multi-colored" ("pestraia"). ("Terrible" ["strashna"] is connected with "Spanish" ["ispanskaia"] only semantically, but in the pair "simple/multi-colored" ["prosta-pestraia"] in addition to the semantic link there is also an auditory one, i.e., the repetition "prst-pstr.") In the first case, the shawl is "lazily" ("lenivo") thrown over her shoulders; in the second, the child is "awkwardly" ("neumelo") covered with it. In the first case, the "you" stylizes itself in the spirit of conventional literary-theatrical Spain; in the second, she reveals her youthful awkwardness in a pleasant domestic setting.

The first two stanzas are deliberately conventional: two image-cliches are introduced through whose prism the heroine is understood (and understands herself). In the first stanza, it is Carmen, an image of deep significance for Blok in that time and entailing an entire complex of auxiliary meanings. In the second, it is the Madonna, a girl-woman combining purity, impassiveness, and maturity. Behind the first stands Spain and the opera; behind the second, Italy and the painting of the pre-Raphaelites.

The third stanza separates the heroine from that image of her which "they" create (and which she does not dispute) in the preceding stanzas.

The dialogue between the heroine and "them" continues in specific terms. Compositionally the poem is constructed as a chain of three links:

I. "They"—verbal text; "You"—the text-gesture.[154] Relationship between texts: complete correspondence.

II. "They"—verbal text; "You"—text-gesture, pose (indicated but not adduced). Relationship between texts: divergence.

III. "They"—no text; "You"—verbal text. Relationship between texts: "You" rejects "them."

The verbal text in the first and third segments is given in the first person. The behavior of the heroine is set forth with growing dynamism: gesture-pose-internal monologue. However, the movement is generally retarded and tends toward picturesqueness. This is conveyed by the meanings of the words "distractedly heeding" ("rasseianno vnimaia") and "you sadly sink into thought" ("zadumaetes' grustno").

The fourth stanza is summational. The dispute with the "them" ends not as a rejection of their thoughts but as a revelation of the great complexity of the heroine, of her ability to combine diverse essences within herself. The last stanza is built on a denial of elementary logic in the name of more complex associations. The last three lines of the final stanza deny "their" words just as the first line does. Two different assertions are equated however:

I am not terrible = I am not so terrible that. . .
I am not simple = I am not so simple that. . .

This is only part of the general principle of the stanza's construction however. The meanings of the words in the last stanza shift somewhat in relation to the others. The same words are used in different senses. This expands the very concept of the word's meaning giving it greater flexibility. The marked increase in the role of local meanings which arise only in a given text (insofar as the last stanza always occupies a special place in a poem) results in a situation where precisely these unusual meanings begin to be perceived as the true ones. The text introduces us into a world where words mean not only what they mean.

When the reply "not terrible am I" ("ne strashna. . . ia") follows the assertion "beauty is terrible" ("krasota strashna"), we find a characteristic substitution before us: the "I" which is connected with the concept of extreme concreteness replaces the abstract concept. (Only from the context does it become clear that in the first and second cases "beauty" ("krasota") is a paraphrastic replacement of the personal concrete concept.) Because "terrible" ("strashna") or "simple" ("prosta") figure as components of different combinations in each of the two cases, their meaning shifts somewhat. But this is only part of the general system of meaning shifts. "Simple am I" ("prosta ia") permits us to interpret "prosta" by inserting it in contexts which will be incorrect in transformations of the expression "beauty is simple" ("krasota prosta").[155] But the expressions "it is simple to kill" ("prosto ubivat' ") and "I am not so simple that I do not know how terrible life is" ("ne tak prosta ia, chtob ne znat', kak zhizn' strashna") show completely different meanings for "simple" ("prostoi") and "simply" ("prosto"). Although both of these meanings can be inserted in the expression "ne prosta ia," they cannot replace each other. It is precisely the homonymy here that reveals the depth of the semantic differences. The word "terrible" ("strashna") is used in the last stanza three times and all three times in contexts excluding synonymy. The point is not only that in the first two cases it is connected with denial and in the last with affirmation, but that the contexts "I am terrible" ("ia strashna") and "life is terrible" ("zhizn' strashna") imply completely different content for this word.

The world of complexity which was created in the last stanza, a grasp of life in all its fullness, the world of *wisdom,* is built in the form of a monologue by the heroine. This contradicts the femininity and youth[156] of the world of the heroine in the first stanzas. This contrast becomes an active constructional factor in that the first stanzas are formulated as a dialogue between two points of view, the "heroine's" and "theirs," while the latter stanza is her monologue. The poet's point of view does not seem to figure in the text. However the lexical level enters into conflict with the syntactic level here. It informs us that although there is no authorial monologue in the text, the question is more complex. The heroine's monologue does not, of course, consist of her actual words, but what she *might* have said. She "repeats" them "to herself." How does the author know them? There can be only one answer: they are his words, his *point of view.*

Consequently, the entire poem is a dialogue. In the first stanzas it is a conversation between "you" and "they" where the "they" dominates, and the "you" follows "them." In the last stanza, there are two voices: "mine" (the author's) and "yours" but they merge to such an extent that they seem to be *one.* It follows from this that the "you" for the duration of the text is not equal to itself, and its complex multi-facetedness, the possibility of being simultaneously wise, like the author, and beautiful with feminine (both worldy and theatrically Spanish) charm enveloped in the enchantment of youthful maternity and poetry, of being naively dependent upon the opinion of others and yet superior to this opinion, creates the text's semantic content on the level of the poem's lexicon and of its syntactic compositional construction.

The complex polyphonism of meanings on this level is supplemented by the special structure of the lower elements. The reader's perception of the text is that it is one of extreme simplicity. Simplicity, however, does not mean "unstructured." The low degree of activeness of the rhythmic and stanzaic levels and the absence of rhyme is compensated for by the active organization of the text's phonology. Insofar as the vocalism and the consonantism afford different schemes of organization and the resulting conflict enters into thè total sum of meanings, let us examine each of these systems separately.

The stressed vowels in the text are arranged as follows:

	a	a	a
		i		i
I	a	a	e
	a	o	a

	a	a	a
II	o	a	e
		o	o
	a	o	u

		e	a
III	a	o	a
	u	u	
	i	a	

	a	a	
IV	a	a	o
	a	a	a
	a	y	a

The distribution of the stressed vowels yields the following:

	A	I	E	O	U	Y	
No.	25	3	3	7	3	1	Total: 42
%	59.5	7.1	7.1	16.7	7.2	2.4	

For comparison we cite the data for the poem "In the street—rain and slush. . ." ("Na ulitse—dozhdik i sliakot'. . .") written in the same period and similar in its basic indices, i.e., the number of lines and stressed vowels per line:

	A	I	E	O	U	Y	
No.	17	10	7	8	5	1	Total: 48
%	35.4	20.8	14.6	16.7	10.4	2.1	

Recognizing that it would, of course, be necessary to compare these data with the corresponding statistical indices in Blok's *entire* lyric output (and there as yet is no such count) and with statistical data for vowel distribution in non-poetic Russian speech, we can nonetheless conclude that these data are quite sufficient for an impression of the text's phonological organi-

233

zation.

Let us pursue certain features of this organization.

Within the vocalism the leading phoneme is "a." The first line not only affords emphatic inertia to this dominance (the framework of the first line's vocalism is "a-a-a-a-a-a-a followed by u"),[157] but also plays the role of the phonological leit-motif for the entire poem: subsequent modifications, up to the total destruction of this inertia, are possible only because it is established so firmly at the beginning. The stressed "a" strings together as on a thread a row of words forming a chain of concepts that display a semantically similar function in the text. (Just as we have spoken of local synonyms and antonyms in a poetic text, one may also speak of local semantic nests that play the same role in a poetic text as mono-radical groups in non-belletristic texts):

beauty	*krasota*
terrible	*strashna*
red	*krasnyi*

The similarity of these concepts creates new meanings actuating some of the traditional ones and suppressing others. Thus at the intersection of the concepts "terrible" ("strashnyi") and "red" ("krasnyi"), the word "blood" arises. It is absent in the text but clearly enters into our perception of the text. The unexpected appearance in the last stanza "to kill" ("ubivat' ") would be completely incomprehensible without this implied but unstated word.

A kind of dialogue on the phonological level is created in the first stanza. Back vowels with the dominant "a" form one group while the front vowels plus "y" form the second. The sounds "i" and "y" dominate in this series. Here too a "kindred" series is formed:

You	*Vy*
lazily	*lenivo*
shoulders	*plechi*

It is curious in this regard that the pair "to you–you" ("Vam–Vy") function not as two forms of a single paradigm but as opposing responses in a dialogue. The "red" ("krasnyi"), "terrible" ("strashnyi") and "beautiful" ("krasivyi") world is the world that the "they" thrust on the "you" ("Vam"). The "they" represent a certain cultural tradition, a certain mold for the understanding of life. The group "i/y" forms the poetic "Vy" ("you"), the reaction of the heroine: "nakinete" ("throw on"), "lenivo" ("lazily"), "plechi" ("shoulders"). "Nakinete" and "ispanskuiu" ("Spanish") represent a synthesis of this sound conflict: "nakinete" with its "a-i-i-e" constitutes a transition from the first group to the second while "ispanskuiu" with its "i-a-u-u" represents a transition from the second group to the series given in the first line, i.e., "a–u." The word "krasnyi" ("red") has a special role in that it represents

234

a merger of the group "krasota" ("beauty")—"strashna" ("terrible") which is built solely on the "a" sound and "Vy" with its lone vowel "y."

The explanatory cliche offered by "them" is attractive, polysemous and terrible, while the heroine is passive and ready to accept it.

The second stanza begins with the same line in terms of its sound organization. True, the first line already displays some difference. Although its vocalism is identical from the point of view of pronunciation, i.e., *a-a-a-a-a-a-a-u*, not all of these "a's" are equally meaningful: some of them are phonemes, others merely pronunciational variants of the phoneme "o." In some measure this also occurred in the first line of the first stanza but the difference is considerable. It is not that there is one such case among the seven "a's" in the first line and two in the second. In the key word of the first stanza, "strashna" ("terrible"), both of the "a's" are phonemic, while in the second stanza the first "a" of "prosta" is only a "masked" "o." This is most important in that the phoneme "o" in this stanza is from the group of "back" vowels being opposed to "a," thus obtaining independent structural meaning. If in the expression "krasota strashna" ("beauty is terrible") with its sequence *a-a/ o-a-a-a*, "a/o" is concealed owing to the general inertia, then in the case of "krasota prosta" ("beauty is simple") we obtain the symmetrical or organization *a-a/o-a-a/o-a* which immediately makes it structurally meaningful. As a consonantal group, as we shall subsequently see, "prosta" ("simple") is connected with "pestroi" ("multi-colored") *(prst—pstr)* and the vocalisms form the group:

pestroi	multi-colored
neumelo	awkwardly
ukroete	you will cover
rebenka	child

Insofar as the special role of "red" ("krasnyi") in the first stanza establishes an inertia of high "coloration," the antithetic character of the general structure predisposes us to seek a color antonym. It is "multi-colored" ("pestryi") which condenses in itself the meanings of domesticity, awkwardness, youth and maternity. The "u" sound assumes a special role in this stanza. It is met in combinations not with "a" but with the group "e-i-o," i.e., "neumelo" *(e-u-e-o)* ("awkward"), and "ukroete" *(u-o-e-e)* ("you will cover"). In the antithetic contrast of the lines

Krasnyi rozan—v volosakh
Krasnyi rozan—na polu

A red rose is in your hair
The red rose is on the floor,

the opposition of the final stressed vowels "a—u" assumes the character of an opposition "above—below" which on the semantic level is easily understood as the triumph or the abasement of "the red rose" ("krasnyi rozan"), that is, of the entire semantic group consisting of the words beauty, terrible and red ("krasota," "strashnyi," and "krasnyi").

Insofar as the first stanza is opposed to the second as "red" ("krasnaia") is to "multi-colored" ("pestraia"), special significance is assumed by the fact that the first is built on the repetition of a single phoneme (namely "a"), while the second stanza contains various combinations. That is, in the first case the phoneme itself is significant while in the second, its elements are. In the establishment of correspondences between the phonological and the color meanings, this may be understood as an iconic sign of multi-coloredness.

The third stanza is "not colored." This is expressed both in the absence of color epithets and in the impossibility of discovering the vocal dominants of the stanza.

The last stanza, forming a compositional ring, is built on the "a" sound just as demonstrably as the first. (This assumes special meaning in that on the word level it denies the first stanza.)[158] Only the stressed "y" sound in the word "zhizn' " ("life") is dissonant. This is all the more significant in that with a single exception it is the only stressed "non-a" in the stanza. It is immediately drawn into a unified semantic group with the "Vy" ("you"). The fact that "zhizn' " ("life"), the broadest and most meaningful concept, is syntactically an antonym of the heroine, i.e., "terrible am not I, but life" ("strashna ne ia, a zhizn' "), whereas phonologically it is a synonym (more accurately, a word "sharing the same root"), assigns to the image of the heroine that complexity which is also the constructional idea of the poem.

The text's consonantism also forms a special structure somewhat parallel to that of the vocalism and simultaneously conflicting with it. Conventionally speaking, the "red" ("krasnyi") group and the "multi-colored" ("pestryi") group are clearly isolated in the text's consonantal organization. The first group is characterized: 1) by the voicelessness of the sounds "k," "s," "t," "shch," "p" and 2) by a concentration of consonants in groups. The second group is characterized: 1) by voicing in that liquids predominate and 2) by the markedly higher proportion of consonants in relation to vowels. While the correlation of vowels and consonants is 1:2 or 1:3 in the first group, it is 1:1 in the second.

The phonological repetitions of consonants form certain connections among the words.

krasota	beauty	*strashna*	terrible	*krasnyi*	red
krst		strshn		krsn	
krasota		*prosta*	simple	*pestryi*	multi-colored
krst		prst		pstr	

The sound transformations occur quite regularly. On the one hand, phonemes which are included in the recurring sound nucleus are activated as, on the other hand, are non-recurrent phonemes such as "sh" in the first case or "k" in the second. They play the role of differential features. It is from this that we have the heightened significance of the combinations "sh" with the dominant "a" in the word "shal'" ("shawl") in the third line of the first stanza and "kr" in the second stanza where this latter combination is repeated both in the discarded (both thematically—"na polu" ["on the floor"] and constructionally) "krasnyi" ("red"), and in the opposing "ukro-ete" ("you will cover") and "rebenka" ("child").

Thus notwithstanding the whole opposition of "red—multicolored" ("krasnyi—pestryi"), these concepts (words) form a neutralized pair on the meta-level not only because they constitute the archiseme "color," but also in that they share a tangible common phonological nucleus. The use of isolated single consonants on a vocalic background is opposed to this accumulation of consonants with its combination of plosives and liquids and of voiceless and voiced sounds. "Vy" ("you") becomes the center of this group. Sonorants and semivowels occupy a major place in the group which contains such words as "neumelo, vnimaia" and "zadumaetes' " ("awkwardly, heeding" and "sink into thought"). Their semantic kinship is evident in that they are all connected with the world of the heroine. These two tendencies are synthesized in the last stanza. Thus, the word "ubivat' " ("to kill") (the poem's sole enjambment) is set in its unique syntactic position in the line. In terms of its consonant organization it belongs to the group with "domestic" meanings which facilitates the unexpectedness, that is, the meaningfulness of its informational load.

If one sums up the picture thus obtained of the coinciding orders, albeit not fully coinciding, on the various structural levels of the text, approximately the following is obtained:

The first stanza contains the quoted speech of some generalized collective observer and a description of the semantically consonant behavior of the heroine. The heroine agrees with this voice. The second stanza is also constructed in this way. The difference lies only in the fact that in each of them the "voice" says opposing things and, accordingly, the heroine's behavior is built in a contrastive fashion. There is, it seems, no authorial judgment, no author's "point of view" in the text.

The third stanza is a transition. It neutralizes the problems of the first two for all structural indices.

The fourth is a reprise which simultaneously contains a repetition and a denial of the first stanzas. The synthesis is given in the form of the heroine's direct speech, that is, it indisputably gives her point of view. However, this is not actual direct speech but an internal monologue known to the author only because it coincides with the authorial explanation of the heroine's personality. (Syntactically it resembles the phrase "In answer to this you might have said.") As well as being the direct speech of the heroine, it is simultaneously the direct speech of the author. In the first stanzas the heroine's point of view coincides with that of general opinion, while in the second it coincides with Blok's voice.

The image of the poetic "Vy" ("you") manifests itself in the following movement:

Carmen	—	Madonna	—	Person whose inner world does not lend itself to the standard explanations, (a poet).

It is evident that an approximation between the "you" and the author's poetic "I" is taking place. But the following is also important: the first two links of the chain are given as something external for Blok; the evaluation is "theirs" and "yours" (not "mine"). We know, however, how important the symbols of Carmen and the Madonna are for Blok's lyrics and the measure in which they belong to his poetic world. This contradiction is not external and accidental but internal and structurally motivated.

The images of Carmen and the Madonna in Blok's lyrics are varieties of the feminine element and are invariably opposed to the lyric "I" as passionately earthly or the exaltedly divine but always external element. The image of the poet in his lyrics is asigned to the inner world of the "I" and therefore the feature "masculine/feminine" is irrelevant for him (as for Lermontov's pines and palms). The image is complex and approximates Blok's lyrical "I." In the above chain a weakening of that which is specifically feminine (very clearly emphasized in the first links) occurs and there takes place a simultaneous migration of the heroine from a world external to the "I" into an inner world.

But the circular composition means that the rejection of the first links is not their destruction. The enchantment of femininity and the separateness of the heroine from the author are preserved, forming only a structural tension with the synthetic image of the last stanza.

The specific nature of the text's structure enables Blok to convey to the reader an idea significantly more complex than the sum of the meanings of the individual words. The interweaving of the various points of view, which are expressed by direct speech proceeding from several subjects, turns out to be the author's complexly constructed monologue. That the authorial text is given in the form of the heroine's monologue (otherwise it would be still another interpretation from aside, which the bystanders offer to the "you" ["vam"]), does not diminish its connection with Blok's world. The concluding "life is terrible" ("zhizn' strashna") is a clear reference to phraseologisms of the type "terrible world" ("strashnyi mir"). This is Blok's explanation of what Akhmatova is and contains distinct features of a translation into Blok's poetic language of the world of the young poetess, a representative, both poetically and humanly, of the new generation which was already succeeding that of Blok. Just as in Altman's portrait of Akhmatova, Altman himself is visible and in Petrov-Vodkin's portrait, the artist who has translated Akhmatova into *his own* language is evident, Blok too is present in his poetic portrait. But the portraits are nonetheless, first and foremost, the poetess depicted in them. Blok's portrait is connected by many threads to the poetry of the young Akhmatova who becomes here an *object* of interpretation, of depiction and translation into the language of Blok's poetry.

M. I. Tsvetaeva

In vain with my eye—as with a nail,
Do I try to pierce the black earth:
In my consciousness—it is more certain than the nail:
Thou art not here—and thou art not.

In vain in the turn of an orb
I ransack the horizon:
—Rain! A tub of rainwater.
Thou art not there—and thou art not.

No, neither of the two:
Bone too much is bone, spirit is too much—spirit.
Where art thou? Where is that one? Where is oneself?
     Where is all?
There is too much there, here is too much here.

I shall not replace thee with sand
And steam. You who took [me] —as kin
For corpse and specter I shall not give back.
Here is too much here, there—too much there.

Not thou—not thou—not thou—not thou,
Whatever the priests may chant to us,
That death is life and life is death—
God is too much God, a worm—too much a worm.

Into corpse and specter—indivisible!
We shall not give you back in exchange for the smoke of
The thuribles,
The flowers
of the graves.

And if anywhere thou *art*—
It is in us. And highest honor to you,
Thou art gone completely. *With everything*—gone.
Those who have gone—scorn the schism:

           —January 5-7, 1935
       • • •
       • • •
Naprasno glazom—kak gvozdem,
Pronizyvaiu chernozem:
V soznanii—vernei gvozdia:
Zdes' net tebia—i net tebia.

Naprasno v oka oborot
Obsharivaiu nebosvod:
—Dozhd'! Dozhdevoi vody bad'ia.
Tam net tebia—i net tebia.

Net, nikotoroe iz dvukh:
Kost' slishkom—kost', dukh slishkom—dukh.
Gde—ty? Gde—tot? Gde—sam? Gde—ves'?
Tam—slishkom tam, zdes'—slishkom zdes'.

Ne podmeniu tebia peskom
I parom. Vziavshego—rodstvom
Za trup i prizrak ne otdam.
Zdes'—slishkom zdes', tam—slishkom tam.

Ne ty—ne ty—ne ty—n ty,
Chto by ni peli nam popy,
Chto smert' est' zhizn' i zhizn' est' smert'—
Bog—slishkom bog, cherv' slishkom cherv'.

Na trup i prizrak—nedelim!
Ne otdadim tebia za dym
Kadil,
Tsvety
Mogil.

I esli gde-nibud' ty *est'*—
Tak—v nas. I luchshaia vam chest',
Sovsem ushel. *So vsem*—ushel.
Ushedshie—prezret' raskol:

The poem is a part of the cycle "Epitaph" ("Nadgrobie") dedicated to the death of N. P. Gronsky.[159] Extremely interesting in a structural regard, this poem of Tsvetaeva is a vivid example of poetic semantics: the dictionary meanings of the individual words are sharply attenuated with the word approximating a pronoun and exhibiting an occasional meaning dependent on the structure of the text.[160]

The poem is clearly apportioned into an entire system of parallelisms which form sense paradigms manifesting the semantic construction of the text. Intuition based on attentive reading enables us to isolate the following stanzas as parallel: 1 and 2, 3 and 5, and 4 and 6. The seventh remains unpaired. As we shall see, there are profound ideational and compositional reasons for this. Let us examine the isolated parallel segments of the text.

The first two stanzas are marked by full parallelism of their syntactic and intonational structures. The rhythmical structure of the stanzas is as follows:

1	2
U–U–U–U–	U–U–U–U–
U–U–U–U–	U–U–U–U–
U–U–U–U–	U–U–U–U–
U–U–U–U–	U–U–U–U–

Marked parallelism is evident. (Variation is created by the rhythmic anomaly in the third line of the second stanza.) The change of degree of unexpectedness in the lines is curious. The first lines of the first and second stanzas belong (according to Taranovsky, whose terminology we have already used) to the type IV rhythmic figure. This is the most widespread variety of Russian iambic tetrameter. According to Taranovsky's tables, in Pushkin's lyrics of the 1830s, it constitutes 44.9 percent of all cases of the use of this meter (the most numerous group). It preserves its dominance in the poetry of the twentieth century, although the absolute figures of its frequency of usage are somewhat smaller. In Blok's poetry, according to the same source, it constitutes 38.7 percent of all iambic tetrameter.

The variety of iambic tetrameter (type V according to Taranovsky)[161] which is twice repeated in the second lines of both stanzas is very rare. V. V. Ivanov calls it "an iamb of an unusual form." (In his terminology it is called type VII.)[162]

In Pushkin's lyrics of the 1830s it is not met at all and in Blok's work it amounts to 0.07 percent. The third line in the first stanza belongs to a rare, but all the same more frequent variety: type III which accounts for 4.7 percent in Pushkin's work of the thirties and 11.6 percent in Blok's poetry. Thus a certain regularity of expectation is created: from the most frequent— to the most rare, with an ensuing softening of the sharpness of this transition. No sooner has this pattern been established however, than it is violated.

The third line of the second stanza which is not in correct iambs at all and which therefore seems unpredictable in the given rhythmic context is projected against the background of the third line of the first stanza. Both stanzas end with a line which, as we shall see, may equally well be read either as type I, type II, or as type II rhythmic figures. But these have sharply differing probabilities. (In the "Pushkin norm" of the 1830s, the probabilities are 34.3 percent, 44.9 percent, and 4.7 percent respectively.) This gives special significance to which variant will be actualized in the reader's declamation and which will be rejected.

The parallelism of the first and second stanzas is especially striking on the level of lexical construction.

> **In vain with my eye—as with a nail. . .**
> **Naprasno glazom—kak gvozdem. . .**
>
> **In vain in the turn of an eye. . .**
> **Naprasno v oka oborot. . .**

The anaphoric element "in vain" ("naprasno") establishes the parallelism between the lines. However, it is parallelism, not identity. Subsequently, the differences are as significant as the similarities: they are mutually activated against each other's background. *Glazom—gvozdem"* ("with an eye—with a nail") and *"oka—oborot"* ("of an eye—a turn") obviously constitute two phonologically connected pairs. This establishes a semantic connection between them.

242

The methodology of demonstrating semantic communality may be represented in the following form: a full list of "semes," i.e., elementary sense units, is given for each of two words. The common "semes" constitute that intersection of semantic fields which is activated by comparison, by sound repetitions and by contiguity in the poetic line.

A less cumbersome way may also be proposed: a list of possible natural language phraseologisms for each of these words may be given. The contexts in which both words can combine with a given third word yields the meaning which is activated in the text. In the case at hand, this will be:

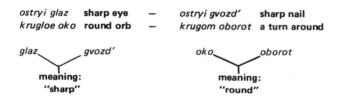

These meanings are reinforced by the verbs "I pierce" ("pronizyvaiu") in the first case and "I ransack" ("obsharivaiu") in the second. These verbs continue to activate the antithesis "sharp—round" ("ostryi—kruglyi") which branches out into a spatial opposition of a uni-directional action, i.e., space in the form of a "beam," and of one that is pan-directional, i.e., space in the shape of a "circle."

The impression may be created that there is an intensification of the degree of opposition taking place against the background of syntactic-intonational and rhythmic parallelism. (The higher the linguistic level, the clearer the difference becomes: intonation shows complete coincidence; rhythm— some differences; and the lexicon—an increase in the opposition of the stanzas.) "Eye" ("glaz") and "orb" ("oko") show only a stylistic opposition but subsequently the semantic opposition "sharp—round" ("ostryi—kruglyi") arises and the antithesis "action in beam-shaped space"—"action in circular space." The parallel is completed by the opposition "horizon—black earth" ("nebosvod—chernozem") which also yields the stylistic opposition "poetic— non-poetic," the spatial opposition "above—below" and the physical opposition "earth—air" or "filled space—empty space." The parallel passes over to the extreme points of the opposition. In the following line the very basis of the contrastive comparison, syntactic and rhythmic repetition, is disrupted:

In my consciousness—it is more certain than the nail. . .
V soznanii—vernei gvozdia. . .

Rain! A tub of rainwater. . .
Dozhd'! dozhdevoi vody bad'ia. . .

But it is precisely here that the previously established inertia of the thematic opposition of "consciousness" and "tub," the spiritual and physical elements which organize the entire system, is manifested. It is not by chance that the following stanza begins with a reference to the two basic elements: "bone" ("kost' ") and "spirit" ("dukh"). "Here—there" ("Zdes'—tam") at the beginning of the fourth line becomes a highly generalized expression of this opposition. If, however, the structure of the oppositions in the first and second stanzas affirms the antithesis of "horizon" ("nebosvod") and "black earth" ("chernozem") and of "there" ("tam") and "here" ("zdes' "), a second construct is deposited on top of the first one. The entire meaning of this second construct lies in its rejection of the characterized structure of the semantic associations.

The coincidence of the beginnings, i.e., "in vain" ("naprasno") and the endings, i.e., "thou art not—and thou art not" ("net tebia—i net tebia") affirms the unity of those seemingly opposed essences. The opposed elements prove to be identical and the poles of the semantic opposition are merely different forms of a single structural sense paradigm.

The identity of both poles of the opposition is to be seen primarily in their stylistic equation: the oppositions "heaven and earth," "above and below," "spirit and bone" do not coincide, tradition and expectation notwithstanding, with the opposition "poetry—prose." Both members of the opposition behave identically in this regard. Initially it might seem (and the line deliberately evokes this false inertia of expectation in the reader) that the stylistic features of an anti-poeticism are attributed to "earth" ("zemlia"): similarly, "eye" ("glaz")and "nail" ("gvozd' ")in opposition to "orb" ("oko") and to the poetically neutral "turn" ("oborot") produce an impression of being physically etiolated. But, subsequently, the crude "I ransack" ("obsharivaiu") is combined with the "poetic" "orb" while "I pierce" ("pronizyvaiu") which sounds poetic in the antithesis is linked with the corporeal "nail" ("gvozd' "). Next the traditional poetic "horizon" ("nebosvod") is joined to "I ransack" ("obsharivaiu") and "black earth" ("chernozem") which clearly lies outside the poetic lexicon is linked to "I pierce" ("pronizyvaiu"). It would seem, finally, that having satisfied the reader's expectation, "poetry" would be identified with "above" and prose with "below." But here again an unexpected substitution occurs: "below" is identified with the spiritual element, with "consciousness" ("soznanie"), and "above" is represented by the word "rain" whose physical character is strikingly underlined by its similarity to "tub" ("bad'ia").

Thus, the high and low spatially prove to be the means for expressing the antithesis of the spiritual and the physical but both equally lie outside the world of "the sublime" in the sense of "the poetic."

The identity of the semantic poles is shown in their uniform relationship to another sense construct in the same text. In the poem's first stanzas the structural centers are: "I" which is expressed by the personal form of the verbs "I ransack" ("obsharivaiu") and "I pierce" ("pronizyvaiu") and "thou." They frame the text of the stanzas by their initial and terminal location. Their relationship is represented in the schema:

In relation to the "I," the entire text is a set of synonyms, variants of a single invariant system: verbs of seeking—the sphere of the search. But they are equally so in relation to the "thou" in that they uniformly fail to contain the "thou." Let us note that if the *relationship* of the "I" and "thou" is designated, then their *essence* (for the "I" is not even directly expressed in a pronoun) coincides with their general language meaning. To determine the structural meaning of these pronouns for a given artistic text means to understand the poetic idea of the text.

The structuring of "thou" begins in these lines:

> **Thou art not here—and thou art not...**
> **Zdes' net tebia—i net tebia...**
>
> **Thou are not there—and thou art not...**
> **Tam net tebia—i net tebia...**

Similar structuring is impossible in a non-belletristic text: one and the same word is united to itself as is another. This immediately forces us to create a structure in which the hemistiches would be semantically distinct and consequently, unification would become possible. The simplest possibility for the opposition of hemistiches is intonational: in the first hemistich the "no" ("net") is considered stressed and in the second—"thee" ("tebia") (or vice versa). We have already noted (see. p. 242) that the degree of rhythmic unexpectedness depends on this. The meaning of the assertion also changes however. Given a change of stress, the assertion changes, i.e., "it is not that one which is thou" and "it is that one—not thou." (The simple repetition of the hemistich, which is also possible in poetry, would have given only an intonation of compression and would be equivalent to the introduction into the utterance of a quantitativeness which is alien to it, i.e., "red-red" ("krasnyi-krasnyi") equals "very red"; whatever intonational interpretation might be chosen, the entire sum of interpretations admissible in a text will be present in its reading as a set from which a choice is realized.

Although eliminating the external logical contradiction in the text of the fourth lines, intonation still does not resolve the question. If the goal were to arrive at a logically non-contradictory judgment, it could be much more easily attained.[163]

A semantically similar construct is possible if one concedes that the first and the second "thou" ("tebia") are not the same, but, as it were, two different words. And this is actually the case: the first "thou" designates the dictionary second person pronoun and, consequently, is applicable to anyone capable of filling the role of the second person. With the second "tebia" there begins the construction of a specifically poetic pronoun which can be assigned only to one person, i.e., the "thou" of the text.

The inequality of a word to itself which is absurd from the viewpoint of general language usage but is nonetheless one of the basic principles of poetic semantics is shown in these lines to be the semantic principle of Tsvetaeva's text.

A certain substantive representation of the "thou" which remains a question is formulated here. Neither "here" (earthly space) nor "there" (non-earthly space) contains the "thou." And if the first "thou art not here (there)" can be understood as an indication of the fact of death ("thou art no longer"), the second is an indication of the incompatibility of the "thou" with that space. But if the "thou" is incompatible with both "here" and "there," that is, *with any space at all,* then the nature of this "thou" begins to seem strange and is seen as a contradiction that the subsequent text is called upon to resolve.

Let us cite the rhythmical scheme of the remaining text:

$$
\begin{aligned}
&\acute{u}-u\acute{\smile}u-u-\\
&\acute{u}\acute{\smile}u\acute{\smile}\acute{u}\acute{\smile}u\acute{\smile}\\
&u\acute{\smile}u\acute{\smile}u-u\acute{\smile}^{164}\\
&\acute{u}\acute{\smile}u\acute{\smile}\acute{u}\acute{\smile}u\acute{\smile}\\[6pt]
&u-u\acute{\smile}u\acute{\smile}u\acute{\smile}\\
&u\acute{\smile}u\acute{\smile}u\acute{\smile}u\acute{\smile}\\
&u\acute{\smile}u\acute{\smile}u\acute{\smile}u\acute{\smile}\\
&\acute{u}\acute{\smile}u\acute{\smile}\acute{u}\acute{\smile}u\acute{\smile}\\[6pt]
&u\acute{\smile}u\acute{\smile}u\acute{\smile}u\acute{\smile}\\
&\acute{u}\,\acute{\smile}u\acute{\smile}u\acute{\smile}u\acute{\smile}\\
&\grave{u}\acute{\smile}u\acute{\smile}u\acute{\smile}u\acute{\smile}\\
&\acute{u}\acute{\smile}u\acute{\smile}\acute{u}\acute{\smile}u\acute{\smile}\\[6pt]
&u\acute{\smile}u\acute{\smile}u-u\acute{\smile}\\
&u-u\acute{\smile}u\grave{\smile}u\acute{\smile}\\
&u\acute{\smile}\\
&u\acute{\smile}\\
&u\acute{\smile}\\[6pt]
&u\acute{\smile}u\acute{\smile}u-u\acute{\smile}\\
&u\acute{\smile}u\acute{\smile}u-u\acute{\smile}\\
&u\acute{\smile}u-u\acute{\smile}u\acute{\smile}\\
&u\acute{\smile}u\acute{\smile}u-u\acute{\smile}
\end{aligned}
$$

Even if one makes the reservation that the last line of the text permits variant readings, the picture remains most striking. Two types of lines dominate in the text: on the one hand, the line with two (!) spondees (/ / U / / / U /) which is extremely remote from the iambic tetrameter norm and, on the other hand, the standard line (U / U / U – U /) (In nineteenth century poetry the type I rhythmic figure was second in frequency, yielding only to type IV; however in twentieth century poetry it has tended to increase its domain. According to Taranovsky's data, its frequency in Blok's poetry almost equaled the usage of type IV, i.e., 30 percent and 38.7 percent while in the pre-revolutionary writings of Viach. Ivanov and S. Gorodetsky, type I predominated—41.4 percent and 36.4 percent, and 44.1 percent and 41.1 percent respectively). One is quickly persuaded that all of the text's more meaningful points lie at these rhythmical extremes. Each of them constitutes a theme which runs throughout the text.

We have already noted that an intersecting parallelism is active in the central part of the line: the third stanza is parallel to the fifth, the fourth to the sixth. Certain refinements must now be introduced into this assertion. The spondaic lines which were connected with the theme of space ("there—here"), unite three stanzas: the third, the fourth, and the fifth. Their rhythmic antithesis which creates the meaning of the "thou" affirms the parallelism of the fourth and sixth stanzas. Finally, the theme of unity brings the fifth and the seventh stanzas together. Thus arises the complex compositional interweaving that makes up the semantic fabric of the poem.

> **Bone too much is bone, spirit is too much spirit. . .**
> **Kost' slishkom—kost', dukh slishkom—dukh. . .**
>
> **There is too much there, here—too much here. . .**
> **Tam—slishkom tam, zdes'—slishkom zdes'. . .**
>
> **Here is too much here, there is too much there. . .**
> **Zdes'—slishkom zdes', tam—slishkom tam. . .**
>
> **God is too much God, a worm too much a worm. . .**
> **Bog—slishkom bog, cherv'—slishkom cherv'. . .**

The constructional parallelism of these lines lies on the surface. They create two series which are mutually antonymic, each forming within itself a kind of semantic paradigm:

bone *(kost')*	—	spirit *(dukh)*;
here *(zdes')*	—	there *(tam)*
worm *(cherv')*	—	god *(bog)*

The structure of such synonymic series in and of itself results in the activation both of a common semantic nucleus "earthly (material)—heavenly (spiritual)" and of differential meanings:

inert material	—	ideal
base	—	exalted
near	—	far

The matter is not, however, reduced to this: the adjunction of a word to itself with the help of the adverb "too" ("slishkom") not only introduces an element of quantitative measurement into non-quantitative concepts, but anew separates the dictionary word from the poetic by showing that the dictionary word can in some, albeit not the usual, measure be contained in the poetic one. Thus a picture is created of the two parts of world space wherein each contains the quintessence of itself, its own essence. Here the spondaic lines enter into a relationship with the second semantic leit-motif which affirms the impossibility for the "thou" of remaining itself either in an exclusively earthly or in an exclusively spiritual world.

> **Where art thou? Where is that one? Where is oneself? Where is all?. . .**
> **Gde—ty? gde—tot? gde—sam? gde—ves'?. . .**
>
> **Not thou—not thou—not thou—not thou. . .**
> **Ne ty— ne ty—ne ty—ne ty. . .**

The first of these lines creates the synonymic series: "thou—that one—oneself—all" ("ty—tot—sam—ves' "). It also reveals the meaning of "thou": it incorporates in itself the meaning of uniqueness (that one, and not this one or any other one), of the personal element,[165] and of integralness ("all"). Thus, the "thou" acquires a series of supra-dictionary semantic features.

The reader, having already become accustomed to the fact that in Tsvetaeva's text the word is not equal to itself, will not perceive the four-fold repetition of "not thou" as a tautology. He will feel that four (here a synonym for "any number") different variants of the "thou" are being offered to him and they are all "not thou." The idea of the singularity, the uniqueness of the "thou" is conclusively affirmed by this. The pronoun becomes its grammatical opposite—a proper noun.

By varying the basic antithesis of the earthly and the heavenly, Tsvetaeva introduces new pairs of semantic poles in order to reject those differential features which the preceding text constructed for their differentiation. The pair "sand—steam" ("pesok—par") removes the opposition "material—immaterial" in that both members of the semantic relationship are material, and for Tsvetaeva—grossly material. "Steam" is no more ideal than "sand." Moreover, insofar as this word stands where we would expect to see the word "soul" or its synonym, it reveals the deliberate crudity of such a replacement.

Compare the description of death:

> **Like steam through a hole went**
> **The celebrated absurd heresy,**
> **Called soul.**
> **The pallid Christian illness!**
> **Steam. Apply poultices!**
> **And it never even existed!**

248

There was the body, it wanted to live.

Parom v dyru ushla
Preslovutaia eres' vzdornaia,
Imenuemaia dusha.
Khristianskaia nemoch' blednaia!
Par. Priparkami oblozhit'!
Da ee nikogda i ne bylo!
Bylo telo, khotelo zhit'.[166]

Steam consonant with poultices ("par—priparka"), the depiction of the moment of the parting of soul and body with the words "like steam it went out through a hole," all this is, of course, remote from idealism.

If, however, both semantic poles seem material and crude in this context, the other antithesis "Smoke of the thuribles,—the flowers of the graves" ("dym kadil—tsvety mogil") represents them both as poetic.

Thus, neither the opposition of the leaden material to the ideal nor the antithesis of the exalted to the base is capable of organizing the text. Not only are all of the initially proposed principles for a division into basic semantic centers discarded but even the division itself is abandoned. The "thou" is opposed to the "not thou" as the undivided to the divided:

No, neither of the two. . .
I shall not replace thee with sand
And steam. That which has taken—*as kin*
Into corpse and specter—indivisible.

Net, nikotoroe iz dvukh. . .
Ne podmeniu tebia peskom
I parom. Vziavshego—*rodstvom*
Na trup i prizrak—nedelim.

[The italics are mine. Y. L.]

The theomachistic and anti-Christian character of the fifth stanza was such that it could not be published in *Sovremennye zapiski* where the poem initially saw light (Paris, 1935, N.. 58, p. 223). However it is not merely a matter of the organic impossibility (according to Tsvetaeva's text) of death. The "thou," whose essence is in indivisibility, in integralness, can exist, can "be" only in non-divided integrated space while the entire text creates a structure of divided space. Real space from time immemorial has been divided into "horizon" and "black earth" and for the poet who does not accept this division the ideal "thou" can neither die nor live its real life in it. This space is not compatible with it. The fact that here the very principle of a division is not accepted is proved by the stanza:

Not thou—not thou—not thou—not thou.
Whatever the priests may chant to us,
That death is life and life is death—
God is too much God, a worm too much a worm.

249

Ne ty—ne ty—ne ty—ne ty.
Chto by ni peli nam popy,
Chto smert' est' zhizn' i zhizn' est' smert'—
Bog—slishkom bog, cherv'—slishkom cherv'.

The stanza is interesting not only as a polemic against the entire church tradition from its lowest manifestations, "priests," to the very highest and most poetic. (The last line is a polemic against the Psalter and the entire Russian tradition of the interpretation of the famed seventh verse from the Twenty-first Psalm).[167] Something more significant is implied, to wit, that integrity of the personality also requires integral space. The affirmation of the "priests" does not destroy the division of life and death, but only changes their places, declaring earthly life, death, and death, real life. But the church concept that the "thou" was dead in life and only now has become truly alive is rejected ("not thou") just as is its opposite, i.e., "thou were alive and became dead." They both proceed from a division but according to the construction of the text, division and "thou" are not compatible.

Thus the last stanza is in opposition to the entire text. The text speaks of that space where the "thou" is absent while the final stanza creates the structure of a possible space which would correspond to the nature of the "thou."

The dynamics of the relationship of the "I" and the "thou" is interesting in this sense. The complex system of the use of the category of number merits attention.

	1st Person Pronoun	2nd Person Pronoun
I-IV Stanzas	sg.	sg.
V-VI "	pl.	sg.
VIII "		
1st and 4th lines	—	sg.
2nd and 3rd lines	pl.	pl.

Prior to the appearance of the "we" ("us") in the text, the first person pronoun is present only in the verbal endings. The second person is always expressed by the pronoun. More important is that although a system of relationships of the "I" and the "thou" ("I" seeks "thou") is set forth, from the very beginning it is realized in the text through what Hegel termed nonfulfillment. All of the verbal forms characterizing the actions of the poetic "I" (and of the "we") are given the denials ("in vain. . .I penetrate," "in vain. . . I ransack. . .," "I shall not replace," "I shall not give back," "we shall not give back"), while the "thou" is present by its absence, ("thou art not," "where art thou?," "not thou").

Thus, a space is created where "thou" cannot exist. The last stanza,

250

where the "thou" is given with the positive feature of existence is opposed to this, i.e., "thou art." The relationships of the text's lyrical centers are built contrastively. In stanzas I-IV the relationship of the "I" and the "thou" is as follows: the proposed place of "thou" is heaven and earth; searches are conducted along the rectilinear "I pierce" and the circular "I ransack," i.e., the entire external universe. In the seventh stanza the relationship between the "I" ("we") and the "thou" is inclusive ("if thou art anywhere, then it is among us"). External space is split; internal space is unified. (Only here is it possible "to scorn the schism". . . ("prezret' raskol").

| Stanzas I-VI | Space external in relation to the "I": space torn apart; not thou. |
| Stanza VI | Space internal in relation to the "I": integral space; thou art. |

Thus the full and integral existence of the "thou" is its sojourn in "I" ("we"). Therefore complete departure from the disrupted world ("completely" ["sovsem"] —"with everything" ["so vsem"]) is not annihilation.

> . . . And the highest honor to you,
> Those who have gone—scorn the schism:
> Thou art gone completely. Gone with everything.

> . . . I luchshaia vam chest',
> Ushedshie—prezret' raskol:
> Sovsem ushel. So vsem ushel.

The absolute totality of the rejection of both heaven and earth, of the total departure expressed by the last line, both hemistiches which in their mutual projection reveal a complex structuring of meaning: "completely" ("sovsem") against the backdrop of the second hemistich means "totality," i.e., he died absolutely. This hemistich is also opposed to the idea of life beyond the grave ("however priests might chant to us") and to the tradition stemming from Horace that death does not completely ravish the poet, a *part* of him is preserved in memory by his glory. Compare:

> Not completely shall I die; but death will leave
> A great part of me, as I end my life. . .
> N. Lomonosov

> Ne vovse ia umru; no smert' ostavit,
> Veliku chast' moiu, kak zhizn' skonchaiu. . .

> Yes!—I shall not die entirely; but a great part of me,
> Having escaped decay, after death will begin to live.
> G. Derzhavin

> Tak!—ves' ia ne umru; no chast' menia bol'shaia,
> Ot tlena ubezhav, po smerti stanet zhit'. . .

251

No, I shall not die entirely. . .
Net, ves' ia ne umru. . .
—A. Pushkin

Traditional immortality in the memory of posterity is rejected precisely because "a great part of me" will remain alive. To this is opposed the *full* preservation of the entire "thou" among "us," among people who knew the "thou" both as a poet and as a man. The second hemistich with the italicized "everything" ("vsem") declines to identify the departed with the material traces of his personality. In accord with Tsvetaeva's maximalism the text proclaims the identity of total preservation and of total annihilation, of preservation of the internal, of annihilation of the external.

The adduced scheme gives only the general semantic skeleton upon which the more individual constructs are superimposed, either refining it or contradicting it. But precisely these numerous derivations give the text life. Thus, for example, the opposition of stanzas I and VI and VII contrasts worlds where "thou art not" and where "thou art." But the conditional form of the first line of the seventh stanza ("And if. . .") introduces doubt in this concept which other structures confirm. It should also be noted that although the "I" and the "we" structurally go back to a single semantic invariant, the play on their transitions creates additional meanings which are by no means indifferent for the whole. In the line "Where art thou? Where is that one? Where is oneself? Where is all?. . ." ("Gde—ty? gde—tot? gde—sam? gde—ves'?. . .") the change of meanings of the pronouns interests us. But another matter can also be remarked upon: the vowels of this line form the sequence *e-y-e-o-e-a-e-e,* where "e" in pairs combines with different vowel phonemes revealing different aspects of its articulation. (In "Where is all?" ["gde-ves' "] the relationship of "e" to itself is activated supporting the meaning of wholeness in this segment of the text.) The exhaustion of the phonological components is parallel to the exhaustion of the possibilities for re-enumeration, to the general meaning of the line. The sequential combinations of "e" with the maximum number of other vowel phonemes establishes the closeness of the above line and *Ne podmeniu tebia peskom* with its vowel sequence *e-o-e-u-e-a-e-o.* In general, insofar as the antithesis "here" and "there" is important in the poem, the role of "e" and "a" as the two opposed phonological centers expands sharply.

Interesting results might be obtained from a detailed analysis of the relationship of the intonation of the poem's first and second parts. Thus, in the first six stanzas there are only two enjambed lines, "with sand/ And steam" ("Peskom/ I parom") and "for smoke of the / thuribles" ("za dym/ Kadil"). On the other hand, there are a great many exclamations and questions. In the four lines of the last stanza, there are two enjambments and not a single emphatic intonation. Furthermore, both of the text's italicized expressions are met here, i.e., "art" ("est' ") and "with everything" ("sovsem"). This, of course, is not by chance. The intonations of declamation (the external world) and of meditation (the internal world) meet. Together with the replacement of "I" by "we," this creates a paradoxical construct. With the transition to the internal world, the intonation becomes less personal. Thus arises the interweaving of individual constructs which do not simply illustrate the basic construct of the lower levels but have their own constructional role in guaranteeing non-predictability for the text, a plenitude of informational meaning at all stages of its development.

V. V. Mayakovsky

A Scheme for Laughter

The wind howled and knew not because of whom,
instilling in our heart a shiver.
Along the road went a baba with her milk,
she went along the railroad track.

And exactly at seven in due form
rushing at full speed from the Oka,
having flashed beyond the semaphores—
the express flew along.

The baba would have been injured,
for naught a hundred whistles fiercely howled—
but a muzhik came along with his mutton
and let her know in time.

Off to the right went the baba,
off to the left went the train.
Had it not been for the muzhik then
It would have cut her in twain.

The smoke has already disappeared beyond the stars,
the muzhik and the baba have vanished.
We shall render tribute to the hero,
by soaring above the prosaic.

Although from the thick of the masses,
he saved her in broad daylight.
Long live the mutton-trading
middle-peasant!

Long shine the sun in darkness!
Burn, stars, at night!
Long live both those and those—
and all the others too!

1923

Skhema Smekha

Vyl veter i ne znal o kom,
Vseliaia v serdtse drozh' nam.
Putem shla baba s molokom,
shla zheleznodorozhnym.

A rovno v sem' po forme,
nesias' vo ves' kar'er s Oki,
sverknuv za semaforami,—
vzletaet kur'erskii.

Byla by baba ranena,
zria vylo sto svistkov revmia,—
no shel muzhik s baraninoi
i dal poniat' ei vovremia.

Ushla napravo baba,
ushel nalevo poezd.
Kab ne muzhik, togda by
razrezalo po poias.

Uzhe ischez za zvezdy dym,
muzhik i baba skrylis'.
My dan' geroiu vozdadim,
nad budniami voskrylias'.

Khot' iz narodnoi gushchi,
a spas sred' bela dnia.
Da zdrastvuet torguiushchii
baraninoi seredniak!

Da svetit solntse v temnote!
Gorite, zvezdy, noch'niu!
Da zdrastvuiut i te, i te—
i vse inye prochie!

Mayakovsky in the "Introduction" to his satiric poem collection "Mayakovsky Smiles, Mayakovsky Laughs, Mayakovsky Mocks" ("Maiakovskii ulybaetsia, Maiakovskii smeetsia, Maiakovskii izdevaetsia") wrote of this poem:

I know satiric work much better than other kinds. . .
There is not a single humorous idea or funny thought in this poem.
There is no idea, but there is correct satiric treatment of the word.
This is not a poem suitable for use. It is a specimen.
It is a scheme for laughter.[168]

The assertion that "A Scheme for Laughter" is "not a poem suitable for use" cannot be accepted without reservation. For Mayakovsky printed it in the journal *Ogonek* (with his own illustrations) not, of course, as a constructional model for poets but as a poem for readers. It is indisputable, however, that Mayakovsky considered this text a model in its own way for the structuring of "satiric work." That the poet was convinced of the existence of structural laws for making a text both comic and satiric is also important. In this same comment, he wrote:

I am convinced that in schools of the future satire will be taught alongside arithmetic and no less successfully. . .
A general awareness of verbal technique has given my satire the

255

power to survive the moment.[169]

All this forces one to look carefully at the structural peculiarities of "A Scheme for Laughter." The key to the text's construction may be found in the poem's very name:

s — khem -- a	s -- mekh — a
"scheme"	"laughter"

A word which we have become accustomed to perceive as an independent lexical item proves to be a displacement, a transposition, a transformation of another word which hitherto has not been associated with it. The entire text consists of such transpositions. Each of its elements appears in a double light. On the one hand, each element is incorporated into a logically consistent system and is well-grounded in it; from this point of view the presence of each element is completely natural and predictable. On the other hand, the element is felt as part of an *alien* system, the result of a shift of structural meanings. From this standpoint it seems unexpected, strange, and unpredictable. The comic effect stems from the fact that elements of meaning with extremely remote evaluational characteristics are drawn into mutual proximity. (Tragedy juxtaposes elements which are found on identical or adjacent evaluational levels in a given system of a culture.)

The Genre Level

During his association with the humor magazine *Satirikon,* the young Mayakovsky was already drawing on the satiric effect of genre displacement by creating "hymns"—works of "high" genre and comic content. The structuring is more complex in the present case: the text in and of itself is clearly understood as belonging to the comic genre. (Its publication in *Ogonek* establishes an even more specific characterization, i.e., that of "poetic subscripts" beneath satiric pictures.) However the lexical structure of a number of the stanzas contradicts our view of the text as comic. It must be noted that the form adopted here—iambic tetrameter with alternating three-foot lines and quatrain stanzaic structure—is neutral as a genre form in the Russian poetic tradition. The genre is determined by several additional features: lexicon, phraseology, theme *[siuzhet]*, the system of imagery, etc.

In the case at hand these features contradict each other: the non-correspondence of intonation and the phraseology of different stanzas is supplemented by the non-correspondence of subject and style, of the hero and the "savior" function attributed to him. An examination of Mayakovsky's drawings for the text is of interest in this regard. These drawings, which belong to the *Satirikon* tradition of satiric comic drawings with poetry subscripts, are simultaneously clearly connected with the verse on posters of the Russian Telegraph Agency (ROSTA) where Mayakovsky worked. This is the source of the text's didactic pathos which concludes with the obligatory apotheosis of the positive hero. In the drawings the didactic moral is expressed by the introduction of a hand with pointed index finger, while the pathos of the concluding lines is conveyed by the final depiction of the hero against the backdrop of the sun's rays. The elegaic fifth drawing, however, flatly contradicts ROSTA painting poetics by approximating book graphics. This entire system of non-correspondences causes us to regard the text as comic.

The Level of the Text's Internal Syntagmatics

The internal textual sequences also are characterized by a series of non-correspondences. Let us examine only one stanza:

> **Although from the thick of the masses,**
> **he saved her in broad daylight.**
> **Long live the mutton-trading**
> **middle-peasant!**
>
> **Khot' iz narodnoi gushchi,**
> **a spas sred' bela dnia.**
> **Da zdravstvuet torguiushchii**
> **baraninoi seredniak!**

The scheme "Although. . . and" ("Khot'. . .a") establishes a concessive construction on the syntactic level.

> In compound sentences, the main clause may contain information contrary to what might have been expected on the basis of the content of the subordinate clause. A relationship of this nature between the main and the subordinate clauses is marked by the conjunctions "although" ("khotia" or "khot' ") or "notwithstanding" ("nesmotria na to chto"). . . In compound sentences with a concessive subordinate element such conjunctions indicate that something in the main clause contradicts what might be expected as a logical consequence of the content of the subordinate clause.[170]

The expression "from the thick of the masses" contains nothing logically contradicting the content of the second clause which specifies the heroic act. On the other hand, there is an allusion to newspaper phraseology here. The poem was written in the heat of a campaign designed to attract cadres from below to administrative positions. This allusion is accompanied by a semantic shift which gives rise to irony. The formula "he saved her in broad daylight" ("a spas sred' bela dnia") contains a contradiction on the phraseological level. There is nothing surprising about a rescue in broad daylight but this phraseologism is clearly derived from another one: "to plunder (or kill) in broad daylight" ("ugrabil" or "ubil"). The key word has been replaced by its antonym. This comic principle which gives rise to texts such as Gogol's "to get well like flies" was often applied by Mayakovsky. The technique of replacing any element by an "alien one" in phraseologisms is analogous. Note in Mayakovsky's poem "About this" ("Pro eto"):

> The words are so
> (or else perhaps from malice):
> "One here broke his leg,
> so now we make merry with what
> God has sent
> we dance a bit for ourselves."
> • • •
> Slova tak
> (ne to chtob so zla):
> "Odin tut slomal nogu,
> tak vot veselimsia, chem bog
> poslal,
> tantsuem sebe ponemnogu."

The general incongruity of the situation ("broke his leg") and of the actions ("we make merry. . ., we dance. . .") is supplemented by the introduction of incompatible elements into the phraseologisms. "We make merry!" ("veselimsia") instead of "we grit our teeth" ("zakusyvaem") and "we dance" ("tantsuem") instead of "we make merry." The lines "Long live the trading/in-mutton middle-peasant!" ("Da zdravstvuet torguiushchii/ baraninoi seredniak!") are clearly connected on the one hand with the newspaper and poster phraseology of the early NEP period, and, on the other, are no less clearly not connected with the content of the poem whose conclusion they mark in terms of compositional position and intonation. It is also important to note that not only are constructional shifts of great consequence but so is the diversity of these shifts. The non-correspondences are developed on various levels thus assuring a constant and high degree of unexpectedness in the combinations of the text's structural elements. The tag ending is characteristic in this sense:

> Long shine the sun in darkness!
> Burn, stars, at night!
> Long live both those and those—
> and all the others too!
> • • •
> Da svetit solntse v temnote!
> Gorite, zvezdy, noch'iu!
> Da zdravstvuiut i te, i te—
> i vse inye inye proichie!

The first non-correspondence is that of the stanza as a whole which imitates a high degree of pathos, of ode-like ecstasy, and of the entire preceding text.

258

The semantic shifts within the stanza go further still. The first and second lines intonationally and compositionally are parallel and are perceived on these levels as analogous. Their incompatibility on the lexico-semantic level is obvious, however: the first stanza contains an "ode-like" appeal to the impossible; the second appeals in pathetic intonations to the natural, to that which ordinarily happens daily. The comic effect of the last two lines lies in the fact that the ode formula which presupposes pathos, "ecstasy," is built on the model of an office form with blanks for the insertion of family names.

The following stanza yields three distinct types of lexical materials:

> The smoke has already disappeared beyond the stars,
> the muzhik and the baba have vanished.
> We shall render tribute to the hero
> by soaring above the prosaic.

> Uzhe ischez za zvezdy dym
> muzhik i baba skrylis'.
> My dan' geroiu vozdadim,
> nad budniami voskrylias'.

The three types are:

stars	*zvezdy*	adult male peasant	*muzhik*
smoke	*dym*	adult female peasant	*baba*

tribute	*dan'*
hero	*geroi*
weekdays,	*budni*
humdrum life	
to soar up	*voskryliat'sia*

The combination of words from the elegaic, the everyday, and the odic vocabularies produces the general effect of the combination of that which cannot be combined.

The Level of Rhyme

Rhyme is among the most active levels in Mayakovsky's poetics. Mayakovsky himself discussed the comic function of rhyme in this text. "Laughter is elicited," he wrote, "by the creation of whip rhymes. . ."[171] The use of pun rhymes was permitted in nineteenth century poetry only in comic poetry. In Mayakovsky's poetry, this limitation is rejected. Stylistically the pun rhyme is in and of itself neutral. It activates a semantic level by brining together diverse kinds of concepts. In the case at hand, however, such rhymes as "drozh' nam—zheleznodorozhnym" ("a shiver for us—railroad"), "kar'er s Oki—kur'erskii" ("full speed from the Oka—express") and others create the effect of a huge machine performing a trifling task. The drawing together of remote concepts unexpectedly fails to give rise to new meaning due to the general insignificance of the content. Mayakovsky defined this as comedy of "absurd hyperbolism."[172]

The rhymes divide the text into three parts. The first three stanzas are completely organized by punning, inexact rhymes of differing numbers of syllables (including compound rhymes) which are typical for Mayakovsky. The fourth quatrain utilizes both inexact and compound rhymes. They are, however, comparatively simple and could well be met in a chastushka, a brief popular ditty often of humorous and/or vulgar content. The chastushka element, incidentally, is felt throughout the intonation of the stanza. Vocabulary of the type "had it not been for the muzhik" ("kab ne muzhik") fosters this impression. Difficult and unusual rhymes are completely absent in the last three stanzas. The hidden complexity of the rhymes of the fifth stanza attest that the simplicity here is deliberate and imitates a type of rhyme alien to Mayakovsky. Let us list the rhymes by groups.

I

znal o kom	knew of whom
s molokom	with milk

drozh' nam	a shiver for us
zhelezhnodorozhnym	railroad

po forme	in due form
semaforami	semaphores

kar'er s Oki	full speed from the Oka
kurer'skii	express

baba ranena	injured baba
s baraninoi	with mutton

svistkov revmia	whistles fiercely
vovremia	in time

II

baba	peasant woman
togda by	then t'would

poezd	train
poias	waist

gushchi	thick
torguiushchii	trading

dnia	day
seredniak	middle-peasant

III

dym	smoke
vozdadim	we shall render

skrylis'	vanished
voskrylias'	soaring up

temnote	darkness
te i te	those and those

noch'iu	at night
prochie	others

The first group concentrates on the "hard" rhymes typical of Mayakovsky, while the second group is neutral, and the third (in conjunction with its specifically ode-like vocabulary) displays rhymes alien to Mayakovsky's poetics. We are speaking mainly of imitation, of the peculiar cozenage of the reader's perception insofar as the rhyme "temnote—te i te" ("darkness—those and those"), for example, is in essence virtuosic and only "pretends" to be elementary. On the whole, however, one obtains the impression of a transition from lines organic to the reader's idea of Mayakovsky's poetry to lines that are not compatible with that conception and that are absurd in this incompatibility.

The transition from the "hard" rhyme to traditional ones also assumes another meaning here: in the history of Russian poetry, the first type of rhyme is closely associated with base, comic, familiar genres; the second, in conjunction with vocabulary such as "we shall render" ("vozdadim"), "soaring up" ("voskrylias' "), is perceived as a sign of the ode genre. Thus the dynamics of the change of rhymes affords a compositional sequence—from the comic to the odic, from the base to exalted.

This progression, however, is realized not as a deliberate transition but as a combination of the incombinable and devoid of internal logic. Also the intonations of the ode are not real but only a mocking imitation. On the level of rhyme, this is shown by the rhyme *"temnote—te i te"* ("darkness"—"those and those") which is reminiscent of the beginning of the poem. It is also shown by the ironic touch that gives this context such pseudo-careless rhymes as "gushchi—torguiushchii" ("thickets—trading") and "dnia—seredniak" ("day—middle-peasant"). From the standpoint of Mayakovsky's poetics, these are masterly rhymes; from the viewpoint of odic poetry, they are impossibly bad. Set in two mutually exclusive contexts, they are simultaneously both very bad and very good.

Mayakovsky considered his poem "an irreproachable formula"[173] for laughter. What is the constructional essence of this formula? Tragic contrast yields an opposition which is arrayed on one structural level and in principle allows a position of neutralization. For tragedy there is an archilevel on which the contrast is removed. The contrast "villainy—virtue" ("zlodeistvo—dobrodetel' ") can be resolved logically but the statement "In the garden there is an elderberry bush and in Kiev there is an uncle" does not permit the construction of an utterance that neutralizes the opposition. Therefore, there is more negative pathos in truly comic situations in art than in more tragic ones.

A text built on incompatibilities does not form a structure. Its structuredness is false. It is a non-system endowed with the external features of a system and, consequently, all the more internally chaotic. Mayakovsky's construction is precisely of this sort and, because of this, it is a scheme for laughter.

N. A. Zabolotsky

The Passerby

Filled with mental anguish,
In his three-flap winter cap, with his soldier bag,
Along the ties of the railroad,
He strides during the night.

It is already late. For the Nara station
The next-to-last train has left.
The moon from behind the edge of a granary
Shines, having risen over the roofs.

Having turned in the direction of the bridge,
He enters a spring wood,
Where pines, bending down toward the graveyard,
Stand, like a gathering of souls.

Here a flier at the edge of the road
Reposes in a snarl of wire,
And a dead propeller whitely shining,
Crowns his monument.

And in the dark palace of the universe
Over this sleepy foliage
Unexpectedly arises that sudden
Peace which transfixes the soul,

That marvelous peace, before which,
Agitated and ever in haste,
Falls silent with lowered gaze
The living human soul.

And in the light rustling of the leaf buds
And in the slow noise of the branches
The invisible youth-flier
Talks about something with it.

And a body wanders along the road,
Striding through thousands of misfortunes,
And his grief and troubles
Run, like dogs, after him.

1948

Prokhozhii

Ispolnen dushevnoi trevogi,
V treukhe, s soldatskim meshkom,
Po shpalam zheleznoi dorogi

Shagaet on noch'iu peshkom.

Uzh pozdno. Na stantsiiu Nara
Ushel predposlednii sostav.
Luna iz-za kraia ambara
Siiaet, nad krovliami vstav.

Svernuv v napravlenii k mostu,
On vkhodit v vesenniuiu glush',
Gde sosny, skloniaias' k pogostu,
Stoiat, slovno skopishcha dush.

Tut letchik u kraia allei
Pokoitsia v vorokhe lent,
I mertvyi propeller, beleia,
Venchaet ego monument.

I v temnom chertoge vselennoi
Nad sonnoiu etoi listvoi
Vstaet tot nezhdanno mgnovennyi,
Pronzaiushchii dushu pokoi,

Tot divnyi pokoi, pred kotorym,
Volnuias' i vechno spesha,
Smolkaet s opushchennym vzorom
Zhivaia liudskaia dusha.

I v legkom shurshanii pochek
I v medlennom shume vetvei
Nevidimyi iunosha-letchik
O chem-to beseduet s nei.

A telo bredet po doroge,
Shagaia skvoz' tysiachi bed,
I gore ego, i trevogi
Begut, kak sobaki, vosled.

The poem "The Passerby" presents certain difficulties not only for literary analysis but also from the standpoint of ordinary comprehension although a first acquaintance with the text is sufficient to assure us that it is one of the late Zabolotsky's poetic masterpieces. The reader may well not understand how the "passerby" and the invisible "youth-flier" are connected and why the "passerby" who appears at the beginning of the poem in a decidedly ordinary guise ("in a three-flap winter cap with a soldier's bag"), is at the end unexpectedly opposed to the dead flier as "a body": "And a body wanders along the road" ("A telo bredet po doroge").

Reconstruction of the general outlines of Zabolotsky's model of the world must precede our analysis of the poem's text. This system, inferable from the poet's *other* texts which provide a context for the present poem, functions as *a language* in relation to the poem while the poem functions as *a text* in relation to the system.

Zabolotsky underwent a prolonged and complex evolution which embraces all of his creative output and which has yet to be thoroughly investigated. It is all the more noticeable in that certain fundamental concepts of his artistic system are extremely stable. Above all the important modeling role assigned to the opposition top/bottom *[verkh/niz]* must be noted in Zabolotsky's poetry. "Top" is always a synonym for the concept "far" ("dal"), and "bottom" ("niz") for the concept "near." Therefore in the final analysis all movement is movement upward or downward. Movement is essentially organized only on one axis, the vertical.

Thus in the poem "The Dream" ("Son") the author dreams that he is "in a mute region" ("v mestnosti bezglasnoi"). Initially the surrounding world is described as being *"far* away" ("dalekii") ("I sailed away, I roamed far away," ["la uplyval, ia stranstvoval vdali. . ."]), as being "remote" ("otdalennyi"), i.e., being very strange. But it subsequently appears that this distant world is extremely "high" ("vysoko"):

> Bridges at an immense height
> Hung over the gorges of the gaps.
>
> Mosty v neobozrimoi vyshine
> Visali nad ushchel'iami provalov.

The earth is far below:

> The lad and I went to the lake,
> He cast his line somewhere below
> And something, which had flown up from the earth,
> He unhurriedly pushed away with his hand.
>
> My s mal'chikom na ozero poshli,
> On udochku kuda-to vniz zakinul
> I nechto, doletevshee s zemli,
> Ne toropias', rukoiu otodvinul.

This vertical axis simultaneously organizes ethical space: evil in Zabolotsky's work is invariably found to be below. Thus in "The Cranes" ("Zhuravli") the moral coloration of the axis "top—bottom" is stark: evil comes from below; salvation is an upward surge:

> A black gaping muzzle
> From the bushes in meeting was raised
> ....
> And echoing the sorrowful sobbing,
> The cranes burst upwards.
> ....
> Only there, where the luminaries move,
> In expiation for their own evil
> To them nature anew has returned
> That which death with itself bore off;
> ....
> Proud spirit, high striving,

Unswerving will to battle. . .

Chernoe ziiaiushchee dulo
Iz kustov navstrechy podnialos'
....
I, rydan'iu gorestnomu vtoria,
Zhuravli rvanulis' v vyshinu.
....
Tol'ko tam, gde dvizhutsia svetila,
V iskuplen'e sobstvennogo zla
Im priroda snova vozvratila
To, chto smert' s soboiu unesla:
....
Gordyi dukh, vysokoe stremlen'e,
Voliu nepreklonnuiu k bor'be. . .

The combination of height and distance and the opposing characterization of "bottom" makes "top" the direction of expanding space: the higher, the more boundless space is; the lower, the more confined. The terminal point of "the bottom" contains all of the space that has disappeared. It follows that only upward movement is possible and that the opposition top/bottom becomes the structural invariant not only of the antithesis good/evil, but also of the antithesis movement/non-movement. Death, the cessation of movement, is movement downward:

And a leader in a shirt of metal
Sank slowly to the bottom. . .

(Ibid.)

A vozhak v rubashke iz metalla
Pogruzhalsia medlenno na dno. . .

In "The Snow Man" ("Snezhnyi chelovek"), the spatial scheme that is customary for twentieth century art, i.e., the atomic bomb as death *from above,* is destroyed. The hero, "the snow man," is borne aloft and atomic death comes *from below* while the hero falls *down* in perishing.

They say that in the Himalayas somewhere,
Higher than the temples and monasteries,
He lives, unknown to the world,
The primordial fosterling of the beasts.
....
Hidden in the mountainous catacombs,
He seems not to know that *beneath him*
Atomic bombs pile up,
True to their masters.
Never will he reveal their secrets
This Himalayan troglodyte,
Even if, like an asteroid,
All aflame, he will fly *into the abyss.*

265

Govoriat, chto v Gimalaiakh gde-to,
Vyshe khramov i monastyrei,
On zhivet, nevedomyi dlia sveta,
Pervobytnyi vykormysh zverei.

....

V gornye upriatan katakomby,
On i znat' ne znaet, chto *pod nim*
Gromozdiatsia atomnye bomby,
Vernye khoziaevam svoim.
Nikogda ikh tainy ne otkroet
Gimalaiskii etot troglodit,
Dazhe esli, slovno asteroid,
Ves' pylaia, *v bezdnu* poletit.

The concept of movement in Zabolotsky's work often becomes complicated as a result of the complexity of the concept "bottom." For a number of Zabolotsky's poems "bottom" as an antithesis to "top—space—movement" is not the final point of descent. The death-related descent into the depths which are lower than the usual horizon is unexpectedly characterized in Zabolotsky's "poetic universe" by features reminiscent of certain qualities of the "top." The absence of frozen forms is typical of "the top." Movement here is interpreted as *metamorphosis,* transformation, while the possibilities of combination are not seen in advance:

> I well remember the external appearance
> Of all these bodies swimming from space:
> The mixture of farms and the convexities of grave stones
> And the wildness of pristine adornment.
> Not even a trace of refinements there,
> The art of forms is obviously not respected there. . .
>
> —"The Dream"

> • • •
> • • •
>
> Ia khorosho zapomnil vneshnii vid
> Vsekh etikh tel, plyvushchikh iz prostranstva:
> Spleten'e ferm i vypuklosti plit
> I dikost' pervobytnogo ubranstva.
> Tam tonkostei ne vidno i sleda,
> Iskusstvo form tam iavno ne v pochete. . .
>
> —"Son"

This redistribution of earthly forms is simultaneously a joining of the forms to a more general cosmic life. But it also relates to the underground, posthumous course of the human body. In an address to his dead friends, the poet says:

> You are in that land where there are no ready-made forms,
> Where all is torn apart, mixed, smashed,
> Where instead of the sky—only a grave mound. . .
>
> —"A Parting with Friends"

266

Vy v toi strane, gde net gotovykh form,
Gde vse raz'iato, smeshano, razbito,
Gde vmesto neba—lish' mogil'nyi kholm. . .

—"Proshchanie s druz'imai"

Thus the earth's surface, the *ordinary space of everyday life,* functions as a static opposition to "top." Motion higher and lower is possible. But this motion is understood in a specific way. Mechanical locomotion of immutable bodies in space is equated with immobility; mobility is transformation.

A new important opposition is advanced here in Zabolotsky's work: immobility is equated not only with mechanical movement but also with any unambiguously preordained, completely determined movement. Such movement is perceived as slavery, while freedom, the possibility of non-predictability, is opposed to it. (In the terminology of modern science this textual opposition might be presented as the antinomy "redundancy/information.") The absence of freedom, of choice, is a feature of the physical world. The free world of thought is opposed to it. Such an interpretation of this opposition which is characteristic of all of the early and a significant part of Zabolotsky's late poems has determined his assignment of nature to a low, immobile and servile world. This world is full of anguish and the absence of freedom and is opposed to the world of thought, culture, technology and creativity which present choice and the freedom of establishing laws where nature dictates only servile execution.

And the sage will leave, reflective,
And live as an unsociable person,
And nature, having instantly become bored,
Like a prison, stands over him.

—"Serpents"

I uidet mudrets, zadumchiv,
I zhivet, kak neliudim,
I priroda, vmig naskuchiv,
Kak tiur'ma, stoit nad nim.

—"Zmei"

Beasts have no names.
Who ordered them be named?
Uniform suffering is
Their invisible lot.
....
All nature smiled,
Like a high prison.

—"The Stroll"

267

U zhivotnykh net nazvan'ia,
Kto im zvat'sia povelel?
Ravnomernoe stradan'e—
Ikh nevidimyi udel.

....

Vsia priroda ulybnulas',
Kak vysokaia tiur'ma.

—"Progulka"

The same images of nature are also found in Zabolotsky's late work.

Culture and consciousness are forms of spirituality participant to the "top," while the beastly, non-creative element constitutes the "bottom" of the universe. The spatial resolution of the poem "The Jackals" ("Shakaly") is interesting in this regard. The poem is imbued with the landscape of the Crimea's southern shore and, on the level of the reality described by the poet, provides a particular spatial setting: a sanatorium is located *below,* by the sea, while the jackals howl *above* in the mountains. The artist's spatial model, however, contradicts this picture and inserts corrections in it. The sanatorium belongs to the world of culture: it resembles an electric motor launch in another poem of the Crimean cycle:

A gigantic swan, a white genius,
At anchorage a motor launch has risen.

He rose *over the vertical abyss*
In the triple harmony of octaves
Having flung fragments of a musical storm
Lavishly from the windows.

He trembled all over from the storm,
He was in the same clef as the sea,
But he was drawn to architecture,
Having raised an antenna on his shoulder.

On the sea he was a *phenomenon of thought. .*

—"At Anchorage"

• • •
• • •

Gigantskii lebed', belyi genii,
Na reide vstal elektrokhod.

On vstal *nad bezdnoi vertikal'noi*
V troinom sozvuchii oktav,
Obryvki buri muzykal'noi
Iz okon shchedro raskidav.

On ves' drozhal ot etoi buri,
On s morem byl v odnom kliuche,
No tiagotel k arkhitekture,
Podniav antennu na pleche.

268

On v more byl *iavlen'em smysla*. . .

—"Na reide"

Consequently the sanitorium standing by the sea is called "high" (the electric motor launch is "over the vertical abyss"), while the jackals, although found in the mountains, are located at *the bottom of the top:*

Only there, *on top, along the ravines*. . .
The lights do not die out all night.
• • •
Lish' tam, *naverkhu, po ovragam*. . .
Ne gasnut vsiu noch' ogon'ki.

But having placed the jackals in the ravines of the mountains (a spatial oxymoron!), Zabolotsky supplies them with "doubles," the quintessence of their base animal nature which is located still deeper:

And the beasts along the edge of the stream
Cowardly flee to the reeds,
Where deep in stone burrows
Rage their doubles.
• • •
I zveri po kraiu potoka
Truslivo begut v trostniki,
Gde v kamennykh norakh gluboko
Besnuiutsia ikh dvoiniki'.

Thought invariably figures in Zabolotsky's lyrics as a vertical ascension of nature set free:

And alive I wandered over the fields,
Entered the wood without fear
And the thoughts of dead ones *like transparent columns*
Around me rose up to the skies.

And Pushkin's voice was heard over the foliage,
And Khlebnikov's birds sang by the water.
....
And all existences, all peoples,
Preserved their imperishable being,
I myself was not a child of nature,
But its thought! But its supple mind!

—"Yesterday, reflecting on death..."

I ia zhivoi skitalsia nad poliami,
Vkhodil bez strakha v les,
I mysli mertvetsov *prozrachnymi stolbami*
Vokrug menia vstavali do nebes.

I golos Pushkina byl nad listvoiu slyshen,

269

I ptitsy Khlebnikova peli u vody.

....

I vse sushchestvovan'ia, vse narody
Netlennoe khranili bytie,
I sam ia byl ne detishche prirody,
No mysl' ee! No zybkii um ee!

—"Vchera, o smerti razmyshliaia..."

True, Zabolotsky's work subsequently showed a certain evolution. The poet understood the danger of an inflexible, stagnant, completely fixed idea which conceals in itself so many fewer possibilities than does nature at its crudest. In the poem "The Opposition of Mars" ("Protivostoianie Marsa") we first see in Zabolotsky's work the idea of the threat of a dogma which congeals thought and "reason" and is described without the positive emotional coloring usual for this image:

Spirit, full of reason and will,
Deprived of heart and soul. . .
• • •
Dukh, polnyi razuma i voli,
Lishennyi serdtsa i dushi. . .

It is not by chance that the poet's usual spatial arrangement of concepts sharply changes in this poem: evil moves upward, and this, together with the negative evaluation of reason, makes the text unique in Zabolotsky's creative works:

Bloody Mars from the blue abyss
Looked attentively on us.
And a shadow of malicious awareness
Distorted his swarthy features,
As if a beast-like spirit
Looked on earth from on high.
• • •
Krovavyi Mars iz bezdny sinei
Smotrel vnimatel'no na nas
I ten' soznatel'nosti zlobnoi
Krivila smutnye cherty,
Kak budto dukh zveropodobnyi
Smotrel na zemliu s vysoty.

Creativity is opposed to all forms of immobility: both material, i.e., in nature and man's ordinary life, and mental, i.e., in his consciousness. Creativity frees the world from the slavery of predetermination and creates a freedom of choice which had seemed implausible. A special concept of harmony also arises here. Harmony for Zabolotsky is not the ideal correspondences of ready-made forms, but the *creation of new,* better correspondences. Therefore harmony is always a creation of human genius.

In this sense, the poem "I seek not harmony in nature" ("ia ne ishchu garmonii v prirode") is Zabolotsky's poetic manifesto. It is not by chance that he placed it first (violating chronological order) in his collected poems of the years 1932-1958. Man's creativity is a continuation of the creative forces of nature, their summit. (In nature a greater and a lesser spirituality is also present; the lake in "A Forest Lake" ["Lesnoe ozero"] is more spiritual than the "overgrown place" ["trushchoba"] surrounding it; the lake "burns directed toward the night sky" ["gorit ustremlennoe k nebu nochnomu"], "The bottomless cup of transparent water/ Shone and thought with independent thought" ["Bezdonnaia chasha prozrachnoi vody/ Siiala i myslila mysl'iu otdel'noi"].)

Thus the basic axis "top/bottom" is realized in the texts through a series of variant oppositions.

Top	Verx	Bottom	Niz
far	daleko	near	blizko
space	prostor	crampedness	tesnota
motion	dvizhenie	immobility	nepodvizhnost'
metamorphoses	metamorfozy	mechanical movement	mekhanicheskoe
freedom	svoboda	slavery	rabstvo
information	informatsiia	redundancy	izbytochnost'
thought (culture)	mysl' (kul'tura)	nature	priroda
creativity (creation of new forms)	tvorchestvo (sozdanie novykh form)	absence of creativity	otsutstvie tvorchestva
harmony	garmoniia	chaos	khaos

Such is the general scheme of Zabolotsky's "poetic world." However a belletristic text is not a copy of a system: it consists of the meaningful fulfillment and meaningful non-fulfillment of the system's requirements. Let us look at the poem under analysis in this light.

The first operation in semantic analysis is the segmentation of the text followed by the comparison of its segments according to their different levels (or of segments from different levels) with the aim of disclosing the differential features which are the bearers of meaning.

The segmentation of the text at hand presents no difficulties: the poem is divided into stanzas which, as a rule, are also sentences. The second stanza which consists of three sentences, and the fifth and sixth stanzas which collectively constitute one sentence (the significance of this will be seen shortly) stand out against this background. The smallest segment on the level of composition is the line which is also a syntagma throughout the text. Initially the text is parsed into its two major parts. The boundary passes through the middle of the text between stanzas I-IV and V-VIII and is determined intuitively, by content: an attentive first reading shows that the beginning of the poem is of markedly mundane content, whereas after the line "And

271

in the dark palace of the universe," *description* yields to *argumentation.* Subsequent analysis must affirm or reject this intuition and, in doing so, accept or reject the propositional character of the text's parsing. If one counts the mass-concrete and abstract nouns in the text's first and second halves the following striking figures are obtained:

	Concrete	Abstract
First half	22	3
Second half	5	12

In each case we find a certain number of nouns originally concrete or originally abstract in meaning which constitute the nucleus of each group. Lexemes which acquire such meanings only in the present context cluster around them. Thus, words in the first half with the meaning "landscape" have concrete meaning, but in the second half, abstract meaning. "Body" and "dogs" in the last stanza acquire meanings opposed to their concrete ones.

Beyond this *external* difference lies a still deeper one: the first half of the poem transports us into an extremely concrete spatial area. Initially it is so geographically concretized that it can be perceived only as a representation of a unique and precisely specified location on the earth's surface. The poem's first publisher, N. L. Stepanov, remarked that "The Peredelkino cemetery is explicitly indicated in 'The Passerby'."[174] Insofar as it was apparently important to the poet that this descriptive feature also be clear to the reader not familiar with the Peredelkino landscape, he inserted a proper name in the geography of this part of the text:

> It is already late. For the Nara station
> The next-to-last train has left.
> • • •
> Uzh pozdno. Na stantsiiu Nara
> Ushel predposlednii sostav.

The reader may not know the location of the Nara station just as he may not know why Pushkin in his missive to V. L. Davydov calls M. F. Orlov "a shorn recruit of Hymen. . . ready to submit to punishment." But just as in the Pushkin poem the reader cannot but sense an intimate hint comprehensible only to a small, almost conspiratorial circle, and, consequently, unerringly perceives the author's intent to draw the text into that intimacy, that inimitable uniqueness of atmosphere in which a poem thrives, so, in Zabolotsky's text, the meaning of the geographic *uniqueness* of that place where the poet has brought him becomes clearer to the reader. He does not know where Nara is and has no personal associations with it. But he knows from personal experience that feeling of geographical uniqueness which is connected with this or that place for each person. The introduction

272

into the text of a proper name, the name of a minor and little known station, provides this indication of spatial uniqueness.

Spatial concreteness is supplemented by substantive concreteness. We have already given quantitative indices of the concreteness of the nouns. Still more meaningful however, is the accretion of the feature of materiality in the meanings of separate words dispersed throughout the poem as a whole. Such words as "three-flap cap" ("treukh"), "soldier's bag" ("soldatskii meshok"), "railroad ties" ("shpaly"), "snarl of wire" ("vorokh lent") are not only concrete in their meaning, but also introduce the semantic feature of meager, everyday, mundane existence. Everyday things are more substantive than festive things in the historically constituted hierarchy of our concepts.

It is interesting that a meaning of materiality may be created where the word in and of itself either may have or may not have this feature. "The moon" ("luna") is between "the edge of a granary" ("kraiambara") and "the roofs" ("krovli") and is thereby introduced into the context of things from that real and meager world. The "spring wood"("vesenniaia glush' ") is ambiguous and may assume either meaning in relation to the opposition concrete/abstract. But in the present context the material surroundings influence it. Note that the concrete words "bridge" ("most"), "monument" ("monument"), "snarl of wire" ("vorokh lent"), etc., and the fact that *the relationship* between details of the landscape is introduced into the text and endowed with the features of a concrete locality. One must turn away from the railroad and the flier's grave "at the edge of the road" ("u kraia allei") "toward the bridge" ("k mostu"). Only the "pine trees" ("sosny") which are equated to "a gathering of souls" ("skpoishche dush") fail to fit into the general system of this part of the text.

Time is no less concrete in this section of the text. We do not know the time in terms of hours (although we could easily calculate it), but we know that it is a *specific* time, *a time with the feature of precision.* It is the time between the movement of the moon from behind the granary roof to a position over the roofs. (It is assumed that the reader knows where to stand for this. The point of view is fixed by the intimacy of this unique world which the author builds.) Further, the time is between the next-to-last and the last train to Nara, actually closer to the next-to-last. The reader is assumed to know when this train departs. In the world of the suburbs, the concept of train and calculable time are synonyms.

If the author had said that the "last train" had left, the meaning of the utterance might be either extremely concrete or metaphorically abstract to the point of introducing the meaning of hopelessness and irretrievable loss. The "next-to-the-last train" can designate only a concrete time.

Against the background of this semantic organization of the first half of the poem, the universal spatial and temporal character of the second part becomes highly significant. The action takes place "in the dark palace of the universe"; the dramatis personae are "a living human soul," "an

273

invisible youth-flier" and "a body wandering along the road." There is no mention of eternity or temporal duration, nor of pictures of the cosmos or of the universe. The characterization of time and space in this part of the text is presented on the level of expression by a zero semantic form. (The mention of the "palace of the universe" is the only exception and it is met on the boundary of the poem's two parts in order to "incorporate" the reader into the new system; there are no further images of this type in the text.) All of this, taken against the background of the first part, is what gives the text its character of *ineffable* universality.

On the other hand, the comparison sharply isolates the feature of the upward striving on the two collocated worlds.

In introducing us into the world of everyday objects, the first half of the poem also introduces everyday dimensions. Only two points tend upward: the moon and the pines. Their nature is different, however. The moon, as we have already said, is "attached" to the everyday landscape and is included in "the space of things." The "pines" are characterized differently: their height is not indicated, but they tend upward. At least it is said that they "bend down." But it is a comparison that is of still more importance here:

> ...the pines, bending down to the graveyard,[175]
> Stand like a gathering of souls. . .
> • • •
> ...sosny, skloniaias' k pogostu,
> Stoiat, slovno skopishcha dush. . .

It excludes them from the material world and simultaneously from all connection with the objects in this half of the poem.

In contrast the second half of the poem transports us into a world of different dimensions. The "palace" introduces the image of an edifice thrusting upward. The metaphor "the palace of the universe" creates a supplementary meaning.[176] It may be roughly represented as a combination of the meanings of a structuredness *[postroennost']*, a horizontal organization by stages (the meaning of "edifice") with the facultative feature of a narrowing, a sharpening, a "towering" upward and of a generality, a universality subsuming everything in itself. The epithet "dark" introduces the element of the obscurity, the incomprehensibility of this structure that unites in its own universality thought and thing, above and below.

All further names are hierarchically organized in relation to the levels of this building and this hierarchy both partitions them off and unites them. "Peace arises" ("pokoi vstaet") (the meaning of verticality and movement is paramount in this verb) *over* the foliage. The "living human soul" ("zhivaia liudskaia dusha") can be understood as a synonym of "living person." ("Soul" ["dusha"] in this case is perceived not as an antonym of "body" ["telo"] but as its metonym).[177] Subsequently this frozen phraseologism

274

is incorporated into a series of oppositions: in its opposition to the "invisible youth-flier" ("nevidimyi iunosha-letchik"), the lexical meaning of the word "living" ("zhivaia") which had been lost in the fixed word combination is activated while the word "soul" ("dusha") is analogously activated in its opposition to "body" ("telo") in the last stanza.

It is important to note that moving nature is represented by trees, a layer of nature that rises above the everyday world and is always more animated in Zabolotsky's work; cf. "Read, O trees, the verses of Hesiod..." ("Chitaite, derev'ia, stikhi Gezioda..."). The merging of human heroism with this moving nature creates that level of animation which rises above the world of things and graves and in which contacts are possible ("they talk about something" ["o chem-to beseduiut'"]) between a living person, nature, and preceding generations.

The last stanza develops in an interesting fashion in comparison with the first. Thematically it returns us to the passerby. This isolates the metamorphosis of the image. The solitary passerby, "filled with mental anguish," ultimately dissociates into three beings: the soul talking in the foliage of the trees with the perished youth-flier, the body wandering along the road, and "his grief and troubles" which run after him. The three are located on different tiers in the hierarchy of the "palace of the universe" along the axis top/bottom. The "soul" is on the level of the trees, the middle zone of animated nature, the "body" is collocated with the everyday world, while the "troubles" that run after him "like dogs" constitute the lowest level of corporeality, reminding one of the jackals' raging doubles. The system of verbs is correspondingly hierarchical: the "soul" talks, the "body" wanders, and the "troubles" run along behind. It seems that this contradicts the scheme central to the other texts according to which the lower the world, the more motionless it is. But here we find the antithesis which is specific for this text, i.e., that of the horizontal axis, the axis of everyday movement, of the anxiety of qualitative immobility and that of the axis of vertical movement, of spirituality, of peace and understanding in the course of internal transformation.

The correlation of the two parts creates a complex semantic structure: the internal essence of man is recognized by being identified with the hierarchy of natural elements.

The system of other textual contrastive-comparison [so-protivopostav-lenie] introduces changes into this general scheme, imposing semantic oppositions which are antagonistic or which simply do not coincide with it. Thus, entering into the general spatial "language" of Zabolotsky's poetry, the concrete world is presented as the lowest. However, in Russian poetic tradition of the nineteenth century with which the poem is clearly correlated, there is another semantic structure: the concrete, which is regarded as synthetic, warm, and intimate and is opposed to the abstract, which is characterized as analytic, cold, non-living, and remote. In this connection, the correlation of the "passerby" will be quite different in the first and second stanzas. In the first stanza the synthetic quality, the integralness of the image, stands out. Spiritual state and external appearance constitute the differential pair arising from a confrontation of the opening stanza's first two lines, while place and time of movement are activated in the confrontation of the last two lines. Initially their *coalescence* is revealed, while their disjunction, the breakdown of the entity into substances is shown at the end. But in the light of that traditional classification of Russian poetry which we mentioned earlier, it is the first that will be regarded as valued and poetic.

Saturating the text with details, Zabolotsky does not accompany them with evaluative epithets. This has profound meaning. Let us cite one example: at the dawn of Soviet cinematography one of the creators of montage theory, L. V. Kuleshov, performed an experiment that won universal fame: having taken a close-up of the indifferent face of the actor Mozzhukhin, he mounted it with another frame which serially showed a plate of soup, a coffin, and a playing child. The montage effect, at that time still unknown but now a well-studied phenomenon, revealed itself in that *for the viewers* Mozzhukhin's face *began to change,* consecutively expressing hunger, grief, and paternal joy. Empirically the indisputable fact, the immobility of the face, is not registered by the senses of the observers. Finding itself in different associational systems, a text fails to equal itself.

Not having established his relationship to the image of the first stanza, Zabolotsky reserved the possibility of incorporating it both into the system of "his own" artistic language and also into associations of the traditional sort. Depending on the choice, the episode's evaluational characterization may change into its direct opposite. But precisely this vacillation, the possibility of a dual understanding, distinguishes the text from the system. The system excludes the intimate experiencing of the image of the "passerby" from the first stanza. The text allows it. And the whole concrete world, within the limits of the text, vacillates between evaluating the image as base and as sympathetic. It is instructive that in the two last stanzas the positive world of spirituality acquires features of concreteness: the endowment of movement and thought with auditory characteristics, e.g., "light rustling" ("legkoe shurshanie") and "slow noise" ("medlennyi shum") (with an obvious onomatopoeic element) is perceived as the introduction of a material element. Simultaneously, transforming the "passerby" into the "body," Zabolotsky introduces an abstraction into the "low" world, activating the possibility of understanding the text in the light of an "antisystem." This poetics of a dual understanding of the text also explains the phenomenon of the oxymoronic combinations and the subject matter's principled obscurity which creates the possibility of pre-comprehension *(doosmyslenie).*

Against the backdrop of these basic semantic organizations, more private ones function.

If we examine the text as a sequence of episodes, reckoning the stanza as an episode, then the relationship of each thematic [*siuzhetnyi*] segment to the following one (apart from the last stanza) and to the preceding one (apart from the first) forms a chain of "montage effects," a sequentiality of thematic development.

The first stanza introduces the personage termed "he." No amplification is given in the text. (The "passerby" is named only in the title and this characterization is structurally extra-textual, related to the poetic text but not entering into it.) His spiritual anxieties are equally nameless.

The anxieties are just as much an inalienable property of the personage as is the three-flap winter cap and the soldier's sack. The ambience and time whose emphatic materiality we have already discussed conform to this personage. Starting in the third stanza the movement of the hero into a new spatial area, a "spring wood," takes place. The fourth stanza begins with the introduction of a new name which in the course of the following three stanzas forces out the first hero who ceases even to be mentioned. This new personage, the "flier," while replacing the first hero, greatly differs from him. For one thing, he is not referred to by a pronoun. Also of importance is that the image of the flier differs from that of the first hero by its oxymoronic duality. The flier buried in the earth and the dead propeller which collectively become the thematic center of these stanzas conceal two elements in themselves: flight and the grave. The oxymoronic quality of the construction of the personage is further developed by the verb system. The verbs which characterize "him" are verbs of motion. Spatial movement is combined with spiritual disquiet. The flier is characterized by a combination of motion and immobility: over his grave peace *arises*. The meeting of the passerby with the flier is a double one: it is the "he" who walks past the grave and the meeting of "his" soul with peace. The feature of the beginning of movement is assigned to peace, i.e., it "rises" whereas the end of movement, tranquillity, is ascribed to the living soul, i.e., it "falls silent." Initially "he" was "filled with spiritual anguish": now before the peace which has arisen over the grave,

> Agitated and ever in haste,
> Falls silent with lowered gaze
> The living human soul.
> • • •
> Volnuias' i vechno spesha,
> Smolkaet s opushchennym vzorom
> Zhivaia liudskaia dusha.

In the following stanza, movement shifts to the youth-flier. This is the puzzling "light rustling of the leaf buds" and "the slow noise of the branches." Both characterizations are demonstrably excluded from the world of everyday experience: the rustling of leaf buds, i.e., the sound of their opening ("a microsound") while an epithet not of sound but of movement is assigned to the sound of the branches. The meeting of two souls takes place in this "strange" world while the newly appeared "he," having been transformed into a "body," continues his movement. But changes have also occurred in the "he." His submissiveness has increased: "he" initially "strides along the ties," whereas now he "wanders." The "railroad," the "ties," have been transformed into a generalized road of life. He goes not along them but "through thousands of misfortunes." He was filled with spiritual anxiety and now

> . . .his grief and troubles
> Run, like dogs, after him.
> • • •
> . . .gore ego, i trevogi
> Begut, kak sobaki, vosled.

Thus examined the poem obtains additional meanings: for the "he" it is the theme of entering upon a higher way of life; for the "flier," the immortality of an expiatory feat of personal destruction which spiritualizes the surrounding world.

But this does not exhaust the numerous supra-meanings created by the structure of the poetic text. Thus, for example, in the fifth stanza the antithesis of sleep ("sleepy foliage") and peace arises. Almost meaningless outside of the context, it here has deep significance: sleep is a state of nature whose immobility is not spiritualized by thought. Peace is a blending of thought and nature. It is not by chance that "peace" is located above "sleep":

> Over this sleepy foliage
> Unexpectedly arises that sudden
> Peace which transfixes the soul.
> • • •
> Nad sonnoiu etoi listvoi
> Vstaet tot nezhdanno mgnovennyi
> Pronzaiushchii dushu pokoi.

One could show that "sudden" does not mean "very fast," but rather, in antithesis to the time of the first two stanzas, not having a temporal feature. Or yet another matter: the third, fifth, and sixth stanzas end in lines containing the word "soul." (It is met only at the end of stanzas.) Each time it obtains a new meaning, however.

We are foregoing an examination of the sublexical levels of the text although this substantially impoverishes the analysis. In regard to syntax, we shall note only that the dissociation of the material world and the unity of the spiritual world are expressed in the antithesis of short and long sentences. The second stanza consists of three sentences while the sixth and seventh stanzas consist of one sentence each.

Only the poetic structure of the text enables us to concentrate in the

278

relatively small space of thirty-two lines a semantic system of such complexity and saturation. One is easily persuaded of the virtual inexhaustability of the poetic text: the fullest description of the system provides only an approximation while the intersection of different systems does not create a final interpretation but *an area* of interpretations within whose limits lie individual treatments. The ideal of poetic analysis is not in the discovery of some eternal uniquely possible interpretation, but in the determination of an area of verities, a sphere of possible interpretations of a given text from the stance of a given reader. For new readers, bearers of new systems of consciousness, Zabolotsky's "The Passerby" will reveal new aspects of itself.

NOTES

PART ONE

Introduction

1. I. A. Goncharov, *Sobr. soch. v vos'mi tomakh* (M. 1954), II, 287.
2. See also Iu. M. Lotman, *Struktura khodozhestvennogo teksta* (M. 1970), 384.

Purposes and Methods of the Structural Analysis of the Poetic Text

3. A similar equation is inherent in our perception of a text but is far from being a general law. Thus in Oscar Wilde's *The Picture of Dorian Grey* the hero's library has different books with the identical composed text and with variously colored paper. In many primitive societies, a text inscribed on stone or copper stands in the same relationship to the identical text not so inscribed as the sacred to the profane, the true to the false.
4. Claude Levi-Strauss, *Anthropologie structurale* (Plon, 1958), 306.

Language as the Materiél of Literature

5. For further detail see B. Uspenskii and Iu. Lotman, "Uslovnost' v iskusstve," in *Filosofskaia entsiklopediia,* V (M. 1970), 287-288.
6. This enumeration, unavoidably quite incomplete, of the aspects of the structure of language in no sense pretends to any depth. Its purpose is merely to acquaint the reader with certain terms that he will meet in the subsequent exposition. Insofar as a knowledge of the basic postulates of modern linguistics is indispensable for an understanding of the subsequent material, we refer the reader to the following books: I. I. Revzin and Iu. Rozentsveig, *Osnovy obshchego i mashinnogo perevoda* (M.), 244; Iu. D. Apresian, *Idei i metody sovremennoi strukturnoi lingvistiki* (M. 1966). For references to more specialized literature, see *Strukturnoe i prikladnoe iazykoznanie. Bibliograficheskii ukazatel'* (M. 1965).
7. For interesting examples and valuable theoretical conjectures, see B. A. Uspenskii, "Vliianie iazyka na religioznoe soznanie," *Trudy po znakovym sistemam, III* (Uch. zap. Tartuskogo gos. un-ta, vyp., 1969), 236.
8. On the dependence of versification systems on the structure of the language, see M. I. Lekomtseva, "O sootnoshenii edinits metricheskoi i fonologicheskoi sistem iazyka," *ibid.*

Poetry and Prose

9. B. V. Tomashevskii, "Stikh i iazyk," in *IV Mezhdunarodnyi s"ezd slavistov. Doklady* (M. 1958), 4. Reprinted in B. V. Tomashevskii, *Stikh i iazyk* (M.-L. 1959), 10. The same point of view is also adopted by M. Iana-kiev in his very interesting book *B"lgarsko stikhoznanie* (Sofiia, 1960), 11.

10. Zygmunt Czerny, "Le vers libre francais et son art structural," in the collection *"Poetics, Poetyka, Poètika"* (Warsaw, 1961), 255.

11. We are here utilizing material from the history of Russian litera-ture, but what interests us in principle is not the specifics of national literary development or even its historical typology but the theoretical question of the correlation of poetry and prose.

12. It is instructive that the criticism of Pushkin's time considered the following as the highest attainments of prose at the beginning of the 1820s: Karamzin's *History of the Russian State (Istoriia gosudarstva rossiiskogo)*, N. Turgenev's *An Essay on the Theory of Taxes (Opyt teorii nalogov)* and D. Davydov's *An Essay on the Theory of Partisan Action (Opyt teorii par-tizanskogo deistviia)*.

13. *"Tvoreniia. . . Kirilla Turovskogo"* (Kiev, 1880), 60.

14. *Slovo Daniila Zatochnika po redaktsiiam XII i XIII vekov i ikh peredelkam* (L. 1932), 7.

15. A. S. Pushkin, *Poln. sobr. soch.*, XI (M. 1949), 19.

16. V. G. Belinskii, *Poln. sobr. soch.* (M. 1955), 523.

17. B. V. Tomashevskii, "Stikh i iazyk" in *IV Mezhdunarodnyi s"ezd slavistov. Doklady* (M. 1958), 7-8.

18. B. Unbegaun, *La versification russe* (Paris, 1958).

19. M. Ianakiev, *B"lgarsko stikhoznanie* (Sofiia, 1960), 10.

20. *Ibid.*, 214.

21. Josef Hrabák, "Remarques sur les corrélations entre les vers et la prose, surtout sur les soi-disant formes de transition," in *"Poetics, Poetyka, Poètika"* (Warsaw, 1966).

22. *Ibid.*, 245.

23. See Josef Hrabák, *Úvod do teorie verše* (Prague, 1970), 7ff.

24. A *generative model* consists of rules whose observance permits one to construct correct texts in a given language. The development of generative rules in poetics is one of the moot problems of contemporary scholarship.

25. Josef Hrabák, *Uvod do teorie verše* (Prague, 1958), 245.

The Nature of Poetry

26. M. Kridl, *Wstęp do badan nad dzielom literackim* (Wilno, 1936);

Teoria badan literackich w Polsce, ed. H. Markiewicz (Krakow, 1960), I-II; Endre Bojtár, "L'école 'intégraliste' polonaise," in *Acta Litteraria Academiae Scientiarum Hungaricae,* XII (1970), No. 1-2.

27. Kiril Taranovski, *Ruski dvodelni ritmovi* (Beograd, 1953).

28. See, for example, M. L. Gasparov, "Aktsentnyi stikh rannego Maiakovskogo," in *Trudy po znakovym sistemam,* Uch. zap. Tartuskogo un-ta, vyp. 198 (1967). Viach. Vs. Ivanov, "Ritm poemy Maiakovskogo 'Chelovek,' " in *"Poetics, Poetyka, Poètika,"* II (Warsaw, 1966).

29. *Redundancy* is the possibility of predicting the following elements of the text conditioned by the limitations imposed on a given type of language. The higher the redundancy, the lower the information content of the text.

30. Ivan Fónagy, "Informationsgehalt von Wort und Laut in der Dichtung, in *"Poetics, Poetyka, Poètika"* (Warsaw, 1961), 592.

31. Our own experiments not only confirm the data of the Hungarian scholar, but also show that poems intuitively felt by a given informant as good were guessed with greater difficulty, that is, they have low redundancy for him. In bad poems, it grows sharply. This permits us to introduce objective criteria into an area that is most difficult for analysis and has traditionally been dealt with by the formula: "De gustibus non disputandem est."

32. L. N. Tolstoi, *Poln. sobr. soch.,* LXIII (M. 1953), 268-269.

33. *Ibid.,* 270.

34. Iu. Tynianov, *Problema stikhotvornogo iazyka* (L. 1924), 9.

Belletristic Repetition

35. Subsequently, we shall utilize the concepts of element and segment. An element is a unit in relation to which structure figures as a universal set. A segment is a syntagmatic element.

36. More accurately, in at least two dimensions.

37. As an example of the displacement of the "level of observation" and the "level of construct" (we utilize terminology whose linguistic use was established by S. K. Shaumian) in poetic studies, we mention the works of A. P. Kviatkovskii and B. Ia. Bukhshtab which display great subtlety of observation but are questionable in their initial premises.

Rhythm as the Structural Basis of Poetry

38. Pierre Quiraud, *Problèmes et méthods de la statistique linguistique* (Paris, 1960), 7-8.

39. G. Shengeli, *Tekhnika stikha* (M. 1960), 13.

40. A. Belyi, *Ritm kak dialektika i "Mednyi vsadnik"* (M. 1929); N. Aseev

also has written on the dialectical nature of the poetic word in his book *Zachem i komu nuzhna poeziia* (M. 1961), 29.

Rhythm and Meter

41. For extremely careful counts of the disposition of the actual stresses in Russian iambs and trochees, see K. Taranovskii's book *Ruski dvodelni ritmovi* (Beograd, 1953).

42. See V. M. Zhirmunskii, *Vvedenie v metriku. Teoriia stikha* (L. 1925). Available in English as *Introduction to Metrics: The Theory of Verse* (The Hague, 1966). B. V. Tomashevskii, *Russkoe stikhoslozhenie: Metrika* (Prague, 1923); B. V. Tomashevskii, *O stikhe* (L. 1929). L. Fleishman has recently shown that B. V. Tomashevskii began as a disciple of Bruisov by polemicizing with Belyi. This does not gainsay Belyi's vast influence on him.

43. B. V. Tomashevskii, *O stikhe* (L. 1929), 12.

44. Tomashevskii, *Stilistika i stikhoslozhenie* (L. 1959), 354-355.

45. Andrei Belyi, *Ritm kak dialektika i "Mednyi vsadnik"* (M. 1939), 55.

46. L. I. Timofeev, *Problemy stikhovedeniia* (M. 1931), 61.

47. Children scan verses while reading them, since for them the reading of a concrete poem is simultaneously the mastering of poetic speech in general.

48. B. Ia. Bukhshtab, "O strukture russkogo klassicheskogo stikha," *Trudy po znakovym sistemam,* III (Uch. zap. Tartuskogo gos. un-ta, vyp. 236, 1969), 388.

49. Viach. Vs. Ivanov's opinion which was expressed at a session of the fourth Summer School on Secondary Modeling Systems (Tartu, 1970) is of particular interest in this connection. He notes that *vers libre* must be examined as a combination of different, usually incompatible, metrical inertias.

50. Taranovskii, "O vzaimootnoshenii stikhotvornogo ritma i tematiki," in *American Contributions to the Fifth International Congress of Slavists* (The Hague, 1963).

The Problem of Rhyme

51. V. Zhirmunskii, *Rifma, ee istoriia i teoriia* (Prague, 1923), 9. Cf. his earlier formulation in the book *Poeziia Aleksandra Bloka* (Petrograd, 1922): "Rhyme is sound recurrence at the end of corresponding rhythmic groups." (91.)

52. See Iu. M. Lotman, "Zamechaniia k probleme barokko v russkoi literature," *Cheskoslovenská rusistika,* XIII, No. 1 (1968), 21.

53. *Russkaia narodnaia drama XVII-XX vekov.* Edited with introductory article and commentary by P. N. Berkov. (M. 1953), 85-89. (My
italics.—Iu. L.).

54. Cited according to V. P. Zubov, *Epifanii Premudryi i Pakhomii
Serb.* Trudy otdela drevnerusskoi literatury, IX. (M.-L. 1953), 148-149.

55. This does not apply to *vers libre* which is regulated by laws that
have been very little studied.

56. Translator's note: the word combination "sivyi merin," literally
a "gray gelding" is best known to Russians as a part of the set expression
"vret kak sivyi merin" meaning someone "lies like a gray gelding," i.e.,
an inveterate liar.

Recurrences on the Phonemic Level

57. This is especially important for languages in which the pronunciation of the phoneme depends on its position in the word. Modern Russian
pronunciation norms had already been adopted for poetry in the 1820s.
However, in the eighteenth century the dependence of the pronunciation
of vowel phonemes on their position was still suppressed.

58. Neither the prose of Classicism nor the paraphrastic style of Karamzin and his school reckoned on such a correlation. A conceptual object rather
than an actual fact played the role of content and corresponded to a unit of
the plane of expression.

The Graphic Image of Poetry

59. For poems in the form of a star or a heart, see the book: *Simeon
Polotskii. Izbrannye sochineniia* (M.-L. 1953), the leaf between 128 and 129.

60. A. Zhovtis recently has examined attention toward this aspect of
the matter. See his book *Stikhi nuzhny* (Alma-Ata, 1968).

61. Cf. the ironic description of the analogous affected use of dots
in Isakovskii's poem "V kazhdoi strochke—tol'ko tochki, Dogadaisia, mol,
sama" ("In each line—only dots, Guess, he said, yourself") "I kto ego
znaet. . ." ("And who knows him. . .").

62. Symbolism with its musical orientation cultivated the tonal elements in graphics. Futurism linked literature not with music but with painting and this influenced the appearance of such elements as Maiakovskii's
"ladder effect" ("lesenka"), the striving toward a synthesis of text and
graphics.

The Level of Morphological and Grammatical Elements

63. R. Jakobson, "Poeziia grammatiki i grammatika poezii," *"Poetics, Poetyka, Poetika"* (Warsaw, 1961), 403 and 405. Also see the above mentioned work of V. V. Ivanov "Lingvisticheskie voprosy stikhotvornogo perevoda."

64. A. S. Pushkin, *Poln. sobr. soch.,* III, kn. 1 (M. 1948), 330 and 418.

65. R. Jakobson, "Poeziia," 438.

66. *Ibid.,* 405.

67. The sign of a contrastive comparative opposition *[kontrastnoe soprotivopostavlenie]*.

68. Exceptions such as Heine's poem "Ein Jungling liebt ein Madchen" ("Devushku iunosha liubit"). [V. Zorgenfrei's translation] only affirms the general rule by its manifest unusualness. All of the text's personages belong to a single person, the third, as in narrational genres.

The Lexical Level of Verse

69. We are deliberately simplifying the question. In fact the text of a poem can be presented as the realization of a series (hierarchy) of languages: "the Russian language," "the Russian literary language of a given epoch," "the work of the given poet," "the poetic cycle as an integral system," "the poem as a self-enclosing poetic world." In relation to each of these systems, the text will constitute a different degree of realization and its relative "size" against the background of the system will change.

70. Cf. N. Khardzhiev and V. Trenin, *Poeticheskaia kul'tura Maiakovskogo* (M. 1970), 195-197.

The Concept of Parallelism

71. A. N. Veselovskii, "Psikhologicheskii parallelism i ego formy v otrazheniiakh poeticheskogo stilia," *Istoricheskaia poetika.* (L. 1940), 125.

72. R. Austerlitz, "Parallelismus," in *"Poetics, Poetyka, Poetika"* (Warsaw, 1961), 439.

73. *Ibid.,* 440.

The Line as a Unity

74. Note P. A. Viazemskii's epigram on S. Bobrov: "Net sporu, chto Bibris bogov iazykom pel; iz smertnykh bo nikto ego ne razumel," "There's no dispute that Bibris sang in the language of the gods; for among mortals,

none could comprehend him." It must be remembered that the epigram was written at a time when comprehensibility and reference to conversational speech were beginning to be required of poetry. The expression "language of the gods" had begun to sound ironic.

75. This was compensated for by the presence of a developed system of differentiations in supra-poetic structures, especially in the system of genres. Subsequently genre diversity loses its significance and the diversity of intra-poetic tonality increases.

76. We give the first stanza:

> Looking over the mountain peaks,
> their infinite arshins,
> jugs filled with wine,
> the whole world like beautiful snow,
> I saw dark torrents,
> I saw the cruel gaze of the storm,
> and the high and peaceful wind,
> and the vain hour of death.

> Osmatrivaia gor vershiny,
> ikh beskonechnye arshiny,
> vinom nalitye kuvshiny,
> ves' mir, kak sneg prekrasnyi,
> ia videl temnye potoki
> ia videl buri vzor zhestokii,
> i veter mirnyi i vysokii,
> i smerti chas naprasnyi.

The Stanza as a Unity

77. Other obligatory segments of the poetic text include the *word* and *sublexical elements* such as phonemes, morphemes, and syllables. These, however, have a derived character. Segmentation into words derives from the fact that the text is in a certain language; segmentation into independently meaningful sublexical units stems from the presumption that the text is poetic.

78. Binarism involves two entities. This principle underlies the structural approach.

79. A. S. Pushkin, *Poln. sobr. soch.,* IV (M. 1937), 373.

80. On the nature of the *zajal,* see Ramón Menéndes Pindal, *Izbrannye proizvedeniia.* (M. 1961), 469-471. The *qaşidah* is a ceremonial eulogistic poem in classical Arabic-Persian poetry. In the first couplet *(bayt),* there is a paired rhyme; the remaining lines are rhymed via a monorhyme in alternate lines. The *zajal* is a Spanish-Arabic folk ballad.

81. See G. O. Vinokur, *Slovo i stikh v "Evgenii Onegine," Pushkina* (M. 1941).

The Problem of Poetic Plot

82. In the poetry of the 18th century there is only one poem about exile, Radishchev's "Ty khochesh' znat', kto ia, chto ia, kuda ia edu. . ." ("Thou wouldst know, who I am, what I am, whither I go. . ."). The theme of the poem is as follows: a central personage is given: *Ne skot, ne derevo, ne rab, no Chelovek. . . (Neither cattle, nor tree, nor slave, but Man. . .).* The text implies that such a hero is incompatible with the world from which he has been exiled. He does not wish to change: "Ia tot, chto byl, i est', i budu ves' svoi vek. . ." ("I am that which I was, and am, and shall be all my life. . ."). The only place in Russia for such a man is "Ilimsk prison."

"The Alien Word" in the Poetic Text

83. For the posing of a number of problems relating to diversity of stylistic layers and polyglotism, see B. A. Uspenskii, "Problema stilia v semi-oticheskom osveshchenii" in *Trudy po znakovym sistemam IV* (Tartu, 1969).

84. From the viewpoint of Karamzinian culture the styles of these two writers were similar. Note Karamzin's programmatic assertion about Bog-danovich as the founder of "light poetry."

85. Not only the structure of the image but also the originality of the rhythm make these lines "Batiushkovian." The line belongs to the rare type VI rhythmic figure according to K. Taranovskii's system. In the poem this type constitutes 3.9% of the whole which curiously coincides with Batiush-kov's 3.4%; Zhukovskii shows 10.9 and 11.6% for the same years. Pushkin in his lyrics of 1817-18 has 9.1% according to Taranovskii's figures. Thus the line is sharply etched. A purely Batiushkovian device is attained through the use of the pause: in an erotic scene the action is unexpectedly interrupted and attention is shifted to details of the estheticized surroundings which consequently acquires the meaning of euphemism, e.g., "timpan nad golovoi. . .," "Razvaliny roskoshnogo ubora" ("the tympanum over the head. . .," "the debris of luxurious attire").

86. M. Bakhtin, *Problemy poetiki Dostoevskogo* (M. 1963); V. N. Voloshinov. *Marksism i filosofiia iazyka.* (L. 1929). [The latter is available in English as *Marxism and the Philosophy of Language.* Translated by Ladi-slav Matejka and I. R. Titunik. (New York and London: Seminar Press, 1973).]

87. V. N. Voloshinov, *Marksism i filosofiia iazyka.* (L. 1929), 136-146.

88. Compare in Annenskii's poem "Ego": "Ia—slabyi syn bol'nogo pokolen'ia. . ." ("I am the weak son of a sick generation").

89. See V. A. Zaretskii, *Semantika i struktura slovesnogo khudozhest-vennogo obraza*. Doctoral dissertation abstract. (Tartu, 1966).

90. Variant: On whom is a frock coat *(na koem frak)*. [Footnote of Koz'ma Prut'kov] .

PART TWO

A. S. Pushkin: "To F. N. Glinka"

91. A word not conforming to the general style *(nestilevoe slovo)* is artistically active precisely because it is alien and does not enter into the system. Consequently, its introduction leads to the activation of the feature of systemicity. On the problem of the artistic function of extra-stylistic elements, see: Iu. Tynianov, *Problema stikhotvornogo iazyka. Stat'i* (M. 1965), 145ff.; V. N. Voloshinov, *Marksizm i filosofiia iazyka.* (L. 1929), 131 ff.; L. Ginzburg, *O lirike* (M.-L. 1964), 20-23.

92. A. Rikhter, *O bardakh, skal'dakh i stikhotvortsakh srednikh vekov* (St. P., 1821), 20.

93. Iu. Tynianov, *Problema stikhotvornogo iazyka. Stat'i* (M. 1965), 143. Italics by Iu. N. Tynianov (Iu. L.).

94. Cf.: A. Kukulevich, "*Iliada* v perevode Gnedicha," *Uch. zap. LGU,* 33, Seriia filologicheskaia, vyp. 2; "Russkaia idilliia *Gnedicha 'Rybaki'." Uch. zap. LGU,* 46, *Seriia filologicheskaia,* vyp. 3, 1939.

95. A. S. Pushkin, *Poln. sobr. soch.,* t. III, kn. 2, (M. 1949), 858.

96. *Ibid.,* kn. 1. The reference to "the marketplace" ("torg") is a polemic attack on literary enemies of 1830.

97. A. S. Pushkin, *Poln. sobr. soch.,* t. XII, (M. 1949), 65.

98. *Ibid.,* t. XIII, 1937, 101. Citation taken from a letter to A. A. Bestuzhev. The "kind, forgetful egoist" is Nikita Vsevolozhskii. On N. Vsevolozhskii, see P. M. Kazantsev, "K izucheniiu 'Russkogo Pelama' Pushkina." In the miscellany *Pushkin. Vremennik pushkinskoi komissii, 1964* (L. 1967), 21-33.

99. Cited according to M. A. Tsiavlovskii, "Stikhotvoreniia Pushkina, obrashchennye k V. F. Raevskomu" in the miscellany *Pushkin. Vremennik pushkinskoi komissii,* 6 (M.-L. 1941), 47.

100. Cf.:

> Only tyrants and slaves
> Rejoice at his sudden death.
> (K. Ryleev. On the Death of Byron)
>
> Odni tirany i raby

Ego vnezapnoi smerti rady
    ("Na smert' Beirona").

Everywhere the yoke, the battle-ax or the crown,
    Everywhere the malefactor or the faint-hearted,
Tyrant   fawner
Or the obedient slave of prejudices.

Vezde iarem, sekira il' venets,
    Vezde zlodei il' malodushnyi,
Tiran   I'stets
Il' predrassudkov rab poslushnyi.

[A. S. Pushkin, *Poln. sobr. soch.* t. II, kn. I (M. 1947), 266.]

101. See Gr. Gukovskii, *Pushkin i russkie romantiki* (M. 1965), 173-222.

102. Poetry involving the coincidence of real facts from contemporary life with their poetically conventional (e.g., Classical) models comes into being when common aspects of life are proclaimed, as it were, non-existent and life seems to be "enlarged." Thus the comic aspects of the personality of Pushkin's good friend F. Glinka did not exist for this text although they were well-known in Pushkin's circle and determined that invariable combination of respect and irony in Pushkin's references to him. For example, in sending the above lines to his brother, Pushkin wrote: ". . . show them to Glinka, embrace him for me, and tell him that he is *all the same* (my italics—Iu. L.) the most respected person in the world." (A. S. Pushkin, *Poln. sobr. soch.,* t. XIII [M. 1937], 55.) It is indicative that outside of poetry, in letters, the "classical" tone in reference to Glinka sounds ironic: "I am glad that Glinka liked my poem—that was my aim. I am not his Themistocles; we are friends and have yet to quarrel over a boy" *(ibid.,* 56). Also compare the epigram "Our friend *Fita,* Kuteikin in epaulets..." and the ironic references to Glinka's psalms in Pushkin's letters.

103. Translator's note: The literal translation of line 2 of the poem is "Me befell ostracism" ("Menia postignul ostrakizm"). This literal rendering is "functionally parallel" to the structure of "was a joy to me" ("mne byl otradoi") in line 2. This structural parallelism is obscured in my initial Englishing of the poem where I gave "I was censured by ostracism." This somewhat loose translation, i.e., "censured" for "befell" ("postignul"), was utilized in order to retain "ostracism" in its line final position where it is paired with its identically positioned rhyme word "egoism" in line 4. Lotman's extended discussion of this pair would have appeared meaningless (in terms of the English text) had this pairing not been preserved.

104. A. S. Pushkin, *Poln. sobr. soch.,* t. II, kn. 2 (M. 1949), 788.

105. In the early text, "the betrayal of friendship" ("izmena druzhby") is a Romantic cliche. However, in 1828, the word "friendship" ("druzhba") in combination with the name F. Glinka sounded like a reference to the recent Decembrist epoch and could not be combined with the base concept

of betrayal. This also apparently influenced the replacement of "friendship" by "glory."

A. S. Pushkin: "Reveille sounds... from my hands..."

106. Translator's note. The Russian expression "zoriu b'iut" (literally, "they beat the twilight"), can mean either to play reveille or taps since *zaria* can refer equally to dawn or dusk. Although the English word "twilight" has both of the two meanings of the Russian *zaria,* it does not figure in any single expression referring collectively to "reveille" and "taps." Hence, to be fully accurate, the English translation must have two variant readings: 1) "Reveille sounds," 2) "Taps sound." Lotman subsequently comments on this ambiguity of the Russian text.

107. Iu. Tynianov, "Ob osnovakh kino" in the collection *Poetika kino* (M.-L. 1927), 61 and 73. Compare Eikhenbaum's statement, "In the film we have the semantics of frames and the semantics of montage." (B. Eikhenbaum, "Problemy kinostilistiki," *ibid.,* 49.)

108. E. V. Paducheva "O strukture abzatsa" in *Trudy po znakovym sistemam. Uch. zap. Tartuskogo gos. un-ta, vyp. 181, 1965, 285.

109. Marcel' Marten, *Iazyk kino* (M. 1959), 92 and 95. [Marcel Martin, *Le Langage cinematographique* (Paris, 1962).]

110. A. S. Pushkin, *Poln. sobr. soch.,* III, kn. 2 (M. 1949), 743.

M. Iu. Lermontov: "We parted; but thy portrait..."

111. On the artistic significance of the basic grammatical opposition in translations of this poem see L. V. Shcherba, *Izbrannye raboty po russkomu iazyku* (M. 1957), 97-110.

112. Such conflict is only one of the varieties of the general Romantic concept of contact as a struggle with the agents of contact. Along with this, the means of the connection are viewed as basic obstacles on the road to it. From this grows the Romantic idea of the struggle with the word as an obstacle to communication in the name of more immanent connections.

113. Among more recent, Pasternak's "The Substitute" ("Zamestitel'-nitsa") might be cited.

114. Formed by a given context.

115. "Govoriu" ("I speak") and "liubliu" ("I love") function here as local synonyms sharing the common semantic invariant "verb of communication."

F. I. Tiutchev: "Two Voices"

116. *Tserkovnyi slovar' ili istolkovanie slovenskikh, takzhe malo-vrazumitel'nykh drevnikh i inoiazychnykh rechenii. . .* Compiled by the former Protopresbyter of the Moscow Arkhangel'skii Cathedral and member of the Imperial Russian Academy of Sciences, Petr Alekseev (St. P. 1818), 4th ed., III, 48.

117. A. S. Pushkin, *Poln. sobr. soch.,* t. XIII (M. 1937), 101. By the expression "or of Lomonosov," Pushkin emphasized that the word "muzhat'-sia" appeared here only in Lomonosov's "overlay." The Biblical text in the Slavonic translation read "Girdst now thy loins like a man"—superfluous evidence of the degree to which biblical phraseology was present in Pushkin's consciousness.

118. Ambivalency—the removal of an opposition. An ambivalent utterance remains true even on the replacement of its basic thesis by its opposite.

119. "Polyphonic construction" is a term coined by M. M. Bakhtin [Translator's note. The interested reader may consult Mikhail Bakhtin's important work *Problems of Dostoevsky's Poetics* which has recently been published in an English translation by Ardis (Ann Arbor, 1973).]

F. I. Tiutchev: "On the Eve of the Anniversary of August 4, 1864"

120. F. I. Tiutchev, *Stikhotvoreniia, pis'ma* (M. 1957), 448-449.

121. Translator's note. This alludes to something quite unusual in Tiutchev's poem. The Russian words "etot" and "tot" approximately correspond to the English "this" and "that," respectively. These words are commonly used in the opposed expressions "Na etom svete" ("in this world") and "Na tom svete" ("in the other world"). Tiutchev has partially reversed this usage in that his "Vot tot mir" ("Here is that world") clearly refers to the earthly world rather than the world beyond.

122. See N. Ia. Berkovskii. "F. I. Tiutchev" in *F. I. Tiuchev. Stikhot-voreniia* (M.-L. 1962), 25-27.

123. See pp. 28-32.

124. Kirill Taranovskii, "O vzaimootnoshenii stikhotvornogo ritma i tematiki," *American Contributions to the Fifth International Congress of Slavists.* (The Hague, Mouton, 1963).

125. Translator's note. Lotman here begins an extended comparison of the Tiutchev poem with Lermontov's seminal "Vykhozhu odin ia na dorogu." The latter, however, is only partially reproduced and that only in disconnected fragments. This is apparently on the assumption that the reader is extremely familiar with the Lermontov poem. For the convenience of the English reader, the full text is given below in both Russian and English:

I Go Out Alone Onto the Road.

I go out alone onto the road.
Through the mist the stony way glistens;
The night is still, the wilderness heeds God,
And star speaks with star.

In the heavens it is solemn and wonderful!
The earth sleeps in a blue radiance...
Why is all so painful and burdensome for me?
Do I await something? Do I regret something?

I no longer expect anything of life,
And regret the past not at all.
I seek freedom and peace;
I would like to find oblivion and to fall asleep...

But not with that cold sleep of the grave:
I would like to fall asleep forever,
So that in my breast might slumber the forces of life,
So that my breast would quietly rise in breathing.

So that all night, all day my ear soothing,
Of love a sweet voice to me might sing;
That o'er me, eternally green
A dark oak might bend and rustle.

Vykhozhu odin ia na dorogu.

Vykhozhu odin ia na dorogu.
Skvoz' tuman kremnistyi put' blestit;
Noch' tikha, pustynia vnemlet Bogu,
I zvezda s zvezdoiu govorit.

V nebesakh torzhestvenno i chudno!
Spit zemlia v siian'i golubom...
Chto zhe mne tak bol'no i tak trudno?
Zhdu l' chego? Zhaleiu li o chem?

Uzh ne zhdu ot zhizni nichego ia,
I ne zhal' mne proshlago nichut'.
Ia ishchu svobody i pokoia;
Ia b khotel zabyt'sia i zasnut'...

No ne tem kholodnym snom mogily:
Ia b zhelal naveki tak zasnut',
Chtob v grudi dremali zhizni sily,
Chtob dysha vzdymalas' tikho grud';

Chtob vsiu noch', ves' den' moi slukh leleia,
Pro liubov' mne sladkii golos pel;
Nado mnoi chtob, vechno zeleneia,
Temnyi dub sklonialsia i shumel.

126. Taranovskii, 343.
127. *Ibid.*
128. The poem "Vykhozhu odin ia na dorogu" has frequently been

examined in the literature. See in particular D. E. Maksimov's monographic analysis in the anthology *Russkaia klassicheskaia literatura: Razbory i analizy* (M. 1969), 127-141.

129. Being written in 1830, it could not have taken into account the specifically Lermontovian understanding of the "road," and, consequently, is of particular interest for us in the case at hand.

130. The "useless path" or "the aimless road" which are characteristic of Pushkin's "Onegin's Journey" and of Lermontov's *Hero of Our Time* are examples of such "anti-movement." The hero's spatial mobility is a sign of his inner immobility. Note the refrain "Ennui, ennui" that accompanies Onegin and the internal immutability of Pechorin.

131. The parallelism of these series is felt as an undoubted kinship of the phonological base with the continual activation of a differential feature: the feature of labialization is activated in "o—u"; in "d—t," that of "voice" vs. "voiceless"; while "i—y" activates the feature "front—back." See S. Tolstaia, "O fonologii rifmy," in *Trudy po znakovym sistemam* (Tartu, 1965).

132. See Zhukovskii's lines "Vedi menia, pustyni zhitel',/ Svyatoi anakhoret" ("Lead me, dweller of the wilderness/ Holy anchorite"). Also note the Old Russian verb "pustynno-zhitel'stvovat' " meaning "to live in solitude."

133. Compare the two possible correlations of the elements of earthly space in Lermontov's poetry:

I. Opposition: city—road and wilderness (functioning as synonyms) Thus, for example, in "The Prophet" ("Prorok"), departure ("ukhod") and road ("put' ") indicate movement from city to wilderness:

> I bestrewed my head with ashes,
> From cities fled I a beggar,
> And now in the wilderness I live...

> Posypal peplom ia glavu,
> Iz gorodov bezhal ia nishchii,
> I vot v pustyne ia zhivu...

II. Opposition: city and wilderness—road (synonyms in the opposition "mobility—immobility")

> Whether goest thou across wilderness
> Or city magnificent and great,
> Offend no one's holy place,
> Nowhere build for thyself a shelter.
>   ("When, to hope inaccessible...")

Poidesh' li ty cherez pustyniu
Il' gorod pyshnyi i bol'shoi,
Ne obizhai nich'iu sviatyniu,
Nigde priiut sebe ne stroi.
("Kogda, nadezhde nedostupnyi...")

134. Note the complete absence of verbs of motion and the abundant indication of states of rest, e.g., "The night is silent" ("Noch' tikha"), "In the heavens it [is] solemn" ("V nebesakh torzhestvenno") with no verb! and "Sleeps the earth" ("Spit zemlia").

135. Compare the song of the fish in Lermontov's poem "Mtsyri."

136. As an example of this type, we cite Lermontov's line from "Meditation" ("Duma"): "I nenavidim my, i liubim my sluchaino" ("And we hate, and we love by chance" where "hate" ("nenavidet'") and "love" ("liubit") are antonyms which are easily neutralized in a single seme of a higher level.

137. It must be kept in view that a similar "reconciliation" arose in connection with the independent existence of the Lermontov text: as a part of the entire lyric output of the poet, in relation to it, the poem revealed tragic aspects just as the voice of the fish is tragic in "Mtsyri." The fish sings lulling songs of love at a moment when the hopes of the hero for an *active* life are being dashed. The tragedy of inaction is revealed in this text only in its relation to other works by Lermontov. Similarly, the Tiutchev text will be understood differently by the reader who projects it against the isolated Lermontov poem and by one who projects it against the same poem *as a part* of Lermontov's lyric output.

138. Compare Tiutchev's letter three days after E. A. Denis'evaia's funeral: "Emptiness, a terrible emptiness. Even in death, I do not foresee relief. Ah, I need her here on earth and not there somewhere." Tiutchev's daughter wrote with conviction that he "was plunged into that tormenting sorrow, into that desperation at the loss of earthly joys that lacks the slightest glimmer of striving toward anything in the least heavenly." Cited from *Tiutchevskii sbornik.* (Prague: Byloe, 1923), 20 and 29. Also see F. I. Tiutchev *Stikhotvoreniia, pis'ma.* (M. 1957), 445.

139. This does not exclude the presence of a different tendency in other texts. The semantics of darkness and light in Tiutchev's poetry is a very broad and completely independent theme.

140. Tiutchev's frequent epithet "living wings" ("zhivye kryl'ia") enters into this same system: "death (down)—life (up)."

N. A. Nekrasov: "Last Elegies"

141. B. Eikhenbaum, *Skvoz' literaturu* (L. 1924), 246.

142. Iu. Tynianov, "Stikhovye formy Nekrasova." *Letopis' doma literatorov,* No. 4 (Prague, 1921) [Compare *Arkhaisty i novatory* (L. 1929)].

143. See K. Shimkevich, "Pushkin i Nekrasov" in *Pushkin v mirovoi literature* (L. 1926); V. V. Gippius, "Nekrasov v istorii russkoi poezii XIX veka," in *Literaturnoe nasledstvo*, Vol. 49-50 *(Nekrasov, I)*, (1949); Kornei Chukovskii, *Masterstvo Nekrasova* (M. 1952).

144. In its turn, Pushkin's "sweet custom" ("privychka milaia") had a distinctly literary and citational character. A. A. Akhmatova has noted that it is a translation of an expression from Constant's *Adolphe*. (See A. A. Akhmatova's " 'Adol'f' Benzhamena Konstana v tvorchestve Pushkina" in *Vremennik pushkinskoi komissii AN SSR*, Vol. I. [M.-L. 1936] 109.) Pushkin himself indicated another source. In his story "The Blizzard" ("Metel' "), he has Burmin say "I have behaved incautiously in surrendering to the sweet custom *[milaia privychka]* of seeing and hearing you daily," and observed that on hearing these words Maria Gavrilovna "recollected Saint-Preux's first letter, " i.e., Rousseau's *La Nouvelle Heloise*. L. N. Shtil'man did not find the appropriate quote in Rousseau's novel, but, having discovered a mention of custom and its dangers for those in love in the eighteenth letter of Rousseau's novel, concluded: "It is most probable that in Pushkin's case we are dealing with a reminiscence from Constant's novel and that the cited lines from this novel in their turn go back to *La Nouvelle Heloise*. (L. N. Shtil'man, "Problemy literaturnykh zhanrov i traditsii v 'Evgenii Onegine' Pushkina," in *American Contributions to the Fourth International Congress of Slavists, 1958)*. One suspects that the matter is simpler: Pushkin simply made a mistake. But it is the character of the mistake that is most interesting: he forgot that it was a quote from *Adolphe* but did not forget that it was a quote. Actually, the source is not so important here as that the text fulfills the function of an alien, a bookish, word.

145. See Gr. Gukovskii, *Pushkin i russkie romantiki.* (M. 1956).

146. Kornei Chukovskii, *Masterstvo Nekrasova.* (M. 1952).

A. K. Tolstoy: "There Sits Beneath a Canopy..."

147. Translator's note. This mock Chinese name is a play on the Russian "sukin syn" ("son of a bitch").

148. The absence of a satiric factor in a fable such as Zhukovskii's "The Hawk and the Dove" ("Sokol i golubka") is regarded as a kind of incompleteness, a violation of an expectation, which may itself be a source of meanings. The presence of a satiric element in a fable is scarcely surprising since it is contained in the very definition of the genre. The A. K. Tolstoy poem being analyzed here, taken from a purely generic point of view, i.e., an untitled poem of the song type, a quatrain in iambic trimeter, is absolutely neutral in this regard: it may equally be or not be a satire.

149. On the semantics of "puppetry" in the satire of the second half of the nineteenth century, see, V. V. Gippius, "Liudi i kukly v satire Salty-

kova," in *Ot. Pushkina do Bloka* (M.-L. 1966).

150. See K. I. Chukovskii, *Ot dvukh do piati,* in *Sobr. soch.* (M.), Vol. 4. On the structure of the text in nonsense poetry, see T. V. Tsiv'ian and D. M. Segal, "K strukture angliskoi poezii nonsensa" in *Trudy po znakovym sistemam,* V. 2 (Tartu, 1965).

A. A. Blok: "To Anna Akhmatova"

151. It is revealing that the system of plots *[siuzhetov]* in lyric poetry varies in dependence on the structure of the language. The presence of a [grammatical] dual number [category] and of the corresponding pronominal forms in Old Russian made possible a thematic development in "The Lay of the Host of Igor": the example "Tu sia brata razluchista" ("the brothers parted" with dual grammatical forms is all the more instructive in that there were not two princes but four. The real life situation is deformed in the process of conversion to a system of standardized plots. (It must be remembered that the difference on the pronominal level between the dual and the plural number is not only quantitative: plural pronouns represent an undifferentiated object which is opposed to the singular while dual pronouns indicate two equal objects).

In those languages where grammatical expression of gender is lacking in pronouns (e.g., in Estonian), lyric texts built on the scheme "first person pronoun-third person pronoun" are possible in principle. Such languages permit the insertion in a single text of both masculine and feminine characters in both positions. In Russian poetry special texts are required for this. Compare this with the well-known dispute over the addressee of Shakespeare's sonnets and the non-expression of the category of grammatical gender in the English language. See Roman Jakobson and Lawrence G. Jones, *Shakespeare's Verbal Art in "Th" expense of Spirit* (The Hague-Paris: Mouton, 1970), 20-21.

152. Compare this with the widespread situation in poetry where the author of a poem addresses as "thou" a woman with whom his actual degree of intimacy does not warrant such a form of address. This lyrical "thou" is more abstract than the pronoun corresponding to it in conversational speech and does not obligatorily imply a degree of intimacy inasmuch as the lyrical "thou," in contrast to non-belletristic language, lacks the "remote" second person pronoun "you" as an alternative.

153. Aleksandr Blok, *Sobr. soch. v vos'mi tomakh* (M.-L. 1960), Vol. III, 550.

154. It is instructive that the "answers" present themselves, as it were, for recoding into visual images, illustrations. They can also be examined as illustrations to "their" words.

155. For example, for the isolated expression "Ia prosta" ("I am

simple" a semantic substitution of the type "simplicity is worse than thievery" is quite possible. Any rephrasing of the expression "krasota prosta" ("beauty is simple") which might proceed from a demand to preserve the basic meaning of the utterance (a meaning such as "glupaia krasavitsa" ("a stupid beauty") clearly does not enter into the given utterance), excludes the substitution of such meanings.

156. Compare in the drafts: "Vas strashit rastsvet Vas rannii" ("Your early flowering terrifies you").

157. The clausula shows a characteristic violation of the inertia but within the limits of the back phonemes. [Translator's note. Graphically there are only six "a's" in the first line. Since, however, unstressed "o's" are pronounced as "a," there are in fact seven—similar confusion arises in other places with "e" which is pronounced as "i" in unstressed positions.]

158. Here at first the heroine is termed not "Vy" ("You"), but "Ia" ("I") which enters into the "a" group.

M. I. Tsvetaeva: "In Vain With My Eye—As With a Nail..."

159. N. P. Gronskii (1904-1934)—a poet who perished in an accident in the Parisian Metro. M. Tsvetaeva greatly valued Gronskii as a person and an artist: "The young man was becoming a great poet." *Marina Tsvetaeva. Pis'ma k Anne Teskovoi* (Prague, 1969), 117. In a posthumous review of Gronskii's book *Stikhi i poema* in *Sovremennye zapiski,* No. 61 (1936), Tsvetaeva contrasted his work with that of the emigre "young poetry."

160. See A. Zaretskii, "O mestoimenii," *Russkii iazyk v shkole* (No. 6, 1940).

161. Kiril Taranovski, *Ruski dvodelni ritmovi* (Beograd, 1953), 85 and table.

162. V. V. Ivanov, "Ritmicheskoe stroenie, 'Ballady o tsirke Mezhirova' " in *"Poetics, Poetyka, Poetika"* (Warsaw, 1966), 285.

163. Even within the narrow limits of its purely logical aspect the problem is, in essence, more complex: it is not simply the elimination of a logical contradiction but the mutual imposition and contention of two logical constructs that are mutually exclusive.

164. An interpretation of the line as unique is also possible, i.e., as being built on four spondees ($\acute{u}$ / $\acute{u}$ / $\acute{u}$ / $\acute{u}$ /) as well as a series of other rhythmico-declamational variants. The abundance of such variants here and below is conditioned by the large number of one syllable words including such semantically critical ones as "kost' " ("bone"), "dukh" ("spirit"), "bog" ("God"), "cherv' " ("worm"), "zdes' " ("here"), "tam" ("there"), and "dozhd' " ("rain").

165. "The emphatic pronoun *sam* is used with animate nouns and personal pronouns in the meaning 'independently,' 'without the help of

others'." *Grammatika russkogo iazyka,* I (M. 1952), 402.

166. Marina Tsvetaeva, *Izbrannye proizvodeniia* (M. 1965), 467.

167. See Iu. Lotman, "S kem zhe polemiziroval Pnin v ode 'Chelovek'?, *Russkaia literatura,* No. 2 (1964), 166-167.

V. V. Mayakovsky: "A Scheme for Laughter"

168. Vladimir Maiakovskii, *Poln. sobr. soch.,* XII (M. 1959), 52.

169. *Ibid.,* 53.

170. *Grammatika russkogo iazyka,* II, Pt. 2 (2 vols.; M. 1952-1954), 337.

171. Maiakovskii, *op. cit.,* 52.

172. *Ibid, Cf.,* M. P. Shtokmar, *Rifma Maiakovskogo* (M. 1959), 14-15 and 26-27 ff.

173. Maiakovskii, *op. cit.,* 53.

N. A. Zabolotsky: "The Passerby"

174. N. Stepanov, "Pamiati N. A. Zabolotskogo," in *Tarusskie stranitsy* (Kaluga, 1961), 309.

175. By calling the grave of the flier a symbol of the twentieth century, a "graveyard" (rendered by the archaic word "pogost" in the original), Zabolotskii not only introduces a lexical archaism into the present but also establishes a manifestation of the ancient, or more accurately, of the eternal, the extra-temporal.

176. If one lists all the possible phraseological combinations of the words "chertog" ("palace") and "vselennaia" ("universe"), the combined meanings will yield the meaning of the metaphor. Insofar as the rules of combinability will be determined each time by the semantic structure of the text (or type of texts) while the number of possible phraseologisms also will vary, the possibility of semantic movement, which is essential for art, arises.

177. Cf., Tvardovskii's "Chto zh, boets, dusha zhivaia,/ Na voine kotoryi god..." ("Well, warrior, living soul,/ At war which year..."). From A. Tvardovskii, Stikhotvoreniia i poemy v dvukh tomakh, II (M. 1951), 161.

A BIBLIOGRAPHY
OF THE WORKS OF YURY LOTMAN
compiled by L. Fleishman

1949

1. "Kratkie nastavleniia russkim rytsariam." (Neizvestnyi pamiatnik agitatsionnoi publitsistiki rannego dekabrizma). — Vestnik L. G. U., N. 7, str. 133-147.

1950

2. Iz istorii literaturno-obshchestvennoi bor'by 80-kh godov XVIII veka (A. N. Radishchev i A. M. Kutuzov). — "Radishchev: stat'i i materialy." izd. L. G. U., str. 81-128.

1951

3. A. N. Radishchev v bor'be s obshchestvenno-politicheskimi vozzreniiami i dvorianskoi estetikoi Karamzina. Avtoreferat dissertatsii na soiskanie uchenoi stepeni kandidata filosoficheskikh nauk. Tartu.

1952

4. O nekotorykh voprosakh estetiki Radishcheva. — "Nauchnye trudy, posviashchennye 150-letiiu T. G. U.," Tartu, str. 158-192.

1955

5. Uusi materjale dekabristide võitlusest balti aadli vastu. — "Edasi," (Tartu), 25 dec.

1956

6. Byl li A. N. Radishchev dvorianskim revoliutioneram? — "Voprosy filosofii," N. 3, str. 165-172.
7. Stikhotvorenie Andreia Turgeneva "K otechestvu" i ego rech' v "Druzheskom literaturnom obshchestve." — "Literaturnoe nasledstvo," t. 60, kn. 1, M.-L., str. 323-333.

1957

8. Evoliutsiia mirovozzreniia Karamzina (1789-1803). — Uch. zai. T. G. U., vyp. 51. str. 122-166.
9. Neizvestnyi tekst stikhotvoreniia A. I. Polezhaeva "Genii." — V. L.,

N. 2, str. 165-172.

1958

10. "Dva slova postoronnego" — neizvestnaia stat'ia P. A. Viazemskogo. — "Voprosy izucheniia russkoi literatury XI-XX vekov." M.-L., str. 301-305.
11. K voprosu o tom, kakimi iazykami vladel M. V. Lomonosov. — "XVIII vek." sb. 3, M.-L., str. 460-462.
12. K kharakteristike mirovozzreniia V. G. Anastasevicha. — T. R. S. F., I, (Uch. zai., T. G. U., 65), str. 12-27.
13, Andrei Sergeevich Kaisarov i literaturno-obshchestvennaia bor'ba ego vremeni. (Uch. zai., T. G. U., 63).
14. A. F. Merzliakov. Stikhotvoreniia. Vstupitel'naia stat'ia, podgotovka teksta i primechaniia. L.
15. O slove "paporzi" v "Slove o polku Igoreve." — T. O. D. L. R., XIV, M.-L., str. 37-40.
16. O tret'ei chasti "Pochty dukhov" Ch. A. Krylova. — "XVIII vek." sb. 3, M.-L., str. 511-512.
17. Radishchev i Mabli. — Tam zhe, str. 276-308.
18. A. N. Radishchev i russkaia voennaia mysl' v XVIII veke. — Uch. zai. T. G. U., 67, (Trudy po filosofii), str. 194-207.
19. Rukopis' A. Kaisarova "Sravnitel'nyi slovar' slavianskikh narechii." — T. R. S. F. I., (Uch. zai. T. G. U., 65), str. 191-203.
20. Neue Materialien über die Anfänge der Beschäftigung mit Schiller in der russischen Literatur. — Wissenschaftliche Zeitschrift der E. M. Arndt. — Universität Greifswald, Gesellschafts — und Sprachwissenschaftliche Reihe, Nr. 5/6, 1958-1959.
21. Matvei Aleksandrovich Dmitriev-Mamonov — poet, publitsist i obshchestvennyi deiatel'. — T. R. S. F. II (Uch. zai. T. G. U., 78), str. 19-92.
22. K biografii Ia. P. Kozel'skogo. — "Voprosy filosofii," N. 8, str. 97-99.
23. Pisatel', kritik i perevodchik Ia. A. Galinkovskii. 1777-1815. — "XVIII vek." sb. 4, M.—L., str. 230-256.
24. Novye izdaniia poetov XVIII veka. — Tam zhe, str. 456-466. Retsenziia na izdaniia proizvedenii Sumarokova i Kantemira.

1960

25. P. A. Viazemskii i dvizhenie dekabristov. — T. R. S. F. III (Uch. zai. T. G. U., 98), str. 24-142.
26. Zapisi narodnykh prichitanii nachala XIX veka. Iz arkhiva G. R. Derzhavina. — R. L., N. 3, str. 145-150.
27. Istoriko-literaturnye zametki. — T. R. S. F. III (Uch. zai. T. G. U., 98), str. 310-314. "Bednaia Liza" Karamzina v pereskaze krest'ianina.—

O tak nazyvaemoi "Rechi D. V. Davydova pri vstuplenii v 'Arzamas'." Zhukovskii — mason. — Neizvestnyi otzyv o litseiskom tvorchestve Pushkina. — Pushkin —chitatel' Sen-Zhusta. — Pushkin i Rivarol'.

28. K evoliutsii postroeniia kharakterov v romane "Evgenii Onegin." — "Pushkin: issledovaniia i materialy." III, M.-L., str. 131-173.

29. Kniga o poezii Lermontova. (Pets.: D. E. Maksimov. Poeziia Lermontova. L., 1959). — V. L., N. 11, str. 232-235.

30. Novonaidennaia povest' XVIII veka "Istoriia o portugal'skoi korolevne Anne i gishpanskom koroleviche Aleksandre." — T. O. D. L. R., XVI, M.-L., str. 490-505 (v soavtorstve s L. A. Dmitrievym).

31. Osnovnye etapy razvitiia russkogo realizma. — T. R. S. F. III (Uch. zai. T. G. U., 98), str. 3-23 (v soavtorstve s B. F. Egorovym i Z. G. Mints).

32. Problema narodnosti i pyti razvitiia literatury preddekabr'skogo perioda. — "O russkom realizme XIX veka i voprosy narodnosti literatury." sb. st. M.-L., str. 3-51.

33. Velikii russkii revoliutsionnyi demokrat. K 150-letiiu so dnia rozhdeniia V. G. Belinskogo. — "Kommunist Estonii," N. 6, str. 13-18.

33a. Suuz vene revolutiooniline demokraat V. G. Belinski. 150. sünniaastapǎeva puhul. — "Eesti Kommunist," nr. 6, lk. 12-16.

34. P. A. Viazemskii i Estoniia. — T. R. S. F. IV (Uch. zai. T. G. U., 104), str. 293-295.

35. Istoriko-literaturnye zametki. — Tam zhe, str. 277-284. Neizvestnoe stikhotvorenie A. Meshchevskogo. — Lermontov: Dve reministsentsii iz "Gamleta." — Iz kommentariia k poeme "Mtsyri."

36. Kto byl avtorom stikhotvoreniia "Na smert' K. P. Chernova." — R. L., N. 3, str. 153-159.

37. Neizvestnye i utrachennye istoricheskie trudy A. O. Kornilovich. — R. L., N. 2, str. 121-125.

38. Poet, uchenyi, patriot. (O M. V. Lomonosove). — "Sovetskaia Estoniia," N. 273, 19 noiabria.

39. Poety nachala XIX veka. Vstupitel'naia stat'ia, podgotovka teksta i primechaniia. L.

40. Prosvetitel'stvo i realizm. — "Problemy russkogo Prosveshcheniia v literature XVIII veka." M.-L., str. 158-162.

41. Puti razvitiia russkoi literatury preddekabr'skogo perioda. Avtoreferat dissertatsii na soiskanie uchenoi stepeni doktora filologicheskikh nauk. L.

42. Puti razvitiia russkoi prozy 1800-1810-kh godov. — T. R. S. F. IV (Uch. zai. T. G. U., 104), str. 3-57.

43. Puti razvitiia russkoi prosvetitel'skoi prozy XVIII veka. — "Problemy russkogo Prosveshcheniia v literature XVIII veka." M.-L., str. 79- 106.

44. (Rets.:) S. N. Chernov. U istokov russkogo osvoboditel'nogo dvizheniia. Izbr. stat'i po istorii dekabrizma. Saratov, 1960. — "Voprosy istorii."

N. 5, str. 137-139.

45. A. Y. Herzen. 150-sünnipäeva puhul. — Looming, nr. 7, lk. 625-632.
46. Vospriiatie idei Russo v russkoi literature kontsa XVIII — nachala XIX v. v. — Tezisy konferentsii, posviashchennoi 250-letiiu so dnia rozhdeniia Zhan-Zhaka Russo. Odessa, str. 78-80.
47. Vystuplenie (v diskussii o barokko). — IV Mezhdunarodnoi s"ezd slavistov. Materialy diskussii. T. 1. Problemy slavianskogo literaturovedeniia, fol'kloristiki i stilistiki. M., str. 149-150.
48. Ideinaia struktura "Kapitanskoi dochki." — "Pushkinskoi sbornik," Pskov, str. 3-20.
49. Istoki "Tolstovskogo napravleniia" v russkom literature 1830-kh godov. — T. R. S. F. V (Uch. zai. T. G. U., 119), str. 3-76.
50. Istochniki svedenii Pushkina o Radishcheve, 1819-1822. — "Pushkin i ego vremia," vyp. 1, L., str. 45-66.
51. Pokhodnaia tipografiia shtaba Kutuzova i ee deiatel'nost'. — "1812 god. K stopiatidesiatiletiiu otechestvennoi voiny." M., str. 215-232.
52. Radishchev — poet-perevodchik. — "XVIII vek." sb. 5, M.-L., str. 435-439.
53. "Slovo o polku Igoreve" i literaturnaia traditsiia XVIII-nachala XIX v. — "Slovo o polku Igoreve — pamiatnik XII veka." M.-L., str. 330-405.

1963

54. Kirjanduse uurimise matemaatilistest meetoditest. — Teaduslik konverents "Kaasaegne matemaatika ja tema rakendusalad." Tartu, 1963, lk. 65.
55. Die Entwicklung des Romans in der russischen Literatur des 18. Jahrhunderts. — Studien zur Geschichte der russischen Literatur des 18. Jahrhunderts. B. 1, ss. 22-51.
56. Iz istorii polemiki vokrug sed'moi glavy "Evgeniia Onegina." (Pis'mo E. M. Khitrovo k neizvestnomu izdateliu). — "Vremennik Pushkinskoi komissii. 1962." M.-L., str. 52-57.
57. Neizvestyni chitatel' XVIII veka o "Puteshestvii iz Peterburga v Moskvu." — T. R. S. F. VI (Uch. zai. T. G. U., 139), str. 335-338.
58. O razgranichenii lingvisticheskogo i literaturovedcheskogo poniatiia struktury. — "Voprosy iazykoznaniia," N. 3, str. 44-52.
59. "Sochuvstvennik" A. N. Radishcheva. A. M. Kutuzov i ego pis'ma k I. P. Turgenev. Vstupitel'naia stat'ia Iu. M. Lotmana. Podgotovka teksta i primechaniia V. V. Fursenko. — T. R. S. F. VI (Uch. zai. T. G. U., 139), str. 281-334.
60. Tarutinskii period otechestvennoi voiny i razvitie russkoi obshchestvennoi mysli. — Tam zhe, str. 8-19.

1964

61. Eesti N. S. V. entsüklopeedia marksonästik proekt. Tallinn. N. S. V. Liidu rahvaste ja valiskirjandus. Kirjandusteooria. Rahvaluule. Raamatukogundus. [Koost: K. Aben, V. Alttoa, S. Issakov, E. Laugaste, M. Loodus, Y. Lotman ja K. Sarv].

62. Sur la délimitation linguistique et littéraire de la notion de structure. — "Linguistics" (The Hague), 1964, N. 6, pp. 59-72.

63. Lermontov ja kaasaeg. — T. R. Ü., 16 X, nr. 25.

64. Vstupitel'noe slovo. — "Programma i tezisy dokladov v letnei shkole po vtorichnym modeliruiushchim sistemam. 19-29 avgusta, 1964 g." Tartu, str. 3-5.

65. Igra kak semioticheskaia problema i ee otnoshenie k prirode iskusstva. — Tam zhe, str. 32-33.

66. Lektsii po stuktural'noi poetike. Vyp. 1. (Vvedenie. Teoriia stikha). Tartu. — T. Z. S. I (Uch. zai. T. G. U., 160). (Brown University, Slavic Reprint 5, Providence, 1968).

67. Problema znaka v iskusstve. — "Programma i tezisy dokladov v letnei shkole po vtorichnym modeliruiushchim sistemam. 19-29 avgusta, 1964 g." Tartu, str. 57-58.

68. S kem zhe polemiziroval Pnin v ode "Chelovek"? — R. L., N. 2, str. 166-167.

69. "Chelovek prirody" v russkoi literature XIX veka i "tsyganskaia tema" u Bloka. — Blokovskii sbornik. Trudy nauchnoi konferentsii, posviashchennoi izucheniiu zhizni i tvorchestva A. A. Bloka, mai, 1962. Tartu, str. 98-156. (v soavtorstve s Z. G. Mints).

70. Gnedich, Nikolai Ivanovich. — K. L. E., t. 2, stb. 204-205.

71. Dmitriev-Mamonov, Matvei Aleksandrovich. — Tam zhe, stb. 706-707.

72. Metodicheskie ukazaniia po kursu "Istoriia russkoi literatury" dlia studentov-Zaochnikov. Tartu. (v soavtorstve s drugimi prepodavateliami kafedry).

73. O poniatii geograficheskogo prostranstva v russkikh srednevekovykh tekstakh. — T. Z. S. II (Uch. zai. T. G. U., 181), str. 210-216.

74. O probleme znachenii vo vtorichnykh modeliruiushchikh sistemakh. — Tam zhe, str. 22-37.

75. Otrazhenie etiki i taktiki revoliutsionnoi bor'by v russkoi literature kontsa XVIII veka. — T. R. S. F. VIII (Uch. zai. T. G. U., 167), str. 3-32.

76. Radishchev — chitatel' letopisi. Publikatsiia i vstupitel'naia zametka. — Tam zhe, str. 213-234.

1966

77. S. Issakov ja Y. Lotman. Vanavene kangelaslugu eesti keeles. (Rets.: Lugu Ygori sõjaretkest. Tlk. A. Annist. Tallinn, 1965) — Keel ja kir-

jandus, nr. 3, lk. 188-189.

78. Beseda A. A. Ivanova i N. G. Chernyshevskogo. K voprosu o spetsifike raboty nad istoriko-literaturovedcheskimi istochnikami. — V. L., N. 1, str. 131-135.
79. Vospriiatie liriki Pushkina v Germanii. (Rets.: H. Raab. Die Lyrik Pushkins in Deutschland (1820-1870). Berlin, 1964). — R. L., N. 2, str. 250-253 (v soavtorstve s Iu. D. Levinym).
80. Istoriko-literaturnye zametki. — T. R. S. F. IX (Uch. zai. T. G. U., 189), str. 137-141. 1. Ob odnoi samootsenke Radishcheva. — 2. Gorodnichii o prosveshchenii.
81. K probleme tipologii tekstov. — Tezisy dokladov vo vtoroi letnei shkole po vtorichnym modeliruiushchim sistemam. 16-26 avgusta, 1966. Tartu, str. 83-91.
82. Kaisarov, Andrei Sergeevich. — K. L. E., t. 3, stb. 314-315.
83. N. M. Karamzin. Polnoe sobranie stikhotvorenii. Vstupitel'naia stat'ia, podgotovka teksta i primechaniia. M.-L.
84. Katenin, Pavel Aleksandrovich. — K. L. E., t. 3, stb. 447-448.
85. Kutuzov, Aleksei Mikhailovich. — Tam zhe, stb. 930-931.
86. O modeliruiushchem poniatii "kontsa" i "nachala" v khudozhest-vennykh tekstakh. — Tezisy dokladov vo vtoroi letnei shkole po vtorichnym modeliruiushchim sistemam. 16-26 avgusta, 1966, Tartu, str. 69-74.
87. O postroenii tipologii kul'tury. — Tam zhe, str. 82-83.
88. Ob odnom chitatel'skom vospriiatii "Bednoi Lizi" Karamzina. (K strukture massovogo soznaniia XVIII veka). — "Rol' i znachenie literatury XVIII veka v istorii russkoi kul'tury," M.-L., str. 280-285.
89. Ob otnoshenii Pushkina v gody iuzhnoi ssylki k Robesl'eru. — "Russko-evropeiskie literaturnye sviazi." Sb., st. k 70-letiiu so dnia rozhdeniia akademika M. P. Alekseeva. M.-L., str. 316-319.
90. Khudozhestvennaia struktura "Evgeniia Onegina." — T. R. S. F. IX (Uch. zai. T. G. U., 184), str. 5-32.

1967

91. "Akadeemilise elu" õhkkond. [Vordlusjõoni üliõpilaselust Tartus ja Tsehhoslovakkia ülikoolides]. Fotoga. — "Edasi," 15 XI, nr. 291.
92. Metodi esatti della szienza literaria sovetica. — Strumenti critici. (Torino), anno I, fasc. 2, 1967, p. 107-127.
93. Problèmes de la typologie des cultures. — Information sur les sciences sociales. vol. 6, No. 2/3, 1967, pp. 29-38.
94. Semiootika ja kirjandusteadus. — Keel ja kirjandus, nr. 1, lk. 1-5.
95. V tolpe rodstvennikov. (Rets.: G. Shtorm. Potaennyi Radishchev. Vtoraia zhizn' "Puteshestviia iz Peterburga v Moskvu," M., 1965.)— Uch. zai. Gor'kovskogo Universiteta, vyp. 78, N. 2, seriia istoriko-

filologicheskaia, Gor'kii, str. 491-505.
96. K probleme tipologii kul'tury. — T. Z. S. III (Uch. zai. T. G. U., 198), str. 30-38.
97. Literaturovedenie dolzhno byt' naukoi. — V. L., N. 1, str. 90-100.
98. Merzliakov, A. F. — K. L. E., t. 4, stb. 775.
99. Sm. n. 72, Pereizdanie.
100. O zadachakh razdela obzorov i publikatsii. — T. Z. S. III (Uch. zai. T. G. U., 198), str. 363-366.
101. Ob oppozitsii ("chest' " i "slava") v svetskikh tekstakh Kievskogo perioda. — Tam zhe, str. 110-112.
102. Ot redaktsii. — Tam zhe, str. 5-6.
103. (Pis'mo v redaktsiiu). — "Literaturnaia gazeta," 1967, 23 avgusta, N. 34 (4112), str. 13.
104. Russo i russkaia kul'tura XVIII veka. — "Epokha Prosveshcheniia. Iz istorii mezhdunarodnykh sviazei russkoi literatury." L., str. 208-281.
105. Tezisy k probleme "Iskusstvo v riadu modeliruiushchikh sistem." — T. Z. S. III, (Uch. zai., T. G. U., 198), str. 130-145.

1968

106. Die Frühaufklärung und die Entwicklung des gesellschäftlichen Denkers in Russland. —Studien zur Geschichte der russischen Literatur des 18. Jahrhunderts. Bd. 3. Berlin, ss. 93-119.
107. Kunsti semiootilise uurimise tulemuse tànapäeve. — Keel ja kirjandus, nr. 10, lk. 577-585.
108. Poetika, rytmus, verš. Praha.
109. Sémantique du nombre et type de culture. — Tel Quel (Paris), N. 35, pp. 24-27.
110. Analiz dvukh stikhotvorenii. — III Letniaia shkola po vtorichnym modeliruiushchim sistemam. Tezisy. Kiaeriku 10-20 maia 1968, Tartu, str. 191-224.
    I. Iu. M. Lermontov. "Rastalis' my; no tvoi portret..."
    II. B. L. Pasternak. "Zamestitel'nitsa"
111. Zamechaniia k probleme barokko v russkoi literature. — Česko-slovenská rusistika, XIII, Nr. 1. str. 21-22.
112. Istoriko-literaturnye zametki. — T. R. S. F. XI (Uch. zai. T. G. U., 209) str. 358-365.
    1. Neizdannoe pis'mo A. M. Kutuzova I. P. Turgenevu. — 2. Kto byl avtorom stikhotvoreniia "Drevnost' "?
113. Problema khudozhestvennogo prostranstva v proze Goglia. — Tam zhe, str. 5-50.
114. Russkaia poeziia 1800-1810-kh g.g. —vkn.: Istoriia russkoi poezii, t. 1, L., str. 191-213.
115. Semantika chisla i tip kul'tury. — III Letniaia shkola po vtorichnym modeliruiushchim sistemam. Tezisy. Kiaeriku. 10-20 maia 1968. Tartu,

str. 103-109.
116. Tekst i funktsiia. — Tam zhe, str. 74-88. (v soavtorstve s A. M. Piatigorskim).
117. Khudozhestvennyi tekst i izuchenie nerodnogo iazyka. — "Russkii iazyk v natsional'noi shkole," N. 1, str. 17-19.

1969

118. O metajazyce typologickych pepicu kultury. — Orientace (Praha), Nr. 2, str. 67-80.
119. O znaczeniach we wtornych systemach modelujacych. — Pamietnik literacki (Warszawa), rocz. 60, zesz. 1, s. 276-294.
120. Semantika broja u tip kulture. — Telegram (Zagreb), N. 28.
121. T. Murnikova ja Y. Lotman. On aeg minna sõnadelt tegudele. [Vere keele tekstidest rahuuskoolides]. Nõuk. Õpetaja, 29 III, nr. 13.
122. Semiotica? Teadus märkidest. — "Edasi," 3 XII, nr. 283.
123. Y. Lotman et A. Pjatigorsky. Le texte et la fonction. — Semiotica, v. 1, No. 2, pp. 205-277.
124. Valmar Adams [70] juubel. — T. R. U., 7 II, nr. 3.
125. Verbum habet professor. — Tam zhe, 30 IV, nr. 15.
126. Aktual'naia mysl'. — V. L., N. 9, str. 195-197. (Kollektivnoe pis'mo).
127. Liudi i znaki. — "Sovetskaia Estoniia," N. 27, I, II.
128. O metaiazyke tipologicheskikh opisanii kul'tury. — T. Z. S. IV (Uch. zai. T. G. U., 236), str. 460-477.
129. O nekotorykh printsipial'nykh trudnostiakh v strukturnom opisanii teksta. — Tam zhe, str. 478-482.
130. O tipologicheskom uzuchenii literatury. — "Problemy tipologii russkogo realizma," M., str. 123-132.
131. Russo i russkaia kul'tura XVIII-nachala XIX veka. — vkn.: Zhan-Zhak Russo. Traktaty. M., str. 555-604.
132. Stikhotvoreniia rannego Pasternaka i nekotorye voprosy strukturnogo izucheniia teksta. — T. Z. S. IV (Uch. zai. T. G. U., 236), str. 206-238.
133. Khudozhestvennyi tekst i izuchenie nerodnogo iazyka. — Literaturovedenie i shkola. Materialy metodicheskoi konferentsii. Tartu, str. 10-16.

1970

134. Kuidas kõneleb kunst? — Nooris, nr. 9, lk. 46-47.
135. Pavel Naumovich Berkov [Nekrolog]. — T. R. S. F. XV (Uch. zai. T. G. U., 251), str. 383-384.
136. Iz istorii izucheniia stilia Lenina. — Tam zhe, str. 11-13.
137. Iz nabliudenii nad strukturnymi printsipami rannego tvorchestva Gogolia. — Tam zhe, str. 17-45.
138. K strukture dialogicheskogo teksta v poemakh Pushkina (problema

avtorskikh primechanii k tekstu). — "Pushkin i ego sovremenniki" (Uch. zai. Leningradskogo gos. pedagogicheskogo instituta im. Gertsena, vyp. 434), Pskov, str. 125-134.

139. V. I. Lenin ob ideologicheskoi sushchnosti dvizheniia dekabristov. — T. R. S. F. XV (Uch. zai. T. G. U., vyp. 251) str. 3-6.

140. O dvukh modeliakh kommunikatsii i ikh sootnoshenii v obshchei sisteme kul'tury. — Tezisy dokladov IV Letnei shkoly po vtorichnym modeliruiushchim sistemam. 17-24 avgusta 1970, Tartu, str. 163-165.

141. O semiotike poniatii "styd" i "strakh" v mekhanizme kul'tury. — Tam zhe, str. 98-102.

142. O sootnoshenii poeticheskoi leksiki russkogo romantizma i tserkovno-slavianskoi traditsii. — Tam zhe, str. 85-87.

143. Kharal'd Raab (Nekrolog). — T. R. S. F. XV (Uch. zai. T. G. U., 251), str. 385.

144. Semiotika kul'tury. — Informatsionnye protsessy, evristicheskoe programmirovanie, problemy neirokibernetiki, modelirovanie avtomatami, raspoznavlenie obrazov, problemy semiotiki. (Materialy Vsesoiuznogo simpoziuma po kibernetike. Tbilisi, 25-29 Tbilisi, str. 307-308 (V soavtorstve s B. A. Uspenskim).

145. Stat'i po tipologii kul'tury. (Materialy k kursu teorii literatury. Vyp. 1). Tartu.

146. Struktura khudozhestvennogo teksta. M.

147. Tezisy k semioticheskomu izucheniiu kul'tur. (V primenenii k slavianskim tekstam). — Semiotyka i struktura tekstu. Studia Swięcone VII międzynarodowemu kongresowi slawistów. Warszawa, s. 9-32 (V soavtorstve s V. V. Ivanovym, A. M. Piatigorskim, V. N. Toporovym i B. A. Uspenskim).

148. Uslovnost' v iskusstve. — Filosofskaia entsiklopediia, t. 5, str. 287-288 (v soavtorstve s B. A. Uspenskim).

1971

149. Doklad B. M. Eikhenbauma o poezii i proze. Publikatsiia. — T. Z. S. V (Uch. zai. T. G. U., 284) str. 476-480.

150. Eshche raz o poniatiiakh "slava" i "chest' " v tekstakh Kievskogo perioda. — Tam zhe, str. 469-474.

151. Zametki o strukture khudozhestvennogo teksta. — Tam zhe, str. 281-287.

152. O semioticheskom mekhanizme kul'tury. — Tam zhe, str. 144-166. (v soavtorstve s B. A. Uspenskim).

153. Ot redaktsii. (Pamiati K. I. Chukovskogo). — T. R. S. F. XVIII (Uch. zai. T. G. U., 266), str. 3.

154. Poety 1790-1810-kh godov. Vstupitel'naia stat'ia sostavlenie Iu. M. Lotmana. Podgotovka teksta M. G. Al'tshullera. L.

155. Problema "Obucheniia kul'ture" kak ee tipologicheskaia kharakteristi-
ka. — T. Z. S. V (Uch. zai. T. G. U., 284), str. 167-176.

1972

156. Analiz poeticheskogo teksta. Struktura stikha. L.
157. Iskusstvoznanie i "tochnye metody" v sovremennykh zarubezhnykh
issledovaniiakh. — "Semiotika i iskusstvometriia." Sost. i red. Iu. M.
Lotmana i V. M. Petrova. M., str. 5-23.
158. Stikhotvorenie Bloka "Anne Akhmatovoi" v perevode Debory Vaaran-
di. (K probleme sopostavitel'nogo analiza). —Blokovskii sbornik. II.
Trudy vtoroi nauchnoi konferentsii, posviashchennoi izucheniiu zhizni
i tvorchestva A. A. Bloka. Tartu, str. 4-24 (v soavtorstve s A. Mal'ts).

1973

159. Different cultures, different codes. — Times Literary Supplement, Oct.
12, pp. 1213-1215.
160. La structure de text artistique. Paris.
161. Zamechaniia o strukture povestvovatel'nogo teksta. — T. Z. S. VI
(Uch. zai. T. G. U., 308), str. 382-386.
162. Znakovyi mekhanizm kul'tury. — Sbornik statei po vtorichnym modeliruiushchim sistemam. Tartu, str. 195-199.
163. Individual'nyi tvorcheskii put' i tipologiia kul'turnykh kodov. — Tam
zhe, str. 96-98. (v soavtorstve s Z. G. Mints).
164. Kanonicheskoe iskusstvo kak informatsionnyi paradoks. — "Problema kanona v drevnem i srednevekovom iskusstve Azii i Afriki."
Sb. st. M., str. 16-22.
165. Mif-imia-kul'tura. — T. Z. S. VI (Uch. zai. T. G. U., 308), str. 282-303
(v soavtorstve s B. A. Uspenskim).
166. Nikolai Ivanovich Mordovchenko. Zametki o tvorcheskoi individual'
nosti uchenogo. — Istoriograficheskii sbornik. Vyp. 1 (4) Saratov,
str. 205-213.
167. O dvukh modeliakh kommunikatsii v sisteme kul'tury. — T. Z. S.
VI (Uch. zai. T. G. U., 308), str. 227-243.
168. O mifologicheskom kode siuzhetnykh tekstov. — Sbornik stat'ei po
vtorichnym modeliruiushchim sistemam. Tartu, str. 86-90.
169. O soderzhanii i strukture poniatiia "khudozhestvennyi tekst." —
"Problemy poetiki i istorii literatury." Saransk, str. 20-36.
170. Satira Voeikova "Dom sumashedshikh." — T. R. S. F. XXI (Uch.
zai. T. G. U., 306), str. 3-45.
171. Semiotika kino i problemy kinoestetiki. Tallinn, 1973.
172. Stat'i po tipologii kul'tury. (Materialy k kursu teorii literatury). Tartu.
173. O. M. Freidenberg kak issledovatel' kul'tury. — T. Z. S. VI (Uch. zai.

T. G. U., 308), str. 482-489.

1974

174. Luuletaja, teadlane õppejõud. — TRÜ, 8, II.
175. Gogol' i sootnoshenie "smekhovoi kul'tury" s komicheskim i ser'eznym
v russkoi natsional'noi traditsii. — Materialy Vsesoiuznogo simpoziuma
po vtorichnym modeliruiushchim sistemam. I (5), Tartu, str. 131-133.
176. Dinamicheskie mekhanizmy semioticheskikh sistem. — Tam zhe, str.
76-81.
177. O glubinnykh elementakh khudozhestvennogo zamysla. K deshifrovke
odnogo neponiatnogo mesta iz vospominanii o Bloke. — Tam zhe, str.
168-175. (v soavtorstve s Z. G. Mints).
178. O reduktsii i razvertyvanii znakovykh sistem. (K problem "Freidizm i
semioticheskaia kul'turologiia"). — Tam zhe, str. 100-108.
179. O sootnoshenii pervichnogo i vtorichnogo v kommunikativno-mo-
deliruiushchikh sistemakh. — Tam zhe, str. 224-228.
180. Teoriia realisticheskoi dramy v Rossii. (Rets.: A. Anikst. Istoriia u-
chenii o drame. Teoriia dramy v Rossii ot Pushkina do Chekhova. M.,
1972). — "Teatr," N. 6, str. 90-92.
181. Khudozhestvennyi ansambl' kak bytovoe prostranstvo. — "Dekorativ-
noe iskusstvo S. S. S. R.," N. 4, str. 48-51.
182. Chetyre ugla zreniia. — "Molodezh' Estonii," 18 aprelia.